S 250

TRAV

02/09

A Geography of the U.S.S.R.

A Geography of the U.S.S.R.

The Background to a Planned Economy

J. P. COLE, M.A., Ph.D.

Reader in the Department of Geography
University of Nottingham

and

F. C. GERMAN, M.A.(Cantab.)

LONDON
BUTTERWORTHS

6-5-71(70

THE BUTTERWORTH GROUP

ENGLAND

Butterworth & Co (Publishers) Ltd
London: 88 Kingsway, WC2B 6AB

AUSTRALIA

Butterworth & Co (Australia) Ltd
Sydney: 20 Loftus Street
Melbourne: 143 Little Collins Street
Brisbane: 240 Queen Street

CANADA

Butterworth & Co (Canada) Ltd
Toronto: 14 Curity Avenue, 374

NEW ZEALAND

Butterworth & Co (New Zealand) Ltd
Wellington: 49/51 Ballance Street
Auckland: 35 High Street

SOUTH AFRICA

Butterworth & Co (South Africa) (Pty) Ltd
Durban: 33/35 Beach Grove

First published in 1961
Second edition 1970

©Butterworth & Co (Publishers) Ltd, 1970

ISBN 0 408 49751 3

Composed by
Peridon Ltd, London

Printed in England by the
Chapel River Press
Andover, Hants

PREFACE

In a review, published in 1968, of a geography of the Soviet Union, R. E. H. Mellor (see General Bibliography, p. 316) remarked: 'Perhaps no other country is so well covered by general regional geographies' as is the Soviet Union: there are at present nine to choose from.' In 1961 *A Geography of the USSR, the Background to a Planned Economy,* by J. P. Cole and F. C. German, was published by Butterworths. This presumably was one of the earlier of the nine referred to by Mellor. Mellor concludes the review with a plea: '. . . the choice of such general regional geographies of the Soviet Union is now so rich as to leave hardly place for more. One feels that students of the U.S.S.R. should now turn their attention from producing more of this kind of work and devote their attention to producing studies of specific systematic aspects, or of selected regions'.

The present book differs from its predecessor in three main respects. First, it has been completely rewritten and brought up to date by about seven years, to take into account the 1966–70 Five Year Plan. Secondly, it is more systematic, in the sense that little regional detail *per se* is included; in general, any information given is relevant to the main theme. Thirdly, some of the new techniques, models and concepts recently introduced into geography have been used.

Among the relatively new items in the book the following may be noted. Some aspects of mathematics, such as Venn diagrams and topological maps, have been used to illuminate situations. Statistical techniques of data description and correlation have been widely used. Several computer programs have been applied to process data; in particular, factor analysis has been adopted to deal with several multivariate situations. A similar approach is used by J. C. Fisher in *Yugoslavia—A Multinational Case* (Chandler, San Francisco, 1966), a study of Yugoslavia. Notes are included on the techniques and programs in Appendixes at the end of the present book. In addition, some attention has been given to decision making and perception, a little to prediction, particularly of population trends, and, implicity, to the idea of general systems. Some titles of books on these topics are given in the General Bibliography at the end of the book.

More use is made in the present book than in its predecessor of maps, particularly topologically transformed ones, of non-cartographical diagrams and of simple networks and flow charts. Much information is given in numerical form in tables and matrices, rather than verbally. Numerical values, while requiring verbal elucidation, often express information both more concisely and more precisely than verbal passages. Some aspects have been largely dropped from the previous edition of the book: the discussion of the Soviet attitude to geography and Soviet political thought (Chapter 3) and the detailed regional accounts (Chapters 6 and 8). On the other hand, the whole of Comecon has been briefly considered since in certain aspects the economy of the U.S.S.R. is becoming influenced and modified by its links with East European partners.

No attempt is made to outline the contents of other books on the geography of the U.S.S.R., but a list of the many titles available in Russian and in other languages is given at the end of the book. D. J. M. Hooson ('The Soviet Union and the Geography Student' *Canadian Geographer,* **VI** (2), 78–82, 1962) provides a useful review of material in English to the early 1960's.

The maps were drawn by Miss Carol Chambers. The continuing interest of Professor K. C. Edwards in the study of Soviet geography at Nottingham University must be noted and his interest in the present book is greatly appreciated. The assistance of Mr. M. J. McCullagh in translating the factor analysis program and in writing the other programs is gratefully acknowledged, as is the help of Mr. M. Anderson in one of the programs.
1970   J.P.C.

Contents

Spelling of Russian Names

For a discussion of transliteration, see end of book.

An English version has been used for most of the Soviet Socialist Republics rather than a cumbersome exact transliteration (eg Azerbaijan instead of Azerbaydzhan). Certain other well-known places have also been anglicised or simplified:

English	Exact transliteration
Archangel	Arkhangel'sk
Caucasus	Kavkaz
Crimea	Krym
Gorky	Gor'kiy
Kharkov	Khar'kov
Kiev	Kiyev
Lvov	L'vov
Moscow	Moskva
Siberia	Sibir'

ABBREVIATED TITLES

Throughout the book, the following abbreviations have been used for the main statistical yearbooks:

NkhSSSR, 1965   for *Narodnoye khozyaystvo SSSR v 1965 godu* (or other year) statisticheskiy yezhegodnik, published in Moscow

NkhRSFSR 1965   for *Narodnoye khozyaystvo RSFSR v 1965 godu* (or other year) published in Moscow

NDSE Part 2-A   (or other volume) for *New Directions in the Soviet Economy* (U.S. Government Printing Office, Washington, 1966) in various volumes.

1

Introduction

The U.S.S.R. can be viewed in many different ways. The political scientist cannot avoid considering the role of the Soviet Communist Party. The economist has to take into account the almost complete absence of a private sector and of a market economy. The historian cannot overlook the grafting operation of Soviet Russia onto Tsarist Russia. The geographer, however, has several approaches to choose from. A 'complete' geography of the U.S.S.R. might be aimed at, though it is difficult to conceive in one volume. The landscape could be stressed; Gregory[1] has given attention to this aspect. The historical geography of Russia is an extensive topic. Both W. A. D. Jackson and R. A. French for example have discussed this in various papers. The variety and extremes of physical conditions in the U.S.S.R. lead also to an interest in man-environment relationships. Alternatively, the economic regions, objects of detailed study in many Soviet geography books, can form the framework for study. Naturally all these aspects and approaches to some extent overlap.

The present book considers the spatial aspects of the U.S.S.R. as a functioning system. The organisation and regulation of the system is perhaps the main preoccupation and *raison d'etre* of the Soviet Communist Party, the aims of which are frequently stated. The manipulation of the people and material resources of the country in an areal framework is the main theme in the present book. Different regions of the U.S.S.R. offer different possibilities and problems, but all regions are now integrated within a single system, and successes or failures in any one region potentially have repercussions throughout the system.

While geographers would agree virtually unanimously on many aspects of knowledge that do not fall within their field, they are far from being in agreement as to what situations and problems do belong to geography. The attitude to geography of Soviet geographers and of persons in other disciplines in the U.S.S.R. influences the work done in geography there, and therefore the material available to people outside. The approach to geography has become more relaxed than in the 1950's and controversies are now common between adherents of different schools. Hooson[2] discusses earlier clashes of the post-Stalin era, Chappell[3] brings the dispute into the 1960's, and Demko[4] gives a general view of Soviet geographical thinking.

Geography contains a dichotomy between physical and human elements. Many schools of geography in the world have managed in some way to pursue simultaneously the two kinds of geography and even to integrate them with some success. Many Soviet geographers have chosen, or have found it expedient to choose, to emphasise the differences between physical geography and human geography rather than their similarities. This apparently is because (naively) Stalin considered the 'natural' laws determining the distribution of physical objects on the earth's surface to differ fundamentally from the (Marxist) laws affecting the distribution of economic activities (in the Soviet Union, at least). Not all Soviet geographers keep to the division in practice, and some, indeed, contest it. For example, Saushkin[5] in 1946 implied the inseparability of human and physical geography. He stressed that man-altered landscapes do not revert to their original state when human activity ceases. He proposed a separate discipline for the study of cultural landscapes.

Unfortunately, the division of geography has tended to split the subject and to leave the physical geographers with the geologists, botanists, meteorologists and other physical scientists, gathering, processing and often mapping data with them, and seeking physical relationships. On the other side, human geographers have worked with economists, grappling with problems of defining economic regions, calculating the best situation for new industries and dealing with demographic data.

At least two sensible reasons may be suggested why the split between physical and human geography has been unfortunate. First, when physical and human geography are di-' vorced it is more difficult to give attention to the interrelationships between the two. The physical environment still influences the activities of man enormously, even in urban areas. Man also alters the physical environment. It is not possible to obtain an integrated picture of the geography of the U.S.S.R. without taking these facts into account. Secondly, quantitative methods and models are increasingly used to show causal relationships between physical characteristics and human ones. These techniques are equally applicable to physical and human information and to showing connections between them. This valuable insight might be lost if the two aspects were separated.

In view of the dichotomy between physical and human geography it is not surprising that the work of geographers in the two branches differs not only in approach but also in quality. On the whole, physical geography is treated in the U.S.S.R. and East Europe very much as it is in Western Europe and North America although there tend to be different emphases, such as a strong interest in soils and in broad soil-vegetation zones, and even a preoccupation with the acclimatisation of plants in difficult environments. In contrast, human geography is treated in a very different way in the communist countries from outside. Since Soviet human (economic) geographers often tend to be critical of the work of their counterparts outside, it seems opportune to note a few of their own faults.

First, quantitative data of use in and indeed indispensable for the development of human geography are sadly deficient in the U.S.S.R. and much of East Europe. The lack of data has often been noted and deplored in Soviet publications. This defect makes planning difficult. Soviet geographers, however, often fail to use to the full the data they do have. This seems to be because they do not want to reveal disagreeable situations. Secondly, Soviet economic geographers have learned, and incessantly and indiscriminately repeat, various outmoded or oversimplified concepts about the location of economic activities. Thirdly, in a search for the best regions, they have followed the trail of supposed objective regions, believed to exist in reality. In this exercise, lasting already several decades, they have witnessed the construction and demolition of various sets of economic regions in their own country and have successively praised the advantages of different sets. It has not become obvious to them yet that any set of economic planning regions is to some extent arbitrary. *Either* you make a set of regions and then use them, *or* you look for regions in the real world and try to define them. The Russians do both, making their regions and then justifying them. Whatever the methods used, the boundaries of economic regions always coincide with existing political boundaries which may divide natural units, such as the Donbass coalfield. Fourthly, they often put labels such as rational *(ratsional'nyy)*, scientific, efficient *(effektivnyy)*, to what they say, thus giving an air of respectability at little cost to themselves. Similarly Marx and Lenin in particular are regarded as having a monopoly of truth and a quotation from them is sufficient to quell any opposition. This inevitably reduces the practical value of the work they might do in pointing out deficiencies in planning and inefficiencies in the economy. Such an escape route makes Soviet human geographers complacent and even arrogant in relation to their counterparts outside. Like the Italian geographers under Fascism, they have to make the ruling Party happy by quoting the prophets, or praising the big men in power.

REFERENCES

1. GREGORY, J. S., *Russian Land and Soviet People: a Geographical Approach to the U.S.S.R.* (Harrap, London, 1968)
2. HOOSON, D. J. M., 'Methodological Clashes in Moscow' *Ann. Ass. Am. Geogr.,* **52**, No 4, 469–75, 1962
3. CHAPPELL, J. E., 'Progress and Ideology in the U.S.S.R.: Marxism and Geography' *Problems of Communism,* Nov.–Dec. 1965
4. DEMKO, G., 'Trends in Soviet Geography' *Survey,* No 55, 163–70, 1965
5. SAUSHKIN, Yu. G., 'The Cultural Landscape' *Soviet Geogr.,* 9, No 7, 562–69, 1968 (Original paper in *Vop. geogr.,* No 1, 1946)

BIBLIOGRAPHY

ANUCHIN, V. A., *Teoreticheskiye problemy geografii* (Moscow, 1960)
HOOSON, D. J. M., 'Some Recent Developments in the Content and Theory of Soviet Geography' *Ann. Ass. Am. Geogr.,* 1, No 1, 73–82, 1959
NOVE, A., *The Soviet Economy–An Introduction* (2 edn, Allen and Unwin, London, 1965)
SCHAPIRO, L., *The Government and Politics of the Soviet Union* (Hutchinson, London, 1968)

2

Technical aspects of the geography of the U.S.S.R.

Any study of the geography of the U.S.S.R. by a Western geographer comes up against several difficulties of a technical nature. Among these are the great size of the country, lack of much data that would be useful and the difficulty of travelling freely in the U.S.S.R. These and other difficulties will be discussed in this chapter.

2.1 SIZE AND ABSTRACTION

In practising his discipline, the geographer makes enormous abstractions. In dealing with an area as large as the U.S.S.R., he has to collapse a piece of three dimensional space, in form like part of an eggshell, onto a sheet of paper, a few feet across if a wall map, a matter of inches across if an atlas or textbook map. So obsessed has the geographer become with maps that he easily forgets the real nature of the object he is dealing with and so drastically reducing.

In studying the objects within his initial space or container, the geographer has to make further abstractions and simplifications, such as using a few hundred dots or some arbitrary shading to represent the distribution of some 200 million people. In representing the U.S.S.R. on a scale of 1:10 000 000, a very generous page size for a map of the whole country, he is reducing the surface $10^7 \times 10^7$, or 10^{14} times. The question is not: What information must be sacrificed? but: What information may be included? In representing 200 million people by 200 dots, a further drastic reduction of 10^6 is made. Similarly, there are probably around 10^{11} individual trees in the U.S.S.R.; the map of forests represents these by a limited number of patches on the map.

Some aspects of abstraction, simplification and generalisation needed, but easily taken for granted, are shown in Fig. 2.1. The U.S.S.R. occupies 4% of the Earth's shell (Fig. 2.1(a)) or 15% of its land. Like the piece of shell of a spherical egg, it is extensive in two horizontal dimensions, but is actually three dimensional, with a relatively short vertical dimension (Fig. 2.1(b)). In spite of the coming of the space age, the U.S.S.R., like other space conscious countries, still only effectively uses, or is directly influenced by, the atmosphere a few miles above and the lithosphere a few miles below. Fig. 2.1(c) shows the spheres of use to man under present conditions of technology. With a little imagination, it is possible to conceive the total Soviet space as a cone-like form with the apex at the centre of the earth and the base placed far out in the universe. The boundaries of the U.S.S.R. represented as lines (one dimension) on the map are really boundary surfaces (two dimensions), intersecting the earth's surface. The resulting object is untidy, but the U.S.S.R. is theoretically a certain part of the object described, any part of the lithosphere below and atmosphere above. Such a space is not currently of economic importance, but it is undoubtedly of scientific interest in Soviet eyes.

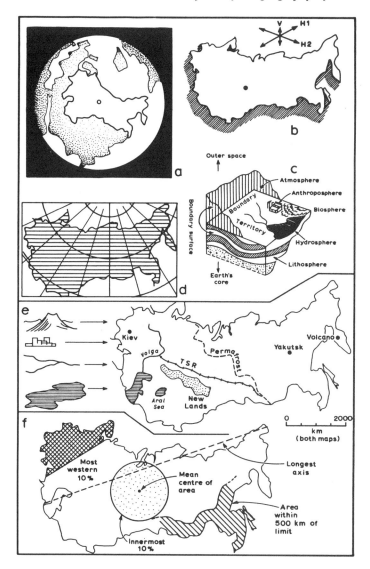

Fig. 2.1.   *Aspects of simplification of the U.S.S.R. in making a map.*

Before it is possible to embark on a study that will eventually turn out an appropriate geographical account of such an enormous and unwieldy object as the U.S.S.R., it is necessary to have various viable maps and diagrams. The first operation is to 'flatten' the piece of shell onto a piece of paper (see Fig. 2.1(d)). Any such projection of the whole of the U.S.S.R. is inevitably considerably distorted in terms of distance, orientation, or both; the distortion, for example, on a good projection may be around 10–15% towards the extremities. Several Soviet atlases[1] describe the type and degree of distortion on various projections. To avoid crowding of information and 'noise', it has generally been the policy to omit parallels and meridians from maps in the present book. It is sometimes useful, however, to include parallels in order to facilitate comparisons between different maps.

Once a suitable base map of the U.S.S.R. has been chosen, various modifications may be desirable. First, since most of the population and economic activities are in the western half, it may be useful to represent all or some part of the western half on a larger scale than the rest, for economies of map space. Secondly, only part of the total area of the U.S.S.R. may be under consideration. Thirdly, a topological transformation may be employed to give fair visual importance to the population of divisions under consideration, rather than to their areas. Topological maps are used in Chapter 3 and throughout the rest of the book.

What does the geographer use his maps for? Often a map is used either as a store of information for reference about the relative location of objects, or to make a direct visual impact about a particular situation, such as a distribution of objects. Often the two functions are combined. In making (or borrowing) maps, the geographer is mapping selected objects from the material or real world into a one to one correspondence with accepted symbols, appropriately located on paper (see Fig. 2.1(e)). The three dimensional space in the real world is fitted into the map frame. The material world objects that interest the geographer themselves exist in three dimensions, but are generally collapsed to symbols (see Fig. 2.1(e)) thought of as dots (no dimensions, eg building, tree, settlement), lines (one dimension, eg railway, river), or patches (two dimensions, eg sea, forest, political division).

In order to identify and refer to particular objects in the space under consideration, labels or names are given to them. It is useful to know a considerable number of these names before one can start thinking quickly about the region one is dealing with, but it must be appreciated that the names are quite arbitrary. It would be possible, for example, to refer to Leningrad as T2, or as the (big) town at 60°N., 30°E., although place names appear to be more convenient, for they are more distinct than say counting numbers or letters plus numbers. Only a small proportion of all the place names in the U.S.S.R. can be memorised and there is no merit in learning as many as possible *per se.* There is a case for trying to learn as soon as possible the names of more important items; the largest towns, the principal coalfields, the major rivers. Real world situations in geography,

whether in regional or systematic geography, need a knowledge of the specific arrangement of real objects in a space.

The place names of the U.S.S.R. cause some extra trouble and even consternation for Western geographers and it is useful for the non-Russian speaker to know the cyrillic alphabet well enough to recognise places in atlases. A widely accepted system of transliteration is given in Appendix 3. When use is being made of place names that are not ambiguous there is no danger in modifying the transliteration system, but for persons dealing with very large numbers of place names it is desirable to be consistent. A rough indication is given of the pronunciation of Russian sounds. Page 11 lists commonly used place names that deviate in this book from the standard system of transliteration (eg Moscow rather than Moskva).

The surface of the U.S.S.R. may for many purposes be dealt with by the geographer as if flat, both in the sense of its original sphericity being projected onto a flat surfaced map, and in terms of more local variation in altitude of the surface. Such a plane surface has certain features (see Fig. 2.1(f)) that might loosely be described as geometrical in a sense of Euclidean geometry. The surface has a mean centre, the location of which can be worked out with considerable precision. It may be calculated approximately by cutting out a cardboard replica of the shape of the U.S.S.R., suspending this successively from several points on the periphery and dropping a perpendicular line in turn from each suspension point. The intersection of the several lines is the mean centre, the two dimensional equivalent of the pivot of a seesaw. The inner and outer parts can be calculated on the basis of the mean centre. The innermost 10% is shown in Fig. 2.1(f). Different innermost and outermost portions may be defined if a replica line is drawn at an appropriate distance in from the coast and the international boundary of the U.S.S.R. It is also possible to draw a longest horizontal axis across the U.S.S.R. Many other such features could be calculated; for example, the quarter of the U.S.S.R. nearest to Moscow. The features outlined are invisible in maps in regional geography books but often implicit in text describing them.

Two other aspects of the space or region under consideration, in this case the U.S.S.R., should not be overlooked. First, the U.S.S.R. does not occupy the same space as it did, for example, three decades ago, or as Russia did a century or several centuries ago (see Fig. 2.2). Nor, presumably, will it remain for ever frozen in its present form. Which space, then, is relevant, the relatively slowly changing physical base on which Russia has rested, or the man-made, analogically 'organic' state of Russia and its successor the U.S.S.R.? Both, presumably.

2.2 THE POLITICO-ADMINISTRATIVE HIERARCHY

In the study at least of the human geography of a region, an appreciation of the politico-administrative arrangement of the country is indispensable. In the case of the U.S.S.R. this is so for several reasons; political units are often the main or only territorial compartments for which data are available, their presence may affect

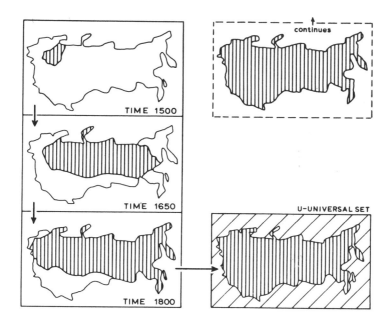

Fig. 2.2.   The territorial growth of Russia.

Secondly (see Fig. 2.2), no region except the world region exists entirely detached from the rest. The U.S.S.R. is touched by neighbouring states, seas and oceans all along its outer limits. If the entire earth's shell is considered to be the 'universal set' of the geographer, then the U.S.S.R. is a clearly distinguishable subset and the rest of the world its complement. If it is considered as a system, then it is an open system, rather than a closed one, even though at times Soviet politicians have tried to make it closed, both economically and culturally.

other distributions, and they are traditionally the discrete elements that form the building bricks for the economic regions. In addition, the Communist Party territorial organisation is based on the system, and the units are used for local government services. One should distinguish between the passive role of the compartments as data containers, and their active role as production, service and trading areas with boundaries that in certain ways (eg the stepping up of freight rates) affect the distribution of other activities.

The highest level in the hierarchy below the U.S.S.R. itself is the set of 15 Soviet Socialist Republics. These are named in Table 2.1. They each have, theoretically, the right to secede from the Soviet Union; they are all on the coast or share a boundary with at least one country outside the U.S.S.R. Schapiro[2] points out that if the right were ever taken up, it would not be difficult for the Communist Party to find a pretext to intervene.

The basic set of major civil divisions comprises roughly 120 *oblasts, krays* and A.S.S.R.'s, most of which are shown in Fig. 2.3. At a lower level still, information is also available for a much larger number of *rayons.* These are used, for example, in the Soviet *Atlas sel'skovo khozyaystva.* In the present book, data will be used where available and convenient for the oblast level units. These are the building blocks or elements that, combined in various ways, form the 15 Soviet Socialist Republics, as well as the 19 economic regions currently in use. It is not necessary for the reader to know where every oblast level division is, but he should acquaint himself with the general features of the system. It is convenient to know the 15 Republics, the 19 economic regions, and certain other combinations of units that are sometimes referred to. Other subsets of oblasts with certain features will be suggested, especially in the chapters on agriculture and on economic regions. It is sobering to note that there are 2^{120} or about 10^{35} different possible subsets of the 120 oblast level regions. Some possible subsets are indicated below:

European U.S.S.R. and Asiatic U.S.S.R.	2
Eastern regions and their complement	2
R.S.F.S.R. and the other 14 Republics	2
Soviet Socialist Republics	15
Economic regions (R.S.F.S.R. in 10, other 14 Republics modified)	19
Economic regions and/or Republics (R.S.F.S.R. 10, Ukraine 3,+13 other)	26
Oblast level units of R.S.F.S.R.+Ukraine 3+13 other	87
Basic oblast level	about 120

In Fig. 2.3 and the corresponding Table 2.2, the R.S.F.S.R. is divided into 71 oblast level units, grouping of which is by economic regions.

Regions 1-10 are subdivisions of the R.S.F.S.R. and 11-13 of the Ukraine. Regions 17-19 coincide with three Republics, Kazakhstan, Belorussia and Moldavia. Regions 14-16 are each composed of several Republics. Region 14, the Baltic Republics, has Kaliningrad oblast, part of the R.S.F.S.R., the only instance where an oblast level unit is transferred across a Republic boundary.

Table 2.1. THE SOVIET SOCIALIST REPUBLICS

1 Russian Soviet Federal Socialist Republic (R.S.F.S.R.)
2 Ukraine
3 Lithuania
4 Latvia
5 Estonia
6 Georgia
7 Azerbaijan
8 Armenia
9 Uzbekistan
10 Kirgizia
11 Tadjikistan
12 Turkmenistan
13 Kazakhstan
14 Belorussia
15 Moldavia

Two, Moscow and Leningrad city oblasts, are merged with their respective ordinary units. The Ukraine is divided first into three parts (Donets-Dnepr, Southwest, South), then (Table 2.3) further divided into a supplementary list of its oblasts, for which, however, few data are readily available to the Western geographer. The list of 71 (R.S.F.S.R.) plus 3 (Ukraine) plus 13 (individual S.S.R.'s) units, a total of 87 units, is used on several occasions later in the book as the best available system for a relatively detailed study of quantitative data, especially in Chapters 9 and 13.

The framework of the Soviet politico-administrative system is based on peoples, which will be discussed in Chapter 8. These are the *raison d'être* not only of the 15 Soviet Socialist Republics, but also of Autonomous S.S.R.'s at oblast level within the R.S.F.S.R. and smaller national units at lower levels. In European U.S.S.R. the system of units is much influenced by the pattern of the pre-Soviet system of provinces or *guberniya,* based on urban centres and their spheres of influence. In the more thinly peopled parts of European U.S.S.R. and in most of Asiatic U.S.S.R., larger, less cohesive areas are found, some defined as krays or territories, with strong central government control or influence. Variations in the territorial extent of units can be judged roughly from Fig. 2.3, although two different scales have been used to accommodate all the relevant information about the system. Variations in population size are revealed in the topological map in Fig. 2.4.

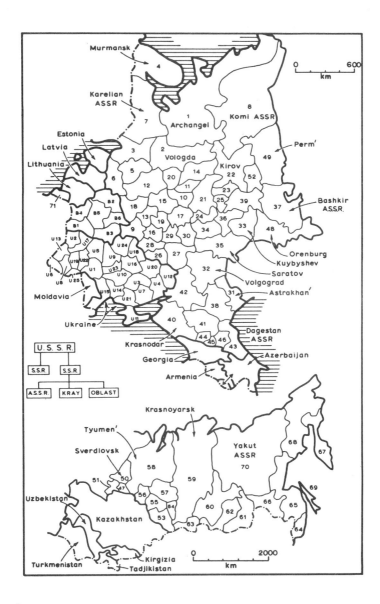

Fig. 2.3. *The distribution of politico-administrative units in the U.S.S.R. See Tables 2.2 and 2.3 for key to the numbering of units.*

Table 2.2. THE POLITICO-ADMINISTRATIVE DIVISIONS OF THE U.S.S.R.

E1	NORTHWEST	RR1	Archangel
		RR2	Vologda
		RR3	Leningrad*
		RR4	Murmansk
		RR5	Novgorod
		RR6	Pskov
		RR7	Karelian (A)
		RR8	Komi (A)
E2	CENTRE	RR9	Bryansk
		RR10	Vladimir
		RR11	Ivanovo
		RR12	Kalinin
		RR13	Kaluga
		RR14	Kostroma
		RR15	Moscow*
		RR16	Orel
		RR17	Ryazan'
		RR18	Smolensk
		RR19	Tula
		RR20	Yaroslavl'
E3	VOLGA-VYATKA	RR21	Gorky
		RR22	Kirov
		RR23	Mariysk (A)
		RR24	Mordov (A)
		RR25	Chuvash (A)
E4	BLACKEARTH CENTRE	RR26	Belgorod
		RR27	Voronezh
		RR28	Kursk
		RR29	Lipetsk
		RR30	Tambov
E5	VOLGA	RR31	Astrakhan'
		RR32	Volgograd
		RR33	Kuybyshev
		RR34	Penza
		RR35	Saratov
		RR36	Ul'yanovsk
		RR37	Bashkir (A)
		RR38	Kalmyk (A)
		RR39	Tatar (A)
E6	NORTH CAUCASUS	RR40	Krasnodar
		RR41	Stavropol'
		RR42	Rostov
		RR43	Dagestan (A)
		RR44	Kabardino-B. (A)
		RR45	Severo-Os. (A)
		RR46	Checheno-Ing. (A)
E7	URAL	RR47	Kurgan
		RR48	Orenburg
		RR49	Perm'
		RR50	Sverdlovsk
		RR51	Chelyabinsk
		RR52	Udmurt (A)

Table 2.2. contd

E8	WEST SIBERIA	RR53	Altay
		RR54	Kemerovo
		RR55	Novosibirsk
		RR56	Omsk
		RR57	Tomsk
		RR58	Tyumen'
E9	EAST SIBERIA	RR59	Krasnoyarsk
		RR60	Irkutsk
		RR61	Chita
		RR62	Buryat (A)
		RR63	Tuvinsk (A)
E10	FAR EAST	RR64	Primorsk
		RR65	Khabarovsk
		RR66	Amur
		RR67	Kamchatka
		RR68	Magadan
		RR69	Sakhalin
		RR70	Yakut (A)
	SPECIAL	RR71	Kaliningrad
E11	UKRAINE	DDN	Donets-Dnepr
		SWE	Southwest
		SOU	South
E14	BALTIC	LIT	Lithuania
		LAT	Latvia
		EST	Estonia
E15	TRANS-CAUCASIA	GEO	Georgia
		AZE	Azerbaijan
		ARM	Armenia
E16	CENTRAL ASIA	UZB	Uzbekistan
		KIR	Kirgizia
		TAD	Tadjikistan
		TUR	Turkmenistan
E17		KAZ	Kazakhstan
E18		BEL	Belorussia
E19		MOL	Moldavia

RR = R.S.F.S.R.

* Leningrad and Moscow City and oblast.

(A) = A.S.S.R.

Major civil divisions of R.S.F.S.R. as in *NKhRSFSR* 1965.

Table 2.3. OBLAST DIVISIONS OF THE UKRAINE AND BELORUSSIA

U	*Ukraine*	U13	Lvov	*B*	*Belorussia*
U1	Vinnitsa	U14	Nikolayev	B1	Brest
U2	Volynsk	U15	Odessa	B2	Vitebsk
U3	Dnepropetrovsk	U16	Poltava	B3	Gomel
U4	Donetsk	U17	Rovno	B4	Grodno
U5	Zhitomir	U18	Sumy	B5	Minsk (City & obl.)
U6	Zakarpatsk	U19	Ternopol'	B6	Mogilev
U7	Zaporozh'ye	U20	Kharkov		
U8	Ivano-Frankov	U21	Kherson		
U9	Kiev (City & obl.)	U22	Khmelnitsk		
U10	Kirovograd	U23	Cherkassy		
U11	Krym	U24	Chernigov		
U12	Lugansk	U25	Chernovtsy		

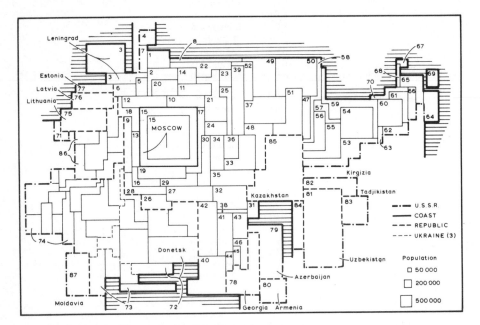

Fig. 2.4.   *The distribution of politico-administrative units of the U.S.S.R. on a topological map with population size of units as the base.*

2.3 AVAILABILITY OF SOVIET QUANTITATIVE DATA

Much has been written in the West about Soviet quantitative data. The reader who wishes to go beyond the following greatly simplified summary of data relevant to this book may refer to Herman.[3] Jasny's[4] commentary on the first major Soviet statistical publication since World War II remains invaluable for its detail and thoroughness; this may be supplemented by a later paper by Jasny.[5] Nove[6] may also be referred to. It is only fair to add that Soviet counterparts of Jasny, Nove and others find some Western statistical data suspect; indeed the title of one publication on this subject by Tsyrlin,[7] 'Bourgeois statistics hide the truth', is self-explanatory.

No country even collects, let alone publishes, every piece of quantitative information that might be useful for some purpose at some time. From the point of view of the Western geographer, it is what is published *and* becomes available in the West that matters, since unpublished material cannot easily be obtained by research workers visiting the U.S.S.R. unless it is at least some decades old. Much of what is actually published is apparently not even widely circulated in the U.S.S.R. itself; in fact, policy generally seems to be to omit data rather than to falsify it. Some of the data published, however, are manipulated if not falsified; for a long time, for example, inflated grain output figures were given. Some figures are given as percentages on an undefined base figure, or on one that is ridiculously small, as were many 1913 industrial production figures, against which present output seems astronomical. Of the material published, some is broken down into regions (sometimes into 15, sometimes 26, sometimes 73), but much is not; the part with a regional breakdown is usually of much greater interest and use to the geographer. A particular set of data, such as town population figures, or area under wheat in R.S.F.S.R. oblasts, may be published periodically with reasonable regularity, or it may appear only occasionally. Thus comparisons and trends through time cannot be established for small regions and as a result, information that can be used for dealing with spatial relations in the U.S.S.R. is very irregular. There is almost nothing, for example, on non-ferrous or precious metals, other than symbols in economic geographical atlases giving little clue as to the size of output. Published statistics in the engineering industry are also given selectively, and certain types of machine tools are a favourite if unrepresentative indicator. There is a great deal, on the other hand, about certain building materials, timber and clothing items.

In general, industrial data are less adequate than agricultural data. Many agricultural figures are however suspect, due to different definitions given to weights and other measures. Thus statistics on grain in the husk, green silage and livestock are particularly difficult to use because of the high proportion of production consumed directly on the farm and the problem of assessing the weight and value of livestock units. The relative value of crops and stock in particular areas can usually only be estimated. Since the publication of the 1959 census, population data have been available in relative abundance, but the census, now out of date, is supplemented only by

meagre estimates of certain aspects. Occasional financial (eg retail sales), social (eg availability of doctors) and transport figures appear, but they are rarely sufficient to support detailed study.

After drawing on the data readily available in the statistical yearbooks one must decide whether to be satisfied with these or to risk what might be a fruitless search through various sources to increase the data available. Since the present book attempts to include all major aspects of the geography of the U.S.S.R. in a relatively small space, use has largely been made of the more readily available sources. The intention is to use such data more intensively than previously with the help of certain mathematical techniques. It may be suggested that even though some sets of figures are absolutely inflated, as grain output has apparently been, the regional breakdown and true relative importance of various regions may still be revealed.

The main sources of quantitative data have, therefore, been the *Narodnoye khozyaystvo SSSR* and the *Narodnoye khozyaystvo RSFSR*. These have been published in most years from 1958 to 1965, but in 1967 they were replaced by the less abundant *Strana sovetov za 50 let* and its R.S.F.S.R. equivalent. Statistical sources are listed in the Bibliography at the end of the book. Finally, the high standard of Soviet atlases deserves mention and several atlases have been referred to continuously in the preparation of the present book. In contrast, large scale topographical maps are very difficult to obtain, even, it seems, for Soviet geographers themselves. Chappell[8] discusses their availability in the West.

REFERENCES

1. e.g., *Geografischeskiy atlas dlya uchiteley sredney shkoly*, pp. IV–V (MVD SSSR, Moscow, 1954)
2. SCHAPIRO, L., *The Government and Politics of the Soviet Union*, 46–47, 83 (Hutchinson, London, 1968)
3. HERMAN, L. M., 'Figures Unfit to Print' *Problems of Communism*, 14–22, Nov.–Dec. 1964
4. JASNY, N., *The Soviet 1956 Statistical Handbook: A Commentary* (Michigan State University Press, East Lansing, 1957)
5. JASNY, N., 'Some Thoughts on Soviet Statistics, An Evaluation' *International Affairs*, **35**, No 1, 53–60, 1959
6. NOVE, A., *The Soviet Economy*, 19–22 (Allen and Unwin, London, 1961)

7. TSYRLIN, L. M. and PETROV, A. I., *Burzhuaz-naya statistika skryvayet pravdy* (Gospolitizdat, 1953)
8. CHAPPELL, J. E., 'Soviet Cartography: Comparisons and Gaps' *Prof. Geogr.*, 15, 1–7, 1963

BIBLIOGRAPHY

KALESNIK, S. V., 'Some Results of the New Discussion about a 'Unified' Geography' *Soviet Geogr.*, 6, No 7, 11–26, 1968

MEDVEDKOV, Yu. V., 'Applications of Mathematics to some Problems in Economic Geography' *Soviet Geogr.*, 5, No 6, 1964
RODOMAN, B. B., 'Logical and Cartographic Forms of Regionalisation and Their Study Objectives' *Soviet Geogr.*, 6, No 9, 3–20, 1965
SAUSHKIN, Yu. G., 'A History of Soviet Economic Geography' *Soviet Geogr.*, 7, No 8, 1966
SMIRNOV, L. Ye., 'The role and significance of objective (mathematical) methods in geographic research' *Soviet Geogr.*, 9, No 1, 55–67, 1968

3

Comecon in figures

The purpose of this chapter is to provide a link between the study of the U.S.S.R. and its Comecon partners in East Europe. A great deal of quantitative information is presented with the help of tables. Comecon in the present context refers to the U.S.S.R. and eight communist countries of East Central Europe. Yugoslavia and Albania, strictly, are not members of Comecon. The eight are referred to for convenience as East Europe when taken in contrast to the U.S.S.R.

3.1 PHYSICAL COMPARISONS

East Europe lies roughly between 55°N. and 40°N., a span of latitude comparable to that from north England to south Italy. It lies between the Baltic, Adriatic and Black Seas, around the meridian of 20°E. (see Fig. 3.1(a)). In Fig. 3.1(d), East Europe is reproduced at its correct latitudes, and to scale, at various places in the U.S.S.R. In Figs. 3.1(b) and (c), it is superimposed on the Volga basin and on Kazakhstan, with meridian 20°E. lying on 45°E. amd 70°E. respectively; the positions of the eight East European capitals are shown in black dots.

Table 3.1 compares temperature, precipitation, and vegetation for four groups of districts of similar latitude selected respectively from (a), (b) and (c) of Fig. 3.1. From the table a striking contrast is seen in conditions in the colder part of the year between East Europe and places in the U.S.S.R. Winter temperatures become progressively colder, far into Siberia. Summer tem-

peratures, however, are somewhat higher towards the east. Altogether, then, there is a much greater range of temperature towards the interior of Eurasia than in East Europe, which itself, however, has greater ranges than are found at comparable latitudes in West Europe. A further contrast between East Europe and the selected areas of the U.S.S.R. is in mean annual precipitation. Increasing cold and aridity towards the interior of the U.S.S.R. bring progressively closer together the coniferous forest of the north, found in Scandinavia in Europe, and the desert of the south, found in North Africa at the longitude of West Europe.

3.2 POLITICO-ADMINISTRATIVE UNITS AND THEIR CONNECTIVITY

The U.S.S.R. is subdivided into 15 Soviet Socialist Republics of greatly varying area and population. It is also divided into 19 so-called economic regions, the layout of which is to some extent related to that of the 15 Republics. In Table 3.2, the 19 Soviet economic regions (referred to as El–E19) are put alongside the eight countries of East Europe and ranked according to area. Their population is also given. The data in the table are presented in graph form in Fig. 3.2. A logarithmic scale is used for area on the horizontal axis, since there is such a great contrast between the largest and the smallest that on an arithmetical scale the small ones crowd together at one end. There is only a fairly weak

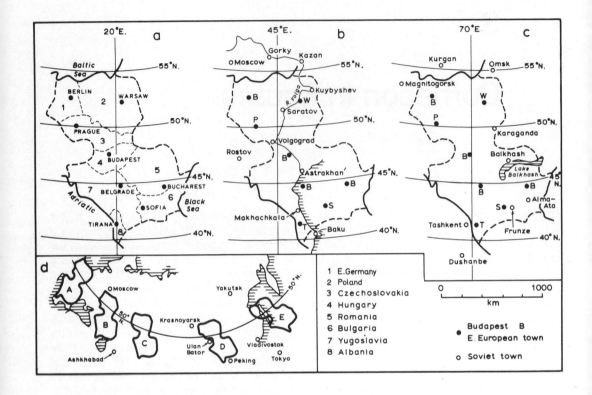

Fig. 3.1.   *Comparison of East Europe and the U.S.S.R. a The position of East Europe. b-c East Europe superimposed on the Volga and Kazakhstan regions of the U.S.S.R., matched according to latitude. d General view of the relation of East Europe to the U.S.S.R.*

Table 3.1. COMPARISON OF SELECTED PHYSICAL INDICES FOR EAST EUROPE AND THE U.S.S.R.

District	Temperature (°C) Mean monthly January	July	Jan.-July range	Days Frost free	Duration of snow cover	Mean annual precipitation (cm)	Soil-vegetation type
Baltic coast	0	15	15	180	70	60	Broadleaf forest
55°N. Kazan'-Kuybyshev	−14	20	34	135	155	42	Mixed-broadleaf forest
Omsk	−19	19	38	115	165	34	Forest steppe
Prague	− 4	18	22	180	60	80	Broadleaf forest
50°N. Saratov-Volgograd	−11	22	33	160	120	35	Steppe
Karaganda	−16	20	36	110	145	30	Steppe
Belgrade	− 2	22	24	200	50	70	Broadleaf forest
45°N. Astrakhan'	− 7	25	32	195	55	20	Desert
Alma-Ata	− 9	24	33	165	100	30	Desert
South Albania	10	20	12	Frost and snow rare		100	'Mediterranean'
40°N. Baku	2	25	27	270	Few	15	Desert
Fergana	− 5	25	30	210	60	10	Desert

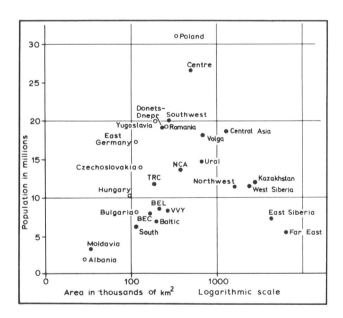

Fig. 3.2.   The comparative area and population of the 19 economic regions of the U.S.S.R. and eight countries of East Europe. Abbreviations on graph: BEC, Blackearth Centre; BEL, Belorussia; NCA, North Caucasus; TRC, Transcaucasia; VVY, Volga-Vyatka.

Table. 3.2. COMPARATIVE AREA AND POPULATION OF SOVIET ECONOMIC REGIONS AND EAST EUROPEAN COUNTRIES IN JANUARY 1968 FOR U.S.S.R., 1967 FOR COUNTRIES

	Country/Region	Area $km^2 \times 10^3$	Population $\times 10^3$	Area Rank	Population Rank	Difference in rank
E10	Far East	6 216	5 709	1	25	24
E9	East Siberia	4 123	7 321	2	23	21
E17	Kazakhstan	2 715	12 678	3	13	10
E8	West Siberia	2 427	12 201	4	14	10
E1	Northwest	1 663	11 855	5	16	11
E16	Central Asia	1 279	18 867	6	7	1
E5	Volga	680	18 004	7	8	1
E7	Ural	680	15 262	8	10	2
E2	Centre	485	26 763	9	2	7
E10	North Caucasus	355	13 867	10	12	2
C2	POLAND	313	32 065	11	1	10
E12	Southwest	269	20 389	12	3	9
E3	Volga-Vyatka	263	8 288	13	20	7
C7	YUGOSLAVIA	256	20 058	14	4	10
C5	ROMANIA	238	19 540	15	6	9
E11	Donets-Dnepr	221	19 922	16	5	11
E18	Belorussia	208	8 820	17	18	1
E14	Baltic	189	7 359	18	22	4
E15	Transcaucasia	186	11 882	19	15	4
E4	Blackearth Centre	168	7 948	20	21	1
C3	CZECHOSLOVAKIA	128	14 333	21	11	10
C6	BULGARIA	111	8 335	22	19	3
E13	South	111	6 070	23	24	1
C1	EAST GERMANY	108	17 090	24	9	15
C4	HUNGARY	93	10 236	25	17	8
E19	Moldavia	34	3 484	26	26	0
C8	ALBANIA	29	1 938	27	27	0

U.S.S.R.   Area 22 402 000
Population 236 689 000
Source *NkhSSSR* 1967 902–4

positive correlation between the area and the population of the 27 units.

The Spearman rank correlation coefficient, r, which lies between +1 and −1, the extremes of complete positive and complete negative correlation respectively, is +0·41 in this case. The regions differ enormously in territorial extent. Thus the Far East (6 216 000 km^2) is almost 200 times as large as Moldavia (34 000 km^2). Even then, however, Moldavia is relatively large compared with many planning regions in West European countries and the Centre (485 000 km^2) is twice as large as Great Britain (244 000 km^2), which is divided into about a dozen regions. The regions also differ widely in population; the Centre with 26 million people,

has about eight times as many as Moldavia or five times as many as the vast Far East region. In general, there is a better balance in population than in area. Changes since the early 1950's resulting in the splitting of the Ukraine and the Centre each into three, have given greater balance than previously in terms of number of inhabitants. In Fig. 3.4, regions 2, 3 and 4 previously formed the Centre, and 11, 12, 13 and 19 formed the South. The two parts of 1, however, the former Northwest and North, have been amalgamated. The extent to which the splitting of the two largest (in population) regions has improved the balance of population can be judged visually in Fig. 3.5.

The overall lack of correlation between area

Fig. 3.3.   *The 19 economic regions of the U.S.S.R. and the eight countries of East Europe. Selected towns are included for identification.*

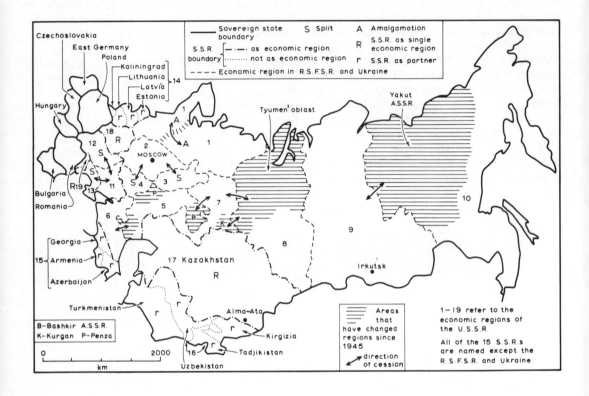

Fig. 3.4.   *The economic regions of the U.S.S.R. (E 1–E 19) in the late 1960's. Numbers on the map refer to economic regions, names to Republics of the U.S.S.R. and to East European countries.*

and population covers two underlying trends. In the first place, among the areally smaller units there is a tendency for population to increase as size increases. But among the larger third, or so, the reverse tendency may be observed; this is evident in Fig. 3.2. The distribution of the units discussed above is mapped in Fig. 3.3. In Fig. 3.3(a) the larger units only are named and the East European units are not distinguished. In the enlarged western part, Fig. 3.3(b), the remaining Soviet units are named, together with the East European countries.

For some mapping purposes, the conventional map of units is unsatisfactory. If, for example, *per capita* consumption of electricity is to be mapped on an areal unit basis, then unjustified prominence will be given visually to East Siberia, as this large area has a high *per capita* consumption though a small total population. East Germany will similarly come high. However, a much greater visual impact is conveyed by East Siberia than by East Germany, if the *area* of each is shaded heavily. East Germany has more than twice as many people, and actually produces more electricity. Such visual dishonesty may either be overlooked, or it may to some extent be remedied. It is possible to make a composite map, with an inflated scale for the part of Comecon with small units but dense population. It is possible also to draw circles

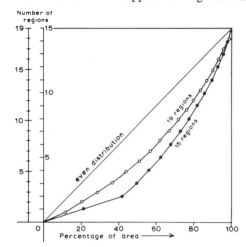

Fig. 3.5.   *A comparison of the distribution of population among the 15 regions of the early 1960's and the 19 regions of the later 1960's. Each set of regions is taken in turn. The regions are ranked in descending order of number of inhabitants. The population of each is then expressed as a percentage of the total population of the U.S.S.R. The percentages are added cumulatively. On the vertical axis of the graph, the scale is divided evenly among the regions (15 or 19). Cumulative population is shown on the horizontal axis. In the system of 15 regions, for example, the three largest had about 50% of population. In the system of 19, the six largest did.*

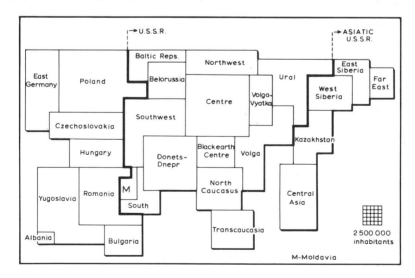

Fig. 3.6.   *A population based topological map of the units of Comecon. Each unit is proportional in area to the population of the economic region or country it represents. Contiguity is correct and orientation is approximately maintained. This map is used as a basis for shading areal variations in several figures in the book.*

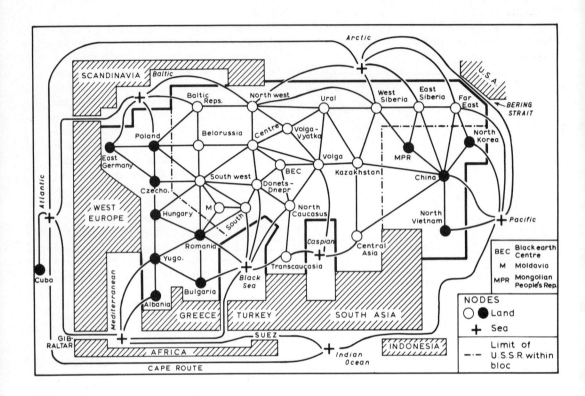

Fig. 3.7.   *Connectivity of regions in Comecon. Arcs (lines) join nodes (circles or crosses) where the countries, economic regions, seas or oceans they represent share a boundary or a coastline. Adjoining seas and/or oceans are also joined. The diagram is a topological map. Non-communist areas are shaded.*

Table 3.3. SOVIET TRADE WITH EAST EUROPE, 1955–66, EXPORTS PLUS IMPORTS

(a) *Value in millions of roubles*

U.S.S.R. with	'old' rouble						'new' rouble					
	1955	1956	1957	1958	1959	1960	1961	1962	1963	1964	1965	1966
Poland	2 874	2 562	2 747	2 568	723	790	907	1 043	1 149	1 240	1 357	1 383
East Germany	3 940	4 791	6 506	6 463	1 728	1 783	1 877	2 201	2 356	2 442	2 383	2 380
Czechoslovakia	2 970	3 081	3 748	3 835	1 066	1 156	1 215	1 436	1 620	1 683	1 764	1 632
Hungary	1 047	991	1 426	1 450	420	504	618	720	780	877	955	915
Romania	1 910	1 790	1 763	1 940	434	487	569	651	728	823	759	713
Bulgaria	996	1 012	1 483	1 615	496	565	614	753	846	991	1 084	1 216
Yugoslavia	136	475	520	408	89	97	81	107	165	230	300	366
Albania	83	106	187	233	57	61	negl.	negl.	negl.	negl.	negl.	negl.
Comecon total	13 955	14 806	18 378	18 511	5 012	5 433	5 881	6 909	7 644	8 285	8 602	8 605
Total Soviet Trade	26 117	29 129	33 277	34 589	9 463	10 072	10 643	12 136	12 898	13 878	14 598	15 079

(b) *% of value of all Soviet foreign trade*

	1955	1956	1957	1958	1959	1960	1961	1962	1963	1964	1965	1966
Poland	11·0	8·8	8·3	7·4	7·6	7·8	8·5	8·6	8·9	8·9	9·3	9·2
East Germany	15·1	16·4	19·5	18·7	18·3	17·7	17·6	18·1	18·3	17·6	16·3	15·8
Czechoslovakia	11·4	10·6	11·3	11·1	11·3	11·5	11·4	11·8	12·6	12·1	12·1	10·9
Hungary	4·0	3·4	4·3	4·2	4·4	5·0	5·8	5·9	6·0	6·3	6·5	6·1
Romania	7·3	6·1	5·3	5·6	4·6	4·8	5·3	5·4	5·6	5·9	5·2	4·7
Bulgaria	3·8	3·5	4·5	4·7	5·2	5·6	5·8	6·2	6·6	7·1	7·4	8·1
Yugoslavia	0·5	1·6	1·6	1·2	0·9	1·0	0·8	0·9	1·3	1·7	2·1	2·4
Albania	0·3	0·4	0·6	0·7	0·6	0·6	0	0	0	0	0	0
East Europe	53·4	50·8	55·2	53·5	53·0	54·0	55·3	56·9	59·3	59·7	58·9	57·2
U.S.S.R. total	100	100	100	100	100	100	100	100	100	100	100	100

Sources: *Vneshnyaya torgovlya SSSR za 1956 god, statisticheskiy obzor*, 7–8 (Vneshtorgizdat, Moscow, 1958)

za 1958 god, 7–8   *za 1963 god*, 10–12
za 1960 god, 7–8   *za 1965 god*, 10–12
za 1962 god, 10–12   *za 1966 god*, 11–12

proportional to population on the areas, and to shade the circles. One can alternatively construct a topological map, in which the units retain correct contiguity but are drawn directly in proportion to their population, rather than to their area. This has been done for Comecon in Fig. 3.6. Such a topological map has drawbacks, one of which is its arbitrariness. However, any projection of an area the size of Comecon is itself considerably distorted and topological. The essential feature of a topological map is its flexibility. Both areal extent and orientation may be ignored. But each pair of regions that is contiguous (ie shares a boundary) on the conventional map must also be contiguous on the topological map. For a description of relevant aspects of topology see Ore[1] for mathematical aspects, and Cole and King[2] for geographical aspects.

Topological maps should be used in conjunction with more conventional maps. On the positive side, the map in Fig. 3.6 forms an honest base for shading maps using data based on people rather than area. The map shown and other topological maps are used considerably in this book. The liability of an areally enormous but demographically empty Siberia is overcome; indeed, Asiatic U.S.S.R. is very much cut down to scale.

The contiguity of the various units has been stressed in Fig. 3.7. In topological terms, each unit of area (eg country, sea, Soviet region) is represented by a node; nodes representing units that are contiguous are linked by arcs. Actual boundaries have mostly been omitted for clarity, but some limits, including coasts and part of the boundary of the Soviet Union, have been shown. The boundaries form a second system of arcs and nodes. From the map, it is possible to work out paths from place to place. For example, which regions does one have to pass through on a journey from Czechoslovakia to the Mongolian People's Republic without passing through non-Communist areas? Can a shipment of goods from Poland reach North Vietnam by land without passing through China? The seasonal nature of the Arctic arcs, and the closure of the Suez Canal, should be borne in mind.

3.3 SOVIET TRADE WITH EAST EUROPE

How strong are Soviet trade links with East Europe? Table 3.3(a) shows the value of total

Soviet trade (imports and exports) with the eight East European countries during 1955–66. Data sources are shown below the table. The introduction of the new rouble in 1959 makes comparison over the whole period difficult. In Table 3.3(b), therefore, values are given in per cent of total Soviet foreign trade with all countries of the world. Actual goods exchanged will be discussed in Chapter 15.

Year to year fluctuations in trade should not be taken too seriously, but some long term trends do appear. During the earlier part of the period shown, Soviet trade with China dropped sharply. From 1960, its trade with Cuba increased. The value and volume of Soviet foreign trade has itself increased fairly steadily throughout the whole period. Its trade, however, with the eight countries rose from a relative low in 1956, when it was some 51% of all Soviet trade, to a high in 1964, when it reached nearly 60%.

Table 3.4. DEPENDENCE ON U.S.S.R. FOR FOREIGN TRADE

Country	Trade in roubles/ inhabitant	Trade with Soviet Union
Bulgaria	149	53%
East Germany	140	over 46%
Czechoslovakia	116	37%
Hungary	91	35%
Poland	44	33%
Romania	38	40%
Yugoslavia	19	12%

A somewhat different picture of the dependence of the seven East European countries (excluding Albania) on the U.S.S.R. for their foreign trade emerges if the figures are re-examined. Table 3.4 shows Soviet trade with each country in terms of roubles per inhabitant in 1966 (first column), and the share of the trade of each country with the Soviet Union as a percentage of the total trade of the country (second column). On these criteria, Bulgaria is the most dependent, Yugoslavia the least.

3.4 AN ASSESSMENT OF COMECON THROUGH MULTIVARIATE ANALYSIS

In this section, the 19 economic regions of the U.S.S.R. (E1–E19) and seven East European countries (20–26 or C1–C7) are studied together. Roughly comparable data for 15 distributions (or variables) are presented: they cover mainly demographic, economic and social aspects. Three of the variables are mapped in Fig. 3.8, urban population, electricity consumption and birthrates. The topological base map (see Fig. 3.6) is used to give a balanced visual picture of population based variables. The mean (average) values for Comecon as a whole for the three variables mapped are: (a) urban population as a percentage of total population, 51%, (b) electricity consumption per inhabitant, 198 kWh, (c) birthrate, 18·8 per thousand population. Shading is graded about the mean in each case. A visual comparison of (a) and (b) suggests a fairly strong correlation between these two distributions. A different pattern, however, emerges in (c).

The rest of this section is concerned with a multivariate view of the 26 regions. Instead of

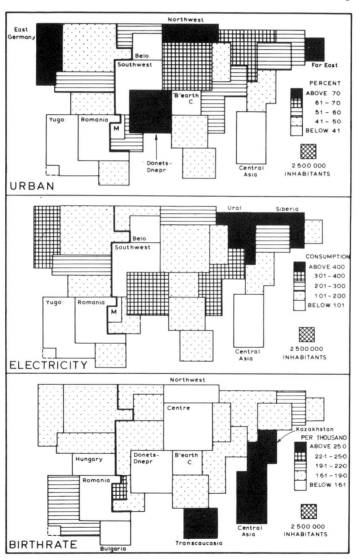

Fig. 3.8.   *Single variable maps of the 19 economic regions of the U.S.S.R. and seven East European countries. Regions on the maps are proportional in area to the population of the regions they represent. Correct contiguity is retained. (a) Urban dwellers as a percentage of total population. (b) Per capita consumption of electricity in kWh/inhabitant. (c) Birthrate per thousand inhabitants.*

comparing a pair of distributions visually, as was done with (a) and (b) above, factor analysis takes a large number of distributions (15 in this case) and compares them mathematically. Multivariate analysis is used at several stages in this book, the first application being in this section. Appendix 1 contains a brief account of the steps in factor analysis, as well as references to works on the subject and to works using it. The technique has been applied already in a number of geographical papers and books, as well as in other disciplines.

Table 3.5 contains selected information about the 19 economic regions of the U.S.S.R. and seven Comecon countries, treated on an equal footing. The original data were drawn from various sources and the 15 variables selected for the study were chosen to give a reasonably representative picture of the human geography of Comecon. Figures are for 1965 or nearest year. Some data that might have been revealing were not available. Some of the variables used, particularly the last three, are not exactly comparable between the U.S.S.R. and the other seven. The data displayed in Table 3.5 have already been processed. As an example, consider the column of figures for electricity. The electricity output of Poland (area 20) in 1965 was 43 800 million kWh. The population was 31 500 000. The *per capita* output of electricity was therefore about 1 390 kWh per inhabitant. The output of Yugoslavia was 15 500 million kWh and its population 20 million. *Per capita* output in Yugoslavia was therefore about 770 kWh. The last zero is omitted in the table, and electricity output therefore represents tens of kWh per inhabitant for each region. Other data have been treated similarly.

Table 3.6 expresses the data in Table 3.5 in a standardised (normalised) way so that the variables may more easily be compared. The Comecon mean for each variable (column) of figures is expressed as 100. It is an unweighted mean, calculated from the already processed data, but does not differ much from the weighted mean. Thus the mean of 197 for electricity is reduced to 100 and the values for each area correspondingly reduced by 100/197. The Polish electricity figure drops from 139 to 70.

The data in Tables 3.5 and 3.6 may be used in several ways. Thus three of the variables have been mapped singly in Fig. 3.8. Another way in which the data can be considered is by ranking

the areal units from high to low. Table 3.7 reveals that for some variables the seven East European countries are dispersed among the 19 economic regions of the U.S.S.R., whereas for others, particularly the last five variables, they crowd at one end. The rest of this section shows the results of factor analysis applied to the 26×15 data matrix.

1. The correlation matrix in Table 3.8 may be studied to detect pairwise correlations. An index of more than about ±0·40 from 0 is fairly strong, and more than about ±0·70 from 0 is very strong. However, no confidence levels are suggested, as the indices are being used for descriptive, not inferential, purposes.

The matrix is square (the number of rows is the same as the number of columns, 15 × 15) and symmetric (the upper right and lower left halves are identical about the principal diagonal, which contains values of 1·00, the perfect positive correlation of each variable with itself).

The highest positive correlations are the following

+0·97 Birthrate and natural change
+0·84 Doctors and students
+0·75 Population density and deathrate
+0·73 Arable and cattle
+0·72 Urban and hospital beds
+0·66 Electricity and cement
+0·64 Cotton manufacturing and students
+0·61 Electricity and urban
+0·60 Electricity and steel

The highest negative correlations are the following

−0·68 Natural change and deathrate
−0·48 Population density and arable

When the meaning of each variable is considered carefully, each correlation index makes sense. For example, natural change (growth) of population, is 'explained' almost entirely by birthrate. Where one is high, so is the other. Hospital facilities tend to be better (ie hospital beds per population more) in urbanised regions than in others. Even from a 15 × 15 correlation matrix, however, it is not easy to pick out multiple interrelations between variables, though it is not difficult to see, for example, that not only are birthrate and natural increase closely correlated (+0·97) but each is negatively correlated (−0·49 and −0·68) with deathrate.

2. Factor analysis helps to group variables that are intercorrelated. Factor I accounts for 3·62 out of 15 units of variation, or about 24% of

Table 3.5. PROCESSED DATA FOR MULTIVARIATE STUDY OF 19 REGIONS OF THE U.S.S.R. AND SEVEN EAST EUROPEAN COUNTRIES. DATA FOR 1965 OR NEAREST AVAILABLE YEAR

	Region	Density: persons per km²	Births (per 10 000 inhabitants)	deaths (per 10 000 inhabitants)	Difference between birthrate and deathrate	Urban population as a percentage of total population	Kilograms of steel produced per inhabitant in 1965	Kilograms of cement produced per 10 inhabitants	Tens of kWh of electricity produced per inhabitant	Metres of cotton cloth produced per 10 inhabitants	Pairs of shoes produced per 100 inhabitants	Hectares of arable land per 100 inhabitants	Cattle per 1 000 inhabitants	Hospital beds per 10 000 inhabitants	Doctors per 100 000 inhabitants	Students per 10 000 inhabitants
E1	Northwest	7	155	75	80	77	170*	349	216	204	358	25	194	111	361	234
E2	Centre	46	137	78	59	66	75*	284	183	1 940	286	53	252	102	329	261
E3	Volga-Vyatka	32	171	76	95	46	25*	117	145	151	238	80	336	88	184	97
E4	Blackearth Centre	46	151	78	73	33	125*	428	109	6	92	136	520	74	169	92
E5	Volga	28	190	72	118	51	150*	468	316	79	176	160	488	86	221	124
E6	North Caucasus	30	188	70	118	47	55	220	131	30	272	123	496	80	239	119
E7	Ural†	9	179	69	110	65	1 970	515	498	9	197	99	337	98	198	114
E8	West Siberia	11	173	66	107	58	1 030	348	289	175	128	175	635	97	204	154
E9	East Siberia	10	203	66	137	57	56	391	595	118	117	116	441	97	193	121
E10	Far East	1	190	58	132	72	36	337	169	22	20	46	254	117	268	124
E11	Donets-Dnepr	88	155	68	87	71	1 890	414	396	9	188	73	425	99	242	132
E12	Southwest	71	174	73	101	34	0	199	72	21	229	65	492	85	223	115
E13	South	48	170	71	99	53	0	60	141	220	197	116	569	94	334	158
E14	Baltic	36	170	83	87	54	21	314	172	314	334	73	505	103	274	132
E15	Transcaucasia	56	308	67	241	49	191	295	169	252	238	21	328	81	296	136
E16	Central Asia	12	350	56	294	37	21	250	94	202	141	35	271	89	181	120
E17	Kazakhstan	4	278	57	221	46	93	340	158	20	126	255	570	97	188	96
E18	Belorussia	40	190	64	126	37	0	206	98	10	328	71	553	88	221	101
E19	Moldavia	92	225	61	164	25	0	174	92	6	218	58	277	88	182	87
20	Poland	101	174	74	100	49	290	304	139	258	168	49	314	67	160	80
21	East Germany	158	165	134	31	73	230	358	315	143	170	28	282	121	151	66‡
22	Czechoslovakia	107	163	99	64	59	610	402	240	336	369	36	310	79	206	100
23	Hungary	109	131	106	25	42	250	234	110	300	252	50	176	76	191	92
24	Romania	80	146	86	60	38	180	282	90	167	220	51	256	75	154	69
25	Bulgaria	82	153	81	72	46	72	326	124	356	128	71	177	61	165	120
26	Yugoslavia	78	204	85	119	30	89	155	77	197	150	52	280	60‡	145	85

† Ural includes Tyumen'. * estimates. ‡ upgraded to allow for very unfavourable definition.

Sources *NkhSSSR* 1965 and *NkhRSFSR* 1965, *Statistical Yearbook of the United Nations* 1965, *Stateman's Yearbook*.

Table 3.6. DATA IN TABLE 3.5 FURTHER PROCESSED

	Region or county	Demographic				Productive								Service		
		Density	Birthrate	Deathrate	Natural change	Urban	Steel	Cement	Electricity	Cotton	Shoes	Arable	Cattle	Hospital beds	Doctors	Students
	Overall mean	100	100	100	100	100	100	100	100	100	100	100	100	100	100	100
E1	Northwest	13	83	99	71	152	58	117	109	99	174	31	52	125	165	194
E2	Centre	87	73	103	53	130	26	95	93	938	139	65	67	115	151	217
E3	Volga-Vyatka	60	91	100	85	91	9	39	73	73	116	98	90	99	84	81
E4	Blackearth Centre	87	80	103	65	65	43	143	55	3	45	167	139	83	77	76
E5	Volga	53	101	95	105	101	51	157	160	38	86	197	130	97	101	103
E6	North Caucasus	56	100	92	105	93	19	74	66	15	132	151	132	90	109	99
E7	Ural	17	95	91	98	129	671	172	252	4	96	122	90	110	91	95
E8	West Siberia	21	92	87	95	114	351	116	146	85	62	215	170	109	93	128
E9	East Siberia	19	108	87	122	113	19	131	301	57	57	142	118	109	88	101
E10	Far East	2	101	76	118	142	12	113	86	11	10	57	68	132	123	103
E11	Donets-Dnepr	166	82	90	77	140	644	139	200	4	92	80	113	111	111	110
E12	Southwest	134	92	96	90	67	0	67	36	10	112	142	131	96	102	96
E13	South	90	90	94	88	105	0	20	71	106	96	90	152	106	153	131
E14	Baltic	68	90	109	77	107	7	105	87	152	163	142	135	116	125	110
E15	Transcaucasia	105	164	88	215	97	65	99	86	122	116	26	88	91	136	113
E16	Central Asia	23	186	74	262	73	7	84	48	17	69	43	72	83	83	100
E17	Kazakhstan	8	148	75	197	91	32	114	80	10	61	313	152	109	86	80
E18	Belorussia	75	101	84	112	73	0	69	50	5	160	87	148	99	101	84
E19	Moldavia	173	120	80	146	49	0	58	47	3	106	71	74	99	83	72
20	Poland	190	92	98	89	97	99	102	70	125	82	60	84	75	73	66
21	East Germany	297	88	177	28	144	78	120	159	69	83	34	75	136	69	55
22	Czechoslovakia	201	87	130	57	117	208	135	121	162	180	44	83	89	94	83
23	Hungary	205	70	140	22	83	85	78	56	145	123	61	47	85	87	76
24	Romania	151	78	113	53	75	61	94	46	81	107	63	68	84	71	57
25	Bulgaria	154	81	107	64	91	25	109	63	172	62	87	47	69	76	100
26	Yugoslavia	147	108	112	106	59	30	52	39	95	73	64	75	67	66	71

Table 3.7. REGIONS AND COUNTRIES IN TABLE 3.5 RANKED FROM HIGHEST TO LOWEST FOR EACH VARIABLE

	Population density	Birthrate	Deathrate	Natural change	Urban population	Steel	Cement	Electricity	Cotton cloth	Shoes	Arable land	Cattle	Hospital beds	Doctors	Students
1	GER	CAS	GER	CAS	NWE	URL	URL	ESB	CEN	CZE	KAZ	WSB	GER	NWE	CEN
2	HUN	TRC	HUN	TRC	GER	DDN	VOL	URL	BUL	NWE	WSB	SOU	FAR	SOU	NWE
3	CZE	KAZ	CZE	KAZ	FAR	WSB	BEC	DDN	CZE	BAL	VOL	KAZ	NWE	CEN	SOU
4	POL	MOL	ROM	MOL	DDN	CZE	DDN	VOL	BAL	BEL	BEC	BEL	BAL	TRC	WSB
5	MOL	ESB	YUG	ESB	CEN	POL	CZE	GER	HUN	CEN	NCA	BEC	CEN	BAL	TRC
6	DDN	YUG	BUL	FAR	URL	HUN	ESB	WSB	POL	NCA	ESB	BAL	DDN	FAR	DDN
7	BUL	VOL	CEN	BEL	CZE	GER	GER	CZE	TRC	HUN	SOU	NCA	URL	DDN	BAL
8	ROM	FAR	BEC	YUG	WSB	TRC	NWE	NWE	SOU	VVY	URL	SWE	WSB	NCA	VOL
9	YUG	BEL	VVY	VOL	ESB	ROM	WSB	CEN	NWE	TRC	VVY	VOL	ESB	SWE	FAR
10	SWE	NCA	NWE	NCA	BAL	NWE	KAZ	BAL	CAS	SWE	DDN	ESB	KAZ	VOL	ESB
11	TRC	URL	POL	URL	SOU	VOL	FAR	FAR	YUG	ROM	BAL	DDN	SOU	BEL	CAS
12	SOU	WSB	SWE	WSB	VOL	BEC	BUL	TRC	WSE	MOL	BEL	VVY	CAS	CZE	BUL
13	CEN	SWE	VOL	SWE	TRC	KAZ	BAL	KAZ	ROM	URL	BUL	URL	VVY	WSB	NCA
14	BEC	POL	SOU	POL	POL	CEN	POL	VVY	VVY	SOU	SWE	TRC	BEL	URL	SWE
15	BEL	VVY	NCA	SOU	NCA	YUG	TRC	SOU	GER	DDN	MOL	POL	MOL	ESB	URL
16	BAL	SOU	URL	VVY	VVY	BUL	CEN	POL	ESB	VOL	CEN	CZE	VOL	HUN	BEL
17	VVY	BAL	DDN	DDN	KAZ	NCA	ROM	NCA	VOL	GER	YUG	GER	SWE	KAZ	CZE
18	NCA	GER	TRC	BAL	BUL	ESB	CAS	BUL	NCA	POL	ROM	YUG	TRC	VVY	VVY
19	VOL	CZE	WSB	NWE	HUN	FAR	HUN	HUN	FAR	YUG	HUN	MOL	NCA	CAS	KAZ
20	CAS	NWE	ESB	BEC	ROM	VVY	NCA	BEC	SWE	CAS	POL	CAS	CZE	MOL	BEC
21	WSB	BUL	BEL	BUL	CAS	BAL	BEL	BEL	KAZ	BUL	FAR	FAR	HUN	BEC	HUN
22	ESB	DDN	MOL	CZE	BEL	CAS	SWE	CAS	BEL	WSB	CZE	ROM	ROM	BUL	MOL
23	URL	BEC	FAR	CEN	SWE	SWE	MOL	MOL	URL	KAZ	CAS	CEN	BEC	POL	YUG
24	NWE	ROM	KAZ	ROM	BEC	SOU	YUG	ROM	DDN	ESB	GER	NWE	BUL	ROM	POL
25	KAZ	CEN	CAS	GER	YUG	BEL	VVY	YUG	BEC	BEC	NWE	HUN	POL	GER	ROM
26	FAR	HUN		HUN	MOL	MOL	SOU	SWE	MOL	FAR	TRC	BUL	YUG	YUG	GER

Table 3.8. CORRELATION MATRIX OF PEARSON PRODUCT MOMENT r VALUES, ROUNDED TO TWO DECIMAL PLACES. THE MATRIX IS SQUARE (NUMBER OF ROWS = NUMBER OF COLUMNS) AND SYMMETRIC (EACH CORRELATION INDEX IS SHOWN TWICE, APART FROM THE 1·00 INDICES ON THE PRINCIPAL DIAGONAL)

Variables →	Density	Birthrate	Deathrate	Natural change	Urban population	Steel	Cement	Electricity	Cotton	Shoes	Arable	Cattle	Hospital beds	Doctors	Students
	1	2	3	4	5	6	7	8	9	10	11	12	13	14	15
1 Population density	1·00	-0·33	0·75	-0·48	-0·12	0·01	-0·13	-0·19	-0·06	0·17	-0·48	-0·37	-0·29	-0·38	-0·43
2 Birthrate	-0·33	1·00	-0·49	0·97	-0·29	-0·18	-0·10	-0·10	-0·22	-0·23	0·09	0·08	-0·00	-0·06	-0·13
3 Deathrate	0·75	-0·49	1·00	-0·68	0·18	-0·03	0·06	0·01	0·16	0·25	-0·37	-0·35	0·00	-0·25	-0·25
4 Natural change	-0·48	0·97	-0·68	1·00	-0·29	-0·14	-0·10	-0·09	-0·23	-0·26	0·17	0·16	-0·00	0·01	-0·04
5 Urban population	-0·12	-0·29	0·18	-0·29	1·00	0·43	0·49	0·61	0·23	0·07	-0·10	-0·12	0·72	0·50	0·51
6 Steel	0·01	-0·18	-0·03	-0·14	0·43	1·00	0·55	0·60	-0·14	-0·03	0·09	0·07	0·16	-0·05	0·03
7 Cement	-0·13	-0·10	0·06	-0·10	0·49	0·55	1·00	0·66	-0·07	-0·18	0·20	0·01	0·23	-0·09	0·05
8 Electricity	-0·19	-0·10	0·01	-0·09	0·61	0·60	0·66	1·00	-0·07	-0·14	0·20	0·13	0·44	0·03	0·13
9 Cotton mf.	-0·06	-0·22	0·16	-0·23	0·23	-0·14	-0·07	-0·07	1·00	0·27	-0·22	-0·30	0·07	0·38	0·64
10 Shoes	0·17	-0·23	0·25	-0·26	0·07	-0·03	-0·18	-0·14	0·27	1·00	-0·35	-0·08	0·01	0·41	0·30
11 Arable	-0·48	0·09	-0·37	0·17	-0·10	0·09	0·20	0·20	-0·22	-0·35	1·00	0·73	0·03	-0·12	-0·05
12 Cattle	-0·37	0·08	-0·35	0·16	-0·12	0·07	0·01	0·13	-0·30	-0·08	0·73	1·00	0·11	0·09	-0·03
13 Hospital beds	-0·29	-0·00	0·00	-0·00	0·72	0·16	0·23	0·44	0·07	0·01	0·03	0·11	1·00	0·47	0·40
14 Doctors	-0·38	-0·06	-0·25	0·01	0·50	-0·05	-0·09	0·03	0·38	0·41	-0·12	0·09	0·47	1·00	0·84
15 Students	-0·43	-0·13	-0·25	-0·04	0·51	0·03	0·05	0·13	0·64	0·30	-0·05	-0·03	0·40	0·84	1·00

all variation, and Factor II accounts for 3·49 or 23%. Together, then, the first two factors do 47% of the 'work' of 15 variables. Factor III is 2·62 or 17·5%.

3. Table 3.9 shows the loading of individual variables on the first three (the strongest) of the 15 possible factors. Factor I shows that there is a strong tendency for urbanisation to be associated with both industry and services. This is to be expected, but the numerical indices give a clearer description of degree of relationship than could be arrived at verbally. Factor II shows the relationship between density of population and demographic changes as well as availability of farm land. Factor III brings out contrasts between heavy industry on the one hand and light industry and services on the other.

One of the most important lessons of factor analysis is that few pairs of variables correlate very highly, but many correlate to some extent.

Table 3.9. FACTOR LOADINGS FROM TABLE 3.8

Factor I		Factor II		Factor III	
Urban	−0·88	Density of pop.	0·86	Doctors	+0·63
Students	−0·64	Deathrate	0·78	Cement	−0·62
Hospital beds	−0·59	Natural increase	−0·62	Students	+0·59
Doctors	−0·57	Arable	−0·59	Steel	−0·58
Birthrate	0·57	Cattle	−0·54	Electricity	−0·57
Natural increase	0·55	Birthrate	−0·49	Cotton mf.	+0·52
Electricity	−0·53	Hospital beds	−0·42	Shoes	+0·43
Cotton mf.	−0·47				
Cement	−0·42				
Steel	−0·41				

Table 3.10. WEIGHTINGS OF INDIVIDUAL AREAS ON FIRST THREE FACTORS

	Factor I		Factor II		Factor III	
1	Centre	−8·3	Kazakhstan	−6·7	Ural	−5·0
2	Northwest	−7·5	West Siberia	−4·7	East Germany	−4·2
3	Donets-Dnepr	−4·7	East Siberia	−4·4	Donets-Dnepr	−3·8
4	East Germany	−4·1	Ural	−3·8	East Siberia	−2·7
5	Ural	−4·0	Central Asia	−3·6	Blackearth Centre	−2·6
6	Czechoslovakia	−2·9	Far East	−3·4	West Siberia	−2·3
7	Baltic	−2·3	Volga	−3·0	Volga	−2·0
8	Far East	−1·5	Transcaucasia	−2·1	Czechoslovakia	−1·2
9	West Siberia	−1·2	Donets-Dnepr	−1·7	Poland	−1·2
10	East Siberia	−1·0	South	−1·5	Kazakhstan	−1·1
11	South	−0·4	Northwest	−1·4	Romania	−0·9
12	Hungary	−0·4	North Caucasus	−0·9	Bulgaria	−0·6
13	Volga	−0·1	Baltic	−0·2	Hungary	−0·3
14	Bulgaria	1·2	Belorussia	−0·2	Yugoslavia	0·3
15	North Caucasus	1·6	Blackearth Centre	0·2	Far East	0·4
16	Volga-Vyatka	1·7	Centre	0·7	Volga-Vyatka	1·1
17	Transcaucasia	1·8	Southwest	1·4	North Caucasus	1·2
18	Romania	1·9	Volga-Vyatka	1·4	Southwest	1·3
19	Poland	2·0	Moldavia	1·5	Moldavia	1·3
20	Southwest	2·4	Poland	3·2	Baltic	1·6
21	Belorussia	2·5	Bulgaria	3·7	Belorussia	1·7
22	Blackearth Centre	2·9	Yugoslavia	4·0	Central Asia	2·7
23	Kazakhstan	4·7	Czechoslovakia	4·2	Transcaucasia	3·1
24	Moldavia	4·8	Romania	4·7	South	3·2
25	Yugoslavia	4·9	East Germany	6·0	Northwest	4·0
26	Central Asia	5·9	Hungary	6·8	Centre	6·2

In the real world there are few black and white situations but many varying degrees of association.

4. Perhaps of greatest interest to the geographer are the weightings of individual areas on the factors. Weightings of each region and country on the first three factors are shown in Table 3.10. The first factor shows extremes of development from an urban/industrial view-point. The extremes are the Centre region (containing Moscow) and the Northwest (Leningrad) at one end, and Central Asia and Yugoslavia at the other. The seven countries are spread through the 19 regions of the U.S.S.R. The top and bottom seven are shaded in Fig. 3.9. The second factor shows the extremes of space and structure of population. At one extreme are the very large regions of the U.S.S.R., with a high natural increase of population but low density, and at the other, the

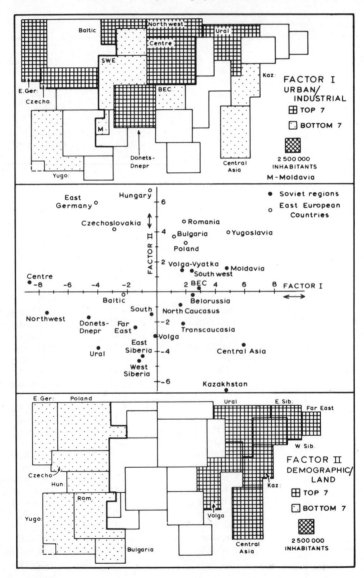

Fig. 3.9.   *Individual weightings of the 19 economic regions and seven countries of East Europe on the first (I) and second (II) factors derived from a consideration of 15 demographic, economic and social variables.*

small densely populated countries of East Europe. On Factor II, in contrast to Factor I, the seven in East Europe all come together at one extreme. The extremes are shaded in Fig. 3.9. Factor III is already more difficult to characterise, but it separates the predominantly heavy industrial areas from the light industrial ones. Weightings on Factors I and II are shown in graph form in Fig. 3.9.

3.5 A COMPARATIVE STUDY OF THE HUNDRED LARGEST TOWNS OF COMECON

In Table 3.11, 2 000 bits of yes/no information are recorded about the 100 largest towns of Comecon, in addition to actual population in thousands. The 100 towns, which are mapped in Fig. 3.10, are ranked in descending order of

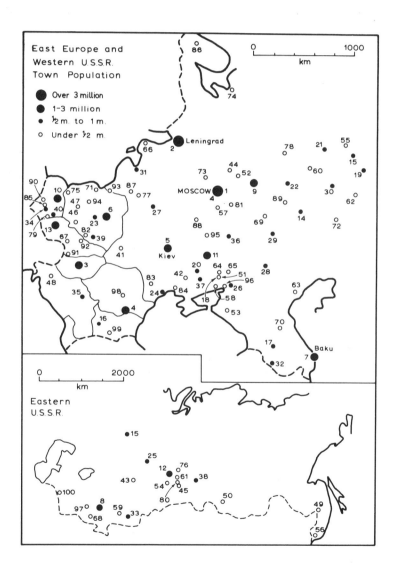

Fig. 3.10.   Location map: the hundred largest towns of the U.S.S.R. and East Europe. The key to the town numbering will be found in Table 3.11.

Table 3.11. 100 LARGEST TOWNS OF THE U.S.S.R. AND EAST EUROPE

Description of attributes in Table 3.11.

1 1 Located on coast or navigable estuary.
2 1 Located on major river or inland waterway system.
3 1 In or adjacent to mountain area.
4 1 Rail junction with at least 4 lines leaving.
5 1 Slav population.
6 1 Town founded before 20th century.
7 1 Increase 1959–65 exceeds 20% (1959 = 100 1965 > 120).
8 1 Larger town within distance of 80 km.
9 1 Sovereign state capital.
10 1 Capital of Soviet Socialist Republic.
11 1 Capital of major civil division.

12 1 Has a University or Technical University.
13 1 On or very close to coalfield (hard or brown coal).
14 1 On or very close to source of oil and/or natural gas.
15 1 On or close to major source of hydroelectric power.
16 1 On or very close to producing area of minerals other than fuel.
17 1 Iron and steel and/or nonferrous metal smelting.
18 1 Chemicals industry.
19 1 Light industry (mainly classes of textiles, clothing, light engineering, various).
20 1 In a food surplus area.

Rank	Location	Population around 1965		1	2	3	4	5	6	7	8	9	10	11	12	13	14	15	16	17	18	19	20
1	CEN	6443	Moscow	0	1	0	1	1	1	0	0	1	1	1	1	0	0	0	0	1	1	1	0
2	NWE	3641	Leningrad	1	0	0	1	1	1	0	0	0	0	1	1	0	0	0	0	1	1	1	0
3	HUN	1928	Budapest	0	1	0	1	0	1	0	0	1	0	1	1	0	0	0	0	0	0	1	1
4	RUM	1372	Bucarest	0	0	0	1	0	1	0	0	1	0	1	1	0	1	0	0	0	0	1	1
5	SWE	1348	Kiev	0	1	0	1	1	1	1	0	0	1	1	1	0	0	0	0	0	1	1	1
6	POL	1232	Warsaw	0	1	0	1	1	1	0	0	1	0	1	1	0	0	0	0	0	0	1	1
7	TRC	1147	Baku	1	0	0	0	0	1	0	0	0	1	1	1	0	1	0	0	1	1	1	0
8	CAS	1106	Tashkent	0	0	1	0	0	1	1	0	0	1	1	1	0	0	0	0	0	1	1	0
9	VVY	1085	Gorky	0	1	0	0	1	1	0	0	0	0	1	1	0	0	1	0	1	1	1	0
10	GER	1071	Berlin	0	1	0	1	0	0	0	0	1	0	1	1	0	0	0	0	1	0	1	1
11	DDN	1070	Khark'ov	0	0	0	1	1	1	0	0	0	0	1	1	0	1	0	0	0	1	1	1
12	WSB	1029	Novosibirsk	0	1	0	1	1	0	0	0	0	0	1	1	0	0	1	0	1	1	1	1
13	CZE	1017	Prague	0	0	0	1	1	1	0	0	1	0	1	1	0	0	0	0	0	1	1	1
14	VOL	948	Kuybyshev	0	1	0	1	1	1	0	0	0	0	1	0	0	1	1	0	0	1	0	1
15	URL	919	Sverdlovsk	0	0	1	1	1	1	0	0	0	0	1	1	0	0	0	1	1	1	1	0
16	BUL	822	Sofia	0	0	1	1	1	1	0	0	1	0	1	1	0	0	0	1	1	1	1	0
17	TRC	812	Tbilisi	0	0	1	0	0	1	0	0	0	1	1	1	0	0	1	1	0	1	1	0
18	DDN	809	Donetsk	0	0	0	1	1	0	0	0	0	0	1	1	1	0	0	1	1	1	0	0
19	URL	805	Chelyabinsk	0	0	1	1	1	1	0	0	0	0	1	0	1	0	0	1	1	1	1	0
20	DDN	774	Dnepropetrovsk	0	1	0	1	1	1	0	0	0	0	1	1	0	0	1	0	1	1	0	1
21	URL	764	Perm'	0	1	0	1	1	1	1	0	0	0	1	1	0	1	1	1	1	0	0	0
22	VOL	762	Kazan'	0	1	0	1	0	1	0	0	0	0	1	1	0	1	1	0	0	1	1	1
23	POL	737	Lodz	0	0	0	0	1	1	0	0	0	0	1	1	0	0	0	0	0	1	1	1
24	SOU	735	Odessa	1	0	0	0	1	1	0	0	0	0	1	1	0	0	0	0	0	1	1	1
25	WSB	721	Omsk	0	1	0	1	1	1	1	0	0	0	1	0	0	0	0	0	0	1	1	1
26	NCA	720	Rostov-on-Don	1	1	0	1	1	1	0	0	0	0	1	1	0	0	0	0	0	1	1	1
27	BEL	717	Minsk	0	0	0	1	1	1	1	0	0	1	1	1	0	0	0	0	0	0	1	1
28	VOL	700	Volgograd	0	1	0	1	1	1	0	0	0	0	1	0	0	1	1	0	1	1	1	1
29	VOL	683	Saratov	0	1	0	1	1	1	0	0	0	0	1	1	0	1	1	0	0	1	1	1
30	VOL	665	Ufa	0	1	0	1	0	1	0	1	0	0	1	1	0	1	1	0	0	1	1	1
31	BAL	658	Riga	1	1	0	1	0	1	0	0	0	1	1	1	0	0	0	0	0	1	1	0
32	TRC	633	Yerevan	0	0	1	0	0	1	1	0	0	1	1	1	0	0	1	1	0	1	1	0
33	KAZ	623	Alma-Ata	0	0	1	0	0	1	1	0	0	1	1	1	0	0	0	0	0	0	1	0
34	GER	595	Leipzig	0	0	0	1	0	1	0	0	0	0	1	1	1	0	0	0	0	1	1	0
35	YUG	585	Belgrade	0	1	0	1	1	1	1	0	1	0	1	1	0	0	0	0	0	0	1	1
36	BEC	576	Voronezh	0	0	0	0	1	1	1	0	0	0	1	1	0	0	0	0	0	1	0	1
37	DDN	550	Zaporozh'ye	0	1	0	1	1	1	1	1	0	1	0	0	0	1	0	1	1	1	0	
38	ESB	541	Krasnoyarsk	0	1	1	0	1	1	1	0	0	0	1	0	0	0	1	0	0	1	1	0
39	POL	509	Krakow	0	0	0	0	1	1	0	0	0	0	1	1	1	0	0	1	1	1	0	1
40	GER	504	Dresden	0	1	1	1	0	1	0	0	0	0	1	1	1	0	0	0	0	0	1	0

Table 3.11. contd

Rank	Location	Population around 1965		1	2	3	4	5	6	7	8	9	10	11	12	13	14	15	16	17	18	19	20
41	SWE	496	Lvov	0	0	0	1	1	1	1	0	0	0	1	1	0	1	0	0	0	0	1	1
42	DDN	488	Krivoy Rog	0	0	0	1	1	0	1	0	0	0	0	0	0	0	0	1	1	0	0	1
43	KAZ	482	Karaganda	0	0	0	0	1	0	1	0	0	0	1	0	1	0	0	1	1	0	1	0
44	CEN	478	Yaroslavl'	0	1	0	1	1	1	0	0	0	0	1	0	0	0	0	0	0	1	1	0
45	WSB	475	Novokuznetsk	0	0	1	0	1	0	1	0	0	0	0	0	1	0	0	1	1	1	0	0
46	POL	466	Wroclaw	0	1	0	1	1	1	0	0	0	0	1	1	0	0	0	0	0	0	1	1
47	POL	432	Poznan	0	1	0	1	1	1	0	0	0	0	1	1	0	0	0	0	0	0	1	1
48	YUG	431	Zagreb	0	0	1	1	1	1	0	0	0	0	1	1	0	0	0	0	0	0	1	0
49	FAR	408	Khabarovsk	0	1	0	0	1	1	1	0	0	0	1	0	0	0	0	0	0	0	1	0
50	ESB	401	Irkutsk	0	1	1	0	1	0	0	0	0	0	1	1	1	0	1	0	0	0	1	0
51	DDN	399	Makeyevka	0	0	0	1	1	0	0	1	0	0	0	0	1	0	0	1	1	1	0	0
52	CEN	389	Ivanovo	0	0	0	1	1	1	0	0	0	0	1	0	0	0	0	0	0	1	1	0
53	NCA	385	Krasnodar	0	0	0	1	1	1	1	0	0	0	1	0	0	0	0	0	0	1	1	1
54	WSB	382	Barnaul	0	1	0	1	1	1	1	0	0	0	1	0	0	0	0	0	0	1	1	1
55	URL	370	Nizhniy Tagil	0	0	1	0	1	0	0	0	0	0	0	0	0	0	0	1	1	1	0	0
56	FAR	367	Vladivostok	1	0	1	0	1	1	1	0	0	0	1	1	0	0	0	0	0	0	0	0
57	CEN	366	Tula	0	0	0	1	1	1	0	0	0	0	1	0	1	0	0	0	1	0	0	1
58	DDN	361	Zhdanov	1	0	0	0	1	1	1	0	0	0	0	0	0	0	0	0	1	1	0	1
59	CAS	360	Frunze	0	0	1	0	0	1	1	0	0	1	1	1	0	0	0	1	0	0	1	0
60	URL	351	Izhevsk	0	0	0	1	0	0	1	0	0	0	1	0	0	0	0	0	0	0	0	0
61	WSB	351	Kemerovo	0	0	1	0	1	0	1	0	0	0	1	0	1	0	0	0	0	1	0	0
62	URL	348	Magnitogorsk	0	0	1	0	1	0	0	0	0	0	0	0	0	0	0	1	1	1	0	0
63	VOL	342	Astrakhan'	1	1	0	0	1	1	0	0	0	0	1	0	0	0	0	0	0	0	1	0
64	DDN	337	Gorlovka	0	0	0	1	1	0	0	1	0	0	0	0	1	0	0	1	1	1	0	0
65	DDN	330	Lugansk	0	0	0	1	1	1	0	0	0	0	1	0	1	0	0	0	1	0	1	1
66	BAL	330	Tallin	1	0	0	0	0	1	0	0	0	1	1	0	0	0	0	0	0	1	1	0
67	CZE	325	Brno	0	0	0	1	1	1	0	0	0	0	1	1	0	0	0	0	0	0	1	1
68	CAS	316	Dushanbe	0	0	1	1	0	1	1	0	0	1	1	0	0	0	0	0	0	0	0	1
69	VOL	315	Penza	0	0	0	1	1	1	1	0	0	0	1	0	0	0	0	0	0	0	0	1
70	NCA	314	Groznyy	0	0	0	0	0	1	1	0	0	0	1	0	0	0	1	0	0	0	1	0
71	POL	314	Gdansk	1	0	0	0	1	1	0	0	0	0	1	1	0	0	0	0	0	0	0	1
72	URL	306	Orenburg	0	0	0	0	1	1	0	0	0	0	1	0	0	0	0	0	0	0	1	1
73	CEN	306	Kalinin	0	0	0	0	1	1	0	0	0	0	1	0	0	0	0	0	0	1	1	0
74	NWE	303	Archangel	1	0	0	1	1	1	0	0	0	0	1	0	0	0	0	0	0	1	1	0
75	POL	303	Szczecin	1	0	0	1	1	1	0	0	0	0	1	1	0	0	0	0	0	0	1	1
76	WSB	302	Tomsk	0	0	0	0	1	1	1	0	0	0	1	1	0	0	0	0	0	1	0	0
77	BAL	298	Vil'nyus	0	0	0	1	0	1	0	0	0	1	1	1	0	0	0	0	0	0	1	1
78	VVY	296	Kirov	0	0	0	1	1	1	0	0	0	0	1	1	0	0	0	0	0	1	1	0
79	GER	294	Karl Marx Stadt	0	0	1	0	0	1	0	1	0	0	1	0	1	0	0	1	0	1	1	0
80	WSB	291	Prokop'yevsk	0	0	1	0	1	0	0	1	0	0	0	0	1	0	0	1	0	1	0	0
81	CEN	287	Ryazan'	0	0	0	0	1	1	1	0	0	0	1	0	0	0	0	0	0	1	1	1
82	POL	284	Katowice	0	0	0	1	1	1	0	1	0	0	1	0	1	0	0	1	1	1	0	0
83	MOL	282	Kishinev	0	0	0	0	0	1	1	0	0	1	1	1	0	0	0	0	0	0	1	1
84	SOU	280	Nikolayev	1	0	0	1	1	1	1	1	0	0	0	0	0	0	0	0	0	0	0	1
85	GER	274	Halle	0	0	0	1	0	1	0	1	0	0	1	1	1	0	0	1	0	1	1	0
86	NWE	272	Murmansk	1	0	0	0	1	0	1	0	0	0	1	0	0	0	0	0	0	0	1	0
87	BAL	269	Kaunas	0	0	0	1	0	1	1	0	0	0	0	0	0	0	0	0	0	0	1	1
88	CEN	267	Bryansk	0	0	0	1	1	1	1	0	0	0	1	0	0	0	0	0	0	0	1	1
89	VOL	265	Ul'yanovsk	0	1	0	1	1	1	1	0	0	0	1	0	0	0	0	0	0	0	1	1
90	GER	265	Magdeburg	0	1	0	1	1	1	0	0	0	0	1	0	1	0	0	1	1	1	0	1
91	CZE	262	Bratislava	0	1	0	1	1	1	0	0	0	0	1	1	0	0	0	0	0	1	1	1
92	CZE	256	Ostrava	0	0	1	1	1	1	1	0	0	0	1	0	1	0	0	1	1	1	0	0
93	BAL	253	Kaliningrad	1	0	0	1	1	1	1	0	0	0	1	0	0	0	0	0	0	0	0	0
94	POL	250	Bydgoszcz	0	0	0	1	1	1	0	0	0	0	1	0	0	0	0	0	0	0	1	1

Table 3.11. contd

Rank	Location	Population around 1965		1	2	3	4	5	6	7	8	9	10	11	12	13	14	15	16	17	18	19	20
95	BEC	245	Kursk	0	0	0	1	1	1	0	0	0	0	1	0	0	0	0	0	0	1	1	1
96	NCA	234	Taganrog	1	0	0	0	1	1	0	1	0	0	0	0	0	0	0	0	1	0	1	1
97	CAS	233	Samarkand	0	0	1	0	0	1	0	0	0	0	1	0	0	0	0	0	0	1	1	0
98	RUM	233	Brasov	0	0	1	1	0	1	1	0	0	0	1	1	0	1	0	0	0	0	1	0
99	BUL	229	Plovdiv	0	0	1	1	1	1	1	0	0	0	1	0	0	0	1	0	0	0	1	1
100	CAS	226	Ashkhabad	0	0	1	0	0	1	1	0	0	1	1	1	0	0	0	0	0	0	1	0

Column totals   16 31 25 64 73 87 41 9 8 15 90 52 19 12 15 21 28 59 72 50

United Nations spelling is used for East European towns.

Notes
5 ie Russia, Ukraine, Belorussia, Poland, Czechoslovakia, Bulgaria, Yugoslavia. Border line are some Soviet towns in non-Slav units but with predominantly Slav population (Karaganda, probably Izhevsk).
7 Some difficulty in obtaining comparable data for East European countries.
19, 20 Very approximate and subjective.

Sources
1 *Atlas SSSR* (Moscow, 1962) topic maps, area maps.
2 *Geograficheskiy atlas dlya uchiteley sredney shkoly* (Moscow, 1954).
3 For Universities (attribute 12): *The World of Learning, 1966–67,* (17 edn Europa Publications Ltd, London).
4 Various years of *Stateman's Yearbook.*

population around 1965. The remaining information is given in binary digits, a 1 (one) representing presence of an attribute, a 0 (zero) representing absence. Some of the information is only available in this dichotomised form (eg whether or not a town is a sovereign state capital). Some information (eg rate of population growth) has been dichotomised from continuous variables. Information about size and location have deliberately been omitted, in order to avoid helping towns of similar size and/or location towards similar classes. Advantages of the table over a verbal inventory of the same facts are its conciseness and its mathematical form.

Table 3.11 exists in its own right as an inventory of information to which reference can be made. More and better information could have been included had space and availability of data permitted. In fact, some later population figures are available for the U.S.S.R. only; these are shown in Table 3.12 for comparison. The data in Table 3.11 may also be further exploited in various ways. One possibility is to derive a similarity index between any pair of towns by counting how many attributes they do and do not have in common. A comparison, for example, of Nizhniy Tagil (town 55) and Magnitogorsk (town 62), both heavy industrial centres in the Ural region, shows that where the former has a 1, the latter always does, and where the former has a 0, the latter always does. The two towns, therefore, agree on all the 20 attributes included in this study. They score a maximum similarity index of 20; if other attributes were included as well as or instead of those actually used, the similarly index of Nishniy Tagil and Magnitogorsk might drop.

In Table 3.11, there are 4 950 unique pairs of towns. This quantity is derived from the formula $n(n-1)/2$, which expresses the number of ways in which two towns can be chosen from n, n in this case being 100. The similarity index between towns A and B is the same as that between towns B and A. Moreover town A is always identical to itself. Thus the 100×100 possible pairs is reduced. It is a lengthy manual calculation to work out 4 950 indices of similarity; a computer program calculates these easily and also sorts the pairs out into similarity classes. Owing to the multivariate and therefore multidimensional nature of the classification it is not possible to represent graphically the relationship (similarity index) of every town to every other on the dimensionally limited flat surface of a piece of paper. It is possible, however, to represent the relationship of any one town to all the others. This has been done for Moscow; the results are mapped in Fig. 3.11.

In addition to Nizhniy Tagi and Magnitogorsk, there are four other identical

pairs scoring 20:

25, Omsk (West Siberia) and 54, Barnaul (West Siberia)

33, Alma-Ata (Kazakhstan) and 100, Ashkhabad (Central Asia)

46, Wroclaw (Poland) and 47, Poznan (Poland)

51, Makeyevka (Donets-Dnepr) and 64, Gorlovka (Donets-Dnepr).

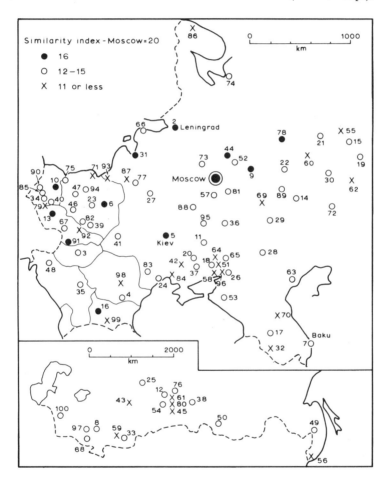

Fig. 3.11.   The similarity of Moscow to the 99 other largest towns in Comecon. No town has a similarity index of more than 16 with Moscow (maximum possible 20). The following is a list of all towns having an index of similarity to Moscow of 11 or less.

32 Yerevan (11)	58 Zhdanov (10)	70 Groznyy (10)	92 Ostrava (11)
42 Krivoy Rog (9)	59 Frunze (11)	71 Gdansk (11)	93 Kaliningrad (11)
43 Karaganda (10)	60 Izhevsk (10)	79 Karl Marx Stadt (9)	96 Taganrog (10)
45 Novokuznetsk (8)	61 Kemerovo (9)	80 Prokop'yevsk (7)	98 Brasov (11)
51 Makeyevka (10)	62 Magnitogorsk (10)	84 Nikolayev (9)	99 Plovdiv (10)
55 Nizhniy Tagil (10)	64 Gorlovka (10)	86 Murmansk (10)	
56 Vladivostok (10)	69 Penza (11)	87 Kaunas (10)	

Table 3.12. TOWNS OF THE U.S.S.R. WITH OVER 97 000 INHABITANTS IN JANUARY 1968.
(All figures are thousands)

E1 NORTHWEST				E6 continued		
1	Leningrad	3 752		6	Astrakhan'	376
2	Archangel	313		7	Penza	343
3	Murmansk	296		8	Ul'yanovsk	312
4	Petrozavodsk	175		9	Syzran'	170
5	Vologda	173		10	Sterlitamak	168
6	Cherepovets	171		11	Tol'yatti	167
7	Severodvinsk	124		12	Engel's	126
8	Pskov	116		13	Volzhskiy	124
9	Novgorod	113		14	Novokuybyshevsk	112
10	Syktyvkar	106		15	Salavat	102

E2 CENTRE				E6 NORTH CAUCASUS		
1	Moscow	6 590		1	Rostov-on-Don	773
2	Yaroslavl'	507		2	Krasnodar	420
3	Ivanovo	415		3	Groznyy	336
4	Tula	384		4	Taganrog	249
5	Kalinin	326		5	Ordzhonikidze	225
6	Ryazan'	322		6	Shakhty	209
7	Bryansk	298		7	Sochi	192
8	Vladimir	218		8	Stavropol'	182
9	Orel	216		9	Makhachkala	170
10	Rybinsk	214		10	Novocherkassk	165
11	Kostroma	213		11	Armavir	142
12	Smolensk	202		12	Novorossiysk	126
13	Kaluga	184		13	Nal'chik	123
14	Podol'sk	166		14	Maykop	109
15	Kolomna	131		15	Novoshakhtinsk	106
16	Novomoskovsk	127				
17	Lyubertsy	124		E7 URAL		
18	Serpukhov	122		1	Sverdlovsk	981
19	Elektrostal'	118		2	Chelyabinsk	851
20	Kovrov	118		3	Perm'	811
21	Orekhovo-Zuyevo	116		4	Izhevsk	391
22	Mytishchi	113		5	Nizhniy Tagil	379
23	Noginsk	102		6	Magnitogorsk	360
24	Kaliningrad	98		7	Orenburg	334
25	Murom	98		8	Kurgan	222
				9	Orsk	216
				10	Zlatoust	180
E3 BLACKEARTH CENTRE				11	Kopeysk	165
1	Voronezh	625		12	Kamensk-Uralskiy	163
2	Kursk	263		13	Berezniki	136
3	Lipetsk	263		14	Miass	124
4	Tambov	216		15	Pervoural'sk	110
5	Belgorod	134		16	Serov	104
6	Yelets	98				

E4 VOLGA-VYATKA				E8 WEST SIBERIA		
1	Gorky	1 139		1	Novosibirsk	1 079
2	Kirov	315		2	Omsk	800
3	Dzerzhinsk	204		3	Novokuznetsk	495
4	Cheboksary	186		4	Barnaul	418
5	Saransk	161		5	Kemerovo	372
6	Yoshkar-Ola	142		6	Tomsk	334
				7	Prokop'yevsk	286
				8	Tyumen'	256
E5 VOLGA				9	Biysk	184
1	Kuybyshev	1 014		10	Rubtsovsk	143
2	Kazan'	837		11	Leninsk-Kuznetskiy	137
3	Volgograd	756		12	Kiselevsk	137
4	Saratov	737		13	Belovo	116
5	Ufa	727		14	Anzhero-Sudzhensk	115

Table 3.12. contd

E9 EAST SIBERIA		
1	Krasnoyarsk	592
2	Irkutsk	428
3	Ulan-Ude	235
4	Chita	208
5	Angarsk	187
6	Bratsk	129
7	Noril'sk	127
8	Cheremkhovo	107
9	Yakutsk	98

E10 FAR EAST		
1	Khabarovsk	448
2	Vladivostok	410
3	Komsomol'sk-A.	210
4	Petropavlovsk-K.	129
5	Blagoveshchensk	125
6	Ussuriysk	124
7	Nakhodka	100

E11 DONETS–DNEPR		
1	Kharkov	1 148
2	Donetsk	855
3	Dnepropetrovsk	837
4	Zaporozh'ye	615
5	Krivoy Rog	523
6	Makeyevka	415
7	Zhdanov	393
8	Lugansk	363
9	Gorlovka	344
10	Dneprodzerzhinsk	228
11	Poltava	192
12	Kirovograd	178
13	Kramatorsk	144
14	Sumy	144
15	Kremenchug	140
16	Kadiyevka	139
17	Kommunarsk	125
18	Melitopol'	123
19	Lisichansk	121
20	Slavyansk	116
21	Nikopol'	114
22	Konstantinovka	104
23	Krasnyy Luch	102

E12 SOUTHWEST		
1	Kiev	1 476
2	Lvov	524
3	Vinnitsa	182
4	Chernovtsy	181
5	Zhitomir	148
6	Chernigov	143
7	Cherkassy	135
8	Rovno	106

E13 SOUTH		
1	Odessa	797
2	Nikolayev	309
3	Kherson	244
4	Simferopol'	229
5	Sevastopol'	215
6	Kerch'	120

E14 BALTIC		
1	Riga	694
2	Tallin	347
3	Vil'nyus	335
4	Kaunas	292
5	Kaliningrad	275
6	Klaypeda	136

E15 TRANSCAUCASIA		
1	Baku	1 224
2	Tbilisi	860
3	Yerevan	698
4	Kirovabad	177
5	Kutaisi	161
6	Leninakan	136
7	Sumgait	110
8	Batumi	102
9	Rustavi	99

E16 CENTRAL ASIA		
1	Tashkent	1 324
2	Frunze	416
3	Dushanbe	345
4	Samarkand	254
5	Ashkhabad	249
6	Andizhan	173
7	Namangan	164
8	Kokand	134
9	Osh	123
10	Bukhara	105
11	Chirchik	104
12	Leninabad	102

E17 KAZAKHSTAN		
1	Alma-Ata	673
2	Karaganda	505
3	Chimkent	227
4	Ust'-Kamenogorsk	218
5	Semipalatinsk	210
6	Tselinograd	185
7	Petropavlovsk	170
8	Pavlodar	162
9	Dzhambul	162
10	Temirtau	159
11	Aktyubinsk	139
12	Ural'sk	127
13	Kustanay	121
14	Gur'yev	104

E18 BELORUSSIA		
1	Minsk	818
2	Gomel'	246
3	Vitebsk	212
4	Mogilev	182
5	Bobruysk	123
6	Grodno	118
7	Brest	102

E19 MOLDAVIA		
1	Kishinev	317

E–Economic region.   Source: *NkhSSSR* 1967, 23–32.

The reader will notice that all five identical pairs are close to each other in location and four of the pairs are close in size. An examination of 40 pairs that each score 19 (ie differ only on one attribute, for example, towns 3 and 6, Budapest and Warsaw) shows links with some of the original 5 pairs, and several clusters. Among the pairs linked are some situated quite far apart, for example, town 72, Orenburg in the Ural region, and town 94, Bydgoszcz in Poland (they differ only in respect of attribute 4; see Table 3.11). Thus an initial large family of relatively similar towns emerges in the northern part of the East European countries and north-central European U.S.S.R. A much smaller family emerges in Central Asia—Kazakhstan.

Which towns, then, are least similar? The lowest similarity index is 5. There are four pairs with such a low score:

    3, Budapest (Hungary) and 45, Novokuznetsk (West Siberia)

    4, Bucharest (Romania) and 45, Novokuznetsk

    10, Berlin (East Germany) and 80, Prokop'yevsk (West Siberia)

    22, Kazan' (Volga) and 45, Novokuznetsk

A consideration of the 17 pairs that have similarity indices of 6 confirms a general maximum dissimilarity between larger multifunctional towns of East Europe and European U.S.S.R. on the one hand, and the Kuzbass coalfield pair on the other. These might be described as the poles of maximum dissimilarity, although at the level of a score of 6, other poles of dissimilarity appear:

    21, Perm' (Ural) and 96, Taganrog (North Caucasus)

    33/100, Alma-Ata/Ashkhabad and 51/64, Makeyevka/Gorlovka

It is possible to calculate how similar any given town is to the other 99 by summing its similarity indices with these towns. A maximum score of 2 000 (including the town with itself) is theoretically possible. In the event, town 78, Kirov (Volga-Vyatka) emerges with the highest score, 1 507, and town 52, Ivanovo (Centre) and town 95, Kursk (Blackearth Centre) next, each

with 1 503. At the other extreme, town 80, Prokop'yevsk (West Siberia), the coal mining centre, emerges as the least similar, with 1 025, and town 45, Novokuznetsk with 1 045, next. 51, Makeyevka and 64, Gorlovka both in the Donets-Dnepr, each score 1 059. Thus four distinguished heavy industrial centres come out as atypical, in so far as the data in Table 3.11 may be considered to typify the larger Comecon towns.

The exercise described leaves a great deal to be desired in the data included, the techniques, and the follow up. The reader may find it helpful, however, to refer to the table from points further on in the book. He will do well, also, to consult a paper by Davidovich[3] in which, among other things, there is an attempt to classify Soviet towns on a multivariate basis.

REFERENCES

1. ORE, O., *Graphs and their Uses* (Random House (New Mathematical Library) New York, 1963)
2. COLE, J. P. and KING, C. A. M., *Quantitative Geography* (Wiley, London, 1968), especially Sections 2.10, 13.1 and 13.2
3. DAVIDOVICH, V. G., 'On the patterns and tendencies of urban settlement in the U.S.S.R.' *Soviet Geogr.*, 7, No 1, 3–30, 1966 (Originally in *Vop. Geogr.*, No. 66)

BIBLIOGRAPHY

KASER, M., *Comecon, Integration Problems of the Planned Economies* (O.U.P., 1965)
Narodnoye khozyaystvo sotsialisticheskikh stran 1965 (Moscow, 1966)
Naseleniye zemnogo shara, spravochnik po stranam (Moscow, 1965)
SINGLETON, F. B., *Background to Eastern Europe* (Pergamon, London, 1965)
Soviet Geogr., 6, No 1, 1965, contains various papers on Comecon

4

Past trends and future prospects

4.1 THE LINES OF RUSSIAN TERRITORIAL EXPANSION

In 1917-18, the Bolshevik Party took control of the Russian Empire and after some years of conflict became at least *de facto* ruler of Russia in the eyes of the whole world. It obtained possession of the largest single sovereign country in the world. Russia contained not only a great variety of environments and resources, but a mixture of peoples, cultures, languages and religions. Some areas were relatively highly developed by world standards of the time, but most were poor and backward. Some were highly industrialised on modern lines; many were deeply agricultural and rural. Parts of the Empire had been under Russian control for many centuries; others had been acquired no more than a few decades before 1917.

Since 1917, the professed policy of the Soviet Communist Party to the situation it inherited has been fairly consistent. First, the productive capacity of the country as a whole has been raised rapidly, in view of internal circumstances and outside pressure (particularly in World War II) and thanks to the natural resources available. Secondly, a more balanced areal spread of wealth has been aimed at. Although the first aim has been pursued with considerable success, the second has not, at least as fully as is desired or was expected by early Soviet leaders, and great anomalies between regions are now revealed in Soviet data. These will be discussed in Chapters 12 and 13.

An appreciation of the general way in which the Russian Empire was built up is vital for an understanding of the anomalies of the present situation, but as the main features of its growth are now available in many books and atlases they will not be described in great detail here. Like the sea empires of Portugal, Spain, England, France and Holland, the Russian Empire was constructed on a grand scale. The great fragmented sea empires, however, collapsed completely or have survived in greatly modified form; the compact Russian Empire remains intact and has had few intruders. There have been losses and fresh gains at places along the periphery, but the form now differs little from that of about 1900.

The main periods of expansion are outlined below. They overlap to some extent because the Russians were often pushing in two or more directions simultaneously.

1. A drive northwards to the Barents Sea and Arctic coast of European Russia in the 16th century.
2. A drive eastwards across Siberia and into North America, rapid in the 17th century, less sure in the 18th.
3. A gradual movement westwards into the Baltic area, Central Europe and the Balkans in the 18th and early 19th century. The area of the present Ukraine was largely absorbed during this period. Late in the 18th century Russia obtained a share of dismembered Poland.

4. A gradual movement southwards in European Russia to the Black Sea and Caucasus late in the 18th century and during the 19th century, culminating in the capture of Transcaucasia in the early decades of the 19th century, followed by the occupation of Central Asia and the Far East in the later decades.

The end product of these lines of expansion is summarised by the divisions shown in Fig. 4.1, which will now be described briefly.

17th century. A thinly spread indigenous population has been gradually outnumbered by Russian settlers along the southern fringe. Russia's North American territories, parts of which were held for over a century, were sold as Alaska to the U.S.A. in 1867.

Ic is an area of Ukrainian and/or Russian settlement which differs from Ia because it has been held or settled for a much shorter period. It was integrated into the Russian Empire by a southward colonising movement from region Ia

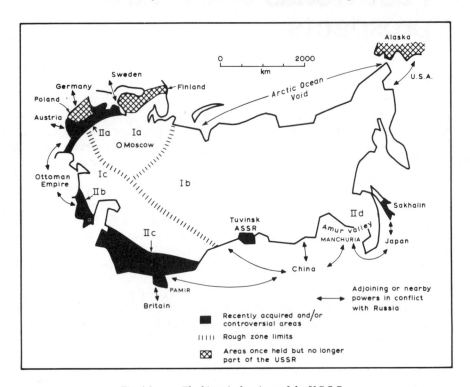

Fig. 4.1.   *The historical regions of the U.S.S.R.*

Ia is roughly the oldest part of the Russian Empire as it emerged in the centuries following the Mongol-Tatar invasions of the 13th century. All parts have been Russian for at least 250 years. There are several million non-Russians (eg Tatars, Mordovs), in the area, but apart from the Karelians, near Finland, they have been isolated from the outside world and their only exposure to European culture and technology has come through the Russians living around and among them.

Ib is Siberia, occupied mainly during the

lasting from the 17th century into the 19th. The population is basically Slav, though non-Slav peoples including the Kalmyks and Kazakhs are found on the southern fringes.

IIa, the western fringe of the Russian Empire, contains lands that have been in Russian hands discontinuously and mostly for less duration than those in areas Ia–Ic. Up to 1917, Russians were only a minority or were virtually absent. Finland and Poland now lie outside the U.S.S.R. The peoples of area IIa have been in contact with other powers in Europe as well as with the

Russians; Latvia and Estonia, in particular, have been influenced by Scandinavia, the central part by Germany, and the south by Balkan powers.

IIb, Transcaucasia, was occupied mainly early in the 19th century. It has many characteristics, both physical and cultural, of southwest Asia and the three main cultural groups, the Georgians, Armenians and Azerbaijanians, differ considerably from one another.

IIc, Central Asia, was occupied mainly in the middle of the 19th century. At that time it consisted of a number of principalities or *Khanates* based on the main oases. The population was Moslem and mostly had Turkic family languages, but the communities had a long tradition of subordination to China and only a limited contact with Arabia or India. Both Transcaucasia and Central Asia had a sophisticated political, religious and urbanised society

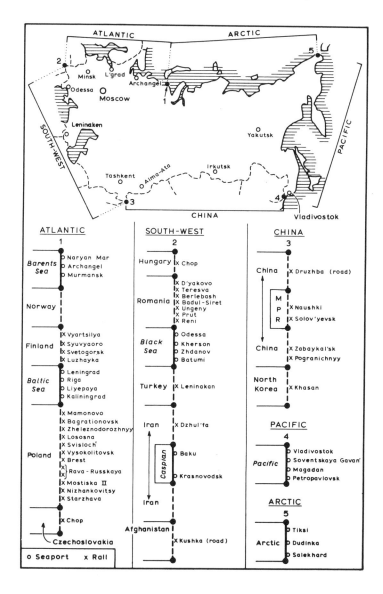

Fig. 4.2. *The boundary and neighbours of the U.S.S.R.*

long before modern Russia began to emerge in the later Middle Ages.

IId. In the later part of the 19th century Russia, Japan and China became involved in a struggle for the Amur valley. Russia made extensive diplomatic gains in this area at the expense of China, but after its defeat by the Japanese in 1906 was content to leave Manchuria, to be later disputed by Japan and China.

Various areas were lost by Russia as a result of World War I and subsequent foreign intervention in the Soviet Union. However, before and at the end of World War II (1941–45), much of the lost area was regained and some new territory was acquired. Although little change occurred in the territorial extent of the U.S.S.R., considerable numbers of people changed hands, and a number of strategic localities were acquired. There have been no boundary adjustments of any consequence since 1945.

Table 4.1. NEIGHBOURS OF THE U.S.S.R., SHOWING LENGTH OF BOUNDARY IN KILOMETRES

European part	Boundary	Asiatic part	Boundary
Norway	120	Turkey	400
Finland	1 000	Iran	1 400
Sweden	Sea	Afghanistan	1 550
Poland	900	Pakistan	Near
Czechoslovakia	80	India	Near
Hungary	80	China	5 000
Romania	900	Mongolian	
Bulgaria	Sea	People's Republic	2 500
		North Korea	30
		Japan	Sea
		U.S.A.	Sea

The U.S.S.R. now shares land boundaries with 12 sovereign states, while two more are within sight. The order in which neighbouring countries and intervening seas touch the boundary of the U.S.S.R. may be followed in Fig. 4.2. For simplicity, the U.S.S.R. is considered to face outward in five different directions, indicated as Atlantic, Southwest, China, Pacific and Arctic. The boundary of the U.S.S.R. has been 'unstrung' from the conventional map and after appropriate rotations rearranged in a topological diagram. Correct order of occurrence of neighbouring states and seas is preserved, but scale is not correct. The main Soviet seaports are shown in the order in which they occur along each stretch of coast, and the railways (or in two cases, railheads) that link the U.S.S.R. through accredited frontier crossing places are all indicated. The rail links with the four adjoining Comecon countries are particularly numerous; compare over 20 rail crossings in some 2 000 km in East Europe with only five in some 7 500 km along the border with China and the Mongolian People's Republic. The main source of information was *Zheleznyye dorogi SSSR*.[1] The length of boundary with each country is given in Table 4.1, in which six relatively near but not contiguous countries are also included.

4.2 THE GROWTH OF INDUSTRY IN THE U.S.S.R.

In Fig. 4.3 the distribution of Russian industry is shown by black dots at three periods in the past, the latter part of the 17th century, around 1780, and about 1900. The first two maps are on the same scale, but the third is slightly smaller in scale. These may be compared with maps in Chapter 10 showing the present distribution of industries.

The picture in the 17th century (Fig 4.3(a)), was one of domestic crafts, small workshops and a considerable exchange of goods. There was already some regional specialisation, both in agriculture and in industry, for example, iron working in the Tula area. Archangel on the White Sea was the only point of contact by sea with the outside world and altogether the Russians had their settlements extremely far north, by any standards in the world, past or present.

Fig. 4.3(b) shows the changes initiated by Peter the Great around 1700 and followed up in the 18th century. Industries were established in and around St. Petersburg and in the Ural region supplementing the existing centres, so that during the latter part of the 18th century Russia possessed the biggest iron industry in the world. Iron goods were shipped by waterways over European Russia and were even exported.

The modern techniques of the Industrial Revolution began to be applied in Russia after the Napoleonic Wars. In particular, textile factories using imported steam drive machinery were built in the Moscow area, particularly to the northeast (eg Ivanovo). A textile industry also grew up in Russian Poland; in Lodz, for example, textile manufacturing was established by German capitalists just inside the Russian customs boundary. With the growth of the railway network from the 1860's, the Ukraine

the building of the Trans-Siberian Railway in the 1890's and early 1900's. Figs. 4.3(b) and 4.3(c) show this spread of industrial centres. Russian productive capacity remained largely in the European part until around 1930. Just as new areas of development tended to supplement old areas rather than to replace them during the pre-Soviet period, so developments in new areas

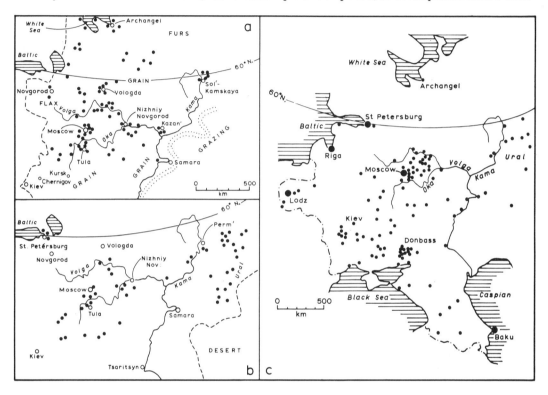

Fig. 4.3.   *Economic activities in Russia: (a) about 1680; (b) about 1780; (c) about 1900. Sources:* Atlas istorii SSSR, *Part 1 (1958), 20, Part 2 (1959), 7, Part 3 (1960), 1.*

area grew in relative importance, the great period of the region being about 1870–1910. (This rise to prominence was in many ways similar to the development of the Middle West and the prairies two or three decades previously in North America.) An agricultural surplus was marketed both in places to the north in European Russia and in foreign markets. Side by side, Russia's biggest iron and steel industry developed in the eastern Ukraine, eclipsing the Ural region, though not replacing it. Two final achievements of the pre-Revolution period were the establishment of the Baku oil industry, which produced about half of the world's oil in the 1890's, and

since the 1920's have been accompanied by modernisation and further expansion of most older areas. This must not be forgotten when present patterns of the location of economic activities are being considered. Moreover, many institutions, attitudes and landscape features have resisted change.

Changes during the Soviet period will be discussed more fully later in the book, but the following outstanding achievements may be noted in anticipation:

1. The creation of the Ural–Kuzbass–Karaganda steel and coal combine, since about 1930.

2. The emergence of the Volga–Ural oilfields (misleadingly also referred to as the second Baku) and Volga hydro-electric power since about 1940.

3. The new lands agricultural campaign, started 1953, losing momentum by 1960. In the 1950's there was a south-facing pioneer frontier in Kazakhstan.

4. The so-called third metal and energy base in central Siberia since the late 1950's. Low cost coal, timber and hydro-electricity are being exploited in this area between the Kuzbass and Lake Baykal.

5. The development of the oil and gas deposits of the West Siberian lowland since the early 1960's. There is now a north-facing pioneer frontier in this area.

The actual achievements on the ground have been paralleled by a number of campaigns, thought up by the Soviet Communist Party and often applied ruthlessly, sometimes with devastating results. In the 1920's the emphasis was on electricity. In the 1930's, a reasonably successful heavy industrial drive was accompanied by the disastrous collectivisation of agriculture, during which farm output dropped to half the level of the late 1920's in some places, and a sector of the farm population, the Kulaks, was largely eliminated. The 1940's were occupied by the war and by postwar reconstruction. Postwar campaigns have included the plan to transform the climate of dry areas by planting tree belts, the propaganda praising maize and recommending its cultivation almost everywhere in the U.S.S.R., the discovery in the late 1950's that oil and gas are cheaper fuels than coal, and the period when chemicals and fertilisers were extolled in the early 1960's. In the late 1960's a meaningless campaign, smacking of numerology, was giving prominence to the passing of targets of 100 million tons of steel, 300 million tons of oil and 600 million tons of coal per year (eg *Pravda* 19 March and 23 December 1968). Round numbers in denary base (base 10) are not round in other bases. The illusion of significance in such arbitrary numbers is commonly found.

On the organisational side, the U.S.S.R. has not been without experiments since the death of Stalin in 1953, even though drastic changes have not occurred. Economic regions, and machine-tractor stations serving collective farms, were both reformed in the late 1950's. In the 1960's there has been talk of decentralisation of responsibility in economic activities, the introduction of a market economy, and even of some kind of profit motive. It is necessary for the geographer to be aware of campaigns and political moves, for the ideas usually find their way into the national plans, and ultimately will involve certain parts of the country in changes. Thus, for example, the recent prominence given to oil and gas is now rapidly bringing the West Siberian Lowland into Soviet economic life, whereas had coal remained the dominant source of fuel this might not have happeed so quickly.

What are the campaigns of the late 1960's? They involve drastic rethinking about planning more than anything else. Is free enterprise to be allowed in the marketing of consumer goods? Can State planning, which is growing impossibly complex as the economy becomes more sophisticated, be saved by the application of electronic computers for data processing? The directives of the 1966–70 Five Year Plan include aspects of consolidation of older areas of settlement. Agricultural improvements and light industrial growth in relatively backward areas such as the Western Ukraine, Belorussia and Central Asia are planned. New irrigation projects for Central Asia and Kazakhstan may materialise in the 1970's.

One surprising development since the mid-1960's has been the willingness of Soviet planners to allow in, or should one say invite, both state and private capital from Western countries to construct industrial complexes in the U.S.S.R. Late in 1965 the Italian firm Montecatini signed agreements to build six major petrochemical and chemical plants. The deal is worth over 100 million U.S. dollars. Similarly, Fiat and Renault are involved in motor vehicle projects (worth about 100 million U.S. dollars) in the U.S.S.R. Another development, described in *The Times,* 19 May 1967, is a possible gas pipeline from the Ukraine through Czechoslovakia and into Italy, France, Austria and West Germany.

4.3 PRESENT PROBLEMS AND POSSIBILITIES

It is fashionable to describe almost anything as a problem; every self-respecting country has many problems, each of which may either be ignored, or solved in various ways. Ever since the Communist regime took power in 1917 it has been spreading its capital widely over its vast territory. Only since 1945 has the U.S.S.R. taken an outward-looking and aggressive attitude towards the rest of the world. For Soviet policy makers and planners, there are many alternative turnings on the road ahead.

One consequence of Russian territorial expansion into the vast relatively empty lands of northern Asia over the period 1600-1900 has been the acquisition of potential agricultural land, timber, minerals and water resources. Until the railway age few settlers moved east, but during the last hundred years there have been sporadic attempts to move people there, either by force or by incentives, financial or simply patriotic. Over the last few decades, however, Soviet planners have spread their investment far more widely, and in places intensively, than their tsarist predecessors did. Much industry is now located east of the Urals and of the many reserves of minerals known to exist there, considerable numbers are now seriously exploited. Productive capacity and communications are being stretched spatially without a proportionate number of people following. Soviet planners, then, are faced with the fact that about 75% of the population is still in the western 25% of the national area, but many of the areas of low cost production lie far to the east. There seem to be two choices, not entirely mutually exclusive: to keep population where it is, making the most of the by no means meagre resources of European U.S.S.R., and exploiting Siberia from a distance, or to move several tens of millions of people distances of 2 000-3 000 km east. The demographic and economic aspects of this dilemma will be referred to frequently in the rest of this book.

A movement of people eastwards would ease pressure of population in European U.S.S.R. if, indeed, there is any pressure, and new markets would be created among the new resources. A more even distribution of population would be achieved, something politicians in all the larger countries of the world must have given thought to. Strategically, also, it may until recently have been thought advantageous to develop the interior parts of the U.S.S.R., those more distant from the U.S.A. Now the border conflict with China provides a new incentive to fill southern Siberia, although it has not been easy to get large numbers of Russians to move east into Siberia. Although they have followed the Trans-Siberian Railway since the 1890's and have been sent east for one reason or another at various times in Russian and Soviet history, their movement has not been as spontaneous or as continuous as, for example, the spread of North Americans to the interior and to the Pacific coast of their continent. Indeed, there seems now to be a revived interest in the longer settled areas as opposed to the newer lands and the desire to occupy and use effectively the vast empty areas of the U.S.S.R. is now accompanied by a desire to catch up in the old areas, to take up the slack by improving existing farmlands, exploring more thoroughly for minerals in European U.S.S.R. and establishing light industry. There is evidence of a campaign, the theme of which is that 'there are riches on our own doorstep'. The recurring theme of drainage of the Poles'ye in Belorussia is raised in *Pravda,* 15 August 1965 and 27 January 1966. The potential of the non-blackearth farmlands of European U.S.S.R. is discussed in several numbers of *Pravda* late in 1966 (eg 20 November) and reference is also made to the iron ore of the Kursk magnetic anomaly in the Blackearth Centre.

REFERENCE

1. *Zheleznyye dorogi SSSR, Napravleniya i stantsii* (Glavnoye upravleniye geodezii i kartografii, Ministerstva geologii SSSR, Moscow, 1966)

BIBLIOGRAPHY

BUDTOLAYEV, N. M. *et al.,* 'Problems of Economic Development of the West and East of the Soviet Union' *Soviet Geogr.,* 5, No 1, 1964

FILIPPOV, B. *et al.,* 'Okean Zovet' *Pravda,* 30 Aug. 1968

5

The Party and planning

5.1 MARXIST–LENINIST ATTITUDES AND VIEWPOINT

The Communist Party of the Soviet Union (C.P.S.U.) had about 11 million full members in the mid-1960's and around 12 million in 1969. There is thus approximately one Party member to every 20 ordinary citizens or 12 adults. Moreover, almost all persons between the ages of 14 and 28 are in the Komsomol (Young Communist) Movement. The Communist Party is the only political party in the Soviet Union and its leaders have made essentially all the major political decisions in the country (see Bialer[1]) since Lenin obtained power early in 1918, shortly after the Revolution of 7 November 1917 (actually 25 October in the Russian calendar of the time; this was 13 days behind our own). Indeed, for a considerable period before his death, J. Stalin was apparently in sole command. The history of the Party and the political organisation of the U.S.S.R. can be studied in Schapiro.[2] Suffice it to say that much of the power lies with the Politbureau of the Central Committee of the Communist Party, a body of some 20 persons meeting weekly. The Central Committee holds Congresses from time to time; on it are 5 000 'elected' representatives of different districts of the U.S.S.R. Since no candidates can oppose the official ones in any Soviet election, votes for the Communist Party are almost unanimous. From a purely academic point of view, the geography of U.S.S.R. is poorer for the absence of an electoral variable.

In the rest of this section only the Marxist-Leninist attitude to the economic life of the country will be considered. This will lead to aspects that are of importance to the geographer; policy regarding the development of different resources, different parts of the country, planning regions and so on.

The influence of Marxist-Leninist thinking on Soviet life in general is discussed by R. N. Carew Hunt in *The Theory and Practice of Communism* (Penguin, 1963), A. Nove in *The Soviet Economy—An Introduction* (2 edn, Allen & Unwin, 1965) and L. Schapiro in *The Government and Politics of the Soviet Union* (Hutchinson, 1968) and will not be repeated here except in bare outline. Throughout the Soviet period the works of Karl Marx, F. Engels and others, as well as the thoughts and writings of Lenin, Stalin and other Communist politicians have provided a mass of preconceived ideas on the course of history, on economic and social changes, and on human relations. Lenin, in particular, still plays a prominent role in Communist thinking and Soviet life, first as an author whose writings are quoted as often as the Bible has been in other contexts, and secondly as a benevolent if stern father figure whose portrait is widely displayed. In 1970, the 100th anniversary of Lenin's birth was given much publicity.

These various thinkers have been followed, modified pragmatically at times (eg New Economic Policy of the 1920's), eroded gradually at the margins, but never openly questioned in total. They predict the downfall of capitalist (now capitalist and colonialist) supported regimes and the triumph of communism through the building of socialism in the U.S.S.R. and subsequently in other countries (eg East Europe). Whether the economic collapse of the leading Western industrial countries is considered imminent seems doubtful, but the idea of their gradual decline is frequently publicised. *Pravda,* 7 February 1968, for example, listed the internal troubles of several Western countries as evidence. In *Pravda,* 18 August 1967, Yeremin wrote on 'The economic advantages of Socialism'. There is an assumption that the Socialist System is superior but that the realisation of the economic advantages of socialism will not happen automatically; the scientific control of the development of the economy is necessary. Among other things, emphasis is placed on economic events rather than cultural or national influences; man, given the right environment, is inherently decent; and the collective interest is always preferable to the interest of the individual. Nature can be overcome by communism, which eliminates the unnecessary duplication and competition between private enterprises, disposes of large amounts of capital and favours large projects and establishments (even farms) in the interests of economies of large scale.

In practice, some cultural hangovers from before the 1917 Revolution remain even now. Wheat, considered more desirable than rye in the eyes of Soviet planners, has failed to supersede Russia's once principal cereal in many areas; pigs are hardly raised at all in former Moslem areas in Central Asia. More strikingly, after decades of brotherly cooperation, Russians and Asians living in the same areas have hardly started to mix and integrate. Furthermore, Soviet planners have generated their own prejudices, independently of Marx and Lenin; there is a hostility towards most service activities including retail sales, and towards almost any form of pure entertainment or leisure; health and education standards, however, are high although housing has been neglected in some ways, as have collective farmers.

It is often suggested in the West that there are in reality many similarities between the U.S.S.R. and the capitalist industrial countries. Another view is that they are becoming more similar. There are marked social classes and income gaps in the Soviet Union, as in the West. There are even private land plots in farms, wage bonuses and incentives in industry and some unplanned production and marketing of goods. The fundamental difference, which will be elaborated in the next section, is that no private individual can invest capital and there are, therefore, no individual shareholders receiving profits (if any) either from their own undertakings or from private companies. Instead, one group, one board of directors, the decision makers of the Communist Party of the Soviet Union, decides in which branches and in which regions all capital investment shall go.

Although it has invested itself with a monopoly of truth on social, economic and political matters, the Communist Party of the Soviet Union has rarely missed the chance to build on the technological experience of capitalist countries, thus where possible taking short cuts. At the same time, advances have been made in many branches of engineering, including electrical, nuclear and space engineering. In 1967, for example, the U.S.S.R. possessed the world's largest proton accelerator *(uskoritel' protonov).*

5.2 WHO MAKES THE DECISIONS?

Large numbers of small decisions made by many people are amenable to statistical techniques and can often be predicted with some confidence. Big decisions taken rarely cannot. The decision, for example, whether or not to construct a railway parallel to the present Trans-Siberian Railway but to the north of it must be decided by some individual or group. The decision either way will have an enormous impact on the spatial development of the Soviet economy. The only comparable decision was that concerning the Trans-Siberian Railway itself. Some insight into the making of big decisions may, however, be obtained by considering the basic thinking of the Soviet Communist Party, and some from a study of those who make the decisions.

The major policy decisions are probably made by a limited number of high party members. They are put into operation by planners. Table 5.1 suggests the similarities and differences between the U.S.S.R., West European countries with a substantial public sector and the U.S.A. The situation in the U.S.A. is complicated by the Federal system, which allows considerable power to States in modifying decisions taken at higher levels; moreover, much spending of public, particularly Federal funds, is on equipment made in the private sector.

One difference between the U.S.S.R. and the West is the relative importance of the public sector. A second difference arises from this one; in the U.S.S.R. the economy can be planned almost exclusively by one body of decision makers. It is like one huge firm that produces nearly everything it needs; its market is its own employees. In the U.S.A., planning is no less important, but it is found within private companies, theoretically competing with each

forests which are at present being wasted at an alarming rate. This article coincides with a rejection in *Pravda* today of the idea that there should be a rigid application of Marx's labour theory of value, according to which the exchange value of an object is represented by nothing more than the cost of the labour spent on its manufacture.
Moskva showed the effect of this law on the Soviet Union's natural resources. Because land, forest and water on which no labour has been spent cannot be valued in roubles, it showed, the most easily accessible timber has the same value as timber in the most remote area. For this reason, accessible forest along rivers, for example, is being rapidly depleted, while less easily accessible reserves are often left untouched.

Considerable evidence will be given in Chapter 13 of marked regional differences in investment, industrialisation, provision of amenities and retail purchasing power. In the

Table 5.1. DECISION MAKERS IN THE U.S.S.R., WEST EUROPE AND THE U.S.A.

	U.S.S.R.	*West Europe*	*U.S.A.*
Agriculture	State planners Collective farm managers Peasant private plots	Mainly small private or tenant farmers	Small private or tenant farmers Bigger companies
Industry	State planners	Public and private	Mainly large private
Services	Largely state planners	Mixed	Varied private

other, but at all events, rarely collaborating in the framework of a national plan. Major decisions, therefore, are made in the U.S.S.R. over one short period for the whole economy, to last for several years and to be modified only in an emergency, but in the U.S.A. private concerns of varying size make their own decisions from time to time and constantly modify their plans.

Another major difference between the U.S.S.R. and the major Western industrial countries is the attitude to land; the reader is referred to a paper by Jensen[3] on changing Soviet attitudes to land evaluation. This important question for geographers is often overlooked; it affects the policy towards marginal farmland, towards the construction of reservoirs and other aspects of Soviet development. The argument is summarised in the following passage *(The Times*, 5 March 1968):

Moskva (a review) argues forcefully for the imposition of a monetary charge on land, water and

R.S.F.S.R., predominantly Russian oblasts are usually much more developed than nearby non-Russian A.S.S.R.'s (eg contrast Gorky oblast and the Chuvash A.S.S.R.). The R.S.F.S.R., moreover, is more highly developed than most other Republics. The encouragement given to the separate cultural life of smaller peoples may have helped to perpetuate their isolation, backwardness and lack of participation; alternatively, the preponderance of Russians (and at times Ukrainians) at the highest levels in the C.P.S.U., may be one reason for the preferential treatment in terms of greater *per capita* investment given to predominantly Russian areas. Bialer[1] makes the point that national distinctiveness is as marked now as in 1939. In the top ranks of the Party, Slavic domination is marked, while Central Asia, Kazakhstan and the Baltic Republics are underrepresented. In the Central Committee of the Party itself, Great Russians are dominant and they thus hold the key to power in the country.

Non-Slavs are well represented at lower levels in the Communist Party membership and no doubt contribute to decision making at local if not regional level.

Some examples of the way in which Russians appear to keep certain key activities within the R.S.F.S.R. are the dominance of the Ural region over the eastern Ukraine in the production of high grade steel, the retention of much of the high grade, skilled engineering in the Moscow and Leningrad areas and the decision to send much Central Asian (Uzbek) gas to the Ural region rather than to use it all locally. Although there is little direct evidence to confirm this, it seems also that much of the aerospace and nuclear power industries is concentrated in Russian areas, as, according to Nove,[4] who suggests that over 50% of Soviet scientific research workers are in Moscow and Leningrad alone, is scientific research.

5.3 BRANCHES AND REGIONS

The Soviet Union has what is loosely termed a command economy (Heilbroner).[5] Two features of such an economy, the first essential, the second likely to follow, are State or public control of most if not all capital investment, and planned investment. Fig. 5.1(a) indicates in a very simplified way the relationship of the command economy to planning and to two distinct questions facing planners. An initial decision must be made as to the proportions of total production to be reinvested and consumed. Two interrelated questions must then be answered: What proportion of investment is each branch or sector of the economy to have? and: What proportion of investment is to go to each region of the country, assuming some system of planning regions is in use?

The branches (Russian *otrasl'*, English *sector*)

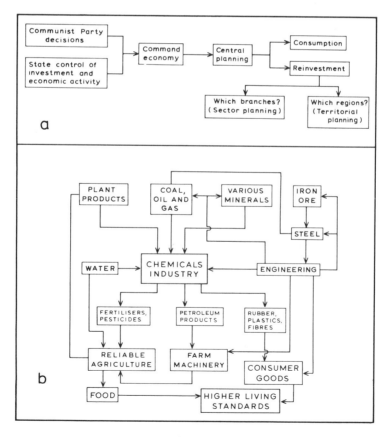

Fig. 5.1.   *(a) Basic relationships in a command economy. (b) Relationships between branches in the Soviet economy viewed from the chemicals industry.*

will be considered first. Preference is bound to be given to some branches rather than to others (eg engineering before clothing, education before housing). The interrelationships, however, of various branches of an economy the size of the Soviet one are very complex. It is possible to gain some appreciation of the complexity with a diagram, but the information that can be included is limited and there is a tendency to see the economy from the viewpoint of one or a few branches. Iron and steel held a key position in the 1930's. Fig. 5.1(b), built round ideas in *Pravda*, 17 December 1963, shows the situation viewed from the chemicals industry, which for a time in

symmetric. The branch at the head of a column pays out the amount indicated to each row or branch. Thus in Table 5.2, Column 7, oil products, buys from branch 6, oil, 1 209 million roubles worth of material. The figure 490 where Column 7 crosses Row 7 represents the transactions within the branch oil products. Sugar, Row 72, is understandably not bought by any of the other branches selected in this table. More of the matrix is shown in Fig. 5.2 in a diagram, which shows almost all transactions in the 1966 Soviet input-output matrix within a branch or between branches, valued at more than 450 million roubles (about £180 million). Of the

Table 5.2. SELECTED ROWS AND COLUMNS OF THE 1966 INPUT-OUTPUT MATRIX OF THE SOVIET ECONOMY

Figures in millions of roubles

		1 Metals	5 Coal	6 Oil	7 Oil products	11 Energy	48 Wood	49 Furniture	72 Sugar
1	Metals	6 573	32	3	9	10	31	4	8
5	Coal	481	1 289	–	–	1 542	23	11	35
6	Oil	–	–	9	1 209	11	–	–	–
7	Oil products	212	12	19	490	450	27	6	70
11	Energy	725	211	78	245	11	90	28	20
48	Wood	32	67	1	4	2	837	389	3
49	Furniture	4	1	–	1	1	1	29	–
72	Sugar	–	–	–	–	–	–	–	934

Source: *NkhSSSR* 1967, 64–111.

the early 1960's was regarded as a leading link in the economy. Such diagrams are both selective and arbitrary, but at least they give some idea of the complexity of the economy.

An input-output table or matrix, containing 72 branches, of the economy for the year 1959 was published in the U.S.S.R. in 1962. In 1967 a comparable table for 1966, with 86 branches, was published, a few selected branches of which are reproduced in Table 5.2, to give an idea of its appearance. The entry at the crossing of each row with each column represents the transaction, if any, between pairs of branches. The matrix is square (86 rows and columns) but not

86 branches in the complete matrix, 47 are actually involved, because they have at least one transaction greater than 450 million roubles; they are listed in Table 5.3. The branch descriptions have been translated freely and most are condensed. Many more branches in the diagram are connected than the arrows indicate, but by smaller transactions.

Forty-five branches are each represented by one box; transport and internal trade (TR) have been split to prevent excessive crossing of transaction lines. Each arrow in the diagram represents a branch-branch transaction. The arrow points towards the branch that receives the

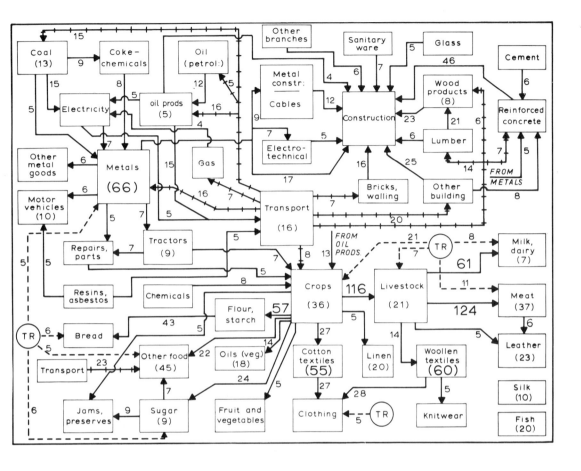

Fig. 5.2.   *Transactions of more than 450 million roubles in the 1966 input-output matrix of the Soviet economy. Numbers of the flow diagram are in hundreds of millions of roubles. Branch titles and definitions are greatly abbreviated in some cases. A number within a box represents transactions within that branch. The size of boxes varies merely for convenience. Transport and Trade (TR) have been represented more than once. Their links with other branches are also distinguished by ticked and broken lines respectively. Note: arrows point in the direction the goods or services go. Payment is in the opposite direction. Thus, for example, in top left of diagram, coke-chemical pays approximately 900 million roubles for coal received from coal branch. Source: NkhSSSR 1967, 63-111.*

materials, manufacturers or services and the payment flows in the opposite direction. Thus, for example (Fig. 5.2, top left), coke-chemicals receives coal worth 9 units from the coal branch, where a unit represents 100 million (10^8) roubles. Fifteen units of coal to electricity represents 1 542 408 000 roubles. Numbers inside boxes represent within branch transactions. A large branch, such as metals, which includes mining, smelting and rolling of all kinds of metal, has big within branch payments.

Table 5.3. SELECTED BRANCHES FROM THE 1959–65 INPUT-OUTPUT MATRIX

1 Metals	61 Cotton textiles
2 Coke-chemicals	62 Silk textiles
5 Coal	63 Woollen textiles
6 Oil	64 Linen textiles
7 Oil products	65 Knitwear
8 Gas	67 Clothing
11 Electricity	68 Leather, etc.
13 Electro-technical	69 Fish
14 Cables	70 Meat
30 Motor vehicles	71 Milk and dairy
31 Farm tractors	72 Sugar
33 Sanitary ware	73 Flour, starch
34 Other metal goods	74 Bread
35 Metal constructions	75 Jams
36 Repairs, parts	76 Vegetable oils
39 Chemicals	77 Fruit and vegetables
45 Resins, asbestos	78 Other foods
47 Lumber	79 Construction
48 Wood products	81 Crops
53 Cement	82 Livestock
54 Reinforced concrete	84 Transport
55 Bricks, walling	85 Trade (TR)
59 Other building materials	86 Other branches
60 Glass	

The appearance of such a matrix depends above all on the kind of economy it portrays (eg industrialised or not). It is also affected first by the subdivisions or branches into which the economy is split (eg engineering is more finely subdivided in the Soviet matrix than in the equivalent U.S. one) and secondly on the order in which the branches are taken (again, the U.S. matrices since 1945 differ not only from Soviet ones, but also among themselves). Many points deserve comment and thought, among them the bottomless pits of construction, clothing and food, even in the consumer starved Soviet economy, the very weak representation of

chemicals and the lack of attention to services (contrast the U.S. economy). Transport, of course, makes the whole thing move. There is some circularity, for example, transport both carries oil products and consumes them; the payments roughly balance, but the direction of materials as they leave the ground (coal, oil, crops) and are then processed and manufactured (textiles and clothing) is usually as would be expected. For comparison, a general picture of the U.S. economy may be gained from reference.[6]

When the emphasis of different branches has been decided and the interrelationships have been worked out, it must then be decided to which regions new investment is to go. Often there is a choice between several localities. Just as a vast spectrum of economic activities must for convenience be grouped into a limited number of discrete branches of the economy, so at least at the present level of sophistication in planning, the continuous territory of the U.S.S.R. must be divided into discrete compartments. The current 19 major economic planning regions will be discussed more fully in Chapter 6. However unrealistically they fit the continuum, with its many spatial variables, they serve a useful purpose in making it possible to see broadly the regional distribution of economic activities, to obtain a spatial balance of investment, and in general to think spatially about the vast and unwieldy territory of the U.S.S.R. Table 5.4 shows how the distribution of each of the branches can be summarised by placing as required the amount of productive capacity, output, existing investment, or new investment, in appropriate entries in the matrix. There is an entry for every contingency, though not every region will have every branch. In this example, only a few selected regions and branches are included. Tables of this type will be used extensively in later chapters to summarise the spatial distribution of branches of the economy and in many cases the information can be transferred to maps for a better visual picture.

Table 5.5 contains information about the interrelationship between regions. If appropriate data are available they can be used in particular to describe the volume and direction of the interregional movements of goods. In this example, a 1 indicates that the movement of coal takes place between a given pair of regions, a 0 indicates no movement.

Table 5.4. PART OF A REGION–BRANCH MATRIX FOR THE SOVIET ECONOMY

Economic region	Meat[1]	Milk[1]	Timber[3]	Electricity[2]	Cement[1]	Cotton textiles[4]
1 Northwest	270	2 653	91	22	3 256	222
2 Centre	848	6 569	31	37	6 114	4 906
3 Volga-Vyatka	314	2 342	33	11	961	111
10 Far East	144	917	23	7	1 692	9
11 Donets-Dnepr	906	4 955	1	59	6 570	16
17 Kazakhstan	665	2 834	2	15	3 425	20
18 Belorussia	430	3 210	8	6	1 266	7
19 Moldavia	144	584	0	1	445	2
U.S.S.R. total	10 195	61 248	370	412	61 018	6 619

Units: 1 $\times 10^3$ ton   3 $\times 10^6 \text{m}^3$
2 $\times 10^{12}$W   4 $\times 10^6$ m

Table 5.5. PART OF A REGION–REGION MATRIX FOR THE SOVIET ECONOMY

From \ To	1 Northwest	2 Centre	3 Volga-Vyatka	10 Far East	11 Donets-Dnepr	17 Kazakhstan	18 Belorussia	19 Moldavia
1 Northwest	1	1	1	0	0	0	1	0
2 Centre	0	1	0	0	0	0	0	0
3 Volga-Vyatka	0	0	0	0	0	0	0	0
10 Far East	0	0	0	1	0	0	0	0
11 Donets-Dnepr	1	1	1	0	1	0	1	1
17 Kazakhstan	0	1	1	0	0	1	0	0
18 Belorussia	0	0	0	0	0	0	0	0
19 Moldavia	0	0	0	0	0	0	0	0

Source: Galitskiy, M. I. *et al.*, *Ekonomicheskaya geografiya transporta SSR* (Moscow, 1965) especially p. 81. Note that the matrix is square (19 x 19 in complete form), but not symmetric, since a two-way flow between each region must be allowed for. The principal diagonal may be used to record within region flows. Where there is a 0 (eg Moldavia (19)), this means that the region itself produces no coal; thus for some purposes the rows for non-producing regions (3, 18 and 19 in this example) are superfluous.

Thus three types of table or matrix may be used to summarise relationships in the Soviet economy. Table types 5.2 and 5.5 are likely to be square matrices but not necessarily symmetric; table type 5.4 will not normally be square. The geographer is concerned more with types 5.4 and 5.5 than with 5.2, although this type should not be overlooked.

Both branch and regional planning are needed in the U.S.S.R. and there has never been an occasion when one or other has been completely abandoned, although there have been shifts of emphasis. The regions were especially strong under Khrushchev during 1957-62, the *sovnarkhoz* era. In 1962-63, the power shifted back towards branches, and industry was reorganised, with 11 national ministries to supervise engineering, gas and transport construction, and 17 Republic-based ones for metals, fuel, oil, power, fishing, geology and trade. The need to use both simultaneously has been stressed in recent years (eg *Pravda,* 29 October 1965). The branch approach is advantageous for stimulating growth sectors (eg chemicals, oil) but the Republics and economic regions are useful for planning complex economic developments within given areas. According to Schapiro,[7] in the late 1960's the ministries were strong at all-Union or Republican level, while local decision making was, if anywhere, with individual enterprises rather than with local regions.

5.4 PLANNING

State ownership and planning are not a new idea; according to Bram[8] and to others, the Inca Empire had some features of both. Similarly, the Crown of Spain had a monopoly of activities such as the mining of mercury in the Spanish American Empire. The governments of Sweden, Italy and Japan in the later part of the 19th century had a hand in the building up of industry and Great Britain, France and Italy now have highly capitalised public sectors. Younger American readers may be surprised to find how strong the trend towards national planning was in the U.S.A. in the 1930's (see, for example, National Resources Committee).[9] The Soviet system, however, has never been paralleled in its completeness, duration and sheer size. From 1917 until 1945 it developed virtually as a closed system; since World War II it has been broadened to include and plan jointly with East European countries. The nature of Soviet Five Year Plans has already been described frequently by Western authors and will not be mentioned here. The reader should bear in mind, however, that the operations of setting targets, checking and discussing these, preparing the plan directives, and approving and making the plan law are all very complicated. No less arduous and hazardous is the job of fulfilling the plan in all its sectors and in the regions of the country.

To be viable and meaningful, a national plan requires at least the following; first, the means (State control) to raise capital by taxation and to enforce (by law) planning directives, secondly, sufficient and accurate information about recent and existing activities of the economy and thirdly, adequate means of communication between planners and producers of goods and services. During the Soviet period all three have caused concern. The first was a serious problem in the 1920's when, under the New Economic Policy, farming was largely outside State planning and even by 1928, only 44% of the national income came from the State run sectors of the economy. After collectivisation of agriculture in the early 1930's, the State became able both to tax and to plan and control activities of almost the whole economy, except the small but important private plots of land still granted to collective farmers, the allotments allowed to non-collective farm workers and some private retail trade.

The problems of obtaining adequate data and of coordination and communication remain. Lack of suitable data hindered progress in planning in the 1920's, but was overcome sufficiently by the end of the decade for the first Five Year Plan to be started in 1928. Since the early plans were relatively simple in scope and limited in the number of branches involved and of large enterprises to be established, lack of data was not apparently too serious a problem, but by the early 1960's, the economy had become so complex that an enormous amount of data was needed to produce a plan. Smolinski,[10] stressing the need for better quantitative data and more statisticians, has suggested that the amount of information needed increases as the square of the amount of production in the plan. This may be an exaggeration, but it brings the point home, for if the current plans are involving eight times as much production as the first, then the data and data processing will require 64 times as many people. It follows that by about 1980 it would require the whole working population of the U.S.S.R. merely to work out the massive calculations required to formulate a plan.[11] According to Kerschner,[12] the electronic computer has been seen by some as the only salvation; Soviet scientists, initially lukewarm towards this idea, were becoming enthusiastic. A few hundred large machines could easily take care of the calculations done by the hypothetical 100 million people. Its widespread application, however, would require really first class data and gradually would tend to take over decision making from human beings. The computer itself does not make the decisions, but arrives at decisions through sensible programs and suitable data given to it by human beings, so this comes back to the need for better data in the first place. *Pravda,* 11 August 1967, going through reader's comments on the information question suggests that data available hitherto have not been suitable for finding the cause of planning failures.

The problem of communication within the economy has not been overcome either. It has tended to be restricted to a flow of information between planners and producers, with little between producers and producers. Indeed, this seems to be one of the fundamental and real differences between the U.S.S.R. and the U.S.A. Satisfactory links between planners and producers and among producers could perhaps be obtained by links with a vast national computer network. Theoretically such a system is feasible; it is used by some large companies in the Western world already. To install such a system in the U.S.S.R., however, would be both costly and difficult. The actual spatial layout would be of great geographical interest, but no hint of the appearance was given by Nemchinov[13] when he talked of the possibility of linking plans of small areas to those of the whole country.

Segal[14] notes an ambiguous attitude towards automation in general in the U.S.S.R. over the last 30 years and apprehension of computers over the last decade. The country was ready for automation and cybernetics in the mid-1950's, but a real fragmentation of organisation following the establishment of sovnarkhoz planning regions delayed progress. Now there appears to be concern that the Party, or at least many Party members individually, could lose their *raison d'être* as decision makers in the face of computerised decisions. According to Tidmarsh[15] such a view is also held by some Soviet mathematicians. Brzezniki[16] argues that the heavy bureaucratic set-up has already weakened the decision making ability of Soviet leaders, compared with the 1930's. The controversy over the computer grid and planning in general, was still prominent in 1968 (eg *The Times,* 29 May 1968).

By the mid-1960's the whole question of planning and indeed the command economy as known in the U.S.S.R. for the previous 40 years was being debated. Kantorovich,[17] for example,

was stressing the importance in planning of mathematical models, especially linear programming. He recommended the study of ways to make fuller use of machinery, to speed up production, to reduce transport costs and to analyse demand. Such high powered media seem to be reaching down. *Pravda,* 13 January 1969, recommends numeracy and accountancy for specialists on farms.

At the same time, a way of reducing the massive calculations foreseen for future national plans was under consideration. A market economy, at least in the sector of consumer goods, would leave out of the plan decisions as to the design, range and quantity of items produced and even the prices; these could then be altered at short notice without affecting the overall plan. The profit motive, introduced alongside, would help to pick out the more efficient producers, or at least might encourage managers to be more efficient and imaginative in the running of their factories. Nove[18] is emphatic that 'the price system should be able to express and transmit consumers' preferences'. The last word has not been said on economic reform, but the crux of the matter seems to be that it is all or nothing. Two Soviet economists are reported in *The Times,* 16 September 1967, as having stated 'that the process of expanding a factory's rights has its limits, and to expand beyond these would undermine the concept of central planning'.

5.5 ADVANTAGES AND DISADVANTAGES OF PLANNING

In the modern world, few large enterprises are run without plans of some kind. The question is not whether planning is needed, but whether it is feasible for an enterprise the size of the Soviet economy, or whether it should be used at the level of individual firms, urban areas or small regions. To many, the idea of a planned economy for a whole country is intellectually attractive; many people were drawn to this by the partial collapse of capitalism in the great depression of the early 1930's. The U.S.S.R., therefore, has been watched with great interest as a laboratory for national planning. Could capital investment be manipulated in such a way that booms or slumps and crises were avoided, balanced expansion achieved and a more consistent and rapid growth rate achieved? Could unemployment be avoided? The laboratory was wrecked for 10 years by World War II and the experimental conditions greatly distorted.

Table 5.6. LIST OF SOVIET NATIONAL PLANS

1928–32	First Five Year Plan
1933–37	Second Five Year Plan
1938–41	Interrupted Third Five Year Plan
1941–45	World War II: no Plan
1946–50	Fourth Five Year Plan
1951–55	Fifth Five Year Plan
1956–57	Abandoned Sixth Five Year Plan
1959–65	Seven Year Plan
1966–70	Five Year Plan

Table 5.6 is given as a guide to the main national plans. The present book is concerned largely with achievements in the 1959–65 Plan and prospects of the 1966–70 Plan. The achievements of the former and main aims of the latter are summarised in Section 5.6. In addition, other national plans of a temporary, emergency or projective nature have been produced from time to time (eg 1964–65). All stem from the Supreme Economic Council established in 1918, GOELRO (electrification plan) of 1920 and GOSPLAN (State Planning in general) set up in 1921.

It is proposed here to start with the assumption that national planning of the Soviet kind is good, and to point out the defects that, in spite of its goodness, have prevented it working smoothly. It is left to the reader to weigh these against the advantages, if any, that remain. The defects are listed briefly below, roughly in increasing order of importance.

1. How far can one usefully plan ahead, before shortfalls in production and unexpected technological innovations erode precision too seriously? The inaccuracy increases exponentially. Is five years a particularly good length? Nowadays this question might be referred to the study of forecasting in general, a subject in which the Russians and Americans are becoming more and more involved. Saushkin[19] remarks: 'Any science that does not provide well founded forecasts is likely to lose its significance' and 'Forecasting is of particular importance in countries with a planned economic system'.

2. Rigidity. A plan must have fairly precise targets to be meaningful at all, but a shortfall may unexpectedly occur, especially in agriculture, through, for example, a bad harvest. Thus the bad harvest in 1963 may have been the reason why revised plans were formulated for 1964 and 1965, the final two years of the 1959–65 Seven Year Plan. Similarly, an unexpected technological innovation, lowering the costs of production of some item in relation to another might make it desirable to switch emphasis in production. The shift of emphasis from coal to oil and natural gas shortly after 1956 has been suggested as a cause of the collapse of the 1956–60 Plan. A serious shortfall in production or shift of emphasis can have a chain reaction through a whole plan, so targets should not be excessively rigid, but rather guides to growth. At the micro-level, too, flexibility is needed in practice, in spite of the egalitarian principles of Soviet society. Tidmarsh[20] writes: 'When a general directive is found to obstruct some action considered more important, or when it is found necessary to waive the regulations and lay down special conditions, . . . the formula *v poryadke isklyucheniya* (there are exceptions to the rule) is invoked'.

3. Bottlenecks have been notorious. Excessive bureaucracy and lack of communication between firms have often been criticised in the Soviet press. *Tolkachi*, professional eliminators of bottlenecks, have played a vital role in smoothing things out, but firms have tended to show excessive self-reliance in making their own components and spares and in processing their own raw materials to ensure supplies which cannot be simply bought elsewhere in the event of a failure of a supplier.

4. Wrong incentives have often induced firms to produce items easy to produce but not really needed. Cases have been cited of firms being penalised for

achieving economies, thereby failing to fulfil targets. Lorry drivers, given credit in the plan for the distance they cover, have been known to make detours in their routes to clock up more kilometres.

5. For a country practising rigid planning, foreign trade causes serious problems. Conversely, a country that depends heavily on foreign trade (having a high import coefficient) finds rigid planning very difficult. The U.S.S.R. has had to trade for various reasons, but its planned economy has not generally been geared to produce surpluses specifically for export. Exceptions include gold, timber, oil, tinned salmon and crab, for which there are accredited export bodies. Foreign trade has been avoided also because of unwillingness to rely on imports from potentially hostile countries and because imports can rarely be guaranteed at fixed prices and in specific quantities, at least outside Comecon.

6. Arbitrariness and failure to correct mistakes. Much capital and enthusiasm has been wasted, and often capital has been invested idly, through the tendency to embark on big development projects and then to abandon them or delay their completion. The shelter belts and large Volga hydroelectric stations are examples.

7. Lack of adequate data, already discussed (*Pravda*, 18 December 1965).

8. Complexity, also discussed. Initially an inventory of a few hundred items sufficed; now hundreds of thousands must be considered. Theoretically the requirements of every family in the U.S.S.R., some 60 million, must be allowed for (*Pravda*, 24 February 1966).

9. Arbitrary prices have contributed to allow firms in high cost locations to remain in production because of the difficulty of detecting low cost locations without a market economy. There has also been a tendency to develop uneconomic resources just because they exist. The expected (if not always observed) competition between private firms and even para-state enterprises in Western capitalist countries is absent. A different kind of competition is encouraged between establishments producing the same thing; Donbass and Kuzbass coal miners, for example, race one another towards production targets.

10. Ultimately consumer sovereignty should come in the U.S.S.R.; Petrov[21] rather optimistically sees something of the kind already. Then the consumer, not the planner, would dictate the range of items produced by consumer industries. This would have repercussions in the planning of capital goods production. On a homely level, Soviet Central Planning has no time for breeding greyhounds or racehorses, for making attractive greetings cards or providing dancing classes in schools. Individuals creep in to provide such needs. According to *The Times,* 3 February 1966, 'an enterprising individual in Kotlas has been found to be making 20 000 roubles a year by setting up ballroom dancing groups all over the Soviet Union'. His inevitable arrest was not unnoticed in *Izvestiya.* Certainly Soviet planners are aware of the impending consumer revolution (eg *Pravda,* 13 June 1968) and of the impact this will have on the notoriously uninspiring sector of Soviet retail trade. In fact, it has even been suggested that retailers might try to sell things, rather than just distribute them.

In conclusion it may be noted that Soviet planners are not the only ones to be aware of the growing complexity of planning. Meier,[22] an American urban planner, remarks: 'The increasing bulk of information flow constitutes another threat to planning and administration' and 'Very few planners do not see their task as becoming increasingly complex'.

5.6 THE PLANS FOR 1959-65 AND 1966-70: SUMMARY

This section is mainly based on material summarised from relevant issues of *Pravda.* * It is

* In particular, 3 February 1966, 29 January 1967, 25 January 1968, 26 January 1969 for achievements in foregoing years, and 20 February 1966 for outline of the 1966–70 Five Year Plan.

not feasible to distinguish precisely which material is quoted directly from which number, nor to distinguish comments of the author.

SUMMARY OF DEVELOPMENTS DURING 1959–65

During the 1959-65 Plan, successes were achieved in economic and cultural construction and in the development of science and technology. The standard of living of the Soviet people rose substantially. The material-technical base of communism was reinforced as the economic strength and defence capacity of the U.S.S.R. was improved. Influence in world affairs grew and the superiority of socialism over capitalism was demonstrated. New levels of competition with the capitalist world will be reached and this will further strengthen the world revolutionary process.

During 1959-65, productive resources grew 1·9 times. The national income used for consumption and accumulation was 53% higher in 1965 than in 1959. New natural resources were exploited and the general education and technological level of the population improved. Industrial production increased during the seven years by 84% and, as shown in Table 5.7, was rapid in several major sectors.

Table 5.7. INCREASE IN PRODUCTION BETWEEN 1958 AND 1965 IN SELECTED BRANCHES OF INDUSTRY

Sector	1965 as percentage of 1958
Electricity output	220
Engineering and metal working products	240
Chemical industry products	250
Oil	220
Natural gas	430
Steel	170
Sea-going merchant fleet	250
Oil and gas pipeline	270

The contribution of industry to total national income rose from 80% to 84%. The share of oil and gas in total fuel consumption rose from 32% to 52% and electric and diesel traction on the railways grew from 24·6% to 85%. The labour force outside collective farm agriculture rose by 21 million.

There were, however, serious failures in the 1959-65 Plan. Agricultural targets were not fulfilled, some branches of heavy industry did not make proper headway, new capacity was slow to be utilised and equipment and labour were under-used. Labour productivity did not rise as it should have done, technically obsolete and poor quality items were produced and scientific and technological innovations tended to be introduced slowly. Much of the trouble arose because there was lack of coordination between rapidly growing material production and planning methods, the direction of the economy and material incentives. The initiative of enterprises was stifled and their rights and responsibilities limited. Decision making was often faulty at local level and arbitrary changes in policy were often made.

CHIEF TASKS OF THE 1966–70 PLAN

During 1966–70 it is essential to:
   (a) Increase national income by 38–41%.
   (b) Increase *per capita* real income by 30%.
   (c) Narrow the gap in living standard between rural and urban population.
   (d) Improve the cultural level of the population.
   (e) Utilise rationally the labour resources of all regions of the country and ensure work for rural population throughout the year.
   (f) Ensure the all-round development of all the Soviet Republics and merge national and republic interests.

To achieve these aims, the following are necessary:
   (a) Increase industrial production by 50% on the basis of heavy industry, especially branches connected with scientific and technological progress; ensure the future re-equipment of agriculture and light industrial establishments, construction and transport.
   (b) Appreciably increase agricultural production (no figure given); improve technology in agriculture and improve incentives to farm workers; concentrate

on increasing grain yields and livestock production.

(c) Raise the efficiency of production
  (i) Modernise products and improve their quality.
  (ii) Quicken completion period of projects involving large amounts of capital.
  (iii) Raise labour productivity, increasing electricity consumption in industry by 50% and in agriculture by 200%.
  (iv) A more rational spatial deployment of productive forces, using new natural resources.
(d) Speed up scientific and technological progress and apply findings to improve production methods. Developments are proposed in particular in mathematics, nuclear physics, outer (cosmic) space research, the earth's interior, chemistry, biology (with farming in view) and the social sciences.
(e) Perfect planning and ensure a satisfactory relationship between centralised planning and individual initiative and independence in industry
  (i) Base central planning on correct branches of the economy, improved location of production, and the complex development of regions; centralise or standardise capital investment, prices, profits, finance and credit.
  (ii) Organise production better actually on the spot in factories, farms and other establishments; improve accounting.

ACHIEVEMENTS DURING 1966–68
IN SELECTED BRANCHES OF INDUSTRY

Table 5.8 brings up to date progress in the main branches of heavy industry and in other selected branches (see Appendix 4, p. 314 for 1969 data). Oil, gas and electricity hold a prominent place, but coal and timber are faltering. The annual increases of 4–6% recorded for pig iron and steel represent by now a massive absolute amount, in fact a yearly increase of considerably more than the whole of Soviet steel output in the late 1920's.

Table 5.8. YEAR TO YEAR INCREASE IN PRODUCTION BETWEEN 1965 AND 1968 IN SELECTED BRANCHES OF INDUSTRY

	1965–66	*1966–67*	*1967–68*
Electricity	108	108	109
Oil	109	109	107
Gas	112	110	107
Coal	101	102	100
Pig iron	106	106	105
Steel	106	106	104
Fertilisers	114	111	109
Motor vehicles	110	108	110
Tractors	108	106	105
Timber	100	104	100
Paper	110	107	104
Cement	110	106	103
Cotton cloth	104	104	103

REFERENCES

1. BIALER, S., 'How Russians Rule Russia' *Problems of Communism*, 45, Sept.–Oct. 1964
2. SCHAPIRO, L. F., *The Government and Politics of the Soviet Union* (Hutchinson, London, 1968)
3. JENSEN, R. G., 'Land Evaluation and Regional Pricing in the Soviet Union' *Soviet Geogr.*, 9, No 3, 1968
4. NOVE, A., 'Soviet research problems' *New Scient.*, 84–5, 11 Jan. 1968
5. HEILBRONER, R. L., *The Making of Economic Society* (Prentice Hall, Englewood Cliffs, 1964)
6. LEONTIEF, W. W., 1. 'Input-Output Economics' *Scient. Am.*, Oct. 1951; 2. 'The Structure of Development' *Scient. Am.*, Sept. 1963; 3. 'The Structure of the U.S. Economy' *Scient. Am.*, Apr. 1965
   The 1959 Soviet table is in *NkhSSSR* 1961, 77–117
   The 1966 Soviet table is in *NkhSSSR* 1967, 63–111
   A reduced version of the 1959 Soviet input-output table is given in English in *NDSE*, Part 2–A, 268
7. SCHAPIRO, L. F., *The Government and Politics of the Soviet Union*, 125 (Hutchinson, London, 1968)
8. BRAM, J., 'An analysis of Inca Militarism' *Monogr. Am. Ethnol. Soc.*, 4 (University of Washington Press, Seattle and London, 1966)
9. National Resources Committee, *Regional Factors in National Planning and Development* (U.S. Govt. Printing Office, Washington D.C., 1935)
10. SMOLINSKI, U., *Pravda*, 18 Dec. 1965
11. *Pravda*, 24 Feb. 1966, stresses the importance of computers and the impossibility of managing with manual calculations, and suggests 10^{16} mathematical operations needed each year could be handled by 4 000 computers, linked for the

circulation of information. Data should be pre-pared in a form suitable to put in the machines.

12. KERSCHNER, L., 'Progress and Ideology in the USSR: Cybernetics' *Problems of Communism,* Nov.–Dec. 1965

13. NEMCHINOV, V., 'Ekonomika i kibernetika' *Pravda,* 31 May 1963

14. SEGAL, G., 'Automation, Cybernetics and Party Control' *Problems of Communism,* Mar.–Apr. 1966

15. TIDMARSH, K., 'Mere mathematics fails to con-vince the party' *The Times,* 8 Mar. 1967

16. BRZEZINSKI, Z., 'Evolution in the USSR: Two paths' *Problems of Communism,* Jan.–Feb. 1966

17. KANTOROVICH, L., *Pravda,* 24 Aug. 1966, 2

18. NOVE, A., 'Planners, Preferences, Priorities and Reforms' *The Economic Journal,* 76, No 302, 1966

19. SAUSHKIN, Yu. G., 'Forecasting in economic geography' *Soviet Geogr.,* 9, No 5, 384–92, 1968

20. TIDMARSH, K., 'When exceptions are the rule in Russia' *The Times,* 2 Oct. 1968

21. PETROV, V., 'Russia Today, The Consumer is the Centre of Attention' *Progress* 2 (Unilever Quarterly, 1966)

22. MEIER, R. L., *Planning,* 287 (Selected Papers American Society of Planning Officials, Chicago, 1965).

6

Spatial aspects of planning

6.1 NON-SPATIAL FEATURES WITH SPATIAL IMPLICATIONS

Changing patterns of distribution can only be fully appreciated if decisions resulting from such aspects as investment policy, strategic policy, technological progress and cultural prejudices are taken into consideration. Only a few of the more important features of these will be given, as examples of what the geographer should bear in mind when dealing with the U.S.S.R.

INVESTMENT POLICY

This involves decisions as to the share of investment between, for example, consumer and capital goods, or coastal and long distance fishing. Suppose at a given time extra capital is allocated to consumer goods industries, then as a result new light manufacturing establishments will be built. Shall they be located in the existing light industrial areas where trained labour already exists, or should they be put into heavy industrial areas to absorb surplus female labour, or into backward rural areas to inject some relatively well paid employment there? The question *where* must be asked and answered.

STRATEGIC POLICY

Information about this is far from complete, but Soviet leaders have frequently taken strategy into consideration. Their outlook has presumably changed from the days of conventional warfare to the days of nuclear warheads on long range missiles. Under conventional conditions, military considerations might lead to a twofold distribution of activities: a concentration of armed forces and supplies as near as possible to the zones in which an enemy might attack and a concentration of key industries out of reach of an invading enemy. The establishment of a new modern heavy industrial base in the Ural region in the 1930's, although not exclusively a strategic move, fits the thinking outlined above. Similarly, the policy of making economic regions self-sufficient could be seen in terms of their self-perpetuation in the event of an invader occupying other parts of the country or cutting off some part by interrupting the tenuous communication system. Fig. 8.9(b) shows the actual area occupied by the Germans from 1941–45 for differing lengths of time. The Soviet Far East was also presumably developed and subsidised artificially to bolster it against Japanese, or more recently Chinese, interference. With the advent of long range missiles, no part can now be considered less vulnerable than any other; the emphasis, then, would seem to be on dispersal of key industries rather than on their concentration in the interior.

PROGRESS IN TECHNOLOGY

Rapid changes and innovations in technology at

the present day make it necessary constantly to weigh and reconsider the advantages of one resource against another, or of the same resource in different localities. Advances in transportation technology as well as production technology have spatial implications. They may make it feasible suddenly to develop a new area or to move some item further than previously. Thus advances in drilling technology may be one of the reasons why it was felt possible to shift emphasis from coal to oil and gas in the 1950's. Advances in the technology of electricity transmission have made it possible to plan the transmission of electricity economically more than 1 000 miles instead of a few hundred. The following directions of technological advance are listed by a team of Soviet economists (Feygin[1]) as likely to affect spatial distributions:

1. The mineral, fuel and energy base will be widened by new methods of exploring, extracting and enriching materials. This means that not only can new areas be further explored, but older areas face prospects of rejuvenation.
2. The amount of labour required in manufacturing processes will be lowered and this will make it more easy to introduce manufacturing into labour deficient regions.
3. Larger establishments, benefiting from economies of large scale, are likely to be required. Obviously such plants will tend to be placed near large or at least medium sized industrial centres, or they may be placed near large sources of raw materials, or on a coast, accessible to ocean shipping.
4. Cheaper transportation will make it possible to assemble materials at big plants.
5. The ability to substitute a new material for an old one may change the importance of one area compared with another. Artificial and synthetic materials also have to be taken into account.

CULTURAL PREJUDICES

This topic was discussed briefly in the previous chapter. The rise of Ukrainians to important posts during the Khrushchev period may be cited; they did not, however, apparently do much to use their influence to boost the interest of the Ukraine, for the western part is currently one of the most backward parts of the U.S.S.R. and has no prospect of changing quickly.

6.2 THE PURPOSES OF REGIONS

It is often pointed out in Soviet publications that the regions used by geographers in capitalist countries are merely for descriptive purposes and are trivial in concept: communist regions on the other hand are designed for planning purposes. The ideal region as defined by Feygin (pp. 13–15)[1] is: 'an economic (*khozyaystven-naya*) territory, standing out within the country for its specialisation and structure of production, its natural and human resources and also its economic–geographical position'. A supposedly socialist region, then, has the following attributes: 'it ensures the most rational use of resources, the planned division of labour on socialist lines, complex and balanced development with planned specialisms, the evening out of economic differences of level among regions and the most rational organisation of inter-regional links'.

Some of the properties of Soviet economic regions deserve a little elaboration.

1. Data collecting and administration of planning. Data are often available only for economic regions, and Western geographers are forced to use the regions as a basis of study simply for this reason. The regions also serve as the first level for the spatial development of investment in planning, their performance may be watched and is a useful indicator for the regulation of the economy in a spatial sense. A preliminary spatial classification of the resource inventory can also be achieved by studying the regions.
2. The regions have been created and used to facilitate the evening out of wealth. The uneven distribution of development and income in the Russian Empire was one of the features the early Communists first committed themselves to eliminate or at least modify. What precise role the regions play in this respect is not stated.

As in many developing countries, wages in industrial employment have tended to be far higher than in agriculture; one way to bring up backward regions, therefore, has been to put new industry in them. As a result, many industries may have been unsatisfactorily located. It might have been better to bring up agricultural wages and therefore allow for the possibility of a prosperous but still predominantly agricultural region, with processing, service, and consumer goods industries arising spontaneously.

3. The regions have been regarded as entities in which some degree of self-sufficiency could be achieved, at least in terms of bulky and/or perishable items. This important aspect will be dealt with in Section 6.5. The regional boundaries could be used to step up freight charges on the carriage of items by rail, waterway or road, thus encouraging (rightly or wrongly) regional self-sufficiency.

6.3 TYPES OF REGION

To the geographer a *formal* region may imply some part of the earth's surface that is reasonably uniform in one, or with a little imagination, several, features (variables). In contrast, a *functional* region is some part of the earth's surface, the elements of which are complementary and mutually related. Division into such regions is convenient for many purposes, because the earth's surface, or a large part of it such as the U.S.S.R., is so complex and varied. For simplification and classification, a number of formal regions may be suggested. On the other hand, for administration and planning, functional regions may be desirable. The first kind of region is often sought, detected and justified by academic geographers, but its limits are rarely visible or precise. The second kind often actually exists on the ground and has precisely defined boundaries, the effects of which are felt in various ways, even though usually the actual boundaries themselves are only recorded in maps or documents, and not physically marked on the ground. In the U.S.S.R., as in most countries, the politico-administrative units (see Chapter 2) form a network of regions of the second kind; usually the network has been partially planned, partially improvised. It could rarely be called ideal. Soviet economists and geographers, on the other hand, have searched for ideal regions of the first kind, with a resource-production, or economic base, round which they could form their system. In practice the 19 regions they have are neither uniform nor functional to more than a slight degree; they are, nevertheless, presumably convenient for various purposes.

Many Soviet authors, including Krzhizhanovskiy[2] and Alampiev[3] have given accounts of systems of regions during the Soviet period. *Voprosy geografii*[4] has papers by various authors on the subject. Twenty-six regions proposed by Kolosovskiy are given by Belousov,[5] several sets of regions are mapped and described by Mellor[6] and Saushkin[7] deals with economic regions in a general economic context. So-called nodal territorial-production complexes are considered by Probst.[8]

Some general points are outlined below:

1. The U.S.S.R. could be subdivided into any number of compartments from two to at least many thousand. For most of the communist period there have been 15–20 regions. For a few years following 1957 reforms, a system of 104 sovnarkhoz regions was in use. By the mid-1960's a system of 19 regions had been established. It is convenient to have a system of regions that can be changed as the basic distributions of the underlying geography change, though this makes comparison over time difficult and in fact Soviet changes have been too drastic to be satisfactory.

2. Unless the area subdivided is reasonably uniform, regions generally vary appreciably in both territorial extent and number of inhabitants. It is possible, theoretically, to hold one or the other constant, but not both unless population is uniformly distributed. In practice there is no merit in being very precise about either. In the U.S.S.R., however, population is very unevenly distributed and the great variations in both area and number of inhabitants tend to be inconvenient.

3. Regions will vary in shape. They can be

fragmented, but usually they are reasonably compact, although they may be elongated. There are methods of measuring compactness but they do not seem useful for applying here.

4. Economic planning regions should, if possible, be reasonably integrated, in the sense of having communications between the various parts and some set of resources that can be used to form the base of an economic complex. The idea of the complex development of regions is in fact being given prominence by Soviet economists and planners, as by Vedishchev[9] and Feygin[1] in works on economic geography and in the press (eg *Pravda,* 20 February 1966).

5. The close connection between economic and administrative regions is a theme often stressed by Soviet economists and geographers. According to Mikhaylov,[10] quoting N. N. Baranskiy: 'a territorial unit with administrative organs within it, a unit that would actively strive for fulfilment of its assignments within the national plan, would actively transform its economy in accordance with its planned specialisation'. Mikhaylov remarks: 'A region is a delicate organism, sensitive to changes in social and economic life. We know that new economic and social phenomena are not always detected at once'. He instances a valley in East Siberia divided into two rayons; interests conflict and there is lack of economic cooperation.

6.4 THE ECONOMIC REGIONS IN THE LATE 1960's

The basis for actually choosing the present regions, as defined in Chapter 3, seems very arbitrary. Reasons for their existence may be suggested:

1. A clearly defined, distinct and/or isolated location, for example, Far East, Transcaucasia, Central Asia.
2. A distinct physical feature giving some unity, for example, Volga, Ural, North Caucasus, Transcaucasia.
3. An industrial complex placed centrally in relation to area and/or population, for example, Centre, Donets-Dnepr, West Siberia.
4. Distinct culturally, for example, Baltic Republics, Belorussia, Transcaucasia, Central Asia.

Several regions, including the Northwest and East Siberia, are dubious either as formal or as functional regions. Some are obviously residual areas; eg Volga-Vyatka, Blackearth Centre, the Southwest and South. Kazakhstan is a meaningless monstrosity, with an empty arid zone separating two main belts of population, northern and southeastern, each like the region adjoining it, namely West Siberia and Central Asia. Unfortunately there is very little information published for the oblasts of Kazakhstan, and the region therefore has to be recognised and used in its entirety. It remains a monument to the obstinacy and deceitfulness of politicians who maintain the myth of a Kazakh people and their Republic.

In several places regional boundaries split particular areas that would benefit from being considered as a single entity for integrated planning. Thus the Donbass coalfield is unequally split between the Donets-Dnepr and North Caucasus regions. The Bashkir A.S.S.R. was transferred from the Ural region to the Volga region leaving an undignified bite out of the flank of the Ural. This was for a time compensated by the transference of Kurgan and Tyumen' oblasts from West Siberia to the Ural, boosting its food supply and replacing Bashkir oil by the new Tyumen' oil. Tyumen' has now reverted to West Siberia, however, leaving the Ural with a poorer energy base than ever before. Such gerrymandering can lead to self-deception, for it makes no difference to the actual location of resources or to the distance over which they must be transported. This question will be discussed again in Chapter 12. The new grain lands are mainly in three regions (Kazakhstan, Ural, West Siberia), the main sugar beet belt also falls in three and the oasis belt of Central Asia continues into Kazakhstan. Other more local anomalies occur. Moreover, integrated planning is presumably hindered in the Baltic Republics, Transcaucasia and Central Asia by the presence of three or four Republics under one economic regional label. Even where boundaries do not cut through some obvious entity, they usually pass arbitrarily through continua, making an unreal break on the ground where none existed.

Only the defects of the existing system have been outlined so far. It would be an extraordinary coincidence if for every economic, agricultural, industrial and service activity, exactly the same 19 subsets were the most meaningful, or even meaningful at all. Nineteen subsets might be too few for some activities, too many for others. A really sophisticated system would have a set of regions for each branch and would consider different sets simultaneously, as required. In practice some kind of three- or four-tier nesting system might prove feasible. Electricity might be planned for the whole country, iron and steel in half a dozen regions, higher educational services in say 20 and potato cultivation in individual oblasts. At macroscopic and microscopic levels respectively, it is reasonably easy to consider the whole U.S.S.R. or an individual farm as meaningful entities; difficulties really arise in trying to define the intermediate 'mesoscopic' levels.

6.5 SELF-SUFFICIENCY VERSUS SPECIALISATION

Self-sufficient regions and specialised regions suggest a dichotomy that does not and could not exist in the U.S.S.R. Outside a completely subsistence economy it would be impossible to have complete local or regional self-sufficiency. At the other extreme, given the size and diversity of the U.S.S.R., it would be unthinkable to have a system with each region possessing only one branch of production. There have been shifts of emphasis as to degree of one or the other and different compromises between the two have been reached at different times. Currently there seems a gradual trend towards more specialisation; on the other hand, the 1957 sovnarkhoz system appears to have encouraged more regional self-sufficiency, though each sovnarkhoz region was to have its specialism or specialisms as well. Many regions, however, were too small to support even one.

The degree of regional specialisation possible depends to some extent on policy, but more on the nature of the branch of production involved and the availability and costs of transportations. The size of the region also matters, for a large region will tend to have more numerous and varied resources than a small one. Similarly, in West Europe, small countries tend to have a higher import coefficient than large ones. Much, of course, depends on how any region is defined. The Ukraine, in total a reasonably self-sufficient unit, turned into three apparently unbalanced new units when split.

Most types of economic mineral are confined in distribution to a few localities and there are few that occur in commercial quantities in all 19 regions, so self-sufficiency in this respect is usually out of the question. In contrast, all 19 regions have some farm land, but soil and climatic conditions do not permit every region to grow every type of crop. Oddly enough, manufacturing establishments are, theoretically, the most flexible in terms of location. There is no reason, other than a cost one, why a steel mill or textile mill should not be located anywhere in the U.S.S.R. In practice, however, it is often advantageous to have large plants and to have various plants in the same vicinity. It would not be desirable for each region to have a fully integrated iron and steel works; or a motor vehicles factory, though several have been given token steelworks to give the appearance of a metallurgical base, and the manufacture of motor vehicles has been decentralised since the 1940's.

One can cite, of course, activities that are found in every region and activities that are confined to one or two. At one extreme, vegetables, potatoes, footwear and cement are produced in all 19 regions, at the other, cotton comes almost entirely from Central Asia, industrial diamonds from the Far East and until the 1950's, motor vehicles almost entirely from the Volga-Vyatka and the Centre. Kistanov[11] proposes a system of indices to measure the degree of regionalisation in major economic regions.

An important point to consider is how far away a given producing area or factory can send its products before its own production costs plus transportation costs exceed production costs elsewhere. This turns out, in practice, to be only a general guide; Ural steel made at Magnitogorsk is theoretically cheaper than local Donbass steel in the Ukraine even after transportation costs, but there is no evidence of much Magnitogorsk steel finding its way to the Ukraine, nor any move to close down the relatively high cost Ukrainian mills.

Currently policy appears to be to encourage regions to be independent for bulky and/or perishable items such as potatoes, milk, domestic fuel and building materials and to leave the major transport lines free to move ores, coking coal, grain and so on. At the same time each region is encouraged to develop its own specialisms based on the best local resources and skills. Some regions, however, are lacking in cheap resources of any kind at all. Belorussia, the Baltic Republics and the Volga-Vyatka, for example, are poorly endowed in material resources, but they have a considerable population. This cannot easily be moved to areas with better resources, so has to be provided with employment, either based on high cost local resources such as peat and flax, or on materials brought in from other regions. Sophisticated engineering goods are now being made, but these are not ideal for areas lacking a skilled industrial tradition. Regional specialisation, self-sufficiency, differences in production costs, and the interregional movement of goods will be considered in greater detail in Chapter 12.

REFERENCES

1. FEYGIN, Ya. G. (ed), VILENSKIY, M. A. and MOSKVIN, D. D., *Zakonomernosti i faktory razvitiya ekonomicheskikh rayonov SSSR,* 201–6 (Moscow, 1965)
2. KRZHIZHANOVSKIY, G. M. (ed), *Voprosy ekonomicheskogo rayonirovaniya SSSR* (Moscow, 1957)

3. ALAMPIEV, P. M., *Ekonomicheskoye rayonirovaniye SSSR* (Moscow, 1959)
4. 'Ekonomicheskoye rayonirovaniye SSSR' *Vop. geogr.,* No 47 (Moscow, 1959)
5. BELOUSOV, I. I., 'O proyekte ekonomicheskogo rayonirovaniya SSSR, sostavlennom N. N. Kolosovskim' *Vop. geogr.,* No 41 (Moscow, 1957)
6. MELLOR, R. E. H., *Geography of the U.S.S.R.* (Macmillan, London, 1964)
7. SAUSHKIN, Yu. G., 'A History of Soviet Economic Geography' *Soviet Geogr.,* 7, No 8, 1966
8. PROBST, A. Ye., 'Territorial-production complexes in the U.S.S.R.' *Soviet Geogr.,* 7, No 7, 47–56, 1966
9. VEDISHCHEV, A. I., *Problemy razmeshcheniya proizvoditel'nykh sil SSSR* (Moscow, 1963)
10. MIKHAYLOV, Yu. P., 'Some aspects of lower-level economic and administrative divisions of the northern part of Transbaykalia' *Soviet Geogr.,* 9, No 2, 120–8, 1968
11. KISTANOV, V. V., 'On indicators of regional specialisation and integration' *Soviet Geogr.,* 6, No 8, 16–25, 1965

BIBLIOGRAPHY

'Ekonomicheskoye rayonirovaniye SSSR' *Vop. geogr.,* No 48 (Moscow, 1959)
'Ekonomicheskoye rayonirovaniye i narodnoye khozyaystvo SSSR' (various papers) *Vop. geogr.,* No 65 (Moscow, 1964)
KOSTENNIKOV, V. M., *Ekonomicheskiye rayony SSSR* (Moscow, 1958)
POKHSHISHEVSKIY, V. V., 'Economic Regionalisation of the USSR' *Soviet Geogr.,* 7, No 5, 4–32, 1966
SAUSHKIN, Yu. G. *et al.,* 'An approach to the economic-geographic modeling of regional territorial-production complexes' *Soviet Geogr.,* 5, No 10, 1964

7

Physical background

Since the emphasis in this book is on economic and social geography, physical features will be introduced and discussed largely in so far as they are related to human geography. At least eight or ten important physical variables suggest themselves in any study of a large region: structure, rock type, rock age, altitude (absolute relief), slope or ruggedness (relative relief), soil, vegetation, atmospheric pressure, temperature, precipitation. Each of these can be expressed in various ways; temperature, for example, by mean annual, mean for coldest month, hottest month, degree days and so on. Some variables can be expressed in combination with others; thus snow cover reflects both temperature and precipitation. In regional studies physical variables are often selected in a rather haphazard way. It is useful to think of the lithosphere, hydrosphere, atmosphere and biosphere and the intricate relationship between these before tackling the complex interrelationships on the ground.

7.1 TECTONIC AND STRUCTURAL FEATURES

Since structural–tectonic features of a region are the result of forces acting beneath the crust of the earth, rather than from above, they make a useful starting point for the study of other physical features. They are closely related to rock age and type, to relief features and to the distribution of minerals. Less directly, through the features mentioned, they affect the hydrosphere, atmosphere and biosphere and economic activities related to mining and water supply. It is only possible to name some of the outstanding variations and features here. In Fig. 7.1 a greatly simplified distinction has been made between areas in which folding is at the surface (1, 3, most of 5, 6) and areas (2, 4) where it is buried some distance beneath the surface by relatively undisturbed sedimentary rocks. The folded areas have been divided into four age groups, 1, Precambrian; 3, Paleozoic; 5, Mesozoic; and 6, Alpine.

Four areas with a cover of sedimentary rocks, in places as thick as several thousand metres, are shown in Fig. 7.1. Much of European U.S.S.R. rests on the so-called Russian Platform. West Siberia, between the Ural Range and the Yenisey, has the West Siberian Platform beneath. The Siberian Platform lies roughly between the Yenisey and the Lena. The Central Asian area has the Turan Platform. In general, the four areas listed above are associated with lowland features. Relative relief may be considerable, but absolute relief (altitude) is not usually great. Mineral deposits exploited in the areas mentioned are mainly non-metallic, iron-bearing minerals being the principal exception. Building materials (sand, clay, limestone) are widely available and coal, oil and natural gas are widespread. Raw materials for the chemicals industry are also found in many places.

The folded areas form the complement of the

sedimentary covered platforms already noted. They consist of two relatively low-lying shield areas, the Baltic Shield (continuing into Scandinavia) and the Ukraine Shield, and of various mountain areas. A broad distinction may be made between the more recent fold mountains of the southwest and east of the U.S.S.R. and the older fold mountains of south-central Siberia and the Urals. Apart from

7.2 RELATIVE AND ABSOLUTE RELIEF

Fig. 7.2 shows some outstanding relief features. Rivers are customarily shown on relief maps, but for the sake of clarity only a few are shown here. The following general relief regions may be suggested:

(a) Excluding peripheral mountain areas (Khibin Mountains of the Kola Peninsula,

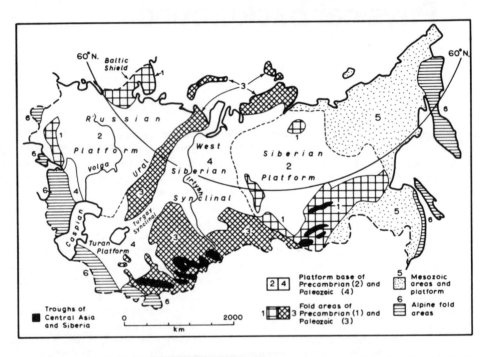

Fig. 7.1.   *Tectonic and structural features of the U.S.S.R. Two Russian words are used for shield:* plita *and* platforma, *the latter only for the 'higher' platform of mid-Siberia. Source: Lyalikov, N.I. (ed.)* Geografiya SSSR, *10 (Moscow, 1955).*

the two shield areas mentioned, the folded areas are mostly both high and rugged, but they contain many depressions and flanking lowland areas. The highest mountain areas of all are mostly associated with the more recent folding (Greater Caucasus, Pamir, some Far East Ranges) but the older (Hercynian) Tyan' Shan and Altay are also high. In contrast to the platform areas, the folded areas are the principal sources of metallic minerals, but are deficient in fuel, though oil and gas deposits commonly occur in sedimentary rocks on their flanks (eg North Caucasus, Central Asia, Volga-Ural oilfields).

Carpathians, Crimea, Caucasus), European U.S.S.R. consists of lowlands and hill country. The northern part has been more profoundly affected by glaciation than the southern (see Fig. 7.3). There are several long, relatively narrow ridges, the remains of moraines (eg the Valday Upland). Further south, there are three main hill areas, sharply dissected in places (1, 3, 4 in Fig. 7.2) which rarely exceed 300 m in altitude and are separated by gently undulating lowlands.

(b) The West Siberian Lowlands are low-lying and in parts almost completely flat. They end abruptly in the west against the Ural Range and in the east against the Mid-Siberian Plateau and rise very slightly southwards to the Kazakh Plateau. A large part of the area is marshy (see Fig. 7.3).

mountains of the U.S.S.R. are here, but there are great lowland areas to the north and east of the Caspian Sea and around the Aral Sea. The Kazakh Plateau (*melkosopochnik*) projects west from the high ranges of the Chinese border, between the Lowlands of Turan and West Siberia.

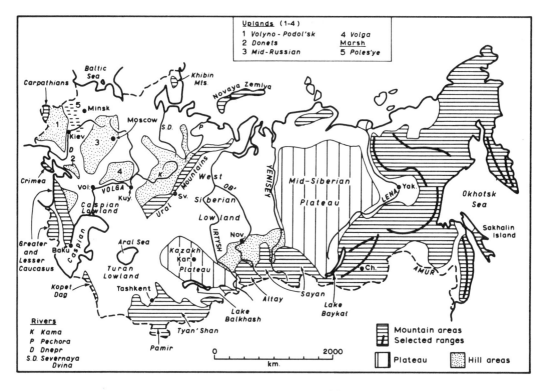

Fig. 7.2.   Selected relief features of the U.S.S.R.

(c) The Mid-Siberian Plateau (*Ploskogor'ye*) is in general around 400 m above sea level, though it rises considerably higher than this in places.

(d) East of the Lena is a complex area of ranges, depressions, and coastal lowlands. Many ranges here reach and exceed 2 000–3 000 m above sea level. The crests of several ranges are shown in Fig. 7.2.

(e) The mountains and lowlands of the south lie between the Caucasus in the west and the Pamir, Tyan' Shan, Altay and Sayan Ranges in the east. Most of the highest

How do the relief features of these five general areas affect economic activities? Steep slopes hinder cultivation mainly in region (d), but also in parts of (c) and (e). The hydroelectric potential is greatest in (c), (d) and parts of (e), although much of that actually exploited so far is in (a). The building of railways and to a lesser extent roads is difficult in much of (d) and parts of (c) and (e). Since all regions except (a) are relatively thinly populated and underdeveloped, the obstacles placed by relief features to the expansion of cultivation and the building of railways and roads are latent rather than active at the moment. Similarly, the hydroelectric potential is little used at present because there is no demand for the electricity and no means of moving it far enough elsewhere to be useful.

In addition to these general features, it is possible to study detailed or local relief features. Some 30 different types of relief are distinguished in a morphogenetic relief map in *Atlas SSSR.*[1] Features commonly found in the

variations in temperature, mean annual temperature is of less interest than a comparison of January or July temperatures. This is shown in Fig. 7.4(a) and (b); sea level temperatures are given.

In the western half of the U.S.S.R., January isotherms run northwest–southeast or in places even north–south, rather than east–west. This is

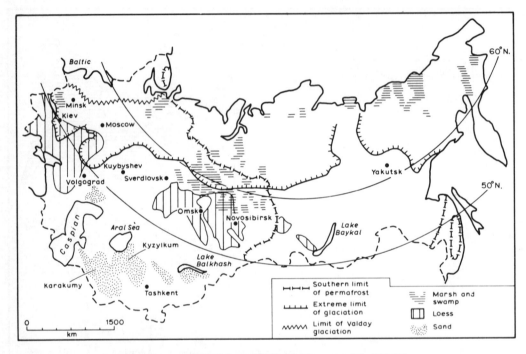

Fig. 7.3.   *Selected geomorphological features of the U.S.S.R.*

northern part of European U.S.S.R. are depositional, with glacial materials, and further south denudational features are developed on widespread loess deposits (see Fig. 7.3). The southern part of the West Siberian Lowland is characterised by lacustrine and alluvial deposits. Shifting and semi-shifting sands are found widely in the lowlands of Central Asia (Fig. 7.3). Many rivers have broad floodplains, particularly in the Ob' basin. These are merely examples of the great variety of landforms found in the more densely populated western part of the U.S.S.R.

7.3 TEMPERATURE AND PRECIPITATION

Since the U.S.S.R. is an area of great seasonal

because moderating oceanic influences from the Atlantic are able to reach northwest U.S.S.R. and penetrate far inland. The only places with a mean January temperature greater than 0°C are small sheltered areas found along the Black Sea coast and by the southern Caspian and a large area in Central Asia. The coldest places in the U.S.S.R. are in northeastern Siberia, away from the coast. Several valleys here have mean January temperatures of less than −40°C. In July, isotherms have roughly an east–west alignment. The coldest places are along the Arctic coast, the hottest in Central Asia; around Ashkhabad in Turkmenistan the temperature sometimes exceeds 32°C.

The range between mean January and mean

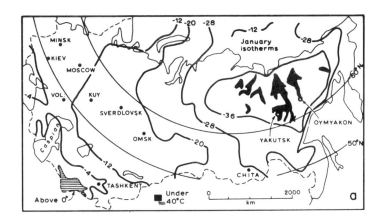

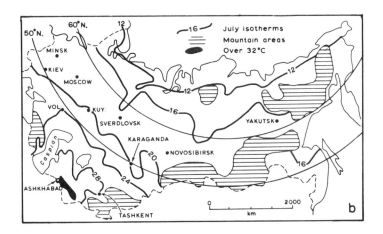

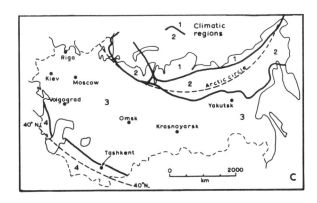

Fig. 7.4. *Mean monthly temperatures for (a) January, (b) July. (c) Four main climatic belts according to* Atlas SSSR, *78.*

July temperatures can be judged roughly from Figs. 7.4(a) and 7.4(b). The areas with the smallest range are in the extreme west, by the Baltic, and along the Black Sea and southern Caspian. The range is greatest in mid-Siberia. In both winter and summer, temperatures fluctuate greatly around the means shown in Fig. 7.4; in places in northeast Siberia, with mean January cover for more than half of the year. Along the Arctic coast, it lasts up to nine months. The areas with the deepest cover are in West Siberia. Another aspect of the extremely cold conditions that prevail in much of the U.S.S.R. is the permafrost, the general area of which is shown in Fig. 7.3. The severity of the winters keeps the moisture in the subsoil permanently frozen to

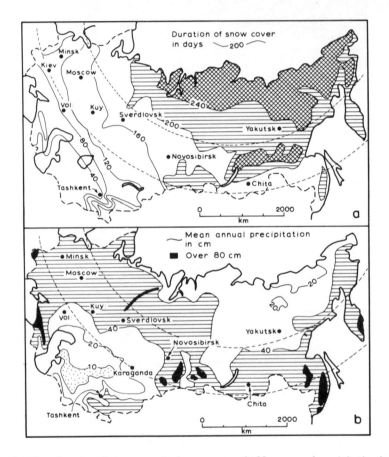

Fig. 7.5.   (a) Mean duration of snow cover in days per year, (b) Mean annual precipitation in centimetres.

temperatures around −45°C, temperatures as low as −65°C are not infrequent. Mountain areas break the general smoothness of the temperature maps, especially in the Caucasus and Central Asia and on a smaller scale, considerable local contrasts occur.

Fig. 7.5(a) shows the mean duration of snow cover (produced by precipitation, preserved by temperature). Almost all Siberia and the northern half of European U.S.S.R. have a snow varying depths. This condition occurs mainly in areas that were not actually glaciated in the Ice Age (Fig. 7.3), but the soil here was deeply frozen and has remained so ever since. Almost all the eastern half of the U.S.S.R. is affected, either continuously or in patches. In summer the uppermost layer of soil thaws and melted water lies upon the frozen subsoil causing marshy conditions and flooding. The permafrost makes construction work difficult, the maintenance of roads and railways costly and cultivation virtually impossible. It contributes to making access to the forests difficult.

Fig. 7.5(b) shows the mean annual precipitation. Fig. 9.4(a) shows the amount falling in the warmer part of the year, the growing season. The wettest parts in general are European U.S.S.R. except the extreme south, the western part of Siberia, and places within a few hundred

as 1, Arctic; 2, Sub-Arctic; 3, Temperate; 4, Sub-Tropical. Table 7.1 gives an approximate idea of conditions in localities representative of familiar regions of the U.S.S.R. The places are shown in Fig. 7.4(c). Other aspects of temperature and precipitation will be considered under agriculture in Chapter 9.

Fig. 7.6 shows the principal drainage basins and rivers. The Caspian and Aral Seas are areas of

Table 7.1. CLIMATE DATA FOR SELECTED TOWNS IN THE U.S.S.R.

| Town | Latitude North in ° | Temperature in °C | | Jan.– July range | Duration of snow cover in days | Frost-free period in days | Mean annual precipitation cm |
		Jan. mean	July mean				
Riga	57	− 5	17	22	100	150	60
Kiev	51	− 6	20	26	90	165	52
Moscow	55	−10	18	28	150	130	57
Volgograd	49	−10	24	34	100	175	36
Tashkent	41	− 5	26	31	60	180	25
Omsk	55	−19	19	38	160	115	34
Krasnoyarsk	56	−18	18	36	180	95	40
Yakutsk	62	−40	18	58	210	90	20

kilometres of the Pacific in the Far East. The driest part is Kazakhstan and Central Asia. A secondary dry area occurs in northeast Siberia, by the Arctic coast. Much of the U.S.S.R. has between about 40 and 60 cm of precipitation per year, which is generally adequate for cultivation of some if not all crops, given the high latitude of the country and the summer maximum of rain. There are small areas, mainly mountainous, with over 60 cm per year. The southern dry area occupies about 15% of the total area of the U.S.S.R. Part of the desert of Central Asia has less than 10 cm (4 in) per year.

Soviet geographers have devised extremely complex climatic types and subtypes. The systems evolved are an elaborate exercise in classification. Definitions illustrate the Russian outlook on climate and in some cases seem amusing. The so-called temperate belt (*umerennyy poyas*) includes the middle Lena valley, one of the coldest places in the world, with an annual temperature range of about 60°C. The sub-tropical belt has high summer temperatures, but long, cold winters, regular frosts and considerable snow. The four basic climates shown in Fig. 7.4(c) are defined (*Atlas SSSR*[1])

interior drainage. Much of European U.S.S.R. and most of Siberia drain to the Arctic Ocean. An approximate idea is given of the volume of water carried by the main rivers. It may be noted here that water resources are receiving increasing attention from Soviet planners.

7.4 VEGETATION

Climate, soil and vegetation are closely related, at least in terms of macro-regions, in the U.S.S.R. Climatic conditions largely determine the broad zones of forest and grassland and climate and vegetation together condition the soils. The tundra climate in the far north has brief warm summers, severe winters, thin rocky soils and a sparse vegetation of flowers, shrubs and lichens. The *tayga* or coniferous forest climate has a four- to five-month summer and severe winters, a grey acid infertile soil with few organic plant foods and is often cold and badly drained because of the underlying permafrost. Coniferous trees are the only tree vegetation that can cope with these conditions. The warmer summers and longer growing period of the broadleaf forest zone give time for deciduous trees to grow. Their leaves provide a better supply of humus and the better drainage usually provides a satisfactory soil for ploughing and cultivation.

The hot relatively dry summers of southern European U.S.S.R. have favoured the growth of annual grasses. These in turn have created a deep rich black soil with good water-absorbing qualities, which is ideal for ploughing, cultivating

the abruptness of the transition. Traverses from north to south in European U.S.S.R. encounter the following features: tundra, tayga, mixed tayga and broadleaf forest, broadleaf forest, forest-steppe transition, steppe and dry steppe (see Fig. 7.7). In West Siberia–Kazakhstan–Central Asia roughly the same sequence is found, but the broadleaf species are largely squeezed out and steppe continues southwards into semi-desert

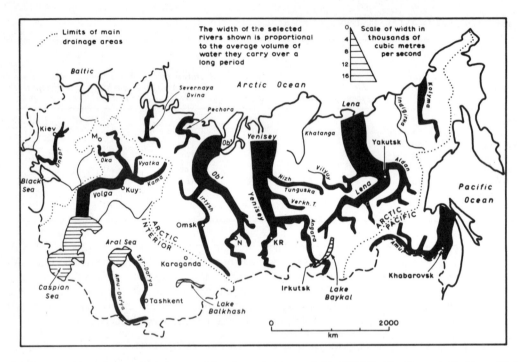

Fig. 7.6.   *The volume of water carried by the main rivers of the U.S.S.R. M = Moscow, N = Novosibirsk, KR = Krasnoyarsk. Source:* Atlas SSSR, 66.

and the growth of cereals. Further south, however, very dry areas have only a brief vegetation cover, soils are thinner and less fertile and often encrusted with salt.

Vegetation and soil belts are associated in the minds of Soviet geographers. Similarly, climate and vegetation are combined, as, for example, in *Atlas SSSR.*[1] It is important, however, to remember that zones or belts, represented as patches on maps, are really arbitrary discrete representations of generally continuously varying features. The forest does not end abruptly in the south against steppe or in the north against tundra. Recognition of forest-steppe and forest-tundra transition zones dilutes

and desert. In East Siberia and the Far East, the more rugged nature of the country distorts the continuity of the east-west belts of vegetation.

A macroscopic view of Eurasia helps to place the vegetation zones of the U.S.S.R. in perspective. In western and central Europe, a reasonably favourable climatic soil-vegetation environment (notwithstanding local interruptions of mountains and arid conditions) lies between the coniferous forest in the north (in Scandinavia about 60°N.) and the desert in the south (Algeria, Libya). In this broad intermediate zone with its relatively long growth season, mild winters and regular rainfall, the growth of deciduous forests of oak, beech and other broadleaf species is possible. This helps to create a less acid soil than in the coniferous forests. The equivalent elements in the U.S.S.R. are as follows:

1. In European U.S.S.R. the southern fringes of coniferous forest or tayga are about 57-58°N. and dry conditions are evident though not marked at 45°N. in the southern Ukraine.

7.5 WATER SUPPLY

The natural resources of the U.S.S.R. derived from the physical environment are described where appropriate under agriculture and industry in Chapters 9 and 10. Water, however, is vital to so many branches of the economy that its availability can best be discussed briefly here. Fig. 7.5 shows the main features of precipitation

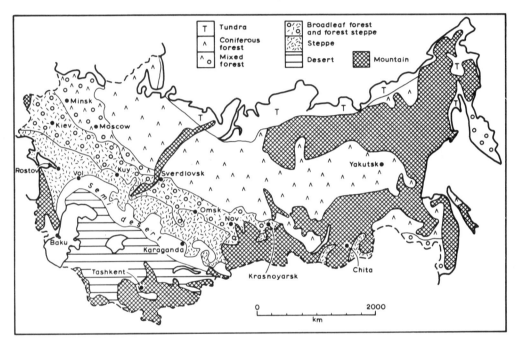

Fig. 7.7.   *Vegetation zones of the U.S.S.R.*

2. From the Volga, east to the upper Ob', coniferous forest at about 56°N. and desert at about 48°N. confront each other across a much narrower, somewhat precarious zone of steppe and mixed forest.
3. East of the upper Ob', mountain forest and Mongolian desert converge to leave only small patches of steppe, fragments of the continuous belt of western U.S.S.R.

It is unfortunate that there has not been a systematic study comparing the distribution of vegetation zones in Eurasia and North America. In spite of different orientations of some zones and of different plant species, some benefit might be gained of common interest.

and Fig. 7.6 the amount and direction of movement of water in the main rivers. The following users of water may be distinguished:

1. Agriculture, either in the form of direct precipitation or of irrigation (usually supplemented by direct precipitation) or water supply in grazing areas.
2. The generation of electricity in hydro-electric stations.
3. Industrial consumers, chemicals and steel works and thermal electric stations are particularly big users.
4. Domestic consumers.
5. Fishing and fish farming.
6. Navigation.

Many projects to improve water supply may benefit more than one user. Others may be carried out for one user but adversely affect another user; industrial pollution of rivers, for example, adversely affects fishing. On a more drastic scale, the construction of dams on the Volga system has created extensive reservoirs, the combined surfaces of which are several times bigger than the surface of the original river. This appears to have accelerated an existing long term trend for the water level in the Caspian Sea to drop, by reducing the volume carried into it by the Volga. One effect has been to put port facilities around the Caspian in need of modification. The considerable effect of the Rybinsk Reservoir (north of Moscow) on local climate is measured by Vendrov and Malik.[2]

In the early 1960's, according to Feygin,[3] the U.S.S.R. was using some 200 cubic km of water per year. This was only 6% of all the water carried in rivers (see Fig. 7.6) but 20% of the reliable amount. There is a further problem of freezing in many areas for much of the year. The greatest need for water occurs where the amount available is limited, but vast amounts are wasted by being emptied by the rivers of Siberia into the Arctic Ocean. It is expected that by the early 1980's the U.S.S.R. will need 650–700 cubic km of water per year. Industrial districts in which water supply is short or is likely to become short are the heavy industrial centres of the Donbass, Kuzbass and Ural, the oilfields of the Volga and new industrial centres in northern Kazakhstan. The Moscow area also has problems. Areas in which big irrigation projects are under way or planned are Central Asia and southern Kazakhstan and the southern part of European U.S.S.R. (see Fig. 14.12). Many large hydro-electric power stations are under construction. The tidying up of the European river system by building reservoirs in gaps along the Volga, Kama, Dnepr and other rivers is nearing completion. Larger sites with lower construction costs per unit of generating capacity installed are being built in Central Asia and East Siberia; the sites are such that the reservoirs will usually be narrower, though deeper, than in European U.S.S.R.

The basic thinking of planners towards water supply is to divert, in some cases at enormous intial construction costs, water flowing into the Arctic, particularly in the Severnaya Dvina, Pechora and Irtysh (see Fig. 7.6) across the watershed into the interior drainage area of the Caspian–Aral Seas. It was announced in *Pravda,* 22 August 1966, that one-third of the volume of the full Irtysh would be raised over 300 km and taken 475 km to Karaganda, with the help of 22 pumping stations. Such a project is only the beginning of what could be the biggest river diversion scheme in the world. One of the most ambitious schemes proposed is to harness the Lena system, the total hydroelectric potential of which is calculated to be capable of producing 250 000 million kWh a year, about three times the whole 1967 Soviet hydroelectric output. Vendrov,[4] discussing the changes of natural conditions that would result if the lower Ob' hydroelectric project were carried out, forecasts a deterioration of natural conditions.

Interference with nature and possible adverse consequences are concerning public-minded individuals in many countries. It is not surprising, then, to find that voices of caution are being raised in the U.S.S.R. against big water projects. An instance was reported in *The Times,* 12 May 1966, of a campaign led by scientists to save Lake Baykal from pollution by pulp and cellulose mills in the vicinity. A growing interest in conservation and similar matters is not confined to water resources. *Pravda,* 3 June 1968, had an article drawing attention to the growing pollution of the atmosphere; many Soviet heavy industrial centres were specified by name as being guilty and means of reducing pollution were suggested in *Pravda,* 16 July 1968.

REFERENCES

1. *Atlas SSSR,* Glavnoye upravleniye geodezii i karto-grafii: morphogenetic relief map, 76–7 (Moscow, 1962)
2. VENDROV, S. L. and MALIK, L. K., 'An attempt to determine the influence of large reservoirs on local climate' *Soviet Geogr.,* 6, No 10, 25–39, 1965
3. FEYGIN, Ya. G. *et al., Zakonomernosti i faktory razvitiya ekonomicheskikh rayonov SSSR,* 134–6, (Moscow, 1965)
4. VENDROV, S. L., 'A forecast of changes in natural conditions in the northern Ob' basin in case of construction of the lower Ob' hydro-electric project' *Soviet Geogr.,* 6, No 10, 3–18, 1965

BIBLIOGRAPHY

FRENCH, R. A., 'The Reclamation of Swamp in pre-Revolutionary Russia' *Trans. Inst. Br. Geogr.,* No 34, 175–88, 1964

GERASIMOV, I. P., and GLAZOVSKAYA, M. A., *Fundamentals of Soil Science and Soil Geography* (U.S. Department of Agriculture, Springfield, Va., 1964)

PETROV, M. P., *Pustyni tsentral'noy Azii* (Leningrad, 1, 1966, 2, 1967)

VENDROV, S. L., 'Geographical Aspects of the Problem of Diverting Part of the Flow of the Pechora and Vychegda Rivers to the Volga basin' *Soviet Geogr.,* 4, No 6, 29–41, 1963

VENDROV, S. L. *et al.,* 'The Problem of Transformation and Utilization of the Water Resources of the Volga River and the Caspian Sea' *Soviet Geogr.,* 5, No 7, 1964

ZHAKOV, S. O., 'The Long-Term Transformation of Nature and Changes in the Atmospheric Moisture Supply of the European Part of the U.S.S.R.' *Soviet Geogr.,* 5, No 3, 1964

8

Population

8.1 INTRODUCTION

At the last census held in the U.S.S.R. on 15 January 1959, the population was 208 800 000. The estimate for January 1969 was 239 million.

CHANGES DURING RECENT DECADES

The following figures show the population of Russia and the U.S.S.R. in selected years:

Table 8.1.

1897	124 600 000
1913	159 200 000
1940	194 100 000
1950	178 500 000
1955	194 400 000

During the years before World War I there was an increase of about two and a half million per year. Between 1913 and 1945, the World Wars and collectivisation affected population growth drastically. In the early 1930's there were food shortages and during collectivisation at that time the class of *kulak* peasants was largely eliminated. Territory changed hands during this period, which also complicates the study of population. Yearly average growth was not greatly above one million per year.

In 1945, the concluding year of World War II, the U.S.S.R. had approximately 164 million people, about 30 million less than in 1940, when the population was 194 million. The 1945 figure is calculated on the assumption that between 1945 and 1950, as between 1950 and 1955, there was an annual gain of about three million people. 1940 and 1950 figures are obtained from *NkhSSSR* 1964, p.7. On the assumption that without the war the 1940 population would have risen by two million per year, then by 1945 it would have reached about 204 million. In other words, it may be inferred that by 1945 the U.S.S.R. had some 40 million people fewer than it would have had without the war. This does not mean that 40 million people actually lost their lives; a figure in excess of 20 million dead is given in *Pravda* (6 April 1966) by Kosygin. Thirty per cent of the Soviet national wealth was also destroyed, families were broken up and the birthrate dropped. Peoples were moved out of the U.S.S.R. and Soviet prisoners of war in some cases opted not to return. There were also boundary changes.

Table 8.2.

Babies born	Births per thousand inhabitants
1960 5 341 000	24·9
1965 4 253 000	18·4
1967 4 093 000	17·4

From 1950 to 1964, the population of the U.S.S.R. increased by more than three million a year. The gain exceeded three and a half million for a time in the later 1950's. Since 1961, however, there has been a sharp decline in the absolute gain, followed by a decline in the relative gain from around 1·8% per year throughout the 1950's to no more than 1·1% in 1965–67. These trends are shown graphically in Fig. 8.1. During the 1960's there has been a marked decline in the total number of babies born, and in the birthrate.

The trends outlined above have not passed unnoticed, but it is too early to foresee all the implications. Comparable trends may be observed in Italy and Japan. The causes probably include the impact of the baby-short years of World War II, the children of that period now being the child-bearing generation and a general move, in the towns at least, towards smaller families. It will be shown in Section 8.6, however, that there are great differences in birthrate not only between town and country, but also between different regions of the U.S.S.R. The non-Slav areas on the whole tend to have a much higher birthrate than the Slav areas.

mid-1960's and a near balance among younger people. The employment implications of the imbalance have been serious throughout the postwar period, but are diminishing, as those less than about 16 at the end of the war, together with postwar babies, form an ever growing share of total population. Though data giving the ratio of male to female have not been available lately for individual regions, it may be assumed that this ratio is greater in areas over which the war was fought than in Central Asia or Siberia.

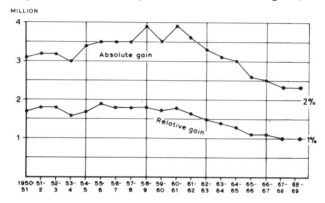

Fig. 8.1.   *Population trends in the U.S.S.R. 1950-67. The upper line, marking the increase in millions during each year, should be read against the left hand scale. The lower line, marking the percentage increase of each year's population over that of the previous year should be read against the right hand scale.*

SEX STRUCTURE[1]

For some decades the population has been characterised by an imbalance in the sexes among adults. This imbalance was accentuated both by collectivisation and by World War II, during which proportionately far more adult males were killed or died than females.

The 1959 census showed females to be 55% of the total population, males 45%. The position had changed to about 54% against 46% in 1967. This overall figure obscures a great imbalance among people over about 40 years of age in the

URBAN AND RURAL

For some decades now, the proportion of urban population to total population has been rising in the U.S.S.R.

Table 8.3.

	Rural	Urban
	%	%
1897	85	15
1913	82	18
1940	67	33
1950	61	39
1959	52	48
1966	46	54
mid-1967	45	55
mid-1968	45	55

Between 1950 and 1967, rural population declined by about one and a half million and urban population rose by about 60 million. In other words, the increase since 1950 has been entirely in urban centres. This is largely the result of changing employment and a shift of population from agricultural to non-agricultural sectors of the economy. Some gain is probably due also to changes in the status of settlements from rural to urban.

During the period 1926–39 the total urban increase according to Feygin[2] was accounted for as follows: 17% by natural growth, 63% by migration from rural areas, 20% by change of status. During 1939–64 the rural contribution was a smaller proportion.

Figures for birthrate (per thousand total population) reveal a sharp contrast between urban and rural areas:

Table 8.4.

	Total	Urban	Rural
1950	26·7	26·0	27·1
1955	25·7	23·5	27·4
1960	24·9	22·0	26·8
1965	18·4	16·2	21·0
1967	17·4	15·5	19·7

Source: *NkhSSSR* 1967, 37.

The continuing trend towards a lower birthrate, noticeable for several decades, carried both urban and rural areas down simultaneously. Since the early 1950's, however, the level has dropped earlier and more sharply in urban areas. As more and more of the population is becoming urbanised, the overall trend towards lower birthrate and smaller families will be accentuated.

CLASS AND EMPLOYMENT STRUCTURE

The following figures summarise changes in the U.S.S.R. since 1928, the year in which the first Five Year Plan started and massive collectivisation was among the targets. Figures are percentages:

State farm workers now number several million. In 1964, therefore, approximately 25% of the Soviet population was still on collective farms, and about 30% connected with agriculture.

The spread of literacy to almost all citizens in recent decades and the attention given to both technical and cultural education have rapidly turned aspirations away from jobs in farming and heavy industry towards services and light industry, from manual jobs to white-collar ones. According to Tidmarsh:[3]

'In spite of the fact that 45% of the population still live in the countryside, agriculture is regarded as the lowest of occupations by the younger generation. One survey of urban school leavers showed that none wanted to live and work in the countryside, while a similar enquiry in a rural area showed that only 8% of school leavers there did not want to move to the city'.

8.2 THE SPATIAL DISTRIBUTION OF POPULATION

The purpose of this section is to describe the main features of distribution of population, both urban and rural, Russian and non-Russian. Since most politicians, planners and people in general appear to assume that a reasonably even spread of people over a national territory or a considerable part of it is desirable, they are rarely satisfied by the existing distribution. The vast empty or thinly populated interior and east of the U.S.S.R. presumably perplex Soviet decision makers as they did the tsarist ones before. Many other countries, notably large ones (eg Brazil, Australia) but even small ones (Britain, Venezuela) also show concern at the concentration of population in certain limited areas.

Fig. 8.2 shows the density of population in persons per square kilometre, for major civil

Table 8.5.

	1928	1939	1959	1965	1967
Total	100	100	100	100	100
Workers*	17·6	50·2	68·3	75·4	77·3
Collective farmers	2·9	47·2	31·4	24·6	22·6
Private small farmers	74·9	2·6	0·3	0·0	<0·1
Private 'capitalists', etc.	4·6	–	–	–	–

* Workers in this context includes *sovkhoz* (state farm) agricultural workers as well as almost all non-agricultural workers.

Source: *NkhSSSR* 1965, 42; 1967, 35.

division units (oblast level). In January 1965 the average (mean) density for the whole of the U.S.S.R. was 10·2 persons per km². In Fig. 8.2 four categories of density are distinguished: more than 50, or more than about five times the national mean, 10–50, 2–10, and less than one fifth the national mean.

The main areas with a very high (by Soviet standards) density of population are the Ukraine, contains less than 5% of the total population. Such an imbalance is not unusual. It occurs in Latin America (as a whole) and probably in China and in North America. At the other extreme, it can be shown that a few per cent of the total national area of the U.S.S.R. contains almost half of the total population. What is more difficult to accept is that this is likely to be so for a long time. It has been noted that each year

The mean density was approximately 10 per km²

Fig. 8.2. *Density of population in the U.S.S.R. in 1965. Oblasts or equivalent units (krays, A.S.S.R's.) are used as the basis for shading. Dotted lines indicate a subdivision of three of the largest units, Tyumen', Krasnoyarsk and Amur. Source:* NkhSSSR, 1964.

the industrial oblasts of the Centre, and Transcaucasia. Information on an oblast basis is not detailed enough to bring out most of the small clusters of very dense population in the oases of Central Asia, but the Tashkent and Fergana oases are evident.

The main area of exceptionally low density of population is Siberia (except for its southern fringe). Smaller areas of very low density occur in the desert of western and central Kazakhstan and Turkmenistan and in the mountain areas of southern Asiatic U.S.S.R. (eg the Pamir).

A calculation based on data for the density of population of major civil divisions shows that the less densely populated half of the national area more people move into the suburbs of Toronto than into the whole of 'empty' Canada. A comparable situation exists in the U.S.S.R.

Fig. 8.3 shows the distribution of population. Each dot represents approximately half of 1% of the national total or about 1 150 000 persons. There are 200 dots altogether. They are distributed on the basis of information about major civil divison and town populations. Their exact location is arbitrary, but in any sizeable part of the national area, the number of dots is correct. With the help of this map it is easy to calculate the approximate number of people in any given part of the country, and the approximate number within a given distance of

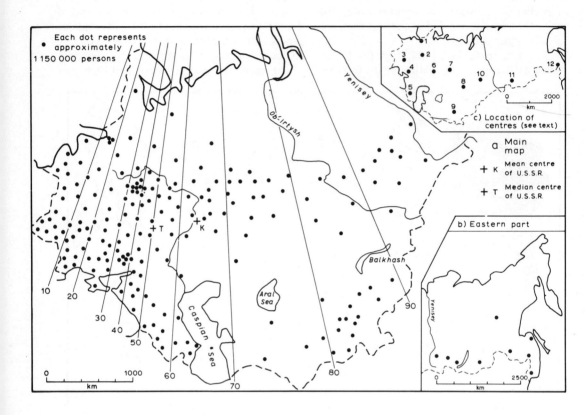

Fig. 8.3. *Distribution of population in the U.S.S.R. The main map (a) is continued on a smaller scale in map (b). There are 200 dots altogether. Map (c) shows the location of places used in Table 8.6. On the main map, T is Tambov (Centre region) and K is Kuybyshev (Volga region).*

any particular place (see Table 8.6).

Since the west-east distribution of population is of particular interest, lines have been drawn along appropriate meridians (lines of longitude) in Fig. 8.4 to divide the dots first into two halves (by a median line), then into deciles (compartments each with 20 dots, or 10% of the population). The north-south median line runs roughly through Gorky and Batumi. Even to the west of Moscow there is 40% of the total population. Other median lines can be drawn with different orientations. Unless a distribution is symmetrical, the various median lines will not all intersect at exactly the same point. The mean and median centres of population are shown. They are near Kuybyshev and Tambov respectively. The mean centre gives extra weight to the more distant dots (such as those in the Far East) and in the U.S.S.R. is thus pulled some way east of the north-south median line. The concepts involved in applying statistical measures of central tendency to two dimensional distributions are discussed by Sviatlovsky.[4]

reference when a large manufacturing plant is to be established, since they show what proportion of the national population is within given distance, time or cost limits.

8.3 RURAL POPULATION

One of the fundamental divisions in the life of the U.S.S.R. is between rural and urban population. The definition is largely based on the function of a place, rather than its size. Three categories of settlement are recognised, rural on the one hand, and urban type and towns, both urban, on the other. The division between town and country is particularly accentuated because there is much less outward spread of services and urban way of life into the countryside than in Western Europe and North America. The strength of the contrast is confirmed by strikingly high correlations between the urbanisation variable and income indicators for economic and social development (see Chapter 13). In the late 1960's rural population

Table 8.6. PERCENTAGE OF TOTAL SOVIET POPULATION WITHIN 100, 200, 400 AND 800 KM RADIUS OF SELECTED PLACES

		100	200	400	800
1	Leningrad	1·5	2·0	4·0	20·0
2	Moscow	4·5	7·5	13·0	36·0
3	Kiev	1·0	3·5	14·0	39·5
4	Donetsk	3·0	5·0	12·5	34·0
5	Tbilisi	1·0	3·0	6·0	11·0
6	Kuybyshev	1·0	2·0	7·0	23·5
7	Sverdlovsk	1·0	3·0	5·5	14·0
8	Tselinograd	0·5	1·0	2·0	6·5
9	Tashkent	1·0	2·5	6·0	8·5
10	Novosibirsk	0·5	1·5	4·0	7·0
11	Irkutsk	<0·5	0·5	1·0	2·0
12	Khabarovsk	<0·5	0·5	1·0	2·0

Fig. 8.3(c) shows the location of places in Table 8.6. With the help of the information in Fig. 8.3, Table 8.6 has been compiled to show what proportion of the total Soviet population lives within given distances of 12 selected places. The figures are only approximate, but they could be calculated with greater precision using more detailed population data and allowing for the communication network. They are useful for

still accounted for approximately 45% of total population. In this and the following section, rural and urban population is discussed separately.

The density of rural population has been calculated for oblast level divisions. Since rural population is more evenly spread than urban population, it is understandable that variations in rural density are less marked than variations in

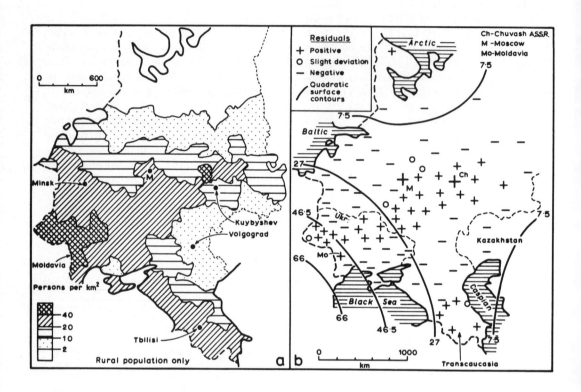

Fig. 8.4. (a) Density of rural population in the western part of the U.S.S.R. in the mid-1960's based on oblast level units. (b) Residuals from trend surface analysis (quadratic surface) applied to the data used in (a).

total density or in urban density alone. Fig. 8.4(a) shows the density of rural population in the western half of the U.S.S.R. The main area of relatively high rural population density is the western Ukraine and Moldavia, but other smaller areas occur in the middle Volga around the Mordov A.S.S.R., in Transcaucasia and particularly in Central Asia.

The distribution, based here on oblast level data, can be studied with the help of trend surface analysis. The density of rural population for each administrative unit is attributed to a point in the centre of the unit; 92 such points are used. An imaginary line or column is raised vertically above each oblast to a height proportional to its rural population density. The distribution now occurs in three dimensions. The first step in trend surface analysis is to fit a plane surface to the three dimensional distribution of points at the top of all the columns to minimise the total distance (actually distance squared) from each point to the surface. In this example, the first (plane or linear surface) is highest in the southwest, Moldavia, and slopes in a northeastern direction. This surface 'explains' 48·6% of the distribution of 92 points.

Table 8.7. LARGEST RESIDUALS FROM TREND SURFACE ANALYSIS

Positive		*Negative*	
Chuvash A.S.S.R.	+32	Kherson	−25
Moldavia	+23	Krym	−22
Moscow	+21	Nikolayev	−18
Vinnitsa	+18	Kalmyk A.S.S.R.	−17
Chernovtsy	+18	Odessa	−16
Ternopol'	+17	Rostov	−14
Khmelnitsk	+13	Volgograd	−13
Cherkassy	+13	Zaporozh'ye	−12
Azerbaijan	+12	Dnepropetrovsk	−11
Mordov A.S.S.R.	+12	Lugansk	−11
Checheno-Ingush			
A.S.S.R.	+12		

Few points fall exactly on or even very close to the surface, but some oblasts deviate more from it than others. The amounts by which they deviate are called residuals. It is possible to improve on the fit of the surface by making it curve through the distribution of points; this second surface is called a quadratic surface. Since the fit is better, most points are found to be

closer to the quadratic surface than to the linear surface. It is the quadratic surface that has been used in this example (further surfaces can be fitted) and illustrated in Fig. 8.4(b). This surface 'explains' some 63% of the distribution. It takes into account not only the general slope in density from southwest to northeast, but a secondary diminution to southeast and northwest from a ridge or 'saddle' of higher densities already noted in Fig. 8.4(a). The contours in Fig. 8.4(b) are the expected rural population densities on the quadratic surface. The observed densities of each place deviate from these. Where the observed are higher than expected they are indicated by a plus sign, where lower, by a minus sign. Where they deviate little they are given a 0 (zero). The largest deviations or residuals are shown in Table 8.7. Although the residuals bring out what is generally appreciated, they pinpoint particular places better and give a more precise value to anomalies than a visual and verbal interpretation. Moscow oblast is presumably very high because its large urban population spills over into districts designated rural by definition. But this does not happen in the industrial areas of the southeast Ukraine. The Chuvash A.S.S.R. and Moldavia are particularly high compared with the general trend and the South region (Black Sea Ukraine) extremely low. Variations and anomalies may be related both to physical conditions (*Poles'ye*, mountains) and to duration of rural settlement (relatively recent colonisation of most of the steppe belt). The ridge of anomalously high residuals coincides fairly closely, however, with the forest steppe vegetation and northern *chernozem* soil belt. European U.S.S.R. and Central Asia carry large pockets of what might be called a rural hangover. If redeployment were possible, much of the rural population would be moved either into newly settled farming areas or into towns.

An instance of the dispersed nature of settlement in the southern part of the coniferous forest, East Siberia, is given by Burmantov:[5] 'The most widespread type of settlement in the district is the agricultural, which accounts for more than 30% of the places. Typical features are a relative decentralisation of the places of work, especially in summer, the seasonal character of work and the scattering of the labour force in summer through temporary field dwellings and its concentration in winter in permanent settlements'. According to Kovalev[6] there are some 700 000 rural places in the U.S.S.R. He proposes that geographical research in rural settlement should focus on the expansion of the size of the main rural communities, the introduction of small-scale industry into rural settlements and the introduction of amenities as good as those in towns. In another paper, Kovalev and Ryazanov[7] consider sizes for farming communities of 1 000 to 2 000 people to be optimum.

8.4 URBAN POPULATION

Some features of the larger towns have already been considered in Section 3.5. Davidovich[8] describes urban agglomerations in the U.S.S.R. In the present section attention is drawn to the variations over the national area in urban population as a percentage of total population; this is mapped in Fig. 8.5 on a topological base.

Urban population is broadly of two kinds, that which is integrated with surrounding rural population, for which it provides services and whose products it processes, and that which bears little or no connection with the immediate rural hinterland. Towns like Vinnitsa, Zhitomir and Cherkassy in the Ukraine are extreme examples of the first kind. Towns like Murmansk, Magadan and Vorkuta are examples of the second kind. Many towns combine something of both. The distribution of the first kind of urban population is closely related to the distribution of rural population (see Fig. 8.4(a)). The second kind may occur in an area with rural settlement and tend to swamp this out numerically, for example, in the oblasts of Moscow, Minsk, or Sverdlovsk, or it may be found far from any but the most meagre sprinkling of rural dwellers. This situation is the reason for the generally high ratio of urban dwellers to rural dwellers in the Northwest region and in most of Siberia.

As noted, some urban population is less

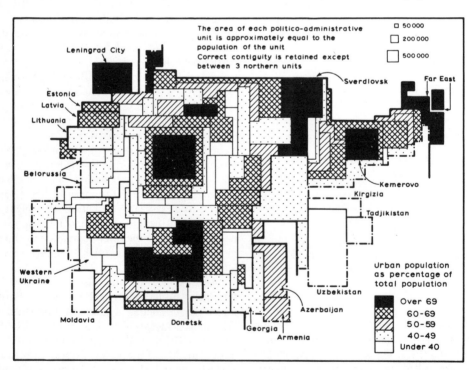

Fig. 8.5. Urban population in the U.S.S.R. A topological map has been used to avoid the absurd visual distortion of shading units of correct areal size. If that were done, visually the highly urbanised divisions would be over-represented since most large, thinly populated divisions are highly urbanised. The black square in left-centre of the map is Moscow city. Where two or more contiguous divisions have black shading, the mutual boundaries are not shown on the map.

directly associated with nearby rural population than other urban population and on the basis of this assumption, a residual urban population figure has been calculated for each oblast level division. It was assumed, somewhat arbitrarily, that for every 100 rural dwellers there would be 30 'basic' urban dwellers serving them directly. The 10 : 3 ratio was calculated on the basis of actual rural-urban data for oblast level divisions. The least highly urbanised divisions have a percentage of urban dwellers to total population of 25–30%. When the 30% basic urban population is deducted from these, little or no residual urban population is left. Where the proportion of urban dwellers is high, on the other hand, the basic number is small compared with the

residual. This new index serves to differentiate more sharply the truly urban areas based on mining, manufacturing and service activities of regional or national importance from those of local importance. This index is shown, together with other information about Soviet towns, in Table 8.8.

8.5 PEOPLES

Peoples exist by definition in the Soviet census. To what particular people (*narod*) an individual belongs depends on his own opinion. Most individuals belong to the *narod* whose language they consider to be their mother tongue.

Table 8.8. URBAN DATA FOR THE 19 ECONOMIC REGIONS OF THE U.S.S.R.

	Economic region	1a	1b	2a	2b	2c	2d	2e	3a	3b
E1	Northwest	3 334	8 315	29	71	63	46	35	29	48
E2	Centre	8 888	17 657	33	67	57	46	32	23	41
E3	Volga-Vyatka	4 363	3 935	53	47	32	24	17	9	21
E4	Blackearth Centre	5 296	2 676	66	34	14	20	7	9	14
E5	Volga	8 432	9 083	48	52	37	37	27	14	26
E6	North Caucasus	6 975	6 253	53	47	31	31	11	19	30
E7	Ural	5 698	10 722	35	65	55	42	24	19	39
E8	West Siberia	4 487	6 356	41	59	46	42	33	12	30
E9	East Siberia	3 014	4 176	42	58	45	31	13	16	36
E10	Far East	1 509	3 918	28	72	64	34	14	23	48
E11	Donets-Dnepr	6 062	13 233	31	69	59	42	27	25*	50*
E12	Southwest	13 280	6 803	66	34	14	17	9	10*	15*
E13	South	2 664	3 057	47	53	39	35	18	20*	35*
E14	Baltic	3 232	3 912	45	55	40	33	25	n.a.	29
E15	Transcaucasia	5 610	5 525	50	50	35	31	23	24	32
E16	Central Asia	10 695	6 348	63	37	18	22	10	18	23
E17	Kazakhstan	6 277	5 576	53	47	31	29	9	9	28
E18	Belorussia	5 263	3 270	62	38	20	22	8	17	21
E19	Moldavia	2 445	858	74	26	4	15	9	13	13
	U.S.S.R.	107 525	121 673	47	53	39	33	20	18	32

Columns   1a, 1b Rural and urban population in thousands, January 1965.

2a–2e Percentages of total population.

(a) Rural; (b) Urban; (c) Residual urban†; (d) in towns with over 50 000 inhabitants; (e) in towns with over 500 000 inhabitants.

3a, 3b Urban population as a percentage of total population in 1926 and 1939.

n.a. not available.

* Estimated from figure for whole of Ukraine.

† Residual urban: Urban population of each region after deducting a number of urban dwellers equal to 30% of the rural population of the region. Residual urban population is then expressed as percentage of total population. Note: residual here is not used in the same technical sense as in Section 8.3.

Sources: *NkhSSSR* 1964, 13–17; *NkhRSFSR* 1964, 12–14. Feygin[2]

Unfortunately few new data about peoples have been published since the 1959 census.[9]

From a spatial point of view there are two basic peoples in the U.S.S.R., those with some territory in the Soviet Union which is their recognised homeland and in which they form usually a majority and those scattered over the national area with no home territory. The first peoples may have many of their members living elsewhere, but retain a core area of their own. They may have members of other peoples living in their core areas. In contrast, the second peoples are de-territorialised. Examples are Poles, Germans, Greeks and Jews, although the latter have a token territory in the Far East.

Of the territory based peoples, some live by the boundary of the U.S.S.R. and in addition are large enough to possess Soviet Socialist Republic (S.S.R.) status. Other groups (eg Tatars) are large enough for S.S.R. status but have an interior territory so achieve no more than A.S.S.R. status. In the 1920's it was decided that full S.S.R.'s should be contiguous with the sea or the international boundary so that they could secede if they desired.

Table 8.9 gives the number of members of the principal peoples in 1959, and Table 8.10 shows the proportion of Russians and Ukrainians in each of the 15 Soviet Socialist Republics. The proportion of Russians and/or of Ukrainians to

Table 8.9. PRINCIPAL PEOPLES OF THE U.S.S.R. IN 1959

Peoples	*1*	*2*	*3*	*4*	*5* $\frac{4 \times 100}{3}$	*6* $\frac{4 \times 100}{1}$
Russians	114 588	R.S.F.S.R.	117 534	97˙845	83	85
Ukrainians	36 981	Ukraine	41 869	31 852	76	86
Belorussians	7 829	Belorussia	8 055	6 444	81	83
Uzbeks	6 004	Uzbekistan	8 106	5 026	62	84
Tatars	4 969					
Kazakhs	3 581	Kazakhstan	9 310	2 755	30	77
Azerbaijanians	2 929	Azerbaijan	3 698	2 481	67	83
Armenians	2 787	Armenia	1 763	1 552	88	56
Georgians	2 650	Georgia	4 044	2 558	63	98
Lithuanians	2 326	Lithuania	2 711	2 151	79	92
Jews	2 268					
Moldavians	2 214	Moldavia	2˙885	1 887	65	86
Germans	1 619					
Chuvashi	1 470					
Latvians	1 400	Latvia	2 093	1 298	62	93
Tadjiks	1 397	Tadjikistan	1 980	1 051	53	75
Poles	1 380					
Mordva	1 285					
Turkmens	1 004	Turkmenistan	1 516	927	61	92
Bashkiry	983					
Kirgiz	974	Kirgizia	2 066	837	40	86
Estonians	969	Estonia	1 197	873	73	90

Column   1: Total population of a particular group in thousands.
2: Soviet Socialist Republic.
3: Population of Republic in thousands.
4: Population of a group residing in its own Republic in thousands.

Example: There are 7 829 000 Belorussians in the U.S.S.R. of which 6 444 000 (83%) live in Belorussia. The population of Belorussia is 8 055 000, so 19% are not Belorussians.

Source: *Pravda*, 4 Feb. 1960, 2.

Table 8.10. RUSSIANS AND UKRAINIANS IN OTHER REPUBLICS

	Russians	Per cent of Republic		Ukrainians	Per cent of Republic
		1959	1926		1959
R.S.F.S.R.	97 845	83·2	78	3 377	2·9
Ukraine	7 400	17·7	9	31 852	76·1
Kazakhstan	4 014	43·1	20	762	8·2
Uzbekistan	1 101	13·6	6	88	1·1
Belorussia	729	9·1	8	150	1·9
Kirgizia	624	30·2	12	137	6·6
Latvia	556	26·6	–	29	1·4
Azerbaijan	515	13·9	10	n.*	n.*
Georgia	438	10·8	4	52	1·3
Moldavia	293	10·2	9	421	14·6
Turkmenistan	263	17·3	8	21	1·4
Tadjikstan	263	13·3	1	27	1·4
Estonia	260	21·7	–	16	1·3
Lithuania	231	8·5	–	18	0·7
Armenia	56	3·2	2	n.*	n.*

n.* Not specified
Sources: *Pravda,* 4 Feb. 1960, 2, and Lorimer, for 1926 data (see Bibliography)

total population in the Republics, economic regions and oblast level divisions is of great interest. It indicates roughly the amount of influence and control the Russians and Ukrainians have over other peoples. Perevedentsev[10] notes that in spite of the fact that several non-Russian Republics, including Central Asia, Transcaucasia and Moldavia are labour-surplus areas, there is little movement of population out, either to the R.S.F.S.R. or to other Republics. Russians are much more mobile, moving readily into labour-deficient regions such as Siberia and Kazakhstan, and into non-Russian Republics. According to Perevedentsev: 'Ethnic factors are thus no obstacle to the migration of Russians to cities in any part of the country'. He hints, also, at the gradual 'Russification' of the country: 'An indisputable fact is the ethnic *rapprochement* of all peoples of the U.S.S.R. This is shown, for example, by the fact that more than 10 million people, ie every eighth non-Russian, listed a language (mostly Russian) other than that of his own nationality, as his native language. Far more people undoubtedly know Russian as a second language'.

Fig. 8.6 shows Russians as a percentage of total population in oblast level divisions by broad categories. In Table 8.11 the proportion has been calculated for the 19 economic regions to the nearest 5%. Since the birthrate in non-Russian areas has tended to be higher than in predominantly Russian areas, it may be assumed

Table 8.11. RUSSIANS AS A PERCENTAGE OF TOTAL POPULATION BY 19 ECONOMIC REGIONS (NEAREST 5%)

E1	Northwest	95
E2	Centre	95
E3	Volga-Vyatka	60
E4	Blackearth Centre	100
E5	Volga	65
E6	North Caucasus	85
E7	Ural	95
E8	West Siberia	95
E9	East Siberia	95
E10	Far East	90
E11	Donets-Dnepr	20
E12	Southwest	10
E13	South	20
E14	Baltic	15
E15	Transcaucasia	10
E16	Central Asia	15
E17	Kazakhstan	45
E18	Belorussia	10
E19	Moldavia	10
	U.S.S.R.	55

Source: *NDSE* Part 3, 633, 1966.

that the percentage of Russians has diminished somewhat since 1959, the year for which figures are available. On the other hand, the outward movement of Russians into non-Russian areas may have compensated for this. Three pre-dominantly non-Russian areas emerge in Fig. 8.6: southwestern European U.S.S.R., Transcaucasia and much of Central Asia. Russian influence is also relatively weak in the six

8.6 REGIONAL VARIATIONS IN BIRTHRATE AND NATURAL INCREASE

Births and deaths per thousand people in 1967 are shown in Table 8.12. Variations in deathrate among the 19 regions, though considerable (extremes Kazakhstan 5·7, Baltic Republics 9·0) are much less marked than variations in birthrate (extremes Centre 12·0, Central Asia 33·1).

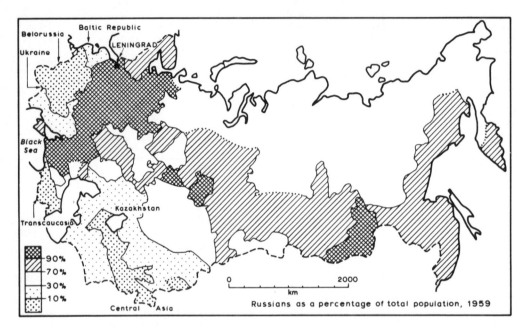

Fig 8.6.   *Russians as a percentage of total population, 1959, on the basis of oblast level data. Note that heavy crossed lines and heavy dots are at the extremes of the shading scale. Source: The Human Resources, NDSE 2, 365.*

A.S.S.R.'s of the mid-Volga–western Ural. Russian penetration of Kazakhstan, particularly the northeastern part, is also clearly revealed. The most solidly Russian area (over 90% Russian) extends between the White Sea and Leningrad in the north and the Black Sea–Volga–Caspian in the south. Russians also account for more than about 75% of the total population in the more densely populated southern part of Siberia. In anticipation it may be noted that on the basis of the 19 economic regions, high correlations have been obtained between percentage Russian and degree of urbanisation, industrialisation, and *per capita* capital investment.

Natural growth (*yestestvennyy prirost*) is calculated by finding the difference between deathrate and birthrate. The simple birthrate figure is sufficient, however, to reveal the main features of spatial variations. The four regions with the lowest birthrate are Centre (12·0) Blackearth Centre (13·0) Donets-Dnepr (13·9) and Northwest (13·1). Three are predominantly Russian and Donets-Dnepr, though in the Ukraine, possibly now also has a majority of Russians. The three with the highest birthrate are Central Asia (33·1) Transcaucasia (25·8) and Kazakhstan (24·0). Since the Soviet mean is 17·4 it is evident that the distribution is a skewed one and the three regions listed stand far above the remainder (Moldavia is fourth with· 20·7). Generally, the non-European peoples have a much higher birthrate than the European peoples; this is confirmed in detail also by 1965 figures for oblast level in the R.S.F.S.R.[11] Contrast figures in the Volga–Vyatka region for the two Russian oblasts and the three largely non-Russian A.S.S.R.'s: Gorky 13·8, Kirov 13·6, Mariysk 19·0, Mordov 18·4, Chuvash 22·3.

to investigate the possibility of distinguishing four periods since about 1890, two (1890–1910, 1930–45) characterised by marked eastward general shift of population, and two (1910–30, 1945–present) characterised by little or no general eastward shift. The stimulus to eastward movement in the first period was the building of railways in the east and in the second period the deliberate investment of capital and move-

Table 8.12. BIRTHS, DEATHS AND NATURAL INCREASE PER THOUSAND IN 1967

	Region	Birthrate	Deathrate	Natural increase
E1	Northwest	13·1	8·2	4·9
E2	Centre	12·0	8·9	3·1
E3	Volga-Vyatka	14·3	8·5	5·8
E4	Blackearth Centre	13·0	8·9	4·1
E5	Volga	15·8	7·8	8·0
E6	North Caucasus	16·8	7·7	9·1
E7	Ural	14·9	7·6	7·3
E8	West Siberia	14·8	7·2	7·6
E9	East Siberia	17·2	7·1	10·1
E10	Far East	16·7	6·4	10·3
E11	Donets-Dnepr	13·9	7·6	6·3
E12	Southwest	16·1	8·4	7·7
E13	South	16·0	8·0	8·0
E14	Baltic	15·7	9·0	6·7
E15	Transcaucasia	25·8	6·6	19·2
E16	Central Asia	33·1	6·3	26·8
E17	Kazakhstan	24·0	5·7	18·3
E18	Belorussia	16·8	7·0	9·8
E19	Moldavia	20·7	6·8	13·9
	U.S.S.R.	17·4	7·6	9·8

Source: *NkhSSSR* 1967, 40–1

In Fig. 8.7, 1965 birthrates are mapped on a topological base for 71 units of the R.S.F.S.R. and 16 further units. The relationship of these figures to other variables will be discussed in Chapter 13 and some projections will be shown.

8.7 POPULATION CHANGE

Unfortunately population censuses in 1926, 1939 and 1959 have come at bad times for intercensus periods to reflect particular periods of characteristic growth. World War II played havoc with 1939–59 trends, while collectivisation distorted trends in the 1930's. Were adequate data available, it would be interesting

ment of people and equipment in the interwar plans and World War II.

Table 8.13 contains population change data for the 19 regions for 1926–39 and 1940–68. The first four columns show the gain or loss in absolute terms; the fifth, sixth and seventh columns show the share (in per thousand of the Soviet total) achieved by each region during the periods 1940–59, 1959–65 and 1959–68. The last five columns show the relative change for the periods, 1926–40, 1940–65 and 1959–68. From the table it can be seen from a comparison of the three periods 1926–40, 1940–59 and 1959–65, that several regions grew in population at a faster rate than the national average in all three periods, namely, East Siberia, Far East, Transcaucasia,

Table 8.13. POPULATION CHANGE BY REGIONS

Economic region	Absolute change (thousands of people)				Per thousand of absolute change			Relative change earlier year = 100				
	1940–65	1940–59	1959–65	1959–68	1940–59	1959–65	1959–68	1926–40	1940–65	1940–59	1959–65	1959–68
E1 Northwest	445	− 341	786	992	−23	38	36	130	104	97	106	109
E2 Centre	−499	−1 326	827	1 045	−90	41	38	118	98	95	103	104
E3 Volga-Vyatka	−550	−595	45	35	−40	2	1	114	94	94	100	100
E4 Blackearth Centre	−1 121	−1 324	203	179	−90	10	6	96	88	86	103	102
E5 Volga	1 866	332	1 534	2 043	22	75	73	104	112	103	109	113
E6 North Caucasus	2 734	1 107	1 627	2 266	75	81	81	113	126	110	114	120
E7 Ural	4 880	3 732	1 148	1 082	253	56	39	123	142	133	107	108
E8 West Siberia	2 686	2 002	684	950	136	32	34	122	133	124	106	109
E9 East Siberia	2 276	1 559	717	848	106	35	30	144	146	133	111	113
E10 Far East	2 272	1 679	593	875	114	29	31	189	172	150	112	118
E11 Donets-Dnepr	2 908	1 379	1 529	2 156	93	75	77	108	118	109	108	112
E12 Southwest	101	−945	1 046	1 352	−64	51	49	108	101	95	106	107
E13 South	751	95	656	1 004	6	32	36	108	115	102	112	120
E14 Baltic	1 279	747	532	747	51	26	29	n.a.*	122	112	107	112
E15 Transcaucasia	2 929	1 299	1 630	2 377	88	81	85	137	136	116	117	125
E16 Central Asia	6 043	2 828	3 219	5 043	192	159	181	138	155	125	123	137
E17 Kazakhstan	5 799	3 100	2 699	3 524	210	133	126	101	196	151	129	139
E18 Belorussia	− 513	−991	478	765	−67	23	27	112	94	90	105	110
E19 Moldavia	835	417	418	599	28	21	21	119	134	116	114	121
U.S.S.R.	35 121	14 750	20 371	27 862	1 000	1 000	1 000	116	118	107	109	113

* n.a. = not available.
Note: the boundaries of the U.S.S.R. and of some of the regions are not the same for 1926, 1940 and the postwar years.

Sources: *NkhSSSR* 1964, 12; 1967, 12. Feygin[2] 156 for 1926–39.

Central Asia and Moldavia. In contrast, certain regions grew at a rate below the national average, or even declined, during all three periods, namely, Blackearth Centre, Belorussia and the Southwest. Several of the eastern regions of the R.S.F.S.R. had much more spectacular rates of growth during 1940–59 than during 1959–65, suggesting that the eastern migration of population began to fade out in the earlier of these two periods.

different areas at different times and for the most part can only partially be controlled by planners. Four influences, to some extent interrelated, will be isolated. They are shown diagrammatically in Fig. 8.8, first singly, then combined. The population of an area will have a greater probability of registering an increase if:

1. It has a high natural increase (see Fig. 8.7 for birthrate).

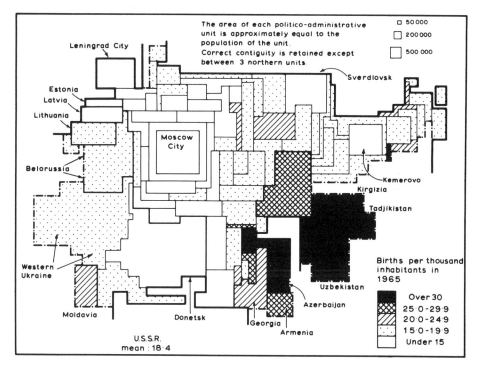

Fig. 8.7.   *Births per thousand inhabitants in the U.S.S.R. in 1965.*

8.8 SUMMARY

The present distribution of population is the result of dramatic changes in the last few decades on an older base of rural population, the previous deployment of which had changed more gradually over the preceding centuries. With particular reference to the Soviet period, several distinct forces have been shaping the total distribution of population. These forces have been working with different intensity in

2. It is predominantly urban (with reservations) (see Fig. 8.5 and Chapter 13).
3. It was not held by the Germans during World War II (see Fig. 8.8(b)).
4. It is receiving immigrants from other regions (see Fig. 8.8(c)).

It must be noted that (1), (3) and (4) may be thought to affect continuous large areas, whereas (2) is above all initially a local matter, with many points as foci of attraction to surrounding areas.

1. Some of the variations in the rate of population growth are caused by dif-

ferences in natural growth, the difference between birthrate and deathrate. Such variations are caused by the propensity or inclination of some peoples to have much larger families than others and by the age structure of different regions. Asian peoples tend to have a greater natural increase than European ones. Within the areas predominantly inhabited by European peoples, areas with younger age groups, such as Kazakhstan and parts of Siberia, tend to have a somewhat higher natural increase rate than the rest.

2. There has long been a general movement of population from rural to urban settlements. Khodzhayev[12] gives the following instances: 'In Voronezh immigration accounted for 73% of the total population increase during 1962–67, in Kiev 69%, in Tallin 80% and in Tula 74%'. Such in-migration into relatively few points means a growing concentration of people in a limited number of small areas. This migration to towns works at several levels. Presumably, as has been noted in other parts of the world, rural dwellers may choose either to settle in a nearby town, usually small or medium in size, or to move to a more distant one, usually large. There may later be a move, either of relative newcomers or of inhabitants of longer standing, from smaller towns to larger ones. Generally migration has been found to take place over relatively short distances. Certainly spontaneous migration, except in such a mobile country as the U.S.A., is not likely to give as many long distance as short distance moves.

According to Feygin[2] one-third of all migration is by skilled or qualified persons. Much seasonal movement also takes place, in particular connected with fishing and farming. One instance is quoted in *Pravda,* 22 July 1968: 700 drivers of combines, tractors and lorries set off from Kishinev in Moldavia to help with the grain harvest in the Ural region and Kazakhstan. Experienced workers, such as those in rail and pipeline construction appear to be on the move from project to project for long periods

(eg *Pravda*, 19 January 1967).

3. The impact of World War II affected in particular several of the regions of European U.S.S.R. This in itself contributed in a negative way to raise the share of total Soviet population to be found in Asiatic U.S.S.R.

4. A resettlement of people from older areas into newly developed ones. Although people have moved, or have been moved, to many places in the north and in Siberia, the main belt of development and new settlement of the last four decades lies between the middle Volga and Lake Baykal. This belt is shown approximately in Fig. 8.8(c). The easterly movement of population occurs regardless of urban or rural origin or destination, involves great distances and is often in some way planned. Among those moving east under compulsion or persuasion have been various deportees, numbering millions according to some sources, demobilised soldiers, komsomols and students. Certain peoples, too, were moved at one time or another, among them the Volga Germans, Crimean Tatars, Kalmyks, Latvians and Estonians. Since 1953 there has been a campaign to settle people, young people in particular, in the new agricultural lands east of the Volga, in rural communities. In general, movement of this type has been in an easterly direction, but it has been followed by a reverse migration in some cases.[13] The general subject of migration may be followed up in a paper by Pokhshishevskiy,[14] in which the slowdown of eastward migration in the 1960's is noted and signs of a reverse trend confirmed.

To appreciate how complex the situation is, it should be noted that even the four influences likely to encourage growth can theoretically be combined in 2^4 or 16 different ways. In Fig. 8.9, the four situations are shown together. It is theoretically possible for any of the four influences to be present or absent in any given place. In Table 8.14, a 1 indicates presence, a 0 (zero) represents absence. Selected places given as examples can be located in Fig. 8.9.

Under Socialism there should theoretically

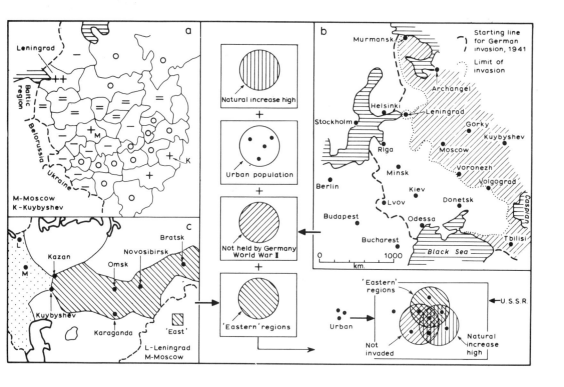

Fig. 8.8. *Features of population change in the U.S.S.R. (a) Selected divisions of European R.S.F.S.R. with significant net migration during 1959-62 (Source: NDSE, 622). Double minus sign: out-migration exceeded natural increase. Single minus: out-migration 50-100% of natural increase. Zero: little migration either way. Plus signs indicate considerable or very considerable in-migration. (b) The maximum extent of the German invasion of 1941-43. (c) The 'East', the main area of new development between the Volga and Lake Baykal. Contrast the 'old' dotted area. The Venn diagrams show four influences separately and combined.*

be no difficulty in getting people to move from one part of the country to another. Until the late 1950's labour could be directed, in practice, if not by any specific regulations. It seems doubtful, however, if the movement of people has ever been planned with any precision. In the 1960's, people have been exhorted and even compelled to move by lack of appropriate jobs in some places. It has been argued that there is a

in terms of clothing, diseases and adaptability of new settlers. Liopo[15] considers clothing and Khlebovich[16] medical geography in the Ob' river region. Newcomers from more southerly regions (eg oil workers from the Volga and North Caucasus) are less likely to adapt quickly to the region than those from more similar environments such as the Volga-Vyatka.

Migration may be permanent or seasonal.

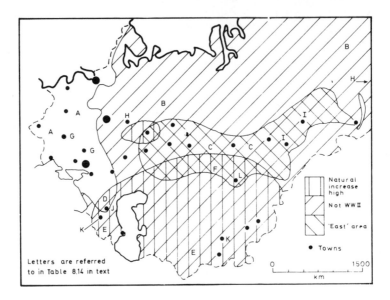

Fig. 8.9.   *Selected places in the U.S.S.R. illustrating various influences on population change.*

moral obligation for people given some skill by State education to move where needed; only the top classes of graduating students have the option of working in such favourable places as Moscow, Leningrad or Kiev. In some areas higher wages, relatively good housing and other attractions have been provided to draw people, but minimum wages for lowest paid workers stated in *Pravda,* 17 January 1968, show only a limited differential for unattractive areas. Instead of 60 roubles per month (about £25) in the rest of the country, 72 roubles per month is offered to workers in distant areas. Roughly three million people 'benefit'; the areas mentioned are in Siberia (Primorsk, Khabarovsk, Chita and Buryat) and the northwest (Archangel, Komi, Karelia). Soviet geographers, among others, have been investigating cold conditions

Men tend to be more mobile than women and younger people more than older ones; in particular the Komsomol (young Communists) have contributed. Some kind of clearing house, or national labour exchange, has been called for in the Soviet press.

In Table 8.13 the total number of people gained (or lost) by each economic region during 1940-59 and 1959-65 is expressed in terms of per thousand of total Soviet change. Between 1940 and 1959, almost the whole increase of 15 million persons occurred in the six eastern regions (Ural, Siberias, Far East, Kazakhstan and Central Asia). During 1959-65, less than half, or about nine million out of a 20 million gain, took place in the same six regions. In absolute terms, the Centre and Donets-Dnepr, together only a tiny fraction of the total area of the U.S.S.R.,

Table 8.14. SELECTED PLACES IN THE U.S.S.R. ILLUSTRATING VARIOUS INFLUENCES ON POPULATION CHANGE

		Natural increase high	*Clear of World War II*	*'East' area*	*Sample location and map reference*
Rural	0	0	0	0	A Rural Ukraine, Belorussia
	0	0	1	0	B Kirov, Yakutia
	0	0	1	1	C Kurgan, Omsk
	0	1	0	0	D North Caucasus A.S.S.R.'s
	0	1	1	0	E Central Asia, Azerbaijan
	0	1	1	1	F Tselinograd oblast
Urban	1	0	0	0	G Kiev, Kharkov
	1	0	1	0	H Gorky, Chita
	1	0	1	1	I Novokuznetsk, Krasnoyarsk
	1	1	0	0	J Groznyy
	1	1	1	0	K Tbilisi, Tashkent
	1	1	1	1	L Karaganda

gained more people than the whole of West and East Siberia and the Far East combined, over half of the national area.

Unlike many Western industrial countries the U.S.S.R. virtually keeps its doors closed to any foreigners other than students which means there is all the more need for it to encourage migration and mobility in its own population. Yet the evidence is that the population of the U.S.S.R. is very inert, apart from relatively short distance migration from the countryside into nearby towns or into more distant special places such as Moscow and the other Republic capitals. Natural conditions, distances, regulations and lack of job incentives all contribute to make this so.

REFERENCES

1. *NkhSSSR* 1964, 8, and 1965, 8
2. FEYGIN, Ya. G. *et al., Zakonomernosti i faktory razvitiya ekonomicheskikh rayonov SSSR,* 162, 164 (Moscow, 1965)
3. TIDMARSH, K., 'Russia runs out of labourers' *The Times,* 9 Oct. 1968
4. SVIATLOVSKY, E. E. and EELLS, W. C., 'The centrographical method and regional analysis' *Geogrl Rev.,* 27, 240–54, 1937
5. BURMANTOV, G. G., 'The Formation of Functional Types of Settlements in the Southern Tayga' *Soviet Geogr.,* 9, No 2, 112–9, 1968
6. KOVALEV, S. A., 'Problems in the Soviet Geography of Rural Settlement' *Soviet Geogr.,* 9, No 8, 641–50, 1968
7. KOVALEV, S. A. and RYAZANOV, U. S., 'Paths of evolution of rural settlements' *Soviet Geogr.,* 9, No 8, 651–64, 1968
8. DAVIDOVICH, V. G., 'Urban agglomeration in the U.S.S.R.' *Soviet Geogr.,* 5, No 9, 34–44, 1964
9. The 1959 data are reproduced, for example, in *Strana sovetov za 50 let* (Moscow, 1967)
10. PEREVEDENTSEV, V. I., 'The influence of ethnic factors on the territorial redistribution of population' *Soviet Geogr.,* 6, No 8, 40–50, 1965
11. Source *NkhRSFSR* 1965, 20–3
12. KHODZHAYEV, D. G., 'The Planning of the Distribution of Production in Population Centers and some Problems in Population Geography' *Soviet Geogr.,* 8, No 8, 619–29, 1967
13. See for example *The Times,* 11 Mar. 1966
14. POKHSHISHEVSKIY, V. V. *et al.,* 'On basic migration patterns' *Soviet Geogr.,* 5, No 10, 3–18, 1964
15. LIOPO, T. N., 'A Method for Computing Optimal Heat-Regulating Properties of Clothing on the Basis of the Probability of Variation of Meteorological Factors' *Soviet Geogr.,* 9, No 2, 95–105, 1968
16. KHLEBOVICH, I. A. and CHUDNOVA, V. I., 'Medical-Geographic Study of the Formation of Population of the Ob' River Region' *Soviet Geogr.,* 9, No 2, 106–12, 1968

BIBLIOGRAPHY

DAVIDOVICH, V. G. *et al., Goroda–sputniki. Sbornik statey* (Moscow, 1961)
'Geografiya gorodov' *Vop. geogr.,* No 38 (Moscow, 1956)
'Geografiya gorodskikh i sel'skikh poseleniy' *Vop. geogr.,* No 45 (Moscow, 1959)
KONSTANTINOV, O. A., *Geografiya naseleniya i naselennykh punktov SSSR* (Leningrad, 1967)

KOVALEV, S. A., *Sel'skoye rasseleniye* (Moscow University, 1963)

LORIMER, E., *The Population of the Soviet Union: History and Prospects* (Geneva (League of Nations), 1946)

NDSE (U.S. Government Printing Office, Washington, 1966)

POD'YACHIKH, P. G., *Naseleniye SSSR* (Moscow, 1961)

POKSHISHEVSKIY, V. V., *Geografiya naseleniya v SSSR*, Geografiya SSSR, vypusk 3 (Moscow, 1966)

POKSHISHEVSKIY, V. V. (ed), *Nauchnyye problemy geografii naseleniya* (Moscow, 1967)

9

Agriculture*

9.1 INTRODUCTION

Almost 10% of the total area of the U.S.S.R. is under field or tree crops. Livestock are raised both within the crop farming area and on natural pastures outside. Cropland and natural pastures together occupy about 25% of the total area of the country and about 25% of the total employed population is engaged in farming. The distribution of farming population, together with persons employed in processing and in services immediately dependent on and support-ing farming, is roughly reflected in Fig. 8.5, showing rural population in the western half of the country. Farming only provides about 15% of the total gross domestic product and, therefore, has considerably lower value of output per worker than manufacturing industry, a feature of many countries.

Farms are either organised on collective lines (*kolkhoz*) or are run directly by the State (*sovkhoz*). Currently the arable land of the U.S.S.R. is shared roughly equally between the two kinds of farm. In general, the productivity of *sovkhoz* farm workers is much higher than that of *kolkhoz* farm workers. On the other hand, both for organisational and environmental reasons, productivity per unit of area is generally higher on *kolkhozes*.

* Numerous data tables are used here and in Chapter 10. Lack of space prevented the mapping of most sets of data for the 19 economic regions, but it was considered useful to present the data for the reader to study and even map.

Although crop and livestock farming are closely associated it is customary to distinguish between arable and livestock in the total value of farm production. In Fig. 9.1 the relationship of plant and animal products to the economy as a whole is shown diagrammatically. During the present century the relative importance of the two has changed considerably. In the period since World War II, an absolute overall rise in total farm output has been accompanied by a growth in the relative importance of livestock farming. Its share of total farm output rose from 40% in 1950 to 44% in 1958 and 49% in 1967. Current policy in farming appears to favour a further strengthening of the livestock sector. Although the weight of vegetable matter consumed by livestock is several times the weight of the meat eventually obtained, rising consumer standards and the greatly enhanced value of livestock production make the changing emphasis desirable. Trends from 1940 to 1965 are shown in Fig. 9.1(b). Between 1965 and 1967 a rise of 10% was claimed in the total value of Soviet agricultural production.

Considerable attention is given to farming in the present book in spite of its relatively small and still diminishing contribution to total gross domestic product. First, more data are available for agriculture than for industry and secondly, agriculture is more of a problem to planners and to politicians than industry. It still uses a large number of low productivity workers whom planners must release for higher productivity industrial jobs if economic growth rates are to be sustained. Farm output must also be raised if the U.S.S.R. is to remain self-sufficient in basic foods and raw materials and to cope with increasing population and rising living standards without the embarrassment and cost of having to buy wheat from Canada and other capitalist countries.

Soviet leaders are anxious to increase total farm output very appreciably and to avoid violent fluctuations in harvest from year to year.

Very broadly, they can increase total production either by modifying the organisation of farming (tenure, incentives and so on) or by overcoming environmental difficulties (farming in new areas, obtaining higher yields in existing areas). In both cases, success will be closely related to the long-due drive to 'technologise' and industrialise agriculture, a need, according to *Pravda,* 7 June 1966, appreciated in some areas but not in others. The fact that vast areas of farmland were

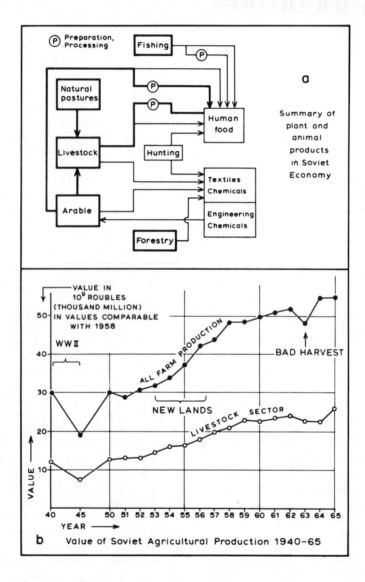

Fig. 9.1.   *(a) The relationship of plant and animal products to the Soviet economy as a whole. (b) The value of Soviet agricultural production 1940–65. Source:* SSSR v tsifrakh v 1965 godu.

almost without electricity supplies in the late 1950's (see eg *Atlas sel'skogo khozyaystva,*[1]) suggests that the degree of electrification of collective (and state) farms could be an indicator of rural progress, or lack thereof. Elsewhere, according to *Pravda,* 3 February 1969, many farms get electricity at great cost from small, unreliable local generators because they are not connected to regional electricity grids.

The recent history of Soviet agriculture dates from 1953 when Stalin died. Incentives in agriculture then were miserable, wages were low or non-existent and State procurement prices low. During 1953-58, thanks to the opening up of the new lands, some good seasons and N. Khrushchev's enthusiasm, Soviet agricultural production increased by about 50%. According to Nimitz,[2] this led Soviet planners to have too high hopes of what might be achieved during 1959-65. Since there were few new lands left to acquire, increased production had to come from higher yields, to be ensured by greater fertiliser output. Unfortunately, not enough capital was put into farming, nor was enough attention paid to big differences in production costs between different regions. Bad management was blamed, rather than poor quality soil. The greatest setback of all was a very poor grain harvest in 1963; State grain procurements were 15 million tons below what was required. By the mid-1960's another attempt was made to restore confidence in agriculture; Brezhnev drew up a programme in March 1965.

9.2 PHYSICAL RESTRICTIONS

In spite of the Soviet attitude that with the resources and initiative of Socialism it is possible to overcome many of the difficulties presented by the physical environment, severe obstacles to farming exist in reality. They make the cost of extending farming into new areas impossible or unthinkably high and they keep down or reduce from time to time the yields of various crops in existing areas of cultivation. The limitations imposed on agriculture by physical conditions are many and can be measured with varying degrees of accuracy. For the purposes of this book, four sets of limitations have been taken: temperature, precipitation, slope and soil. Each

of these can be assessed in various ways, each carries with it associated features (eg soil and vegetation) and all four are to some degree interrelated causally (eg saline soils are frequently found where precipitation is low and temperature high). The four sets of limitations will be discussed in turn, their relationship to arable land will be noted and measures used or planned to combat them will be outlined.

Both the absolute and the commercial limits set by physical conditions vary greatly from plant to plant. It is impossible to cultivate the rubber tree (*Hevea brasiliensis*) or the palm oil tree in the U.S.S.R. at all. Cotton is cultivated successfully only in the south. Rye, barley, cabbages and grasses grow very far north. Fig. 9.2 shows that theoretically there are 16 possible combinations in any given place of the four adverse physical conditions: temperature (growing season) inadequate, precipitation (after evaporation) inadequate, slope too great and soil too poor. To preclude the cultivation of a given plant or set of plants it needs only one physical condition (temperature *or* precipitation *or* slope *or* soil) to be unfavourable. Any combination of two, three or all four of these merely strengthens the case for preventing the cultivation of the plant. Conversely, temperature *and* precipitation *and* slope *and* soil must all be suitable for a given plant or for a given range of plants to be cultivated successfully. The intersection of the four favourable sets of conditions is only one out of 16 combinations. All 16 are summarised in Table 9.1 with the help of binary digits.

In practice, the four influences on agriculture are not entirely independent, since to some extent they are causally related. Thus where conditions are rugged and slopes steep, soil tends to be poor or non-existent. Similarly, where temperatures are very low for much of the year, precipitation cannot be high.

In reality the situation is much more complex than is suggested in Table 9.1 and Fig. 9.2. First, it is not usually possible to give a yes/no answer to a question such as: is temperature or is precipitation adequate here for farming? There is a continuum ranging from hopeless through possible to good. Secondly, no two basic crops cultivated have the same limits. Thus, for example, temperature and/or precipitation may be inadequate for the cultivation of maize in a given area, but barley may be cultivated very successfully.

1. Temperature comes to mind as the major limiting influence in Soviet agriculture. That this thought merits serious reconsideration will emerge later in the section. Certainly, the influence of temperature on agriculture is very powerful. In a direct way it may be assessed reasonably well in terms of length of growing season or of degree days (accumulated temperatures). Indirectly, it affects the possibilities of farming by freezing moisture in the soil for varying periods during the year (permafrost, winter freezing). The duration of the frost-free period, snow cover (Fig. 7.5(a)) and other features of temperature must also be noted. Temperature, together with other physical forces, also affects the formation and fertility of soils.

January and July mean temperatures are shown in Fig. 7.4. A more satisfactory introduction to the limitations of temperature on cultivation is given in Fig. 9.3, which shows the number of days with an average air temperature

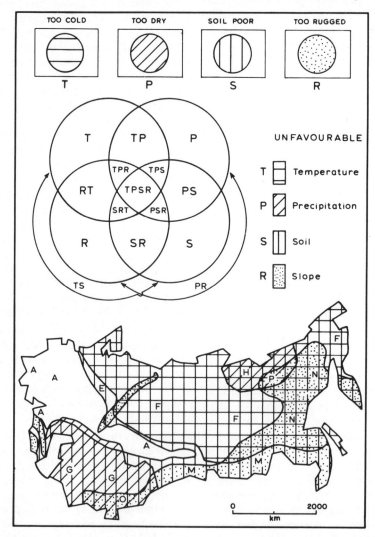

Fig. 9.2.   *Physical conditions affecting farming in the U.S.S.R. The four sets of unfavourable conditions (upper Venn diagrams) combine to give 16 situations, including the situation, not shown, in which all four adverse conditions are absent. The letters on the map correspond to the letters used in Table 9.1.*

Table 9.1. FOUR PHYSICAL CONDITIONS AFFECTING CULTIVATION

Rugged	Poor soil	Too dry	Too cold	Type	Example areas
0	0	0	0	A	Zhitomir, Orel, Krasnodar, Omsk
0	0	0	1	B	Rare
0	0	1	0	C	Rare
0	0	1	1	D	Rare
0	1	0	0	E	Much of Kirov, Vologda
0	1	0	1	F	Ob' lowland, mid-Lena
0	1	1	0	G	Most of Turkmenistan, south Kazakhstan
0	1	1	1	H	Some Arctic coastlands
1	0	0	0	I	Rare
1	0	0	1	J	Rare
1	0	1	0	K	Rare
1	0	1	1	L	Rare
1	1	0	0	M	Most of Southern Siberia
1	1	0	1	N	Much of the Far East
1	1	1	0	O	Central Asia mountains
1	1	1	1	P	Verkhoyansk area (Far East)

1 indicates presence of negative attribute.

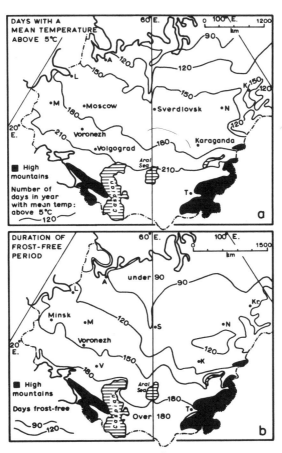

Fig. 9.3.   *(a) Days with a mean temperature above 5°C. (b) Duration of frost free period. Source:* Atlas sel'skogo khozyaystva SSSR *(Moscow, 1960). Initials of places on map: A–Archangel, Kr–Krasnoyarsk, L–Leningrad, T–Tashkent.*

above 5°C (other thresholds may also be used). Very few crops will grow in the area where the number of such days is less than 120, notably the extreme north of European U.S.S.R. and much of Siberia. Between about 120 and 180 days, conditions improve enough to allow progressively southwards, grasses, vegetables, rye, oats, barley and wheat, and flax. Between 180 and 210 days, several important industrial crops can be

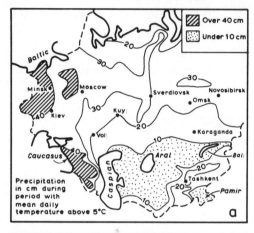

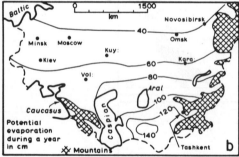

Fig. 9.4.   *(a) Precipitation falling approximately during growing season. (b) Potential evaporation during year.*

Source:
Atlas sel'skogo khozyaystva SSSR *(Moscow, 1960).*

grown including sugar beet, the sunflower and hemp, while maize and millet can also be cultivated. So-called sub-tropical crops including tea, citrus fruits and cotton are cultivated mainly south of about 240 days. Inadequacy of heat sets an absolute limit to commercial agriculture only in about the coldest 30–40% of the area of the U.S.S.R. Since only 10% is cultivated, there must either be no need for more farmland or there must be other limiting influences as well. Indeed,

temperature should be considered as a limit to progressively more individual plants as one moves northwards, rather than as the key limit to cultivation.

2. Adequate water is no less vital to crops than adequate heat. The distribution of mean annual precipitation was discussed in Chapter 7 and shown in Fig. 7.5(b). Two relatively dry areas were noted: the extreme northwest of the U.S.S.R. and the southern part, particularly Central Asia and much of Kazakhstan. The usefulness or effectiveness of a given amount of precipitation must, however, be assessed in relation both to the period in which it falls and to evaporation in the area in which it falls. Thus 40 cm of rain in Belorussia, where evaporation is not great, is more useful than 40 cm in Central Asia, where evaporation is very great. Figs. 9.4(a) and 9.4(b) show growing season precipitation and potential evaporation in the western half of the U.S.S.R. In Fig. 9.4(a), precipitation occurring during the period in which mean daily temperature exceeds 5°C is a rough measure of availability of moisture during the growing period and is, therefore, of interest agriculturally. Fig. 9.4(b) shows potential evaporation during the year (most of it during the period with temperatures over 5°C), ie the moisture that can be lost through evaporation. Fig. 9.5(a) shows the ratio of total precipitation in a year to total potential evaporation; it reflects roughly the relationship between the two previous distributions. To the west of the Yenisey River, much of the northern part is excessively humid. The middle part generally has a satisfactory moisture balance, though this may be upset in some years by droughts. The southern part is deficient, utterly so in most of Central Asia and Kazakhstan, where little can usefully be cultivated except with irrigation. Fig. 9.5(b) shows the main areas in which irrigation is practised and areas into which it might be introduced.

3. Degree of slope affects possibilities and methods of cultivation. Slope is not easy to measure without detailed relief maps, since it is an assessment of micro-relative relief. For the purposes of this book, therefore, altitude (absolute relief) has been the first consideration; the mountain areas defined in this way have been considered bad in general from a slope point of view. The dissected hill country of much of

mid-European U.S.S.R., although not high in an absolute sense, has also been counted as somewhat adverse for reasons of slope. Steep slopes hinder cultivation both on account of the difficulties of mechanisation and movement of crops and materials and because erosion of soil occurs more easily and is more difficult to regulate than on gentler slopes. Farming areas

great damage caused by these storms to agriculture, especially in recent years, control measures have still not been adopted on a wide scale'. *Pravda,* 2 April 1967, draws attention to the urgent need for measures against wind and water erosion. Reference is made specifically to dust storms in Kazakhstan, West and East Siberia, the southern Ukraine and North

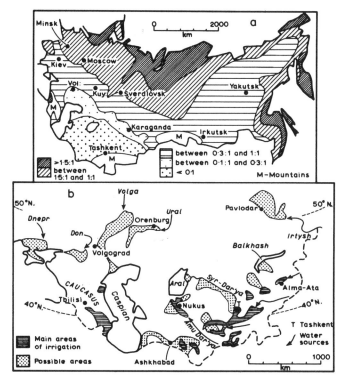

Fig. 9.5.   (a) Precipitation and evaporation. The ratio of mean annual precipitation to potential evaporation is the index given. For example, 1.5:1 means 50% more precipitation than evaporation. Thus the driest area shown has more than 10 times as much potential evaporation as actual rain falling. Source: Cherdantsev, G. N., Ekonomicheskaya geografiya SSSR, 176 (Moscow, 1958). (b) Areas of irrigation.

already affected by soil erosion are shown in Fig. 9.6(b). Widespread soil erosion occurs both in the hill country of the Ukraine and middle Volga and in the high mountains of the Caucasus and Central Asia. An additional area in the new lands around Tselinograd may be added in the 1960's. N. Khrushchev has been blamed for sponsoring the New Lands campaign without sufficient protection against soil erosion, which in the late 1960's affected some 20 million hectares in Kazakhstan. In a paper on dust storms in West Siberia and Kazakhstan, Zhirkov[3] concludes: 'It should be noted that despite the

Caucasus and to water erosion in the Ukraine, Moldavia, the Blackearth Centre and Volga. Mountain areas are also badly affected.

4. The quality of soil and its suitability for agricultural purposes cannot be assessed and expressed in simple numerical terms. There are, however, enormous contrasts between the best chernozem soils on the one hand and northern podzols or southern saline desert soils on the other. Soil fertility varies and is obvious to farmers on the ground, even if its quantification defies soil scientists.

Soils west of the Yenisey are summarised in

Fig. 9.6(a). The main belt of chernozems, extending from Moldavia through the Ukraine and Volga and east to the Altay Mountains, has the most fertile soils. The modified chernozems to north and south of this belt are generally good. North again, the deciduous and mixed forest soils of European U.S.S.R. (2 on map) are usually moderate to poor. South of the chernozem belt, the chestnut soils (3 on map) have been cultivated particularly since 1953. South again, in the semi-desert and desert area (4 on map), soils are generally very poor and may be affected by salinisation or are arid and easily blown by the wind. Locally, if irrigated, they may be satisfactory. In mountain areas in general, quality falls off sharply with altitude. Higher mountain soils are usually thin, easily eroded, and tend to be wet, leached and heavily

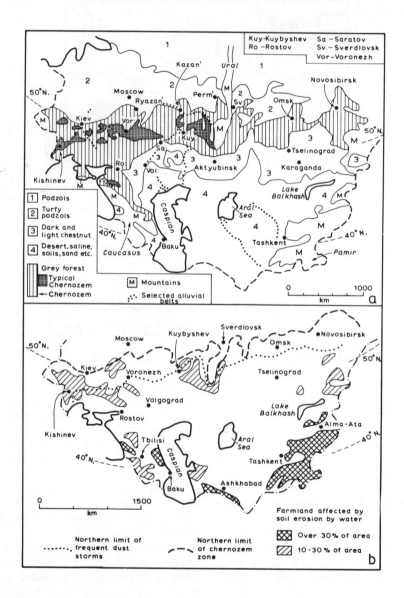

Fig. 9.6.   (a) *Soils in the western half of the U.S.S.R. (b) Areas affected by soil erosion in the western half of the U.S.S.R. Source:* Atlas sel'skogo khozyaystva SSSR, *(Moscow, 1960).*

podzolised, with many of the characteristics of tayga or tundra soils. Finally, the northern tayga and tundra belts (1 on map) have generally very poor soils for cultivation.

In order to have a general assessment of the influence of physical conditions on the distribution of sown land (*posevnyye ploshchadi*) data were collected for 87 administrative units (see Table 2.2 and Fig. 2.3). A rating

shows the general distribution of favourability of conditions in the western part of the U.S.S.R. on the basis of the consensus. Not one unit in the rest of the country reached 10 points. Four possible categories have been arbitrarily distinguished:

Over 16 points out of 20 maximum: much of the Ukraine, Blackearth Centre and the western part of the North Caucasus.

13-15 points, most of the rest of the

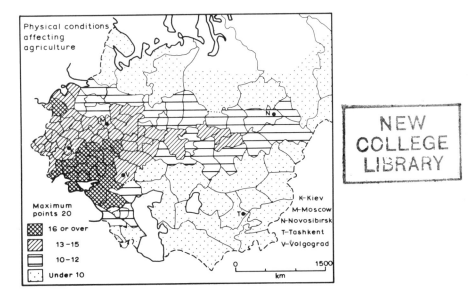

Fig. 9.7.   *Physical conditions affecting agriculture. As there is almost no cultivation at all in the northeast part of the map, this has been left blank. Note: locally there are districts with very favourable conditions even in the areas rated under 10.*

ranging from a minimum of 0 to a maximum of 5 was given to each of the 87 units (areas) according to its suitability for agriculture on the basis of relief-slope, temperature, precipitation and soil. Both the choice of these variables and the rating given each area were, of course, subjectively made. The separate variables were then summed for each unit to give a consensus of the four conditions, with a possible maximum of 20. Small modifications were also made for bad drainage, soil erosion and other influences. Extremes ranged from Yakutsk 2, Magadan 3 and Tuvinsk 4, to Krasnodar, Rostov and Lipetsk each 17, Moldavia, Voronezh, much of the Ukraine 16, and so on. Table 9.2 shows the ratings for each of the four variables for 87 regions and the sum of the four ratings. Fig. 9.7

southern half of European U.S.S.R. and parts of the New Lands.

10-12 points, the fringes of the belt with 13-15.

Under 10, the rest of the U.S.S.R., with small patches that in a more detailed study would emerge as better, eg parts of Uzbekistan, Primorsk.

The four single variables, slope, temperature, precipitation and soil, the consensus of these four and the variable expressing sown area as a percentage of total area in each district were all correlated. The data matrix consisted of 87 areas and the five variables in Table 9.2, as well as sown area. The product moment correlation matrix, Table 9.3, shows the *r index,* expressing degree of correlation, for each pair of variables. Some

Administrative unit	Slope	Temperature	Precipitation	Soil	Consensus
1 Archangel	4	1	4	0	9
2 Vologda	4	2	4	1	11
3 Leningrad	4	2	5	1	12
4 Murmansk	2	0	4	0	6
5 Novgorod	4	2	4	2	12
6 Pskov	4	2	4	2	12
7 Karelian(A)	4	1	4	0	9
8 Komi(A)	4	1	4	0	9
9 Bryansk	4	3	4	3	14
10 Vladimir	5	2	4	3	14
11 Ivanovo	5	2	4	2	13
12 Kalinin	4	2	4	2	12
13 Kaluga	5	2	4	3	14
14 Kostroma	5	2	4	3	14
15 Moscow	4	2	4	3	13
16 Orel	4	3	4	4	15
17 Ryazan'	5	2	3	3	13
18 Smolensk	4	2	5	3	14
19 Tula	4	3	4	3	14
20 Yaroslavl'	5	2	4	3	13
21 Gorky	5	2	3	3	13
22 Kirov	4	2	4	2	12
23 Mariysk(A)	4	2	4	2	12
24 Mordov(A)	5	2	3	3	13
25 Chuvash(A)	5	2	3	3	13
26 Belgorod	4	3	4	5	16
27 Voronezh	5	3	3	5	16
28 Kursk	4	3	4	5	16
29 Lipetsk	5	3	4	5	17
30 Tambov	5	3	3	5	16
31 Astrakhan'	5	4	1	1	11
32 Volgograd	5	3	2	3	13
33 Kuybyshev	4	3	3	4	14
34 Penza	5	2	3	4	14
35 Saratov	5	3	2	5	15
36 Ul'yanovsk	4	2	3	5	14
37 Bashkir(A)	4	2	3	4	13
38 Kalmyk(A)	5	4	1	1	11
39 Tatar(A)	4	2	3	4	13
40 Krasnodar	4	5	4	4	17
41 Stavropol'	4	4	4	4	16
42 Rostov	5	4	3	5	17
43 Dagestan(A)	3	4	2	1	10
44 Kabardino-B.(A)	1	3	5	1	9
45 Severo-Os.(A)	1	3	5	1	9
46 Checheno-Ing.(A)	3	4	3	2	12
47 Kurgan	5	2	2	4	13
48 Orenburg	4	2	2	4	12
49 Perm'	3	2	4	2	11
50 Sverdlovsk	3	2	3	2	10
51 Tyumen'*	4	1	3	1	9
52 Chelyabinsk	3	2	2	3	10
53 Udmurt (A)	4	2	2	3	12
54 Altay	2	2	3	4	10
55 Kemerovo	2	2	4	2	10
56 Novosibirsk	4	2	3	3	12
57 Omsk	5	2	2	3	12
58 Tomsk	4	1	3	1	9
59 Krasnoyarsk*	2	1	3	1	7
60 Irkutsk	2	1	2	1	6
61 Chita	1	1	2	1	5
62 Buryat(A)	1	1	2	1	5
63 Tuvinsk(A)	0	1	2	1	4
64 Primorsk	1	2	5	1	9
65 Khabarovsk*	2	1	5	1	9
66 Amur	2	1	4	2	9

Table 9.2. contd

Administrative unit	Slope	Temperature	Precipitation	Soil	Consensus
67 Kamchatka	1	0	5	0	6
68 Magadan	1	0	2	0	3
69 Sakhalin	2	1	5	0	8
70 Yakutsk*	1	0	1	0	2
71 Kaliningrad	5	3	5	2	15
72 Donets-Dnepr	4	4	3	5	16
73 Southwest	3	3	4	5	14
74 South	5	4	2	5	16
75 Lithuania	5	3	5	3	16
76 Latvia	4	3	5	3	15
77 Estonia	4	2	5	3	14
78 Georgia	1	4	5	2	12
79 Azerbaijan	1	4	2	2	9
80 Armenia	1	3	2	2	8
81 Uzbekistan*	4	5	1	1	11
82 Kirgizia	0	4	2	1	7
83 Tadjikistan	1	4	2	1	8
84 Turkmenistan	4	5	0	0	9
85 Kazakhstan*	4	3	1	1	9
86 Belorussia	4	3	5	3	15
87 Moldavia	4	4	3	5	16

A=A.S.S.R.   * Too large for generalisation.

The following criteria were used:

1. Slope
   Relief and altitude.

2. Temperature
   Degree days over 5°C
   Over 240 per year rated 5
   210–240 4
   180–210 3
   150–180 2
   120–150 1
   Under 120 per year 0

3. Precipitation
   Mean annual
   Over 600 mm rated 5
   500–600 4
   400–500 3
   300–400 2
   200–300 1
   Under 200 0

4. Soil
   Assessed entirely subjectively.

5. Consensus
   Sum of columns 1–4.

Sources:

1. Various maps.
2. Atlas sel'skogo khozyaystva SSSR, 24 (Moscow, 1960).
3. Atlas sel'skogo khozyaystva SSSR, 32.
4. Atlas sel'skogo khozyaystva SSSR, 50–1 and other atlases.

weaknesses of the data are the large size and/or unsatisfactory shape of certain units (eg Tyumen' oblast, Kazakhstan) and the fact that soil itself is known to be affected by other physical features and, therefore, is bound to correlate to some extent with these.

between 1963 and 1966. Any increase in farm production must now be achieved either by obtaining higher yields in existing farming areas or by the slow and costly reclamation of new land by drainage, irrigation and so on.

To overcome the physical limitations listed

Table 9.3. CORRELATION MATRIX OF INTERRELATED PHYSICAL VARIABLES

		1	2	3	4	5	6
1	Physical consensus	1·00					
2	Slope	0·76	1·00				
3	Temperature	0·22	−0·02	1·00			
4	Precipitation	0·22	−0·07	−0·23	1·00		
5	Soil	0·82	0·52	0·15	0·02	1·00	
6	Sown area	0·80	0·53	0·17	0·04	0·92	1·00

The indices are considered simply as numerical descriptions of closeness of correlation. As such they reveal clearly that in total, soil is by far the strongest limiting influence, although relief-slope is also fairly strong. Comparable indices of correlation could be derived for any part of the U.S.S.R. rather than for the whole; then, on a regional or local level, temperature, precipitation and relief would emerge as influences. Thus, for example, in northern European U.S.S.R. there is clearly a strong positive correlation between growing season and sown area as percentage of total area since both increase progressively southwards. Further south, however, temperature continues to increase while sown area falls off towards the lower Volga; the correlation here is negative. The result is to produce no correlation for the U.S.S.R. as a whole.

Various methods have been adopted to overcome limits set by the physical environment to cultivation. These will be more important now than previously, because until the late 1950's there have always been new areas into which cultivation could be extended. Any movement into new areas required new transport facilities and settlements, rather than extensive land reclamation and improvements. With the completion of the New Lands campaign, for the first time in Russian and Soviet experience there remained no large areas left to bring under cultivation without drastic improvement. Indeed, the sown area diminished slightly each year

and to improve conditions, the following have been tried:

1. Temperature: plants that will mature quickly, particularly wheat; the use of hothouses (very limited feasibility); the introduction of substitute crops to replace tropical crops (eg latex-bearing shrubs, sugar beet for cane sugar).
2. Precipitation: drought-resisting plants; tree shelter belts to reduce evaporation of moisture from the soil; wells in arid pastoral areas to support livestock; irrigation works; dry farming; drainage of humid areas.
3. Rugged areas: terracing; reafforestation to reduce erosion.
4. Soil fertility: liming; fertilisers; desalination in arid areas; new crop rotations and new crops; livestock for manure feedback; drainage, especially in the Baltic and Belorussia.

Fig. 9.8 shows the main uses of land in the U.S.S.R. To avoid overlap, only those areas in which any one of the three types occupies more than 60% of the surface are shown. Arable (*pashnya*) extends along the already familiar belt from Moldavia to the Altay Mountains. Natural pastures other than reindeer grazing lands occur in the arid area to the south, forest to the north. Owing to widespread swampy conditions, the forest is notably thinner in the West Siberian Lowlands than in northern European U.S.S.R.

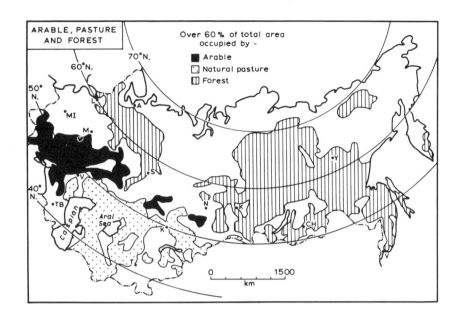

Fig. 9.8.   The main land uses of the U.S.S.R.

Key to letters on map:

A−Archangel	N−Novosibirsk
CH−Chita	S−Sverdlovsk
K−Krasnoyarsk	TB−Tbilisi
L−Leningrad	T−Tashkent
M−Moscow	V−Vladivostok
MI−Minsk	Y−Yakutsk

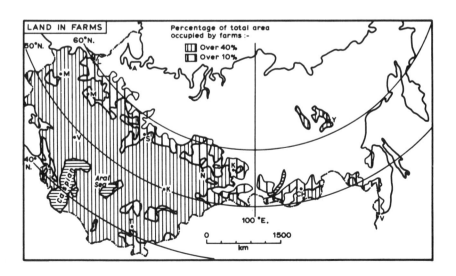

Fig. 9.9.   The main farming belt of the U.S.S.R. Source: Atlas sel'skogo khozyaystva SSSR (Moscow, 1960).

(in spite of clearing) or in East Siberia and the Far East. Fig. 9.9 shows the main farming belt, excluding reindeer herding lands in the northern forest and tundra. The belt contains both the arable land and the natural pasture (see Fig. 9.8) and the mixed arable/forest zone of middle European U.S.S.R.

9.3 FARM PRODUCTION–GENERAL

Crop farming may be assessed in the following three ways, among various others: area occupied by a given crop, weight of crop and value of crop. By taking these three into consideration the relative importance of various crops may be obtained. Unfortunately, data for a regional breakdown of crop farming are available in adequate quantity only for the area cultivated, though some information is available about the weight and, therefore, yield of certain crops.

Some crops give a far higher value of output per unit of farm land than others. The position is shown very broadly by comparing the area occupied by four main groups of crops and the value they contribute. It is roughly as follows for the period 1958–62 and is based on information in Feygin[4] and various yearbooks.

converted almost exclusively into livestock products and would seem, therefore, to merit greater value than it is given, but so also is some of the cereal crop. The vegetable-melon-potatoes group does not include bush and tree crops, such as the vine and tea, which also have a very high output value per unit of area.

At first sight a possible answer to the Soviet agricultural problem might seem to be to increase the cultivation of industrial crops and vegetables at the expense of cereals or fodder. High value crops, however, receive much more attention and, therefore, man hours than low value ones and there is certainly no such sharp discrepancy in value of output per worker as there is in value of output per unit of area. Moreover, there is a limit to the current demand even for individual industrial crops. Vegetables and industrial crops require a far more intensive form of cultivation, in terms of scarce investment, labour, fertilisers and machinery per unit of area. This limits their useful area to the best soils and to places most accessible to labour and markets. The continued attention they need can often only satisfactorily be given to land closest to farm settlements.

The relative importance in terms of value of different kinds of crop and livestock product, region by region, shown in Table 9.4, is perhaps

	Area occupied (millions of hectares)	Percentage of area	Percentage of value	Ratio of value to area (fodder = 1)
Cereals	122	60	32	1·1
Industrial	13	6·5	19	5·8
Vegetables	11	5·5	35	12·8
Fodder	58	28	14	1
Total	204	100	100	

100 hectares = 1 square kilometre.

The calculation shows that the value of output per unit of land under cereals is roughly equal to that of land under fodder. But industrial crops give about six times the value, vegetables (including potatoes) about 13 times. Even if the relative values are deflated to a round five times for industrial crops and 10 times for vegetables, it is clear that the latter two groups are far more important than their areas suggest. The calculation for fodder is dubious as the fodder is

the best brief introduction to the geography of Soviet agriculture. Weight of crops produced and area under different crops will be discussed more fully, but the value indices in this table must be borne in mind. The data are for around 1960 and would need some revision in detail in the late 1960's, but unfortunately the necessary information is not given in the standard yearbooks.

A defect of Table 9.4 is that it does not include the complete range either of crop groups

Table 9.4. CROP AND LIVESTOCK FARMING BY ECONOMIC REGIONS

Rank	Economic Region		Percentage		Livestock			Crops				
			Livestock	Crops	Meat	Milk	Wool	Cereals	Industrial	Potatoes	Vegetables-Melons	Fruit-Berries
1	Northwest	(E1)	58·4	41·6	22·5	27·1	0·5	3·6	7·2	18·4	4·2	1·1
2	Baltic	(E14)	58·2	41·8	25·4	24·7	0·5	5·1	2·9	20·5	3·5	2·2
3	East Siberia	(E9)	55·7	44·3	25·4	17·2	5·2	19·4	0·6	12·7	2·7	0·2
4	Far East	(E10)	51·3	48·7	17·2	17·2	0·4	8·0	14·5	13·5	5·7	0·8
5	Ural	(E7)	49·0	51·0	21·4	17·7	1·7	23·5	1·6	14·7	3·1	0·3
6	North Caucasus	(E6)	48·7	51·3	19·7	11·4	6·4	22·0	8·0	2·3	5·0	5·8
7	Centre	(E2)	48·4	51·6	19·4	20·2	0·7	6·7	7·0	24·6	5·4	1·7
8	Donets-Dnepr	(E11)	47·7	52·3	20·4	15·9	0·8	17·7	10·6	7·0	6·5	3·0
9	West Siberia	(E8)	47·3	52·7	20·5	17·8	2·1	25·9	1·5	13·6	2·3	0·2
10	Volga	(E5)	47·0	53·0	20·6	14·5	2·9	26·1	4·2	10·3	4·7	1·1
11	Kazakhstan	(E17)	46·3	53·7	24·3	10·4	7·5	35·5	2·9	2·9	2·1	0·9
	U.S.S.R.		**45·8**	**54·2**	**19·9**	**15·3**	**2·4**	**16·3**	**9·7**	**13·1**	**4·1**	**3·8**
12	Volga-Vyatka	(E3)	45·3	54·7	19·0	17·8	1·2	12·1	5·0	26·6	5·0	0·7
13	Belorussia	(E18)	43·5	56·5	20·9	17·0	0·3	5·9	7·3	32·1	2·8	2·7
14	Blackearth Centre	(E4)	43·5	56·5	17·8	15·5	1·2	17·7	12·2	15·2	2·9	1·6
15	South	(E13)	43·2	56·8	18·1	14·3	2·1	20·0	7·5	2·3	6·6	10·9
16	Southwest	(E12)	42·5	57·5	19·7	14·2	0·4	13·1	11·4	19·1	3·7	4·0
17	Transcaucasia	(E15)	37·1	62·9	14·7	10·2	3·5	6·3	20·3	2·5	5·2	22·9
18	Central Asia	(E16)	31·7	68·3	13·0	6·6	5·9	3·5	49·1	1·0	3·8	5·9
19	Moldavia	(E19)	30·0	70·0	13·5	8·2	1·2	14·2	12·6	2·5	5·4	28·5

Source: Feygin,[4] 74

or of livestock product groups. Fodder crops appear to be the main omission under crops and probably account for 7% of total Soviet farm output value, but they are counted again under livestock products. Livestock products equal to some 8% of the total Soviet farm output value are also omitted; they probably include items such as eggs and karakul lamb skins. In spite of these deficiencies, the table is useful. The data in it could be further processed (eg to express the ratio of cereals to industrial crops for each region). The 19 regions in the table have been ranked according to percentage contributed by livestock (first column). From the table as it stands, the following points may be noted.

1. If it is advantageous (and virtuous in the eyes of planners) to emphasise livestock rather than crop farming, then the bad position of Central Asia and Moldavia, each with only about 30% of their output from livestock, contrasts greatly with the good position of the Northwest and the Baltic, about 58%. The view may also be taken, however, that it is more the humid and/or cold conditions of the northern part of European U.S.S.R. and much of Siberia that make fodder crops and livestock raising more suitable here than general crop farming.

2. The relative importance of livestock raising for meat and for milk in the regions emerges from Columns 3 and 4. Dairying only exceeds meat production in the Northwest and Baltic regions, where a mild climate favours nutritious grasses which dairy cattle need and

where the urban market is relatively close at hand. In Central Asia where sheep outweigh cattle in importance, meat products are twice the value of milk products.

3. Cereal cultivation is most strongly developed relatively in Kazakhstan (35% of all farm output), West Siberia (26%) and the Volga (26%). The former granary of Russia, the Ukraine, now figures less prominently. This is a result of the increased area under industrial crops such as sugar and sunflowers and of attempts to build up a labour intensive livestock industry based on pigs and stall-fed cattle. Anderson[5] studies increased fodder production on an oblast basis in the Ukraine in the 1950's.

4. Certain regions stand out for industrial crops (Central Asia about 50% of the value of all farm output, mainly cotton, Transcaucasia 20%) potatoes (Belorussia 32%, Volga-Vyatka 27%, Centre 25%) and fruit-berries (Moldavia 28·5%, Transcaucasia 23%). The proportion of vegetables, on the other hand, remains fairly constant around 4%, presumably because of the high perishability and difficulties of transporting, together with the relative ease of growing some kind of vegetables in almost any kind of climate.

9.4 FARM PRODUCTION—CROPS

The distribution of arable or crop land in the U.S.S.R. is the key to the distribution of Soviet agriculture, since the great bulk of livestock

Table 9.5. ASPECTS OF CROP FARMING IN 1967

(a) *General*

Type of land	Millions of hectares	Percentage of total
Total area of U.S.S.R.	2 227	100
All farm land	609	27
Ploughed land[1]	232	10
Arable[2]	224	
Sown area[3]	207	
Meadows[4]	48	2
Pastures[5]	325	14

1 *Pakhotnyye zemli* (including long fallow lands)   4 *Senokosy*
2 *Pashnya*   5 *Pastbishcha*
3 *Posevnyye ploshchadi*

Table 9.5. ASPECTS OF CROP FARMING IN 1967

(b) Economic regions

	Economic region	1	2	3	4	5	6	7	8	9	10	11	12
E1	Northwest	166·3	8·0	3·2	100	5	2	3·1	2·8	89	−0·3	25	6
E2	Centre	48·5	23·2	15·1	100	48	31	12·3	13·7	111	+1·4	51	7
E3	Volga-Vyatka	26·3	10·9	7·9	100	42	30	6·2	6·5	105	+0·3	78	7
E4	Blackearth Centre	16·7	13·6	11·2	100	81	67	8·5	11·0	130	+2·5	139	8
E5	Volga	68·0	46·8	29·9	100	69	44	19·7	28·2	143	+8·5	157	14
E6	North Caucasus	35·5	26·6	16·3	100	75	46	12·4	16·0	129	+3·6	115	10
E7	Ural	211·6	27·9	18·0	100	13	9	11·5	16·0	139	+4·5	105	16
E8	West Siberia	99·2	35·7	19·8	100	36	20	9·9	18·0	182	+8·1	147	23
E9	East Siberia	412·3	22·4	8·9	100	5	2	3·9	7·5	192	+3·6	103	17
E10	Far East	621·6	6·4	2·8	100	1	0·4	1·4	2·6	186	+1·2	46	12
E11	Donets-Dnepr	22·0	17·4	14·4	100	79	65	12·9	13·8	107	+0·9	69	5
E12	Southwest	27·0	16·7	13·0	100	62	48	12·2	13·1	108	+0·9	64	4
E13	South	11·1	8·5	6·7	100	76	60	5·6	6·5	116	+0·9	107	6
E14	Baltic	18·9	8·6	5·3	100	46	28	4·8	5·0	104	+0·2	68	6
E15	Transcaucasia	18·7	8·2	2·7	100	44	14	2·4	2·4	100	0	20	2
E16	Central Asia	127·9	68·2	6·2	100	53	5	5·2	5·9	113	+0·7	31	3
E17	Kazakhstan	271·5	183·4	33·6	100	68	12	7·8	29·9	383	+22·1	236	19
E18	Belorussia	20·7	9·9	6·3	100	48	30	4·9	6·1	124	+1·2	69	4
E19	Moldavia	3·4	2·7	1·9	100	80	56	1·9	1·9	100	0	55	3
	U.S.S.R.	2 227·2	545·1	223·2	100	24	10	146·3	206·8	141	+60·3	88	7

Columns
1–3   In millions of hectares, 1967
1   Total area of region
2   Total farm land
3   Total arable *(pashnya)*
4–6   In percentages, 1967
4   Total area of region
5   Farm land as percentage of total

Columns
6   Arable land as percentage of total
7, 8, 10   In millions of hectares
7, 8   Sown area *(posevnye ploshchadi)* in 1950 and 1967
9   1967 as percentage of 1950
10   Absolute change 1950–67
11   1967 sown area in hectares per 100 inhabitants
12   1964 sown area in hectares per collective farm *(kolkhoz)* household (1967 not available)

Source: (a) *NkhSSSR* 1967, 342
          (b) *NkhSSSR* 1967, 343, 354, *NDSE* 442 for Col. 12

production also comes from those areas where cultivation is important. Only about 25% comes from natural pastures in the less intensively used parts of the country. Farm land is broken down as shown in Fig. 9.5(a); data are for the mid-1960's but other near years do not differ greatly.

The total area of each of the economic regions, the total agricultural area and the total arable area, are shown for 1967 in Table 9.5. Agricultural and arable are then in turn expressed as a percentage of total area. All land used for farming purposes (excluding reindeer grazing) occupies some 27% of the total area of the U.S.S.R. This is composed of about 16-17% meadows or natural pastures and about 10% ploughed land (see Fig. 9.9). The total ploughed land is cut down somewhat by subtracting long fallow and temporary fallow. The residue, representing field crops and known as sown area (*posevnyye ploshchadi*) will be used throughout this section to represent cropland. It does not include tree and bush crops, which it should be remembered are important in some regions (see Table 9.4).

In 1940 the sown area was 151 million hectares. By 1945 it was only 114 million, a reduction largely due to World War II. The prewar level was only exceeded again in the early 1950's.[6] The growth of land under crops in the postwar period is fairly well illustrated by the change between 1950 and 1967. This is shown in Table 9.5, Columns 7-10, with sown areas 1950 and 1967 and relative and absolute gains. The year 1950 represents roughly the middle of the postwar period of rehabilitation and stagnation preceding the 1953 New Lands campaign. Sown area in 1950 was 146 million hectares. It reached a record 219 million hectares in 1963, having thus increased by 45%, or by an area roughly six times the size of England, in a decade. The gain, both relative and absolute, varied greatly among the 19 regions.

The absolute gain in millions of hectares 1, and percentage of total absolute gain 2, were as follows:

	1	2
U.S.S.R.	+60·3	100
Kazakhstan	+22·1	37
Volga	+ 8·5	14
West Siberia	+ 8·1	13
Ural	+ 4·5	7

About half of the new land brought under cultivation was in Kazakhstan and West Siberia alone, but impressive amounts were also added in several other regions. Gains in peripheral regions with particularly difficult conditions (Transcaucasia, Far East, Northwest) and/or a long history of crop farming (Southwest, Baltic) were small. The biggest additions were during 1953-59, after which little was added. Since 1963 there has been a general contraction of sown area (millions of hectares): 1963—218·5; 1964—212·8; 1965—209·1; 1966—206·8; 1967—206·9.

The amount of sown area per inhabitant varies greatly from oblast to oblast and even from region to region (Table 9.5(b)). There is approximately 14 times as much sown area per inhabitant in Kazakhstan as in the Northwest, Central Asia, or Transcaucasia, though the sown area is more intensively cultivated in the last two regions. Such contrasts imply surpluses of crop products in some regions and deficits in others. Care must be taken, however, in relating sown area to other variables. Very broadly, three ratios are frequently derived and referred to (see Fig. 9.10, lower right, for examples):

Total area (A1) : sown area (A2)
Total area (A1) : population (P)
Sown area (A2) : population (P).

The availability of sown area per 100 (or other appropriate number) inhabitants varies between one extreme where an oblast, usually small, has a sown area as a large percentage of total area, together with a small total population (largely rural) and the other extreme where, either total area is large, sown area small and population moderate (eg Archangel) or total area is fairly small, sown area a large percentage of it, but total population large (eg Donetsk, Moscow).

Fig. 9.10 is a topological map with the area of each administrative unit proportional to the sown area of the unit; correct contiguity is retained. Differences in population per sown area at oblast level are shown by shading. Deficient areas range from most of the northern part, through the major urban/industrial concentration, to the dry mountainous southern lands. Since the assessment is based on area of sown land, not value of farm output, areas of intensive cultivation appear unfavourably on the map. Areas that would be expected to have a surplus are mainly along the chernozem belt away from

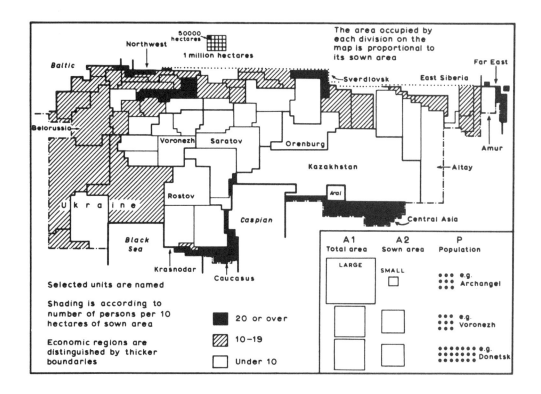

Fig. 9.10. The density of population per sown area in persons per 10 hectares. Note: Sown area, not population, determines the size of each compartment.

Table 9.6. MAIN TYPES OF SOWN AREA *(posevnyye ploshchadi)*

	1963	1964	1965	63–65 Total	63–65 Mean	1966	1967 Total area	1967 Percentage of total area
Cereals	1 300	1 333	1 280	3 913	1 304	1 248	1 222	59·0
Industrial	149	155	153	457	152	151	148	7·2
Potatoes and vegetables	105	106	106	317	106	103	103	5·0
Fodder	631	534	552	1 717	572	566	596	28·8
Total	2 185	2 128	2 091	6 404	2 135	2 068	2 069	100·0

Areas in all columns (except the last one) are in km$^2 \times 10^3$
Sources: *NkhSSSR* 1965, 288–9, and 1967, 348–9

Table 9.7. SPATIAL DISPERSION OF SELECTED CROPS IN THE U.S.S.R.

Regions	More than 8% of total	2–8%	Less than 2%
>15	Spring wheat	Oats Potatoes Annual grasses Perennial grasses	Vegetables
11–15	Non-grain maize Winter wheat Barley	Winter rye	Millet Chickpeas
6–10		Sugar beet Sunflower	Grain maize Tobacco/*makhorka*
5 or less			Rice Cotton Hemp Flax

the urban clusters, though no area would be expected to require and consume exactly the same share of the total volume or value of farm products as it has of population.

The main types of crop grown over the period 1963–67 are shown in Table 9.6. Adjustments to take into account the greater value of industrial crops and vegetables (with potatoes) show a very different picture. Fig. 9.11 shows the absolute and relative importance of each category in five selected years. The four main categories will be broken down as appropriate in turn. First, however, Table 9.7 summarises the spatial dispersion of selected crops grown in the U.S.S.R. Crops are classified according to the proportion of total sown area they occupy (the columns) and how widespread they are among the 19 economic regions (the rows). The criterion for the former is whether they occupy more than 8% of total sown area, 2–8%, or less than 2%. For the latter, the distribution of appropriate crops by regions in *Atlas sel'skogo khozyaystva*[1] has been consulted and the criterion of commercial cultivation in more than 15 regions, 11–15, 6–10, or 5 or less, has been used.

Table 9.8 shows the distribution among the economic regions of the four main categories of crop by area occupied; figures are for 1967. The relative importance to each region of each of the four categories is brought out by the calculation of the share (in per thousand) that each category occupies of total sown area in the region. There is

Table 9.8. THE DISTRIBUTION OF THE MAIN CATEGORIES OF CROP BY ECONOMIC REGION IN 1967

		Areas in thousands of hectares				Per thousand of total			
		Total sown	Industrial crops	Potatoes and other vegetables	Cereals	Fodder	Industrial crops	Potatoes and other vegetables	Cereals	Fodder
E1	Northwest	2 836	213	296	973	1 354	75	104	344	477
E2	Centre	13 729	665	1 406	6 833	4 821	48	102	498	352
E3	Volga-Vyatka	6 539	147	573	4 200	1 618	23	88	642	247
E4	Blackearth Centre	10 973	1 397	489	5 805	3 270	127	45	530	298
E5	Volga	28 157	1 347	684	18 795	7 249	48	24	669	259
E6	North Caucasus	15 992	1 716	324	8 845	5 009	116	20	551	313
E7	Ural	16 001	188	489	11 072	4 244	12	31	691	266
E8	West Siberia	18 036	316	483	12 180	5 053	18	27	675	280
E9	East Siberia	7 498	25	247	4 925	2 300	3	33	657	307
E10	Far East	2 562	854	162	1 078	466	334	63	421	182
E11	Donets-Dnepr	13 754	1 861	708	6 541	4 563	136	52	476	332
E12	Southwest	13 075	1 537	1 605	5 876	4 044	118	123	450	309
E13	South	6 459	708	193	3 084	2 413	110	29	478	373
E14	Baltic	5 018	120	477	2 028	2 393	24	95	404	477
E15	Transcaucasia	2 409	288	121	1 359	622	120	50	565	258
E16	Central Asia	5 850	2 306	140	2 130	1 189	394	24	364	204
E17	Kazakhstan	29 904	381	227	22 686	6 571	13	8	759	220
E18	Belorussia	6 135	317	1 039	2 856	1 922	52	168	466	314
E19	Moldavia	1 910	390	97	906	508	204	51	475	266
	U.S.S.R.	206 837	14 776	9 760	122 172	59 609	71	47	592	290

Small discrepancies between parts and whole are due largely to the omission of tree crops, affecting especially regions 6, 11, 13, 15, 16, 19.

Source: *NkhSSSR* 1967, 354–5, 361, 364–6.

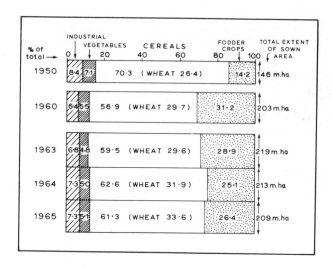

Fig. 9.11. Four categories of crop land in five selected years. The thickness (vertical) of each bar is proportional to the sown area that it represents. *Sources:* NkhSSSR *1964, 269 and* SSR v tsifrakh *1965, 71–2.*

Table 9.9. THE LEADING AND MOST SPECIALISED ECONOMIC REGIONS OF THE U.S.S.R. FOR CROP CATEGORIES, 1967

(a) *Absolute (10⁵ha)*

Rank	Industrial crops		Potatoes/vegetables		Cereals		Fodder crops	
1	C. Asia	23	Southwest	16	Kazakhstan	227	Volga	72
2	Donets-Dnepr	19	Centre	14	Volga	188	Kazakhstan	66
3	N. Caucasus	17	Belorussia	10	W. Siberia	122	W. Siberia	51
4	Southwest	15	Donets-Dnepr	7	Ural	111	N. Caucasus	50
5	Blackearth C.	14	Volga	7	N. Caucasus	88	Centre	48
19	East Siberia		Moldavia		Moldavia		Moldavia	

(b) *Relative (percentage of total sown of region)*

	Industrial crops		Potatoes/vegetables		Cereals		Fodder crops	
1	C. Asia	39	Belorussia	17	Kazakhstan	76	Baltic	48
2	Far East	33	Southwest	12	Ural	69	Northwest	48
3	Moldavia	20	Northwest	10	W. Siberia	68	South	37
4	Donets-Dnepr	14	Centre	10	Volga	67	Centre	35
5	Blackearth C.	13	Baltic	9	E. Siberia	66	Donets-Dnepr	33
19	East Siberia		Kazakhstan		Northwest		Far East	

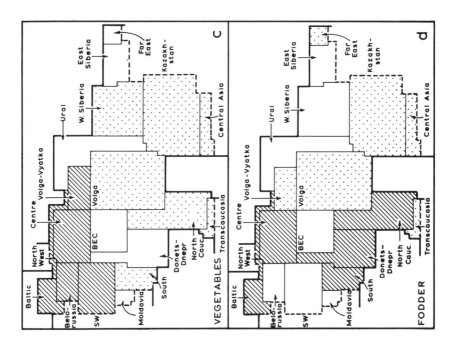

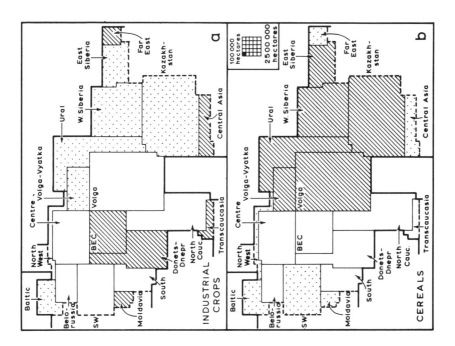

Fig. 9.12.   The distribution of cultivation of the four main categories of cropland. The area of each region is proportional to the sown area of the region. Shading of the maps is as follows: first six regions ranked on percentage of a given category are shaded with diagonal lines, the last six are dotted. (a) Industrial crops. (b) Cereals. (c) Vegetables including potatoes. (d) Fodder.

a small discrepancy in some regions since tree crops are not included in totals.

To bring out the main agricultural regions in both an absolute sense and a relative sense, the top five regions and the 19th are listed in Table 9.9 for each category. Table 9.9(a) shows where the largest areas are under the four main categories, industrial crops, potatoes and vegetables, cereals and fodder crops. Naturally, the larger regions tend to figure among the top five. Table 9.9(b) shows where the different categories are relatively most important and, therefore, distinguishes areas of specialisation. Fig. 9.12 shows the data in Tables 9.8 and 9.9. The base is topological, each of the 19 regions being proportional in area to its sown area; correct contiguity is preserved. Shading is by three categories for each of the four users of sown land: the six highest and the six lowest are shaded and dotted respectively. This makes comparison of the relative importance of each type possible.

POTATOES, VEGETABLES AND FRUITS

Potatoes and vegetables are clearly distinguished in Soviet agriculture, presumably because while both are used for human consumption, potatoes are also fed to livestock and are, or have been, widely used as an industrial raw material. The distribution of vegetable cultivation is fairly close to the distribution of total population, though in Central Asia it is poorly represented. The distribution of potato cultivation, on the other hand, tends to be more specialised, with Belorussia, the Baltic Republics, the Centre and Volga-Vyatka standing out. This is partly because potatoes need a mild moist growing season and partly because they will grow readily in areas that are too damp and cool for successful grain crops.

The cultivation of fruit is much more localised. In general the southern part of European U.S.S.R., together with Central Asia specialise, while fruit growing is of local

Table 9.10. MAIN TYPES OF INDUSTRIAL CROP BY AREA IN HUNDRED THOUSAND HECTARES

	1963	1964	1965	1963–65 Total	1963–65 Mean	1966	1967	1967 Percentage of total
Cotton	25	25	24	74	25	24	24	16
Sugar beet	38	41	39	118	39	38	38	26
Sunflower	44	46	49	139	46	50	48	32
Flax (fibre)	15	16	15	46	15	14	14	9
All industrial	149	155	153	457	152	151	148	100

Sources: *SSSR v tsifrakh v 1965 godu*, 71–2, *NkhSSSR* 1967, 361–3.

INDUSTRIAL CROPS

Table 9.10 shows the principal industrial crops grown according to area occupied; many other industrial crops not listed are also grown. These are of more limited extent and/or value and include hemp, cultivated mainly in mid-European U.S.S.R., tea in Transcaucasia, linseed in Central Asia and soybeans in the Far East. The regional distribution of the four principal industrial crops is shown in Table 9.11. The main areas of cultivation of these crops are shown in Fig. 9.13.

importance or almost absent elsewhere. Grapes, apples and plums are grown in Moldavia, the Crimea and Transcaucasia and nuts and citrus fruits are produced in favoured parts of Transcaucasia. Tree fruit growing has been curiously neglected, however, possibly because of the delay in bearing; Soviet output *per capita* is appreciably lower than in most other European countries.

CEREALS

While increasing absolutely during the present

Table 9.11. MAIN TYPES OF INDUSTRIAL CROP IN THE U.S.S.R. BY ECONOMIC REGION IN THOUSANDS OF HECTARES, 1967

	Region	Total	Flax	Sugar beet	Sunflower	Cotton
E1	Northwest	213	213	–	–	–
E2	Centre	665	440	166	–	–
E3	Volga-Vyatka	147	80	34	–	–
E4	Blackearth Centre	1 397	–	814	468	–
E5	Volga	1 347	–	227	849	–
E6	North Caucasus	1 716	–	309	1 183	–
E7	Ural	188	39	5	121	–
E8	West Siberia	316	42	61	76	–
E9	East Siberia	25	5	3	–	–
E10	Far East	854	–	11	–	–
E11	Donets-Dnepr	1 861	–	602	1 124	–
E12	Southwest	1 537	228	1 112	106	–
E13	South	708	–	116	484	–
E14	Baltic	120	67	52	–	–
E15	Transcaucasia	288	–	9	24	212
E16	Central Asia	2 306	–	53	–	2 184
E17	Kazakhstan	381	–	67	104	46
E18	Belorussia	317	261	50	–	–
E19	Moldavia	–	–	106	223	–
	U.S.S.R.	14 776	1 375	3 797	4 767	2 442

– negligible production or no production.

Source: *NkhSSSR* 1967, 361–3.

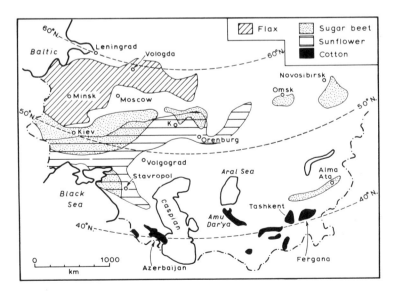

Fig. 9.13.   *The distribution of flax, sugar beet, the sunflower and cotton in the western part of the U.S.S.R. Source:* Atlas sel'skogo khozyaystva SSSR *(Moscow, 1960).*

century the area occupied by cereals has tended to diminish as a percentage of total sown area, owing to an increase in both industrial crops and, particularly since the mid-1950's, fodder crops. The New Lands campaign has taken the major areas of cereal surplus eastwards, and the Ukraine, formerly dominant, probably only achieves a balance now.

During the present century the type of cereal grown has changed, the main loser being rye. Wheat has tended both to replace rye in older areas and to become the dominant cereal in most areas of new development. The cultivation of spring wheat, in particular, has spread in northern areas and in the new lands. More recently, grain maize has been tried in many regions, although by the late 1960's the area where grain maize could be considered a dominant crop had contracted to the eastern Ukraine and North Caucasus. Barley and oats are both grown very widely and barley in particular seems to be a useful cereal both in the coldest and the driest areas of cereal cultivation. Millet is grown fairly widely, especially in northern Kazakhstan, but rice is very localised and production is small. Table 9.12 shows the area occupied by the main cereals and by beans during the period 1963–67.

Since cereals are to some extent interchangeable, both as human and as animal food, it is becoming less relevant to look for regions of specialisation in one type. Moreover, there is now so much overlapping of cultivation of different

cereals that it is no longer meaningful to talk of regions being devoted to particular types. It is still possible, however, to distinguish regional preferences. For example, in the agricultural lands north of the blackearth belt rye is still very widely grown and in northern Kazakhstan for some time spring wheat was virtually a monoculture. During the Soviet period there has been a policy to make the consumption of wheat bread popular, so, for reasons of diet as much as climate, wheat has become more widespread than previously.

Table 9.13 shows the regional distribution of cultivation of four cereals in 1967. More than half of the area under cereals is in the four regions Kazakhstan, West Siberia, Ural and Volga. Since these have less than one-quarter of the total population it may be assumed that they have a large surplus of grain, at least in years when yields are comparable with those in regions further west. During 1962–64 they together accounted for 40–45% of the actual tonnage (volume) of grain harvested, but their share has tended to diminish since 1964.

The virgin and idle lands campaign is now recent history. Since it revolved largely round an attempt to increase Soviet wheat production it is relevant to this section. The actual area brought into use was shown in Table 9.5. The role of durum wheat, the need for crop rotations and the danger of exhausting the soil and causing a dust bowl are discussed in detail by Jackson.[7]

Table 9.12. MAIN CEREALS AND BEAN CROPS BY AREA IN HUNDRED THOUSAND HECTARES

Crop	1963	1964	1965	1963–65 Total	1963–65 Mean	1966	1967	1967 Percentage of total
Winter wheat	164	190	198	552	184	198	197	16
Spring wheat	482	489	504	1 475	492	502	473	39
Rye	150	168	160	478	159	136	124	10
Barley	205	217	197	619	206	192	191	16
Oats	57	57	66	180	60	72	87	7
Maize	70	51	32	153	51	32	35	3
Beans	108	106	68	282	94	59	55	5
Total	1 300	1 333	1 280	3 913	1 304	1 248	1 222	100

Sources: *SSSR v tsifrakh v 1965 godu*, 71–2, *NkhSSSR* 1967, 348, 355–60.

Table 9.13. DISTRIBUTION OF RYE, WINTER AND SPRING WHEAT AND MAIZE BY ECONOMIC REGIONS BY AREA AND OF ALL GRAIN BY VOLUME

Economic region	All cereals	Area in thousands of hectares				Weight of grain	
		Rye	Winter wheat	Spring wheat	Grain maize	Thousands of tons	Per thousand of total
E1 Northwest	973	410	45	102	–	1 102	7
E2 Centre	6 833	2 191	1 156	516	–	8 186	55
E3 Volga-Vyatka	4 200	1 996	230	686	–	4 277	29
E4 Blackearth Centre	5 805	473	1 531	497	142	8 665	59
E5 Volga	18 795	2 476	1 230	8 722	35	22 500	152
E6 North Caucasus	8 845	55	4 806	254	620	15 598	106
E7 Ural	11 072	1 140	3	6 861	–	11 657	79
E8 West Siberia	12 180	313	–	9 008	–	9 684	65
E9 East Siberia	4 925	42	–	3 214	–	6 340	43
E10 Far East	1 078	4	–	572	5	1 241	8
E11 Donets-Dnepr	6 541	209	2 746	154	1 207	12 926	87
E12 Southwest	5 876	712	2 772	24	407	12 263	83
E13 South	3 084	28	1 874	–	361	6 659	45
E14 Baltic	2 028	653	237	31	–	3 617	25
E15 Transcaucasia	1 359	–	762	34	216	1 746	12
E16 Central Asia	2 130	–	876	356	66	1 753	12
E17 Kazakhstan	22 686	116	847	16 278	48	14 408	97
E18 Belorussia	2 856	1 576	219	9	–	3 219	22
E19 Moldavia	906	7	866	–	378	2 046	14
U.S.S.R.	122 172	12 418	19 708	47 318	3 485	147 887	1 000

Source: *NkhSSSR* 1967, 355–9, 371.

9.5 FARM PRODUCTION–LIVESTOCK

Livestock are raised on fodder derived from four basically different types of lands:

1. Sown land other than that devoted specifically to fodder. Part of the production of potatoes, vegetables, industrial crops (eg sugar beet waste) and grains are presumably fed, but in unrecorded quantities, to stock.

2. Sown land devoted by definition to fodder crops. The main categories are silage maize and maize used as green fodder, lucerne (alfalfa) and grasses, either perennial or annual. In 1967 these occupied 28% of the total sown area.

3. Natural meadow land (*senokos,* or hay land) found mainly in the areas of arable farming along river flood plains and comparable areas and shared among farms.

4. Natural pasture (*pastbishche*) mainly in drier or mountainous areas away from the

main arable belt (see Fig. 9.8). Although the total area of natural pasture considerably exceeds the total sown area, the amount of fodder obtained from it is small. Indeed, much of the natural pasture land occurs in semi-desert and desert areas and has a very low stock carrying capacity, used mainly for sheep raised for their wool and skins and for goats. Additional but scanty animal fodder is obtained in the reindeer herding lands of the north of Siberia and waste food from the larger towns is also used.

It is not possible to say with accuracy what proportion of the livestock is supported by each of the four main sources of fodder, but a rough estimate is about 40% from the sown land specifically defined as producing fodder crops and about 20% from each of the other three sources.

The regional distribution of the three types of land directed specifically to supporting livestock is shown in Table 9.14. A study of the relative importance and the distribution of

Table 9.14. 1 MEADOW (*senokos*),
2 NATURAL PASTURE (*pastbishche*),
3 FODDER CROPS (*kormovyye kul'tury*),
IN THOUSANDS OF HECTARES, 1967,
BY ECONOMIC REGION

Economic region	1	2	3
E1 Northwest	2 670	1 650	1 354
E2 Centre	3 960	3 430	4 821
E3 Volga-Vyatka	1 290	1 440	1 618
E4 Blackearth Centre	590	1 620	3 270
E5 Volga	2 930	13 740	7 249
E6 North Caucasus	1 260	8 400	5 009
E7 Ural	2 890	6 770	4 224
E8 West Siberia	7 030	8 220	5 053
E9 East Siberia	3 030	10 140	2 300
E10 Far East	1 810	1 660	466
E11 Donets-Dnepr	570	1 880	4 563
E12 Southwest	1 860	1 370	4 044
E13 South	60	1 250	2 413
E14 Baltic	1 630	1 510	2 393
E15 Transcaucasia	400	4 150	622
E16 Central Asia	380	60 450	1 189
E17 Kazakhstan	6 980	141 070	6 571
E18 Belorussia	1 980	1 440	1 922
E19 Moldavia	10	360	508
U.S.S.R.	41 330	270 550	59 609

Source: *NkhSSSR* 1967, 346–7, 366.

livestock is complicated somewhat by the fact that cattle in particular are much larger and consume much more fodder, than pigs, sheep and goats. To overcome this and to have standard comparable livestock figures, all main livestock except horses and poultry have been converted to livestock units. The calculation is only an approximate one; each head of cattle is considered to be one unit and each pig, sheep or goat one-sixth of a unit. There are more subtle and precise ways of calculating livestock units, but the complete information that would be needed about age and purpose of livestock is not readily available. Horses have not been taken into consideration, since very recent data are not available. They have largely been replaced by mechanisation in the last 30 years, but about 10 million remained in the early 1960's and were therefore still a considerable consumer of fodder. Table 9.15 shows the regional distribution of different types of livestock, both in actual numbers and as proportions of all livestock.

Cattle account for about three-quarters of all livestock units. As a proportion within regions, however, they vary greatly, ranging from 90% in the Far East to only about 55% in Kazakhstan and Central Asia. Pig raising is much more closely associated with cattle raising than with sheep and goats. Moreover, a comparison of the distribution of different types of livestock and different sources of fodder shows that sheep and goats are raised largely on the natural pastures (*pastbishcha*) of dry U.S.S.R. and on the southern mountain ranges and cattle and pigs are fed from the other three sources.

Cattle themselves may be divided into dairy cows and others. In 1967, 43% of all cattle in the U.S.S.R. were classified as dairy cows, but the proportion of these varies very considerably from region to region (see Table 9.15). Thus in five regions of northern and central European U.S.S.R. they exceed 50% of all cattle, but in four southern regions they are less than 40%. Western European U.S.S.R. has the best conditions for dairying, with many large urban markets. Beef cattle are found more widely in hotter, drier or more remote parts. More locally there are areas that specialise in dairying (eg parts of the Baltic Republics, the Centre) and others with a meat orientation.

9.6 YIELDS OF SELECTED FARM PRODUCTS

Before Soviet planners can seriously improve agriculture they must consider the variations in yield of crops and of livestock products. Yields vary both from year to year and from place to place. Little can be done to modify temporal variations in yield until climate is adequately controlled, or battery farming and better storage facilities for fodder provided. On the other hand, yields in many areas can be improved by growing the most suitable crops and by keeping the most suitable types of livestock in each area, by using fertilisers to raise yields and by reorganising land tenure and incentives. Yields of selected crops and livestock products will be briefly discussed and the complexity of the problem shown.

1. Spring wheat is grown commercially in almost every region and on a large scale in most. Initially this is surprising since winter wheat yields tend to be higher in almost every region where the two are grown. Spring wheat is, however, more easy to cultivate, particularly in areas with severe winter conditions. Spring wheat

Table 9.15. LIVESTOCK BY ECONOMIC REGIONS IN 1967

		1	*2*	*3*	*4*	*5*	*6*	*7*	*8*
E1	Northwest	2 273	55	990	1 392	2 382	397	2 670	85
E2	Centre	6 845	51	3 535	4 015	7 550	1 258	8 103	85
E3	Volga-Vyatka	2 834	50	1 430	2 280	3 710	618	3 452	82
E4	Blackearth Centre	4 248	46	3 323	3 260	6 583	1 097	5 345	80
E5	Volga	8 993	39	4 392	16 885	21 277	3 546	12 539	72
E6	North Caucasus	6 656	37	4 472	16 085	20 557	3 426	10 082	66
E7	Ural	5 852	41	2 427	4 607	7 034	1 172	7 024	83
E8	West Siberia	7 262	39	2 552	6 121	8 673	1 446	8 708	83
E9	East Siberia	3 401	38	1 445	8 953	10 398	1 733	5 134	66
E10	Far East	1 420	42	741	207	948	158	1 578	90
E11	Donets-Dnepr	7 855	41	5 668	2 980	8 648	1 441	9 296	85
E12	Southwest	10 132	45	7 140	2 713	9 853	1 642	11 774	86
E13	South	3 178	37	2 187	3 281	5 468	911	4 089	78
E14	Baltic	3 773	51	3 036	791	3 827	638	4 411	85
E15	Transcaucasia	3 951	40	757	9 373	10 130	1 688	5 639	70
E16	Central Asia	5 130	40	610	25 105	25 715	4 285	9 415	54
E17	Kazakhstan	7 527	37	1 849	33 682	35 531	5 921	13 448	56
E18	Belorussia	4 892	51	3 189	711	3 900	650	5 542	88
E19	Moldavia	945	42	1 124	1 600	2 724	454	1 399	68
	U.S.S.R.	97 167	43	50 867	144 041	194 908	32 485	129 652	75

Columns

1, 3, 4	Cattle, pigs and sheep/goats in thousands.
2	Cows as a percentage of all cattle.
5	Pigs plus sheep/goats in thousands.
6	Data in Column 5 divided by six to obtain cattle equivalent.
7	Total livestock units, Column 1 plus Column 6.
8	Cattle as a percentage of all livestock units.

Source: *NkhSSSR* 1967, 428–31.

yields have varied greatly from year to year, being, for example, 55 tsentners (10 metric tsentners = 1 metric ton) per 10 hectares in 1965, 120 in 1966, and 89 in 1967. It will be noted in Table 9.16 that even greater fluctuations have occurred in certain regions than in the country as a whole. Such fluctuations pose serious problems for planners because they involve a large part of the Soviet grain supply. In a year of shortage such as 1963 the situation can be saved only by drawing on stocks, provided these are available, by importing grain, or by cutting down consumption. Partial remedies would appear to be to grow more of other cereals in the hope that they would suffer less severely from fluctuations in weather, or to put effort into raising grain yields in the Ukraine and North Caucasus, where yields already tend to be higher and the weather less variable than in the worst sufferers, Kazakhstan and West Siberia.

2. Grain maize was regarded in the late 1950's as a crop that could improve the grain situation and supplement though not of course replace wheat. In 1964, however, only about 14 million tons of maize grain were produced (cf, U.S.A. about 100 million tons) compared with 74 million tons of wheat. Like wheat yields, maize yields fluctuate considerably from year to year but, region for region, are consistently much higher. Commercially maize is only worth about 70% of wheat prices. From Table 9.16, showing data for 1965–67, it is clear that the most promising regions for grain maize cultivation are in the southern part of European U.S.S.R. High maize yields could also be obtained on irrigated land in Central Asia and elsewhere in the south, but such land can usually be better used.

3. Sugar beet is an example of a crop that was

Table 9.16. YIELDS OF SPRING WHEAT AND GRAIN MAIZE IN TSENTNERS PER 10 HECTARES AND OF SUGAR BEET IN TSENTNERS PER HECTARE IN 1965–67 BY ECONOMIC REGION

| | | Spring wheat | | | Grain maize | | | Sugar beet | |
Economic region	1965	1966	1967	1965	1966	1967	1965	1966	1967
E1 Northwest	86	72	102						
E2 Centre	103	90	136				90	112	172
E3 Volga-Vyatka	72	71	104				71	107	131
E4 Blackearth Centre	126	141	149	157	173	212	134	151	186
E5 Volga	82	110	117	78	132	112	80	109	156
E6 North Caucasus	79	145	104	255	243	280	169	209	256
E7 Ural	63	137	104				72	72	89
E8 West Siberia	48	132	76				100	115	138
E9 East Siberia	89	147	139				49	67	79
E10 Far East	72	89	114	175	213	214	86	56	84
E11 Donets-Dnepr	110	149	115	240	226	249	223	208	195
E12 Southwest	141	174	165	309	332	349	245	231	299
E13 South	87	79	116	261	277	210	211	216	175
E14 Baltic	164	141	163				154	195	247
E15 Transcaucasia	80	71	79	182	138	193	303	298	365
E16 Central Asia	44	61	51	234	262	276	347	387	374
E17 Kazakhstan	31	110	61	227	288	323	285	348	350
E18 Belorussia	116	118	142				152	197	254
E19 Moldavia	84	144	102	291	351	286	196	194	219
U.S.S.R.	55	120	89	252	260	262	188	195	230

Source: *NkhSSSR* 1967, 376, 380, 388.

mostly grown in a limited area, southern European U.S.S.R. Cultivation has been deliberately decentralised in the interests of regional self-sufficiency, but in some regions, at the expense of yield. The highest sugar beet yields are found in irrigated lands of the south, but Moldavia and the Southwest, traditional areas, also give consistently high yields by Soviet standards. In contrast, several regions lying further north in European U.S.S.R. and in Siberia have yields far below the Soviet mean.

4. Cotton can be cultivated commercially only in the hottest parts. Attempts were made to grow it in the Ukraine and North Caucasus, but currently almost all (over 90%) comes from Central Asia, a little from Transcaucasia and Kazakhstan. Even within this area, however, yields vary considerably, as shown in Table 9.17. In contrast to sugar beet, cotton cultivation tends to have contracted spatially more and more and is now largely confined to the most suitable oases of Uzbekistan, Tadjikistan and Turkmenistan. It is grown exclusively in irrigated areas.

Table 9.17. COTTON YIELDS IN TSENTNERS PER 10 HECTARES IN 1965–67 BY REPUBLICS

Republic	1965	1966	1967
Azerbaijan	156	154	159
Uzbekistan	241	251	252
Kirgizia	229	253	244
Tadjikistan	267	274	266
Turkmenistan	215	245	255
Kazakhstan	188	196	206
U.S.S.R.	232	243	245

Source: *NkhSSR* 1967, 385

Soviet agricultural planners are faced with the problem of whether to concentrate the cultivation of each crop in the areas that have consistently shown relatively high yields for that crop, thus increasing the length of haul of many products, or to grow crops in less favourable areas. Further, in the case of crops that can replace one another, particularly grain crops, they can choose to increase the cultivation of some at the expense of others. There is considerable scope for manipulating crops in the ways suggested, but whether this can be done as successfully under centrally planned agriculture as when each farmer makes his own decisions is doubtful. How success itself is assessed is indeed one of the main questions of Soviet Communism: by volume in tons, by value in roubles, by profitability in roubles per man hour, or even by volume or value per unit of land.

9.7 LAND TENURE

Since the two basic types of farm, *kolkhoz* (collective farms) and *sovkhoz* (state farms), occur in greatly differing proportions over the agricultural area of the U.S.S.R. it is relevant to consider how the two types of farm are run and how efficient they are. Both interregional differences in yield and within region differences in yield may be caused by variations in land tenure.

After the winding up of the New Economic Policy in the U.S.S.R. in the 1928–32 Five Year Plan, land tenure was reorganised. Most of the agricultural land was collectivised, but some was allocated to state farms. Since that period there has been a fairly consistent tendency to increase the number and extent of sovkhozes in relation to kolkhozes. Whereas at first sovkhozes occupied only 20–25% of the sown area, in 1967 they occupied nearly half. Their share has been increased both by the creation almost exclusively of sovkhozes in the new lands and by the conversion (in title) of kolkhozes to sovkhozes. A comparison of selected 1967 data brings out marked differences between the two types of farm, even now that they have become more similar (Table 9.18).

In 1967 there were about three times as many kolkhozes as sovkhozes, but the average sovkhoz has more than two and a half times as much sown area as the average kolkhoz. Although kolkhoz *households* and state farm *workers* are not directly comparable, there are clearly more persons per unit of farmed land in kolkhozes than in sovkhozes. This may not be deliberate policy, however, but just the result of the situation of sovkhozes in general in the more thinly peopled rural areas, including marginal areas such as parts of northern Kazakhstan, since 1953.

Kolkhoz households are allowed to have private plots. Sovkhoz workers have less freedom, though even they have some private land. Kolkhoz families have been criticised for

Table 9.18. COMPARISON OF KOLKHOZ AND SOVKHOZ FEATURES

(a) *Kolkhozes*

	1958	1965	1967
Total number of farms	69 100	36 900	36 800
Total number of households	18 800 000	15 400 000	15 300 000
Average number of households per farm	275	422	418
Total sown area in hectares	131 400 000	110 846 000	102 980 000
Average sown area per farm in hectares	1 900	3 000	2 800

(b) *Sovkhozes*

	1958	1965	1967
Total number of farms	6 002	11 642	12 783
Total number of workers	3 835 000	7 650 000	7 889 000
Average number of workers per farm	639	657	615
Total sown area in hectares	53 894 000	95 687 000	97 090 000
Average sown area per farm in hectares	9 000	7 700	7 600

Sources: *NkhSSSR* 1959, 423, 443.   *NkhSSSR* 1967, 466 *et seq.*

devoting much more effort to their private plots, which occupy only a small part of the farm area, but are used intensively and have high yields, than to the collective land. The two types of farm differ also according to payment of workers and to produce. In the past kolkhoz farmers have often fared very badly since they have depended on a small, sometimes non-existent surplus made by their collective and distributed among them according to work days put in. A more reliable and generous wage has been paid on state farms. Against the state farm system of payment, according to *The Times,* 4 November 1965, is the fact that work is often paid by piece rates, which encourages workers to chase after the number of formally completed assignments rather than worry about the success of the farm in total. Collective farm workers, on the other hand, theoretically benefit from the success of their farm as a whole, and individually from sidelines. Long hours of work to squeeze that little extra from the cow or the vegetable plot suggest low productivity, however, characteristic of an underdeveloped country with no more lucrative ways of spending one's time.

Recent information for the two types of farm suggests that the kolkhozes are not such a liability as they have often been pictured. To make them more efficient in terms of output per worker would release a large labour surplus in areas with little alternative employment, possibly without affecting total farm output. In spite of rumours and hints, little appears to have been done to change the basic systems of land tenure to something fundamentally different, although *The Times,* 12 December 1966, reported that near Omsk, six farmers had been allotted pieces of land and equipment and that in one year they had achieved a six-fold increase in production.

It is clear from Table 9.19 that the proportion of total sown land occupied by kolkhozes and by sovkhozes varies greatly from region to region. Table 9.19(b) ranks sovkhoz sown land as percentage of all sown land; the Soviet mean is 46%. Other data show, surprisingly, that production costs for most items are lower on kolkhozes than for sovkhozes. This may partly be due to the higher standard of living provided for sovkhoz workers, partly to the fact that kolkhozes are dominant in easier environmental conditions (Ukraine, Blackearth

Centre). Soviet data also reveal other regional variations. In particular, the number of families per kolkhoz varies greatly, ranging in 1967 from 184 per kolkhoz in the Baltic to 1 037 in Moldavia. Such variations (see Table 9.19) reflect to a considerable extent the size of agricultural settlements and reveal older features of the cultural landscape not yet eliminated. Large nucleated villages, for example, have long been common in the southern part of European U.S.S.R., but small villages and dispersed settlements are characteristic further north. Very marked regional variations in income per kolkhoz household have also been revealed for recent years in Soviet statistical yearbooks. The extreme regions are ranked in Table 9.19(c) (U.S.S.R. mean in 1967 was 1 346 roubles).

The trend generally in the late 1960's seems to be for the differences between kolkhoz and sovkhoz to be gradually reduced. In 1964, a kind of guaranteed basic wage was stipulated for kolkhoz workers; later, pensions for retired kolkhoz workers were introduced for the first time. Equipment and fertilisers seem to be finding their way to kolkhozes more readily than before.

9.8 AGRICULTURAL REGIONS

In many Soviet atlases and geography texts, 25 agricultural regions are mapped and described. They vary somewhat in number and exact location among publications. Rakitnikov[8] proposes a more detailed system of 41 regions for the Ukraine and main agricultural belt of the R.S.F.S.R. Several proposals are shown and discussed by Jackson,[9] who points out the difficulty experienced in the U.S.S.R. of combining physical and economic criteria for regional demarcation. In *A Geography of the USSR* 1 ed, a set used by N. Cherdantsev was shown and described in some detail. In this edition, the regions of Nikitin[10] are used. No attempt is made to describe the regions, but they are mapped in Fig. 9.14 and their main specialisms are shown in Table 9.20. Nikitin has 26 regions, the last of which (26) is largely forest or other non-agricultural land within the agricultural belt, and is not included in Fig. 9.14. Region 25, 'suburban' vegetables, potatoes and dairying, is greatly fragmented, occurring around

Table 9.19. ASPECTS OF FARM TYPE IN 1967 BY ECONOMIC REGIONS

(a) *Basic data*

	Economic region	1	2	3	4	5	6	7
E1	Northwest	1 580	1 520	48	1 172	572	226	1 282
E2	Centre	7 500	7 090	47	3 303	1 679	271	1 384
E3	Volga-Vyatka	5 440	2 180	27	1 935	337	336	1 041
E4	Blackearth Centre	7 740	3 010	27	1 754	363	527	1 283
E5	Volga	16 330	13 140	44	2 804	910	382	1 650
E6	North Caucasus	9 120	6 800	42	1 500	804	646	1 838
E7	Ural	8 240	9 510	53	1 479	678	304	1 538
E8	West Siberia	6 340	13 220	67	968	932	286	1 835
E9	East Siberia	3 410	5 370	60	710	368	230	2 251
E10	Far East	640	2 040	73	287	406	192	3 368
E11	Donets-Dnepr	10 560	3 180	22	3 061	620	486	1 489
E12	Southwest	10 570	1 150	9	5 561	361	583	908
E13	South	4 210	2 320	35	1 017	437	524	1 846
E14	Baltic	3 180	1 730	33	2 816	741	184	1 566
E15	Transcaucasia	1 800	680	25	3 141	718	280	778
E16	Central Asia	3 750	2 230	36	1 907	532	704	1 723
E17	Kazakhstan	4 170	29 270	87	470	1 539	448	2 000
E18	Belorussia	3 810	1 990	32	2 356	695	374	1 021
E19	Moldavia	1 540	260	14	543	91	1 037	1 300
	U.S.S.R.	109 930	106 690	46	36 784	12 783	418	1 346

Columns 1, 2   Area in thousands of hecares of arable land (*pashnya*) in 1 Kolkhozes, 2 Sovkhozes.
       3   Arable land in sovkhozes as percentage of total.
       4, 5   Total number of 4 Kolkhozes, 5 Sovkhozes.
       6   Average number of households (*dvor*) per kolkhoz.
       7   Income per kolkhoz household in roubles in 1967.

Source: *NkhSSSR* 1967, 345, 470, 474–5, 481.

(b) *Sovkhoz cropland as a percentage of all sown land in selected regions (data from Table 9.19(a))*

Rank	Region		Rank	Region	
1	Kazakhstan	87%	16	Transcaucasia	25%
2	Far East	73%	17	Donets-Dnepr	22%
3	West Siberia	67%	18	Moldavia	14%
4	East Siberia	60%	19	Southwest	9%

(c) *Kolkhoz family income in roubles in 1967 in selected regions (data from Table 9.19(a))*

Rank	Region		Rank	Region	
1	Far East	3 368	16	Volga-Vyatka	1 041
2	East Siberia	2 251	17	Belorussia	1 021
3	Kazakhstan	2 000	18	Southwest	908
4	South	1 846	19	Transcaucasia	778

the larger urban clusters. Each of the other 24 regions corresponds to a particular part or zone of the country. Some regions are defined by a single high value crop (eg region 8, sugar beet) which may occupy only a small proportion of total area. Most regions are defined by several specialisms, for example, region 7 (Baltic area) is 'dairying, pigs and fodder'. In Table 9.20, the specialisms of each region are referred to in order

sheep 4 in this order. X indicates no clear place in the ordering. The right-hand total shows the frequency of mention (maximum possible 25) of each agricultural item among the 25 regions. In the second part, for example, the Northwest (economic region E1) contains parts of agricultural regions 1, 2, 3, 5 and 25. A 1 (one) indicates presence of the agricultural region in the economic one (and vice versa).

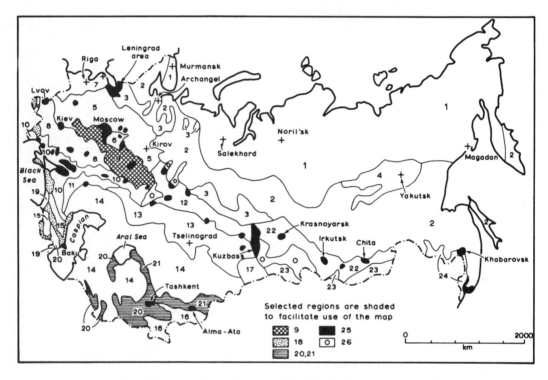

Fig. 9.14.   Agricultural regions of the U.S.S.R. See text for explanation.

of mention, thus being ranked in assumed importance. The usefulness of this classification lies in the fact that it brings together, though very crudely, the many possible single distribution maps. It bears no positive relationship, however, to the distribution of the 19 economic regions; its relationship to these is shown in the lower part of Table 9.20.

The table is used as follows. In the first part, for example, region 11 (roughly the lower Volga) has in its column 3, 1, 2 and 4. This means that its description is Grain 1, meat 2, milk 3,

9.9 AREAL RELATIONSHIPS IN SOVIET AGRICULTURE

It is profitable to devote some space to showing results of the application of factor analysis, since Soviet geographers do not appear to have done this, at least publicly, with any of their data, although they have, for example, with Canadian data. In this study, 21 variables have been used for 87 areas. The areas are 71 units of the R.S.F.S.R., 3 for the Ukraine and 13 other, 1 for each remaining S.S.R. Some areas are large and

Table 9.20. AGRICULTURAL REGIONS OF THE U.S.S.R. SEE TEXT FOR EXPLANATION AND FIG. 9.14 FOR LOCATION

Agricultural items	Agricultural regions																									Total
	1	2	3	4	5	6	7	8	9	10	11	12	13	14	15	16	17	18	19	20	21	22	23	24	25	
Hunting	1	1																								2
Reindeer		2																								1
Agricultural			2																							1
Livestock			2	1											×	×	×					2	1	3		8
Arable				2																						1
Milk (= dairy)			1		2	1	1	3	4	3	3	1	3	1	1	3	2				3				3	16
Flax					1																					1
Potatoes						2			2																2	3
Pigs							2	5	6																	3
Fodder (Korm)										2																1
Sugar beet								1																		1
Grain								2	1	1	2	3	1	3							2	1				9
Meat								4	5	4		2	2	1	2	2	1				2				1	11
Hemp									3																	1
Oil seeds										2																1
Sheep											4			2	3	1		3			4					6
Natural pasture														1												1
Mountain															×	×	×									3
Fruit																	1									1
Vine																	2									1
Tobacco																		3								1
Subtropical perennial																			1							1
Cotton																				1						1
Southern intensive																					×					1
Rice–soybeans																								2		1
'Suburban' vegetables																									1	1

Table 9.20 contd

Economic region		Agricultural regions																									Total
		1	2	3	4	5	6	7	8	9	10	11	12	13	14	15	16	17	18	19	20	21	22	23	24	25	
E1	Northwest	1		1			1		1																		1	5
E2	Centre		1	1			1		1																		1	5
E3	Volga-Vyatka			1		1			1		1																1	5
E4	Blackearth Centre								1						1													2
E5	Volga				1						1	1	1		1												1	6
E5	North Caucasus											1	1			1			1								1	5
E7	Ural		1	1									1	1				1										5
E8	West Siberia		1	1							1	1	1	1										1			1	8
E9	East Siberia		1	1									1											1	1			5
E10	Far East		1	1	1								1											1	1	1		7
E11	Donets-Dnepr						1				1																1	3
E12	Southwest									1	1								1								1	4
E13	South													1					1								1	3
E14	Baltic							1													1							2
E15	Transcaucasia										1					1			1	1	1							5
E16	Central Asia					1											1			1		1					1	5
E17	Kazakhstan														1					1	1	1					1	5
E18	Belorussia							1						1	1													3
E19	Moldavia													1	1				1									3

Table 9.21.

(a) *Matrix of correlation coefficients (r) for 21 agricultural variables*

	1	2	3	4	5	6	7	8	9	10	11	12	13	14	15	16	17	18	19	20	21
1	10																				
2	8	10																			
3	2	0	10																		
4	2	1	2	10																	
5	8	5	2	0	10																
6	8	5	2	0	9	10															
7	6	3	4	2	6	7	10														
8	5	4	1	1	6	5	2	10													
9	3	2	4	2	4	4	4	4	10												
10	3	2	4	1	3	3	4	2	6	10											
11	3	1	6	1	4	4	5	2	5	3	10										
12	3	2	1	3	3	3	5	0	3	4	1	10									
13	1	1	2	2	1	1	2	2	5	4	2	4	10								
14	2	2	2	4	4	4	1	7	5	4	2	2	4	10							
15	2	2	2	5	1	0	2	4	2	1	1	2	2	7	10						
16	0	1	3	1	1	1	2	3	0	0	2	2	0	6	4	10					
17	2	1	5	3	4	3	2	6	5	4	3	0	5	8	5	0	10				
18	5	4	1	0	5	4	2	7	2	0	1	0	2	4	2	1	4	10			
19	3	3	6	5	2	2	0	0	3	1	3	3	1	2	4	0	3	0	10		
20	1	2	6	4	1	1	0	3	3	1	5	4	2	6	7	1	6	1	5	10	
21	1	2	6	4	0	0	1	2	5	5	3	1	4	6	4	0	7	0	5	6	10

(b) *Percentage weight of factors*

Factor	Weight	Cumulative weight
Factor I	31·4	31·4
Factor II	21·3	52·7
Factor III	12·0	64·7
Factor IV	8·7	73·4

(c) *Factor loadings*

Rank	Factor I	Loading	Factor II	Loading
1	Fodder (17)	−0·83	Physical consensus (1)	−0·73
2	Cereals (14)	+0·79	Sheep (19)	+0·69
3	Urban (9)	−0·72	Cows (20)	−0·65
4	Persons per sown (8)	−0·71	Relief (2)	−0·61
5	Soil (5)	+0·69	Wheat (15)	+0·61
6	Sown per total (6)	+0·66	Sown (6)	−0·58
8	Milk yields (21)	−0·60	Soil (5)	−0·54
9	Kolkhoz size (11)	+0·59	Precipitation (4)	−0·54
10	Kolkhoz/sovkhoz	+0·58		
11	Physical consensus (1)	+0·58		

Variable reference number is shown in brackets

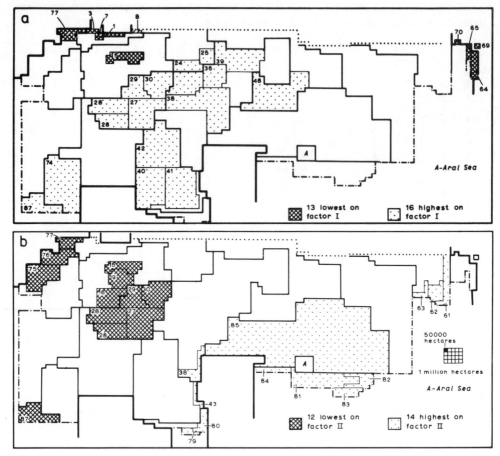

Fig. 9.15.   Factors I and II derived from 21 agricultural variables. The area of each division on the map is proportional to the sown area (in 1965) of the economic region or oblast level unit it represents. Divisions of the economic regions are distinguished only if they belong to highest or lowest groups on each factor. Numbering of regions is standard throughout (see Table 2.2). Numbers of selected units: 15 Moscow, 77 Estonia, 85 Kazakhstan.

diverse, particularly Kazakhstan.

The following 21 variables were used:

1-5 Physical
 1 Consensus of 2-5
 2 Relief
 3 Temperature
 4 Precipitation
 5 Soil

6-9 Land and people
 6 Sown area as percentage of all land
 7 Rural population density
 8 Persons per unit of sown area
 9 Urban population as percentage of total population

10-13 Organisational
10 Collective farms as a percentage of all farms
11 Size of collective farm
12 Income of collective farm family
13 Specialists in agriculture

14-21 Crops and livestock
14 Cereals as a percentage of total sown area
15 Wheat as a percentage of sown area
16 Industrial crops and vegetables as a percentage of sown area
17 Fodder as a percentage of sown area
18 Cattle per sown area
19 Sheep per cattle
20 Dairy cows as percentage of all cattle
21 Milk yields.

Table 9.22. WEIGHTINGS OF EXTREME AREAS ON FACTORS I AND II

	Factor I *(fodder versus cereals)*			*Factor II* *(dairying versus wheat/sheep)*	
Rank	*Area*	*Weighting*	*Rank*	*Area*	*Weighting*
1	Moldavia	+10·3	1	Kirgizia	+10·0
2	Kursk˙	7·6	2	Tadjikistan	9·9
3	Krasnodar	7·1	3	Tuvinsk (A)	9·8
4	Belgorod	7·1	4	Chita	8·5
5	Voronezh	6·9	5	Yakut (A)	8·0
6	Stavropol'	6·9	6	Kazakhstan	7·9
7	Chuvash (A)	6·6	7	Azerbaijan	7·9
8	Tambov	6·5	8	Buryat (A)	7·7
9	Rostov	6·5	9	Turkmenistan	7·6
10	Mordov (A)	5·9	10	Uzbekistan	7·2
11	Orenburg	5·9	11	Kalmyk (A)	6·7
12	Tatar (A)	5·9	12	Dagestan	6·6
13	South	5·8	13	Astrakhan'	6·4
14	Saratov	5·8	14	Armenia	5·6
15	Lipetsk	5·8			
16	Ul'yanovsk	5·6			
75	Moscow	−5·8			
76	Primorsk	−6·4	76	Moldavia	−4·2
77	Estonia	−6·7	77	Tula	−4·3
78	Archangel	−7·3	78	Voronezh	−4·6
79	Khabarovsk	−8·8	79	Orel	−4·8
80	Yakut (A)	−10·3	80	Belgorod	−4·8
81	Komi (A)	−11·6	81	Moscow	−4·9
82	Leningrad	−11·9	82	Estonia	−5·0
83	Karelia	−16·0	83	Tambov	−5·2
84	Sakhalin	−17·2	84	Kursk	−5·5
85	Kamchatka	−18·6	85	Latvia	−5·5
86	Murmansk	−21·8	86	Lipetsk	−6·2
87	Magadan	−22·3	87	Lithuania	−6·3

Factor analysis is used in this study first to describe the correlation between each pair of distributions, and secondly to facilitate a classification of the 87 units on a multivariate basis. None of the pairs would be expected to show complete intercorrelation. Some, on the other hand, must to some extent be correlated, either positively or negatively. Thus 14 and 15 will be positively correlated because wheat is such a large component of all cereals, while 14 (cereals) and 17 (fodder) will be negatively correlated, because together they make up nearly all the sown area and complement each other.˙

To save space, the complete 21 × 21 correlation matrix is included only in very compact form (Table 9.21). Each correlation has been rounded to one decimal place. The decimal point has then been removed. Negative correlations have a bar underneath. Thus,

+ 1·000 becomes 10,
+ 0·356 becomes 4 and
− 0·613 becomes 6.

The correlation between variables 1 and 2 is 0·7645; this becomes 8 in the correlation matrix. From the matrix it is possible to find which pairs of variables are strongly intercorrelated; this task is, however, greatly simplified by the factors, as they group families of interrelated variables. In this study, the first four factors take up 73·4% of all the variation in 21 variables. The 'weights' are shown in Table 9.21(b). Table 9.21(c) shows the loading of the more heavily correlated variables on Factors I and II.

Factor I shows the connection on the one hand between cereals (14), abundant sown land (6), superior physical conditions (1), especially soil (5) and large collective farm size (11), and on the other between fodder (17), lack of sown land (8), urban population (9) and high milk yields (21). Factor II associates wheat cultivation (15) and sheep orientated livestock (19), and contrasts these with favourable physical conditions (1) and cows as a percentage of cattle (20).

From the foregoing it can be seen that even on the basis of 21 variables, Soviet agriculture is full of complexity and contradictions. There are only partial relationships in reality. Which relationships are directly causal and which are worth further investigation is left to the discretion of the individual. A different picture of Soviet agriculture emerges, however, from the mapping of the first two factors according to the individual scores or weightings of each of the 87 areas. Extreme values are given in Table 9.22 and are mapped in Fig. 9.15. On Factor I, the cereal orientated middle belt, from the Ukraine through the Blackearth Centre, North Caucasus and Middle Volga, contrasts with the fodder orientated Northwest and Far East. On Factor II, the cattle raising Baltic and Centre contrasts with the sheep raising Caspian and desert U.S.S.R.

9.10 AGRICULTURE IN THE 1966–70 FIVE YEAR PLAN: SUMMARY

In March 1965 various resolutions were passed stressing the need to increase the volume of production of both foodstuffs and industrial raw materials. During the 1966–70 Plan it was proposed to double state capital outlay in agriculture, strengthen the technical facilities of farms and give better material incentives to workers.

1. During 1966–70 the average yearly output of agricultural products should be 25% higher than in 1961–65. Emphasis is placed in particular on grain and livestock.
2. The output of grain during the period should average 30% higher than during the preceding five years. A sound grain base should be established outside the Blackearth lands. Rice should be grown more in the Syr-Dar'ya and Amu Dar'ya valleys (Central Asia), North Caucasus

and southern Ukraine; more reliable harvest should be obtained in the new lands. The importance of the following is also stressed: cotton, sugar beet, oil seeds, flax, potatoes, vegetables, tea, fruits, berries, vines. Grain targets for 1970 for the major Republics are: R.S.F.S.R. 110–112 million tons, Ukraine 37–38 million tons, Kazakhstan 21–22 million tons.
3. Higher yields are desirable. Improve crop rotation, apply more fertilisers, combat soil erosion, and plant tree belts to protect fields.
4. By 1970, 55 million tons of fertilisers should be delivered to farms each year. The quality of fertilisers should be improved. They should be used by farms on a scientific basis. Loss during their transportation and storage should be reduced. The importance of pesticides is also stressed.
5. Land improvement programme:
   (a) Drainage of humid areas (non-Blackearth part of European U.S.S.R., also Far East). Total area: drain 6–6½ million hectares, improve 9 million hectares, lime 28 million hectares.
   (b) Irrigation in dry areas. Total area 2½ million hectares in Central Asia, Transcaucasia, North Caucasus, Trans-Volga, Southern Ukraine, Kazakhstan, Moldavia. Increase rice cultivation.
   (c) Create a system of specialist centres to carry out improvement and serve in a technical advisory capacity for farms.
6. Increase meat, milk, eggs and wool production. Improve fodder base for livestock. Improve the quality of livestock.
7. Incentives to increased production will be achieved by paying higher prices for items produced on farms above the firm targets fixed by plan. This would not only affect grain, but also industrial and other crops.
8. Links should be greatly strengthened between farms and organisations that process farm products. Perishable products should have direct access to the traders who are to dispose of them.

9. More capital should be made available to agriculture, more construction work carried out in rural areas and more tractors, combines and lorries made available.

10. Other improvements mentioned include the establishment or reorganisation of machine-tractor stations, the extension of electricity availability and 40-45% higher productivity of labour. State planning of agriculture should be fused with local initiative. Credit should be more readily available. Farms should specialise more. More processing and local manufacturing is needed on farms themselves. Experts should be more widely available and advances in biology and other sciences applied. Amenities should be improved in rural areas.

A report in *Pravda*, 31 October 1968, on agriculture during 1965-67 noted the heavy capitalisation in terms of tractors, machinery and fertilisers. The total output for the three years 1965-67 was 15% higher than for 1962-1964. Table 9.23 compares progress over two periods of three years. Note that the middle period (1962-64) included the very bad harvest of 1963. The impression given is one of satisfactory progress, with overall production higher thanks

to increased yields rather than the development of new land. The fertiliser campaign of the early 1960's may be showing results but this is only the beginning, for it is proposed to raise fertiliser production from 47 million tons in 1968 to 95 million in 1972.

REFERENCES

1. *Atlas sel'skogo khozyaystva SSSR*, 73 (Moscow, 1960)
2. NIMITZ, N., 'The Lean Years' *Problems of Communism*, May-June 1965
3. ZHIRKOV, K. F., 'Dust Storms in the Steppes of Western Siberia and Kazakhstan' *Soviet Geogr.*, **5**, No 5, 33-41, 1964
4. FEYGIN, Ya. G. *et al.*, *Zakonomernosti i faktory razvitiya ekonomicheskikh rayonov SSSR* (Moscow, 1965)
5. ANDERSON, J., 'Fodder and livestock production in the Ukraine: a case study of Soviet agricultural policy' *E. Lakes Geogr.*, **3**, 29-46, Oct. 1967
6. *NkhSSSR* 1964, 267
7. JACKSON, W. A. D., 'Durum Wheat and the expansion of dry farming in the Soviet Union' *An. Ass. Am. Geogr.*, **46**, No 4, 405-10, 1956
JACKSON, W. A. D., 'The Russian Non-Chernozem Wheat Base' *An. Ass. Am. Geogr.*, **49**, No 2, 97-109, 1959
JACKSON, W. A. D., 'The problem of Soviet agricultural regionalization' *Slavic Review*, **20**, No 4, 656-78, 1961
8. RAKITNIKOV, A. N. and MUKOMEL, I. F., 'Agricultural regionalisation' *Soviet Geogr.*, **5**, No 9, 24-34, 1964
9. JACKSON, W. A. D., 'The Virgin and Idle Lands Program Reappraised' *An. Ass. Am. Geogr.*, **52**, No 1, 69-79, 1962
10. NIKITIN, N. P., *Ekonomicheskaya geografiya SSSR*, 184-5 (Moscow, 1966)

Table 9.23. TOTAL SOVIET FARM OUTPUT IN THREE PERIODS

	1962–64 as percentage of 1959–61	1965–67 as percentage of 1962–64
U.S.S.R.	103	115
R.S.F.S.R.	104	113
Ukraine	101	116
Belorussia	99	131
Uzbekistan	107	118
Kazakhstan	109	108
Georgia	104	119
Azerbaijan	96	120
Lithuania	101	129
Moldavia	117	122
Latvia	89	126
Kirgizia	119	119
Tadjikistan	114	121
Armenia	98	118
Turkmenistan	106	130
Estonia	97	118

Source: *Pravda*, 31 Oct. 1968.

BIBLIOGRAPHY

ARMSTRONG, T., Farming on the Permafrost, *Geogrl Mag.*, **40**, 11 Mar. 1968
DIBB, P., *The Economics of the Soviet Wheat Industry* (Bureau of Agricultural Economics, Canberra, Australia, 1966)
GRANOVSKAYA, A. Ye., 'Specialisation of Agriculture in Relatively Similar Natural Environments of the U.S.S.R. and the United States' *Soviet Geogr.*, **9**, No 10, 830-37, 1968
KOVALEV, S. A., *Geograficheskoye izucheniye sel'skogo khozyaystva* (Moscow, 1960)
KUZNETSOV, G. A., 'An Economic Appraisal of Lands in Connection with the Organization of Lands on State Farms of the Virgin Lands' *Soviet Geogr.*, **4**, No 9, 10-16, 1963
Sel'skoye khozyaystvo SSSR (Sel'khozgiz, Moscow, 1958)

10

Industry

10.1 INTRODUCTION

Although Soviet industrial capacity has grown many times since 1917 the pre-existing distribution of industry has left a profound mark on the present one. Modern Soviet industry exists in both old and new regions. The old regions already have problems of depletion of their initial attractive resources (eg Donbass coalfield), antiquated factories still in use (Moscow area, Ural) and other features common also in West European and North American equivalent areas.

The dominant position of European Russia in 1908 is shown by its share of 96·5% of the total factory industry, as seen in Fig. 10.1 and Table 10.1. Regions 1, 2 and 4 are roughly equivalent to the following present ones: Centre, Northwest and Baltic, and Donets-Dnepr. With the loss of the Baltic and Poland in the interwar period, industrial Russia of the 1920's was left with an even more restricted base round Leningrad, Moscow and the Donbass. Only in the 1930's did the revival of the Ural region and the establishment of completely new bases such as the Kuzbass and Transcaucasia begin to resemble the present distribution. The *Bol'shoy Sovetskiiy Atlas* (1940) reveals in many maps the still dominant role of the older areas right up to 1940. During World War II, industrial growth was almost exclusively along the Volga or to the east of it and the general effect of the period 1930–50 was to raise the eastern regions relatively, a trend

that will be illustrated later. The return to the U.S.S.R. of the Baltic Republics and of such places as Lvov bolstered the west a little, but the emergence of Comecon has been more important in that respect since it has given new outlets for Soviet resources located in the western part of the Soviet Union. Hooson,[2] describing the planners' dilemma as the 'east-west see-saw' suggests:

'There may well be some validity in the hypothesis that when the politico-economic atmosphere is one of aggressive, optimistic expansiveness and/or comparative affluence, there is a tendency to invest more in some of the eastern regions, even though the expectation of return may be very long-term and the yield less than might be obtained from a similar investment in places closer to home.'

He suggests the Volga, North Caucasus, and eastern Ukraine to be attractive regions for development in the mid-1960's.

The picture of Soviet industry has also been profoundly modified by the shift from light to heavy industry and the continued expansion, or completely new development, of coal, oil, iron ore and other metals, chemicals and so on. Soviet industry is divided into two basic types of production referred to as groups A and B. The former represents the production of means of production and the latter the production of consumer goods. Almost invariably since 1928

Table 10.1. REGIONAL DISTRIBUTION OF RUSSIAN INDUSTRIAL CAPACITY IN 1908

Region	*Percentage of* industry	*Percentage of* population	*Roubles per capita*
1 Central industrial	27·5	11·0	78
2 Northwest and Baltic	16·1	5·7	87
3 Poland (now)	11·4	7·5	48
4 Southern mining and industrial	8·4	7·1	37
5 Southwest	10·3	15·6	21
6 Other European Russia	22·8	38·7	19
7 Asiatic Russia	3·5	14·4	8

Source: Feygin,[1] 64

Fig. 10.1.   *Distribution of Russian Industrial Capacity in 1908. Source: Feygin,[1] 64.*

production figures have shown a faster growth in group A than in group B. In 1928, group A accounted for 40% of capacity, group B for 60%, but by 1965 the proportions were 75% to 25%. Total production has grown many times since 1928 and for the period 1960–67 alone an overall increase of 80% is claimed (1960 = 100, 1967 = 180; group A = 190, group B = 160).

Soviet industrial growth figures have been questioned and are no doubt in some respects suspect. It has, however, become an unpalatable fact to many Western politicians that fast sustained growth is still being maintained in the U.S.S.R. The subject is discussed in a very readable way by Powell.[3] Growth during 1960–67 was, however, very uneven among branches, as shown in Table 10.2(a). These figures are extremely relevant to the study of the regional distribution of industrial capacity since some regions have a larger share of fast growing branches than other regions. During this period population grew by about 12%. A roughly similar range of growth emerges in Table 10.2(b) showing the figures for the 1960–67 growth of 'industrial-productive' basic funds in selected branches.

Selected major items of Soviet industrial

Table 10.2.

(a) *Growth rates of selected branches of industry, 1960–67 (1960 = 100)*

Capital		Consumer and food	
Chemicals, etc.	249	Knitwear	217
Engineering	232	Fish	188
Electricity	211	Fats and dairy	167
Glass	201	Meat	162
Building materials	184	Sugar	144
Iron and steel	169	Leather, etc.	139
Fuel	155	Woollen	138
Wood and paper	142	Flour	137
		Cotton	123

(b) *Growth of 'industrial-productive' basic funds, 1960–67 (1960 = 100)*

Capital		Consumer and food	
Chemicals	277	Food	184
Electricity	221	Light industry	166
Engineering, etc.	199	Fuel	161
Iron and steel	198	Wood and paper	157
Building materials	193		

Sources: *NkhSSSR* 1967, 189, 215.

production are shown in Table 10.3. Absolute figures are given, but the data, although mainly in tons, are not comparable down the columns. Unfortunately it is not easy to calculate the value of each item. The 1958–65 figures represent the performance during the Seven Year Plan. A particular feature to note is the slow growth of coal production compared with that of oil and particularly of natural gas. The impressive achievements in cement, steel and fertiliser production should also be noted. By 1970, however, doubts were being expressed about reaching many targets of the 1966–70 Five Year Plan outlined at the end of this chapter. With regard to Soviet industrial production figures in general, the following points should be borne in mind. First, some items (eg oil, iron ore, timber) are exported in large quantities. Secondly, some must be nearing saturation (footwear, soap). Thirdly, some began from little or nothing in 1928, which makes subsequent percentage growth appear astronomical. A careful comparison with West European, U.S. and Japanese *per capita* figures is needed to put the Soviet achievements in perspective.

Workers in industry (*promyshlennost'*) have

Table 10.3. MAJOR ITEMS OF INDUSTRIAL PRODUCTION IN SELECTED YEARS FROM 1928–68

	1928	1940	1958	1965	1967	1968
Electricity (10^9 kWh)	5	48	235	507	589	638
Oil (10^6 ton)	12	31	113	243	288	309
Gas (10^9 m^3)	0·3	3·4	29·9	129·4	159	171
Coal (10^6 ton)	36	166	493	578	595	594
Cement (10^6 ton)	2	6	33	72	85	88
Pig iron (10^6 ton)	3	15	40	66	75	79
Steel (10^6 ton)	4	18	55	91	102	107
Rolled steel (10^6 ton)	3	13	43	71	82	85
Iron ore (10^6 ton)	6	30	89	153	168	177
Coke (10^6 ton)	4	21	51	68	*n.a.	155(?)
Fertilisers (10^6 ton)	negligible	3	12	31	40	43
Motor vehicles ($\times 10^3$)	1	145	511	616	729	801
Tractors ($\times 10^3$)	1	32	220	355	405	423
Paper (10^3 ton)	284	812	2 169	3 231	3 800	4 000
Cloth (10^6 m)	3 010	4 522	7 539	9 127	*n.a.	8 326
Footwear (leather) (pairs $\times 10^6$)	58	211	356	486	561	597
Meat (10^3 ton)	678	1 501	3 372	5 245	6 400	6 600
Fish (10^3 ton)	840	1 404	2 936	5 774	6 500	6 700
Soap (10^3 ton)	311	700	1 365	1 926	1 650	1 700

*n.a. – not available

Sources: *NkhSSSR* 1965, 130–9
  Pravda, 25 Jan. 1968, *Pravda,* 26 Jan. 1969

more than doubled between 1940 (9 971 000) and 1965 (22 206 000).Between 1958 and 1965 the number increased by 29%, but as already noted industrial production rose by 84% over this period, so much slack was still being taken up by increasing labour productivity. The Soviet press frequently stresses the need both to increase industrial output by making more efficient use of capacity and to improve the quality of output. For example, *Pravda, 30*

ratio of one proportion to the other (×100) gives an index of deviation about the national mean (= 100) for heavier and lighter branches.

The figures in Table 10.4 must be supplemented by a consideration of the relationship of labour to raw materials and to fuel and energy. In Table 10.5 the relative importance of labour is expressed in terms of the proportion (in percentages) for each industry of the expenditure *(struktura zatrat)* on industrial

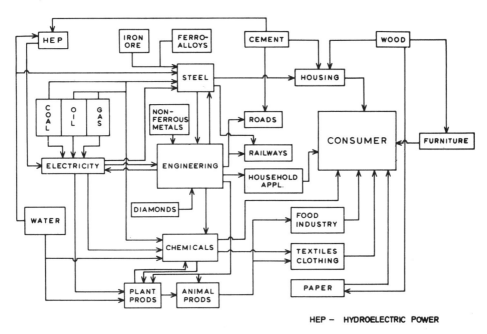

Fig. 10.2.   The interrelationship of selected branches of the Soviet economy.

November 1967, refers to quality, reliability and durability of output, while *Pravda, 31* January 1969, talks of automation, organisation, special-isation and technology. It is common to read of a particular factory or farm squeezing more out of its plant or land than was specified in the national plan and although this is obviously gratifying to all concerned, it suggests that the plan itself was underestimated.

The total labour force in industry was 28,997 000 in 1967, 81% being the workers *(rabochiye)*, over 10% technical, and 4% clerical. The workers were distributed among selected leading branches of the economy in 1967 in the proportions shown in Table 10.4. Capital investment was shared out very differently. The

production going on raw materials, fuel and energy, and wages. For all industry, the 1967 figures are: raw materials 64·4%, fuel and energy 5·8%, wages 16·9%, all other outlays 12·9%. The importance of raw materials to light industry and of wages in coal mining may be seen. In a country still short of manpower, especially male labour, the attractiveness of oil and gas against coal is obvious. The data in the table should also be considered in the light of the distribution of different branches of industry in the economic regions and the composition of industry in them.

Other aspects of industrial organisation should not be overlooked: size of firm, employment of female labour and so on; in particular the complexity of the interrelationship of branches in Soviet industry should be stressed. Lack of space prevents a discussion of this aspect, but it should be appreciated that agriculture is easier than industry to plan from the point of view of items involved, but more difficult because of its vulnerability to unpredictable weather conditions. Some idea of the complexity even of a

bare minimum of selected items in industry is suggested in Fig. 10.2. The prominent position of electricity, steel, engineering and chemicals, key growth industries and leading links, is reflected in the diagram. The consumer puts capital back into the system, but absorbs an ever increasing amount of what is produced, to the disgust, one feels, of Soviet planners.

Table 10.4. DISTRIBUTION OF LABOUR AND CAPITAL AMONG MAJOR BRANCHES OF INDUSTRY, 1967

Branch	Total employment	Percentage employment	capital	Capital/Employment ×100
Electricity	428	1·8	15·3	850
Coal	1 009	4·3	6·1	142
Iron and steel	1 086	4·6	10·5	229
Chemicals	1 149	4·9	8·9	182
Engineering	8 173	39·7	19·7	50
Wood, paper	2 341	9·9	5·3	54
Building materials	1 545	6·6	6·3	95
Light	4 005	17·2	4·4	26
Food	2 246	9·5	8·9	94
All branches	23 594	100·0	100·0	100

Source: *NkhSSSR* 1967, 207, 216–7.

Table 10.5. RELATIVE IMPORTANCE OF RAW MATERIALS, FUEL, AND WAGES IN MAJOR BRANCHES OF INDUSTRY

Raw Materials		Fuel and Energy		Wages	
Food Industry	85·9	Electricity	54·3	Coal	39·0
Light Industry	84·5	Iron and Steel	14·2	Wood	31·5
		Oil	13·3	Engineering	27·6
		Building Materials	11·8	Building Materials	25·2
		Chemicals	9·6	Oil	17·3
		Gas	9·1		
All Industry	**64·4**	**All Industry**	**5·8**	**All Industry**	**16·9**
Chemicals	58·3	Wood, etc.	5·5	Gas	15·2
		Coal	4·0	Chemicals	15·0
Engineering	56·1			Electricity	14·3
Iron and Steel	55·0	Engineering	3·5	Iron and Steel	14·1
Wood and Paper	41·6				
Building Materials	40·2	Food	1·7	Light	10·0
Gas	34·4				
Coal	25·8	Light	0·9	Food	5·7
Oil	0·0				
Electricity	0·0				

Source: *NkhSSSR* 1967, 225.

10.2 THE REGIONAL DISTRIBUTION OF INDUSTRY

Soviet industrial capacity, both total and in specific branches, is distributed very unevenly (in per population terms) among the economic regions according to various criteria. Unfortunately data are almost non-existent for some branches, patchy for others and adequate only for a few (eg timber, footwear, textiles). Table 10.6 is mainly for the early 1960's because data were superior then. Perhaps the best single measure of the industrial importance of the 19 regions is the *per capita* basic funds brought into

action during 1959–65. The mean for the U.S.S.R. was 97, the extremes being the Far East with 170 and Moldavia with 44. The spread is shown in Column 1 of Table 10.6 and is mapped in Fig. 10.3(a). *Per capita* consumption of electricity in Column 2 is another index; it correlates fairly strongly with *per capita* basic investment, though the Far East in particular is anomalous. Electricity consumption only represents industry roughly because it has other users as well and is bound to be very high in heavy industrial regions (Ural, Donets-Dnepr); moreover it is extensively moved across regional boundaries. Column 3 and Fig. 10.3(b) show

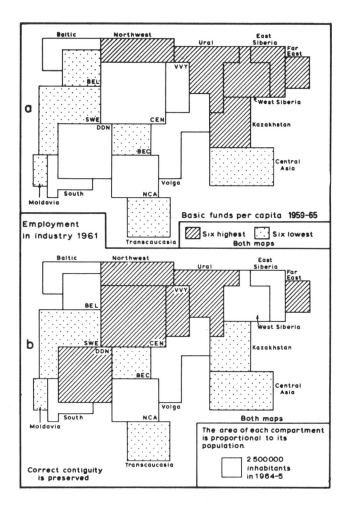

Fig. 10.3. *(a) The distribution of basic funds per capita during 1959-65. (b) Employment in industry in 1961.*

1961 employment in industry. Columns 4 and 5 show other aspects of industry related to the effectiveness of use of labour. Unlike Columns 1 and 2, they do not indicate relative size or strength of industry in *per capita* terms. Column 4 shows the relative weight of labour supply *(trudovykh resursov)* as percentages of national mean. In column 5 three types of region are distinguished:

A Regions with adequate labour using this at the level of the national average or above.

B Regions with an excess of labour and a low level of use.

C Newly opened up regions with a shortage of labour and a low level of use.

Column 6 shows the use of labour supply, occupied in general production in 1963.

Quite a different picture of the regions is given by the data in Column 7, which shows the rate of growth of industrial capacity during 1960-67. The least industrialised European regions (Moldavia and Belorussia) join the new Asiatic regions (Kazakhstan and East Siberia) at the top end of the scale, but the Centre and Northwest show the lowest growth indices. There can be few more difficult tasks for Soviet planners than to decide whether to allow some

Table 10.6. THE REGIONAL DISTRIBUTION OF SELECTED ASPECTS OF SOVIET INDUSTRY

Economic region		1	2	3	4	5	6	7	8
E10	Far East	170	75	122	106	C	97	189	147
E9	East Siberia	159	274	106	99	C	99	194	154
E17	Kazakhstan	135	73	56	93	C	93	200	138
E1	Northwest	133	98	164	108	A/C	110	159	144
E8	West Siberia	121	133	113	100	C	102	180	144
E7	Ural	116	227	139	101	A	105	177	149
E2	Centre	112	84	174	107	A	111	154	136
E6	Volga	109	133	115	98	A	102	197	151
E11	Donets-Dnepr	103	168	146	107	A	100	172	142*
E13	South	99	64	81	108	B	100	195	142*
	U.S.S.R.	97	100	107	100		100	180	142
E14	Baltic	94	77	111	109	A	101	199	145†
E6	North Caucasus	82	60	81	99	B	96	183	142
E3	Volga-Vyatka	70	67	127	99	A	102	178	146
E15	Transcaucasia	66	78	65	91	B	89	173	127†
E4	Blackearth Centre	64	50	71	96	B	97	193	146
E18	Belorussia	62	46	72	99	B	99	211	144
E16	Central Asia	61	43	44	82	B	91	184	126†
E12	Southwest	49	36	63	101	B	92	192	142*
E19	Moldavia	44	40	43	100	B	93	211	132

1 Basic funds put into action during 1959–65 (inclusive) in roubles per inhabitant.
2 Electricity consumption in 1965 *per capita* (U.S.S.R. mean = 100).
3 Employment in industry in 1961, persons per 1 000 total population.
4 Distribution of work resources *(trudovykh resursov)* 1963, U.S.S.R. = 100.
5 Threefold grouping of regions according to the nature of the labour force and the availability of work resources.
6 Use of work resources 1963.
7 Overall growth of industrial production 1960–67, 1960 = 100.
8 Growth of labour productivity, 1958 = 100.

* Ukraine mean.
† Unweighted mean for constituent S.S.R.'s.

Sources: 2 *NkhSSSR* 1965, 170.
             4 Feygin,[1] 184.
             5 Feygin,[1] 185.
             6 Feygin,[1] 188.
             7 *NkhSSSR* 1967, 191.
             8 *NkhSSSR* 1965, 146, *NkhRSFSR* 1965, 71–2.

regions to grow faster than others, and if so, which regions these should be. Fortunately R.S.F.S.R. oblast level data were available at the time of writing for 1958–65 and the detail for these plus the 14 other individual Republics gives a good idea of preferences during that period. The extremes are mapped in Fig. 10.4 and listed in Table 10.7.

Table 10.7. GROWTH OF INDUSTRIAL PRODUCTION DURING 1958–65

Rank	Division	Growth rate	Rank	Division	Growth rate
1	Mordov (A)	285	78	Chita	159
2	Orel	269	79	Vladimir	159
3	Tuvinsk (A)	255	80	Yaroslavl'	157
4	Yakut (A)	248	81	Kirov	156
5	Volgograd	248	82	Leningrad City	156
6	Kalmyk (A)	246	83	Karelia (A)	154
7	Belgorod	245	84	Sakhalin	151
8	Kabardino-B. (A)	232	85	Moscow City	143
9	Pskov	229	86	Kostroma	136
10	Ryazan'	229	87	Ivanovo	127
11	Lithuania (R)	224			
12	Chuvash (A)	223		U.S.S.R. mean	184
13	Bashkir (A)	221			
14	Kurgan	217			
15	Kaliningrad	216			
16	Kursk	215			
17	Saratov	214			
18	Kazakhstan (R)	212		(A) = A.S.S.R.	
19	Moldavia (R)	211			
20	Belorussia (R)	207		(R) = S.S.R.	

Sources: *NkhSSSR* 1965, 128 and *NkhRSFSR* 1965, 50–1.

Five of the 10 slowest growing oblasts were in the Centre economic region. The fastest growing were dispersed widely over the national area and included divisions in Belorussia, Blackearth Centre and Volga-Vyatka as well as in Siberia and Central Asia. Most though not all of the slower growing divisions already had a substantial industrial capacity, whereas many of the fastest growing were mainly agricultural and included several backward A.S.S.R.'s. The absolute increase in capacity was probably greater, therefore, in many slow movers than in the fast growing ones.

Labour productivity has also grown at different rates in different regions. Growth is partly a consequence of capital investment, but potential slack to be taken up in labour productivity must also attract more capital. As shown in Column 8 of Table 10.6, the increase in labour productivity has been least in Central Asia, Transcaucasia and Moldavia, regions already lagging behind in many respects. East Siberia and the Volga have the best indices. Within the 71 R.S.F.S.R. divisions, the range is naturally greater than for the 10 R.S.F.S.R. regions. Table 10.8 shows performances of extreme divisions compared with the R.S.F.S.R. mean of 144.

It is tempting to suggest reasons for the particular performance of individual units, but the overall correlation of productivity growth with other industrial variables or with particular

Table 10.8.

(a) *Growth of labour productivity during 1958–65 in extreme divisions of the R.S.F.S.R.*

Rank	Division	Productivity growth	Rank	Division	Productivity growth
1	Kamchatka	190	62	Tyumen'	136
2	Yakut (A)	179	63	Moscow	136
3	Admurt (A)	174	64	Orenburg	135
4	Kurgan	169	65	Komi (A)	135
5	Vologda	167	66	Primorsk	132
6	Novgorod	167	67	Stavropol'	132
7	Ryazan'	167	68	Murmansk	131
8	Volgograd	167	69	Kabardino-B. (A)	130
9	Kalmyk (A)	165	70	Severo-Os.	127
10	Pskov	162	71	Ivanovo	122
11	Orel	162			
12	Mariysk (A)	162		R.S.F.S.R. mean	144
13	Bashkir (A)	161		(A) = A.S.S.R.	

(b) *Growth of labour productivity during 1958–65 (1958 = 100)*

Industry	Growth	Industry	Growth
Oil extraction	190	Food industry	138
Building materials	172	Timber	
Engineering	162	(*lesogotovki*)	135
Chemicals	151	Coal	129
Iron and steel	141	Light industry	113
		All industry	142

Source: *NkhSSSR* 1965, 143.

regions is low for the period 1958–65. An important clue is given by the figures in Table 10.8(b), showing increase in labour productivity in selected branches of industry. Places with industry in which labour productivity is increasing fast would themselves be expected to have higher indices.

The regional distribution of major branches of industry is shown in Table 10.9. Presence of a branch in a given region is indicated by X. This

since Republics have greatly different absolute amounts.

A more directly quantitative method is now used to describe the regional distribution of those branches of industry for which 1965 data are available. At the time of writing, not all data were available for 1967. Table 10.11 shows the share possessed by each of the 19 regions of population and of production in 12 selected branches of industry. All figures except those for

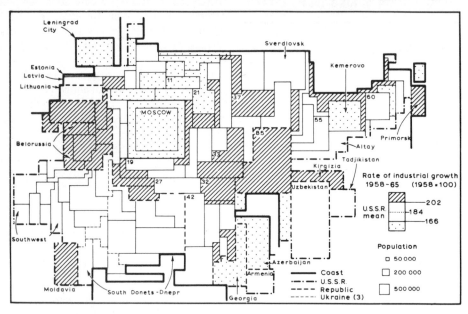

Fig. 10.4.   *Rate of industrial growth, 1958-65 (1958 = 100). Sources:* NkhSSSR 1965, 128 *and* NkhRSFSR 1965, 50-51. *Shading is arranged about the Soviet mean of 184. Diagonal shading and dots represent opposite extremes. The base is topological, with areas proportional to population of units. Numbering of selected units:*
11 Ivanovo,   19 Tula,   21 Gorky,   27 Voronezh,   32 Vologurad,   33 Kuybyshev,   37 Chelyabinsk, 42 Rostov, 55 Novosibirsk, 60 Irkutsk, 85 Kazakhstan.

does not mean that the branch is not present at all in other regions. It is unfortunate that there is no readily available breakdown of employment in manufacturing by 71 divisions of the R.S.F.S.R. and that for 1965 even the 10 economic regions of the R.S.F.S.R. are not revealed. Figures for 1961 give a reasonable idea, however, and are included in Table 10.6, Column 3. The number employed in manufacturing in 1967 is given in Table 10.10 for the 15 Soviet Socialist Republics, the number per 1 000 total population is calculated and the relative importance of major branches is given. Figures are not directly comparable down the columns

steel are based on Soviet tables, but the steel split for the R.S.F.S.R. regions is estimated and will be discussed in a later section in this chapter. Data for chemicals, engineering and several other important branches are inadequate and are not included here, though estimates are used elsewhere in the book. Light industry is the main theme of the table, then, and it should be remembered that this accounts for only a few per cent of the value of total Soviet industrial output, though it represents much of what the consumer actually gets.

A comparison of the columns in the table shows that some industries, particularly elec-

Table 10.9. THE DISTRIBUTION OF MAJOR BRANCHES OF INDUSTRY BY ECONOMIC REGION

Industry		*Northwest*	*Centre*	*Volga-Vyatka*	*Blackearth Centre*	*Volga*	*North Caucasus*	*Ural*	*West Siberia*	*East Siberia*	*Far East*	*Donets-Dnepr*	*Southwest*	*South*	*Baltic*	*Transcaucasia*	*Central Asia*	*Kazakhstan*	*Belorussia*	*Moldavia*	*Total*
Ferrous metals	B1							X	X			X									3
Non-ferrous metals	B2							X										X			2
Coal	B3						X		X	X	X							X			5
Oil extraction	B4					X	X	X			X										4
Gas extraction	B5					X	X														2
Electricity	B6					X				X											2
Engineering	B7	X	X	X		X		X	X			X							X		8
Metal-working	B8	X	X	X		X		X	X			X							X		8
Chemicals	B9	X	X	X	X	X		X	X			X									8
Timber	B10	X		X				X		X	X				X				X		7
Wood manufacture	B11	X		X				X		X	X				X				X		7
Paper	B12	X		X				X		X	X				X				X		7
Building materials	B13				X						X	X	X	X	X	X					7
Light manufacturing	B14	X	X												X		X				4
Food	B15	X				X	X					X	X	X	X	X			X	X	10
Total		8	4	6	2	7	4	9	5	5	6	6	2	2	6	2	1	2	6	1	

Table 10.10. THE INDUSTRIAL STRUCTURE OF THE 15 REPUBLICS IN 1967

	1	*2*	*3* *Electricity*	*4* *Fuel*	*5* *Steel*	*6* *Chemicals*	*7* *Engineering*	*8* *Wood*	*9* *Building*	*10* *Light mf.*	*11* *Food*
U.S.S.R.	28 997	122	153	135	105	89	197	53	63	44	89
R.S.F.S.R.	18 839	147	154	118	85	98	222	70	59	42	80
Ukraine	5 475	118	113	175	220	74	183	17	55	27	99
Lithuania	359	117	213	30	3	73	190	63	100	83	214
Latvia	371	161	201	28	23	86	188	76	76	75	221
Estonia	215	165	272	132	0	30	119	60	83	88	196
Georgia	358	76	233	59	139	86	120	27	63	60	152
Azerbaijan	292	60	135	495	36	75	62	7	36	37	41
Armenia	232	101	256	0	4	160	184	13	72	71	90
Uzbekistan	522	46	205	116	6	99	139	11	121	109	64
Kirgizia	170	60	211	158	0	1	180	14	102	99	143
Tadjikistan	117	43	290	39	0	54	89	15	127	194	122
Turkmenistan	85	42	169	433	0	76	40	8	94	69	67
Kazakhstan	872	69	184	135	128	73	49	18	93	33	68
Bęlorussia	875	99	198	77	3	115	249	55	77	93	108
Moldavia	215	62	225	0	0	9	110	25	85	76	441

Columns
1   Persons employed in industry in thousands, 1967.
2   Persons employed in industry per thousand total population.
3–11 Relative importance (percentage of value) of branches of industry by Republic (compare along rows) in *per thousand* of industrial-productive funds *(promyshlenno-proizvodstvennyye osnovnyye fondy)*

Notes: 0 indicates either negligible proportion or complete absence. A few small branches are not shown (eg glass, non-ferrous metals).
Source: *NkhSSSR* 1967,9, 208, 216–7.

Table 10.11. REGIONAL INDUSTRIAL FIGURES FOR 1965

Economic region	1 Population	2 Electricity	3 Cement	4 Steel	5 Timber	6 Cotton	7 Woollen	8 Linen	9 Silk	10 Footwear	11 Hosiery	12 Underwear	13 Knitwear
1 Northwest	51	50	56	20	265	34	36	51	67	85	79	81	93
2 Centre	116	97	104	40	66	727	543	636	668	156	212	156	237
3 Volga-Vyatka	36	24	13	10	80	18	6	32	0	41	53	36	15
4 Blackearth Centre	34	17	47	30	4	1	36	0	0	15	18	24	14
5 Volga	76	111	114	20	27	20	82	49	0	64	41	51	51
6 North Caucasus	58	35	40	20	11	6	33	3	0	74	51	25	27
7 Ural	66	150	117	349	164	2	19	2	0	66	16	38	44
8 West Siberia	52	69	52	59	76	27	6	7	0	28	12	27	25
9 East Siberia	31	85	39	4	162	12	4	0	41	17	0	13	18
10 Far East	24	18	25	2	60	2	0	0	0	2	0	5	4
11 Donets-Dnepr	84	141	110	406	2	2	33	1	0	75	86	88	75
12 Southwest	87	31	55	0	38	6	23	51	35	95	89	92	77
13 South	25	16	5	0	0	18	9	71	17	26	26	26	22
14 Baltic	31	24	31	0	20	31	62	0	32	49	78	81	84
15 Transcaucasia	49	38	45	24	3	40	34	0	42	55	71	94	54
16 Central Asia	76	33	59	4	0	50	9	0	86	49	44	50	56
17 Kazakhstan	52	38	56	12	4	3	11	0	0	31	31	42	37
18 Belorussia	37	17	24	0	18	1	54	0	3	57	76	59	53
19 Moldavia	15	6	8	0	0	0	0	97	9	15	17	12	14

All figures per thousand.

Table 10.12. MATRIX OF CORRELATION COEFFICIENTS (r)

		1	2	3	4	5	6	7	8	9	10	11	12	13
Population	1	1·0												
Electricity	2	0·6	1·0											
Cement	3	0·8	0·9	1·0										
Steel	4	0·4	0·8	0·7	1·0									
Timber	5	0·0	0·3	0·2	0·2	1·0								
Cotton	6	0·6	0·2	0·4	−0·1	0·1	1·0							
Woollen	7	0·6	0·3	0·4	−0·0	0·0	1·0	1·0						
Linen	8	0·5	0·2	0·3	−0·1	0·1	1·0	1·0	1·0					
Silk	9	0·6	0·2	0·3	−0·1	0·1	1·0	1·0	1·0	1·0				
Footwear	10	0·9	0·4	0·6	0·2	0·2	0·7	0·7	0·7	0·7	1·0			
Hosiery	11	0·7	0·2	0·4	0·1	0·0	0·8	0·8	0·8	0·8	0·9	1·0		
Underwear	12	0·7	0·3	0·5	0·2	0·0	0·7	0·7	0·6	0·7	0·9	0·9	1·0	
Knitwear	13	0·7	0·3	0·5	0·1	0·1	0·9	0·9	0·8	0·9	0·9	0·9	0·9	1·0

tricity, cement and footwear and clothing, are represented in all regions, whereas others, particularly steel and textiles, are not present in some regions at all. To describe the relationship of each branch in the table to population and to every other branch, each branch was correlated as a variable with every other. Correlation indices are shown in Table 10.12. A regional shareout such that each region had exactly the same per thousand of a particular branch as of population would give a correlation of +1·0. The correlation matrix shows indices rounded to one decimal place. The indices are valid as numerical descriptions of relative closeness of distribution, but cannot be the basis of statistical inference, as a correlation of 0 (zero) is not the basis for any conceivable null hypothesis. The four textile and the four clothing branches show very strong intercorrelations and, therefore, distributions. Table 10.13 shows the correlation indices to two decimal places of each branch of industry with population and with electricity respectively. The indices are ranked in descending order of strength.

Table 10.13. CORRELATION INDICES OF POPULATION AND OF ELECTRICITY WITH OTHER INDICES

Population		Electricity	
Footwear	0·85	Cement	0·89
Cement	0·80	Steel	0·78
Knitwear	0·74	Population	0·60
Underwear	0·73		
Hosiery	0·69	Footwear	0·42
Woollen	0·62	Timber	0·34
Silk	0·60	Knitwear	0·34
		Underwear	0·29
Electricity	0·60	Woollen	0·28
Cotton	0·59	Cotton	0·24
Linen	0·54	Silk	0·22
Steel	0·36	Linen	0·19
Timber	0·02	Hosiery	0·18

The factors derived from the correlation matrix are as follows, in percentages of total variation among the 13 variables: Factor I, 60%; Factor II, 20%; Factor III, 8%. Factor loadings are shown in Table 10.14. Population and all the textile and clothing variables load heavily on Factor I. Factor II picks out electricity, cement

Table 10.14. FIRST THREE FACTORS

		I	II	III
1	Population	−0·85	0·33	−0·25
2	Electricity	−0·46	0·83	0·12
3	Cement	−0·61	0·72	−0·08
4	Steel	−0·20	0·86	−0·11
5	Timber	−0·12	0·32	0·89
6	Cotton	−0·90	−0·30	0·14
7	Woollen	−0·93	−0·25	0·08
8	Linen	−0·87	−0·33	0·16
9	Silk	−0·91	−0·31	0·16
10	Footwear	−0·91	0·10	−0·07
11	Hosiery	−0·91	−0·21	−0·16
12	Underwear	−0·87	−0·03	−0·20

and steel. Timber has almost a whole factor of its own and is evidently going very much its own way. The individual weightings of the 19 regions on Factors I and II are shown in Table 10.15.

In Britain and the U.S.A. nearly all regions are highly industrialised in terms of a high ratio of manufacturing to farming employment. Distinctions are made between the types of industry in different regions and many problems arise from the need to replace old and/or declining sectors of industry in some regions. Soviet planners face the same problem, in addition to the difficulties of greater regional discrepancies in actual degree of industrialisation already described. In other words, some regions of the U.S.S.R. are not only relatively very weakly industrialised, but in addition possess less desirable branches from the growth point of view. According to Feygin,[1] this applies to Moldavia, Central Asia, Kazakhstan, Transcaucasia, the Southwest and the Baltic. Certain branches are described as forming the 'basis of technical progress', namely electricity, engineering and chemicals. Together in the U.S.S.R. as a whole they contribute about one-third of total national production in industry. They range however from about 50% in Volga-Vyatka to 10% in Moldavia. Their combined share is shown in Column 5 of Table 10.16, in which four divisions of industry are also shown. They are mapped in Fig. 10.5.

Can the 19 regions be usefully divided into classes in order to group regions with like industrial features and problems? There are 2^{19} or about 10^6 (ie 1 million) possible subsets of 19

Table 10.15. WEIGHTINGS OF THE 19 REGIONS ON FACTOR I AND FACTOR II

	Factor I (population and light industry)			Factor II (heavy industry)	
1	Centre	−30·3		Centre	−3·1
2	Donets-Dnepr	− 5·0		Moldavia	−2·6
3	Southwest	− 3·4		South	−2·4
4	Northwest	− 2·9		Baltic	−1·9
5	Volga	− 2·1		Belorussia	−1·8
6	Ural	− 1·2		Volga-Vyatka	−1·4
7	Transcaucasia	− 0·3		Far East	−1·3
8	Central Asia	+ 0·3		Blackearth Centre	−0·9
9	Baltic	+ 0·4		Transcaucasia	−0·8
10	Belorussia	+ 1·7		North Caucasus	−0·5
11	North Caucasus	+ 2·0		Central Asia	−0·4
12	Kazakhstan	+ 3·1		Southwest	−0·3
13	West Siberia	+ 3·5		Kazakhstan	−0·3
14	Volga-Vyatka	+ 4·0		East Siberia	+0·7
15	East Siberia	+ 5·1		Northwest	+0·8
16	Blackearth Centre	+ 5·4		West Siberia	+1·0
17	South	+ 5·4		Volga	+2·6
18	Moldavia	+ 6·8		Donets-Dnepr	+6·1
19	Far East	+ 7·7		Ural	+6·9

Table 10.16. RELATIVE IMPORTANCE OF FOUR DIVISIONS OF INDUSTRY AND OF GROWTH SECTORS BY ECONOMIC REGION

	Economic Region	Mining and heavy	Wood etc.	Building materials	Manufacturing	Growth sectors
E1	Northwest	14·0	12·7	3·5	66·0	35·2
E2	Centre	12·2	3·4	2·8	77·1	34·3
E3	Volga-Vyatka	15·4	11·3	2·3	69·4	49·0
E4	Blackearth Centre	17·0	1·9	3·5	76·2	38·7
E5	Volga	26·4	4·1	4·1	62·6	40·5
E6	North Caucasus	17·6	4·2	4·2	70·6	26·3
E7	Ural	39·8	7·7	3·4	47·2	35·6
E8	West Siberia	29·2	5·0	4·0	59·2	38·8
E9	East Siberia	18·5	17·2	5·6	47·3	30·5
E10	Far East	15·2	12·1	6·3	64·7	23·7
E11	Donets-Dnepr	41·9	1·4	3·9	51·0	31·7
E12	Southwest	7·6	7·8	4·9	76·1	24·4
E13	South	6·0	2·1	4·9	83·8	28·7
E14	Baltic	6·0	8·5	3·9	78·6	23·3
E15	Transcaucasia	23·7	2·8	4·3	66·6	22·8
E16	Central Asia	9·6	2·2	5·1	81·3	18·0
E17	Kazakhstan	29·3	3·6	7·9	57·8	20·5
E18	Belorussia	4·9	8·2	4·3	79·6	29·8
E19	Moldavia	1·5	3·1	5·1	88·0	9·7
	U.S.S.R.	21·1	5·7	3·9	66·5	32·1

Figures are percentages of the regional totals.

Source: Feygin,[1] 72

elements; the ones actually chosen depend on the criteria used for classification. A single variable classification offers a single scale that can be subdivided as desired. Thus on the basis of percentage in mining and heavy industry or on the basis of growth industries (Table 10.16) the regions could be subdivided, for example, into two classes either side of the mean, into three, four, or up to 19 classes. On the basis of more than one variable, the classification becomes more complex, as is illustrated in Table 10.17, in which three variables and three classes, 0, 1 and 2 are used according to how much population

Table 10.17. SIMPLE CLASSIFICATION OF THE 19 ECONOMIC REGIONS ON THREE CRITERIA

Economic region		1	2	3	4	5	6
E1	Northwest	1	2	1	0	1	0
E2	Centre	2	2	0	1	1	0
E3	Volga-Vyatka	2	1	0	1	0	0
E4	Blackearth Centre	2	0	0	1	0	0
E5	Volga	1	1	2	0	0	1
E6	North Caucasus	2	1	1	1	0	0
E7	Ural	1	2	1	0	1	0
E8	West Siberia	0	1	2	0	0	1
E9	East Siberia	0	0	2	0	0	1
E10	Far East	0	0	2	0	0	1
E11	Donets-Dnepr	2	2	1	1	1	0
E12	Southwest	2	0	0	1	0	0
E13	South	2	0	0	1	0	0
E14	Baltic	2	1	0	1	0	0
E15	Transcaucasia	2	1	1	1	0	0
E16	Central Asia	2	0	1	1	0	0
E17	Kazakhstan	1	0	2	0	0	1
E18	Belorussia	2	0	0	1	0	0
E19	Moldavia	2	0	0	1	0	0

1, 4 Population 2, 5 Industrial capacity.
3, 6 Material resources.
Columns 1–3   2 = abundance.
                       1 = some.
                       0 = little.
Columns 4–6   1 = plenty.
                       0 = little.
Classes on basis of columns 4–6:
001 *Resources plentiful*
     East Siberia, Far East, West Siberia, Volga, Kazakhstan.
010 *Industry highly developed*
     Ural, Northwest.
100 *Abundant population*
     (relative to industry and resources)
     Southwest, South, Belorussia, Moldavia, Blackearth Centre, Central Asia, Volga-Vyatka, Baltic, Transcaucasia, North Caucasus.
110 *Population and industry*
     Centre, Donets-Dnepr.

and industry, and how many resources, a region possesses; 3^3 or 27 classes are then possible. On this basis the 19 regions fall into 12 classes out of 27 theoretically possible. A more simplified and drastic classification giving 0 for lack of, 1 for abundance of the three ingredients, reduces the possible classes to eight and the actual classes to four, shown at the foot of Table 10.17.

10.3 ENERGY

From about 240 million tons in 1940 Soviet fuel output (in conventional fuel) rose to about 310 million in 1950 and 1 080 million in 1967. During this time the contribution of coal to the total declined from over 60% to under 40%. By 1963, gas and oil combined overtook coal, and by 1967, oil alone had almost overtaken coal. Peat, oil shales and especially wood have declined relatively. The contribution of hydroelectricity, not shown in Table 10.18, has been no more than a few percent throughout and the contribution of nuclear fuel, geothermal power and other sources was still negligible in the late 1960's. The organisation of the energy industry is shown diagrammatically in Fig. 10.6(a) and the competition of coal with oil and gas in Fig. 10.6(b). According to *Pravda,* 5 September 1965, the cost of producing oil is only one-sixth that of producing equivalent coal and the cost of producing gas only 1/30. One must surely ask when Soviet coal production will actually begin to decline.

As coal output in conventional fuel units rose from 362 million tons to 416 million, or by 15%, during 1958–65, oil production rose from 162 million to 347 million, or by 114%, and natural gas output rose nearly four and a half times. The shift from coal to oil and gas, confirmed in 1957 as the Five Year Plan was abandoned, has indeed been dramatic. Output in the major hard coalfields has more or less stagnated, specialising more and more in coking coal. The increase in coal output has come particularly from opencast sources. Many of these are so far to the east that their exploitation for thermal-electric power stations, long considered a possibility, has been delayed for lack of east-west transmission facilities over long distances. Since the late 1950's many new oil discoveries have been made, especially in Tyumen' oblast, known gas deposits have been opened up and new ones found. In this section the oil and gas industry will be given the most attention, since the pattern of coal production has already been described often and has not changed much. The possible vast reserves of the Tunguska and Lena coalfields in East Siberia and

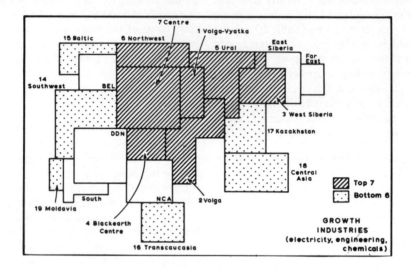

Fig. 10.5.   Growth industries (see text) as a percentage of all industries. The number against top and bottom regions is their position on the rank scale. Source: Feygin,[1] 72.

Table 10.18. SOVIET FUEL BALANCE IN 1945, 1950, AND FROM 1955 TO 1967

	Total in ton × 10⁶	Percentage of total fuel				
		Coal	Oil	Gas	Peat and shales	Wood
1945	185	62·2	15·0	2·3	5·1	15·4
1950	311	66·1	17·4	2·3	5·2	9·0
1955	480	64·8	21·1	2·4	5·0	6·7
1956	514	63·2	23·3	3·0	4·3	6·2
1957	575	61·2	24·5	4·0	4·6	5·7
1958	616	58·8	26·3	5·5	4·1	5·3
1959	659	56·1	28·1	6·4	4·2	5·2
1960	693	53·9	30·5	7·9	3·6	4·1
1961	733	50·5	32·4	9·7	3·4	4·0
1962	779	48·8	34·2	10·9	2·4	3·7
1963	847	45·9	34·8	12·4	3·3	3·6
1964	912	44·2	35·1	13·9	3·2	3·6
1965	969	42·9	35·9	15·6	2·5	3·1
1966	1 033	40·7	36·7	16·5	3·0	3·1
1967	1 079	39·2	37·8	17·4	2·8	2·8

In Column 1, each ton is equivalent to 7 000 kcal of conventional fuel. Thus within and between source types can be compared.

Sources: *NkhSSSR* 1965, 174; *NkhSSSR* 1961, 203; *NkhSSSR* 1967, 235; *Strana sovetov za 50 let*, 68.

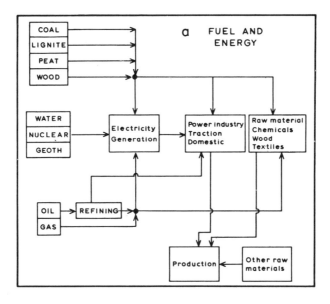

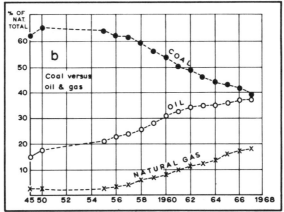

Fig. 10.6. *(a) Fuel and energy in the U.S.S.R. (b) The relative importance of coal, oil, and natural gas.*

the Far East (see Fig. 10.7) are as much of academic interest as ever.

Reasonably complete data for the early 1960's are used in Table 10.19 to show production of energy and the assumed regional surplus and deficit. The major changes in Table 10.19 since 1962 have been the development of oil in the Volga, Ural and West Siberia, and gas in several regions, particularly the Ukraine, North Caucasus and Central Asia. The ambiguous position of the Bashkir A.S.S.R. and Tyumen' oblast with respect to the Volga, Ural and West Siberia economic regions is a monumental example of Soviet gerrymandering

with economic regions; it causes considerable confusion. With the Bashkir A.S.S.R. in the Volga region and Tyumen' in West Siberia, these two regions, together with the new gas regions mentioned, have increased their share of total Soviet output at the expense of the other regions. Several regions in European U.S.S.R., particularly in the northern half, have gone further into deficit. Table 10.19 does not show which regions supply which, but serves as a basis for the study which will be carried out mainly in Chapter 12 on interregional flows of goods. The figures in Column 7 are mapped in Fig 10.8.

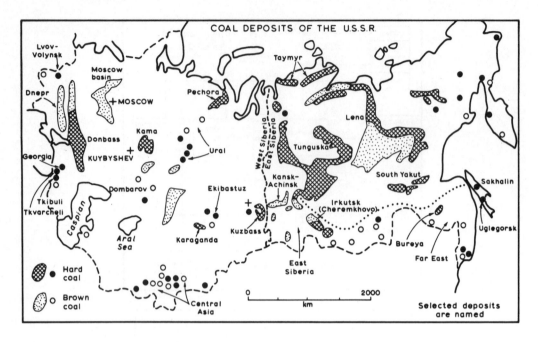

Fig. 10.7.   *Coal deposits of the U.S.S.R. In the eastern half of the U.S.S.R., almost no production comes from fields north of the dotted line. Source: Galitskiy,5 77.*

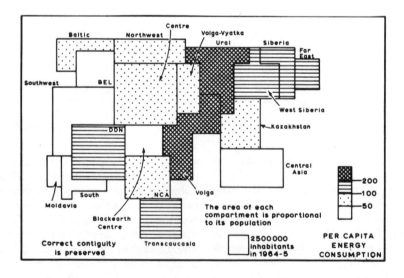

Fig. 10.8.   *Per capita energy consumption. The Soviet mean is 100.*

Table 10.19. REGIONAL DISTRIBUTION OF ENERGY PRODUCTION AND CONSUMPTION
IN THE EARLY 1960's

	Economic region	1	2	3	4	5	6	7
E1	Northwest	33	51	65	47	70	−14	92
E2	Centre	28	116	24	88	32	−60	76
E3	Volga-Vyatka	6	36	17	27	22	−21	75
E4	Blackearth Centre	1	34	3	17	6	−16	49
E5	Volga	261	76	343	176	148	+85	232
E6	North Caucasus	93	58	160	54	172	+39	93
E7	Ural	60	66	83	183	33	−123	254
E8	West Siberia	103	52	219	71	145	+32	151
E9	East Siberia	36	31	116	39	92	−3	126
E10	Far East	24	24	100	26	92	−2	108
E11	Donets-Dnepr	199	84	237	140	142	+59	167
E12	Southwest	28	87	32	32	88	−4	36
E13	South	0	25	0	12	0	−12	48
E14	Baltic	8	31	26	16	5	−8	52
E15	Transcaucasia	48	49	98	59	81	−11	120
E16	Central Asia	29	76	39	28	104	+1	38
E17	Kazakhstan	38	52	73	30	127	+8	58
E18	Belorussia	5	37	13	13	38	−8	35
E19	Moldavia	0	15	0	2	0	−2	14

Column

1 Per thousand share contributed by each region to the national energy total of 779 million tons of conventional fuel in 1962.

2 Per thousand share of the total population of the U.S.S.R. in each region.

3 Relative *per capita* production (U.S.S.R.= 100, column 1 ÷ column 2).

4 Actual consumption in each region per thousand of Soviet total.

5 Relative deficit or surplus,1 output as percentage of 4 consumption.

6 Absolute amount of units (thousandths) deficient or surplus (column 1 − column 4).

7 Relative *per capita* consumption (column 4 ÷ column 2).

Source: Feygin,[1] 146.

COAL

Table 10.20 shows the distribution of coal production by S.S.R.'s in millions of tons during 1965-67. A better breakdown, by fields, is available for 1963 and is shown in Table 10.21. Regions are indicated. The asterisk indicates a large proportion of brown coal or lignite. The lignite and brown coal totals should be reduced for comparison with the others. Fig. 10.7 shows the distribution of coal deposits, including those in Table 10.21. The effect of reducing brown coal to hard coal equivalent and all types of coal to conventional fuel units of 7 000 kcal is as follows for 1965: the combined tonnage of anthracite, other hard coal (347) and brown coal (149), becomes 416 million tons according to *NkhSSSR 1965*, p.174. As in the U.S.A. and West Europe, anyone predicting coal needs over the next decade has a difficult task. If Soviet production continues to rise as slowly in the 1970's as the 1960's, the present 'geography' of the industry is likely to freeze as it is. A possible output of 1 200 million tons by 1980, suggested in one source in 1963, is another matter.

OIL AND GAS

The main producing areas of oil and natural gas do not generally occur together, though commercial quantities of natural gas are obtained from the oilfields. Organisationally the gas industry is simpler than the oil industry for several reasons. The two are contrasted in the Fig. 10.9(a). Gas is usually fed direct from

Table 10.20. SOVIET COAL PRODUCTION BY REPUBLICS IN 1967 IN MILLIONS OF TONS

Area	Mined			Opencast			Coking†		
	1965	1966	1967	1965	1966	1967	1965	1966	1967
U.S.S.R.	437	440	444	141	146	151	139	143	148
R.S.F.S.R.	216	214	216	110	115	118	49	51	55
Ukraine	185	187	189	10	10	10	77	76	77
Georgia	3	3	2	–	–	–	2	2	2
Central Asia*	5	5	5	4	4	4	–	–	–
Kazakhstan	30	31	32	16	17	19	11	13	14

* Uzbekistan, Tadjikistan, Kirgizia. Source: *NkhSSSR* 1967, 241.
† Coking coal is a subset of all mined coal.

Table 10.21. PRINCIPAL SOURCES OF COAL IN THE U.S.S.R.

		Total (ton × 10⁶)	Percentage
	U.S.S.R.	531·7	100·0
E1	Pechora basin (Northwest)	17·3	3·3
E2	Moscow basin* (Centre)	37·1	7·1
E7	Ural basins*	60·9	11·5
E8	Kuznetskiy (Kuzbass) basin (West Siberia)	89·5	16·8
E9	East Siberia deposits*	42·4	8·0
E10	Far East deposits*	23·2	4·4
E11	Donetskiy (Donbass) basin (Donets-Dnepr)	192·4	36·2
E12	Lvov-Volynsk deposits*	8·7	1·6
E15	Georgia deposits (Transcaucasia)	2·7	0·5
E16	Central Asia deposits*	8·7	1·6
E17	Ekibastuz deposits* (Kazakhstan)	10·0	1·9

Source: Nikitin,[4] 95

Table 10.22. OIL AND NATURAL GAS PRODUCTION

	Oil	Gas		Oil	Gas
1901	11·6	*neg.	1961	166·1	59·0
1930	18·5	*neg.	1962	186·2	73·5
1940	31·1	3·2	1963	206·1	89·8
1945	19·4	3·3	1964	223·6	108·6
1950	37·9	5·8	1965	242·9	127·7
1955	70·8	9·0	1966	265·1	143·0
1960	147·9	45·3	1967	288·0	159·0

Oil: ton × 10⁶; Gas: m³ × 10⁹; *neg.: negligible.

Sources: *NkhSSSR* 1965, 175; *Promyshlennost' SSSR* 1957 and 1964;
Pravda, 25 Jan. 1968.

producing wells to markets by a branching network of pipelines. Oil has first to be refined, either in the oilfields or in market areas or at some intermediate place; it may be transported crude or refined by various transport media; much Soviet oil is exported.

Soviet oil and gas output have both increased enormously since World War II. The growth of production of the two is compared in Fig. 10.9(b) and production figures for selected years are shown in Table 10.22. The regional distribution of oil production is difficult to locate exactly, but for 1965 or 1966 it is possible to find enough data to give a reasonable idea. In Table 10.23 the divisions are arranged in the

familiar order of the 19 regions. In 1967, 21 601 000 tons of oil shales were extracted, about 75% in Estonia, the rest in various parts of the U.S.S.R.

The most striking change in the regional distribution of oil production in the Soviet period has been the relative decline of Azerbaijan from 75% of all production early in the century gradually to about 60% at the end of World War II, then dramatically to 12% in 1960 and 7·5% in 1967. The Volga-Ural oilfields, now almost exclusively within the Volga region, accounted for a mere 15% in 1945, but around 70% by 1960. The share of the Volga region has remained around 70% in the 1960's and will presumably

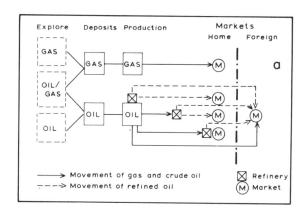

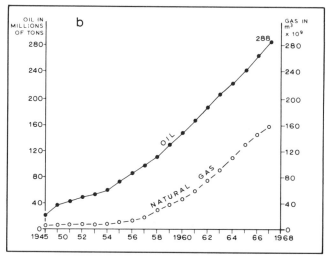

Fig. 10.9. (a) Comparison of the organisation of the gas and oil industries. (b) Comparison of natural gas and oil production, 1950-67.

Table 10.23. REGIONAL DISTRIBUTION OF SOVIET OIL PRODUCTION IN MILLIONS OF TONS, 1965, 1966 AND 1967

Region	1965	Production 1966	1967	Percentage of Soviet total in 1966
U.S.S.R.	242·9	265·1	288·1	100
R.S.F.S.R.	199·9	218·0	235·0	82·3
E1 Komi (A)		3·1		1·2
E5 Tatar (A)		86·2		32·6
Bashkir (A)		43·4		16·4
E6 Checheno-Ingush (A)		11·2		4·2
Dagestan (A)		1·2		0·5
Rest of R.S.F.S.R.		72·9		27·4
E11–13 Ukraine	7·6	9·3	11·0	3·5
E15 Azerbaijan	21·5	21·7	21·6	8·2
E16 Turkmenistan	9·6	10·7		4·0
Uzbekistan	1·8	1·7	1·8	0·6
Kirgizia	0·3	0·3	0·3	0·1
E17 Kazakhstan	2·0	3·1	5·6	1·2
E18 Belorussia		0·2	0·8	0·1

Sources: *NkhSSSR* 1965, 175; *NkhSSSR* 1967, 236
         RSFSR za 50 let, 181–234

begin to decline as the Tyumen' oil in West Siberia is exploited. Oil extraction started in West Siberia in 1964 and an output of nine million tons in 1967 is attributed to West Siberia and Western Kazakhstan in *Strana sovetov za 50 let* (p. 69). According to *Pravda*, 18 June 1966, West Siberian oil production, largely from Tyumen' and Tomsk oblasts, is expected to be 22–25 million tons per year by 1970, although this is still only a few percent of all Soviet oil. Fig. 10.10(a) shows new names connected with the area. Of the divisions shown in Table 10.23, the rest of the R.S.F.S.R. consists largely of Kuybyshev oblast in the Volga region, together with Saratov and Volgograd, but includes the modest output of West Siberia and the Far East, as well as part of the North Caucasus. The Checheno-Ingush and Dagestan A.S.S.R.'s make up 4·7% of the 9% share of the Soviet total accounted for by the North Caucasus region; Krasnodar kray includes other producing districts.

The cost of exploring for oil, extracting it and moving it to markets varies very much among the oilfields. Differences in costs are discussed in Chapter 12 and the pipeline system is described in Chapter 11. The distribution of oil refineries can be found in table and map form in Section 10.4 under chemicals.

The regional breakdown of natural gas reserves and production has similar limitations to that for oil. Table 10.24 shows production by economic regions as far as this is revealed, and Table 10.25 lists important producing centres. The A.S.S.R.'s that are prominent oil producers in the Volga and North Caucasus regions are only secondary gas producers. Areas of gas production are mapped in Fig. 10.10 and the network of gas pipelines is discussed in Chapter 11. Among the newest names in the gas industry are Gazli, Uchkyr and Achak in Central Asia. According to *The Times,* 18 December 1967, West Siberian gas deposits were already about six times as large as those of the North Sea (West Europe) by 1967. In 1967, according to *Pravda,* 8 June 1968, large deposits of gas were discovered between the Ob' and Irtysh. Places mentioned are Luginetsk, Verkhne-Salatsk, Sobolin, Yuzhno-Myl'dzhensk, Olen'ye and Yubileynoye (Fig. 10.10(a) gives the general area).

ELECTRICITY

The dictum of Lenin that 'Communism is Soviet power plus the electrification of the whole country' sounds somewhat outmoded now, although it summarises the Soviet obsession with

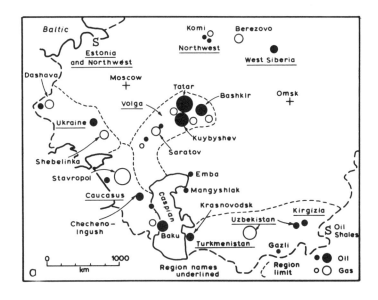

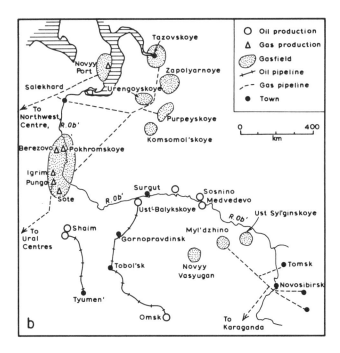

Fig. 10.10.   (a) Regional distribution of Soviet oil and gas production. (b) New names in the oil and gas industry of Tyumen' and Tomsk oblasts, West Siberia. Most of the gas pipelines were still under construction or proposed in the late 1960's. Sources: Pravda 19 July 1966, Pravda 15 Mar. 1968, Atlas razvitiya khozyaystva i kultury SSSR (Moscow, 1967).

Table 10.24. REGIONAL DISTRIBUTION OF SOVIET NATURAL GAS PRODUCTION IN THOUSANDS OF MILLIONS OF CUBIC METRES IN 1965-67

| | Production | | | Percentage | | |
	1965	1966	1967	1965	1966	1967
U.S.S.R.	127·7	143·0	157·4	100	100	100
R.S.F.S.R.	64·3	69·0	74·8	50·4	49·2	47·5
E1 Komi		0·9			0·6	
E5 Bashkir		3·2			2·2	
Tatar		2·7			1·9	
E6 Checheno-Ingush		1·7			1·2	
Dagestan		0·4			0·3	
Rest of R.S.F.S.R.		61·3			43·0	
E11–13 Ukraine	39·4	43·6	47·4	30·8	30·5	30·1
E15 Azerbaijan	6·2	6·2	5·8	4·8	4·3	3·7
E16 Uzbekistan	16·5	22·6	26·6	12·9	15·8	16·9
Turkmenistan	1·2	1·3	2·2	0·9	0·9	0·8
Kirgizia	0·2	0·2	0·3	0·2	0·1	0·2

Sources: *NkhSSSR* 1965, 177; *NkhSSSR* 1967, 238
Strana sovetov za 50 let, 68
RSFSR za 50 let, 39, 183 *et seq.*

Table 10.25. SELECTED AREAS OF NATURAL GAS PRODUCTION

Place	Region
Stavropol'	North Caucasus
Bukhara (Gazli)	Central Asia
Shebelinka	Ukraine
Dashava	Ukraine
Saratov	Volga
Kuybyshev	Volga
Azerbaijan	Transcaucasia
Volgograd	Volga
Bashkir	Volga
Tatar	Volga
Ukhta	Northwest
Berezovo	West Siberia

·electrification of the U.S.S.R. and particularly with the exploitation of the hydroelectric potential. The electricity industry is a heavy user of capital. It is one that depends for success on economies of large scale in its plant, and in the Soviet context, for innovations in technology to overcome long distance transmission problems. Soviet electricity generating capacity has grown impressively as shown in Table 10.26.

Over the years, the actual amount of electricity generated from hydroelectric stations has tended to be appreciably below its share of capacity owing to the closure or slowing down of some stations in the winter. In 1966 the U.S.S.R. produced 588 000 million kWh of electricity; 91 800 million kWh or about 17% came from hydroelectric sources. At the moment coal, oil and gas are the main sources of heat for thermal stations. The contribution of nuclear power is negligible. It is worth noting, however, that according to *Pravda,* 31 August, 1968, there are four sizable nuclear power stations, Voronezh (300 MW by 1969) Melekess (Volga) Beloyarsk (Ural) and one in Siberia. Another is reported elsewhere at Obninsk near Kaluga. Smaller users of nuclear power are in remote places such as the Arctic, Altay Mountains, Chita and Armenia. In Volgograd and Groznyy there are 'radiation-chemical' establishments. According to *New Scientist,* 28 March 1968, p.89, it may be possible to obtain geothermal power from very hot water sources beneath the West Siberian Lowland.

The Soviet electricity industry has been characterised by the appearance in recent years of both hydro and thermal stations of very large capacity. In 1940, only 42% of the output came from stations with a capacity of over 100 MW; by 1966 this proportion was only 15·8%, 27% having come from stations of over 1 000 MW capacity. Some of the largest stations will be

Table 10.26. THE GROWTH OF SOVIET ELECTRICITY GENERATING CAPACITY IN MILLIONS OF KILOWATTS

Year	Absolute			Percentage		
	Total	Thermal	Hydro	Total	Thermal	Hydro
1940	11·1	9·5	1·6	100	86	14
1950	19·6	16·4	3·2	100	84	16
1958	53·6	42·7	10·9	100	80	20
1965	115·0	92·2	22·2	100	80	20
1966	123·0	99·9	23·1	100	81	19
1967	131·7	103·3	24·8	100	81	19

Sources: *NkhSSSR* 1965, 169; *NkhSSSR* 1967, 230
 Strana sovetov za 50 let, 65

Table 10.27.

(a) *Regional distribution of electricity*

Economic region	Production in 10^6 kWh		Per thousand of Soviet total		Per capita
	1958	1965	1958	1965	(1965)
E1 Northwest	15 719	25 237	67	50	216
E2 Centre	24 217	48 858	104	97	183
E3 Volga-Vyatka	7 514	12 044	32	24	145
E4 Blackearth Centre	3 741	8 675	16	17	109
E5 Volga	23 570	55 974	101	111	316
E6 North Caucasus	8 380	17 693	36	35	131
E7 Ural	43 576	75 680	186	150	498
E8 West Siberia	16 512	34 898	70	69	289
E9 East Siberia	9 973	43 148	42	85	595
E10 Far East	4 325	9 300	18	18	169
E11 Donets-Dnepr*	33 000	71 000	141	141	396
E12 Southwest*	7 300	15 700	31	31	72
E13 South*	3 700	7 950	16	16	141
E14 Baltic	3 368	12 433	14	24	172
E15 Transcaucasia	11 111	19 303	47	38	169
E16 Central Asia	6 897	16 764	29	33	94
E17 Kazakhstan	8 525	19 204	36	38	158
E18 Belorussia	2 741	8 410	12	17	98
E19 Moldavia	487	3 110	2	6	92
U.S.S.R.	235 350	506 709	1 000	1 000	219

* 1961 proportions were: Donets-Dnepr 75%, Southwest 16·6%, South 8·4%.

Sources: *NkhSSSR* 1965, 170.   *NkhRSFSR* 1965, 82.   Nikitin.[4]

(b) *Distribution of electricity production by Republics in 1967 in millions of kWh*

U.S.S.R.	587 699	Latvia	2 583	Uzbekistan	14 407	Belorussia	10 877
		Estonia	8 620	Kirgizia	2 968	Moldavia	4 932
R.S.F.S.R.	379 759	Georgia	6 703	Tadjikistan	2 245		
Ukraine	108 722	Azerbaijan	11 164	Turkmenistan	1 573		
Lithuania	4 691	Armenia	4 682	Kazakhstan	23 773		

Source: *NkhSSSR* 1967, 231.

mentioned below. An experimental generator of 800 MW has been installed in the Slavyansk thermal station, Donbass.

The main user of electricity was industry, which in 1965 took nearly 70% of the output, compared with a mere 4% in agriculture and only 7% in transport. Losses also accounted for 7%. The regional distribution of electricity production is shown in Table 10.27. In 1965, the *per capita* production, shown in Table 10.28, ranged from almost 600 kWh in East Siberia to about 70 kWh in the Southwest.

The ability to transmit electricity economically at least several hundred kilometres has been an essential consideration in the planning and

Table 10.28. NINETEEN REGIONS RANKED IN ORDER OF *per capita* ELECTRICITY PRODUCTION, 1965

Region	Production	Region	Production
1 East Siberia	595	10 Transcaucasia	169
2 Ural	498	11 Kazakhstan	158
3 Donets-Dnepr	396	12 Volga-Vyatka	145
4 Volga	316	13 South	141
5 West Siberia	289	14 North Caucasus	131
6 Northwest	216	15 Blackearth Centre	109
7 Centre	183	16 Belorussia	98
8 Baltic	172	17 Central Asia	94
9 Far East	169	18 Moldavia	92
		19 Southwest	72
		U.S.S.R.	219

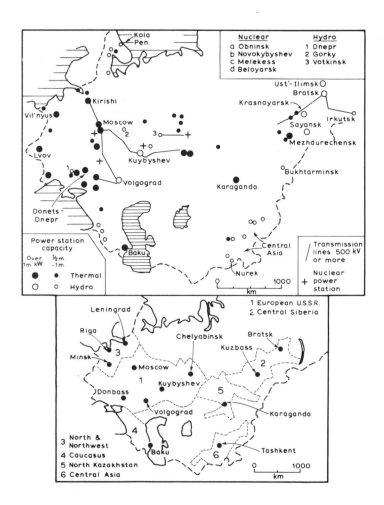

Fig. 10.11.   Electricity. Upper map: Main power stations, and transmission lines of 500 kV or more. Lower map: Regional electricity systems.

development of electricity grids on a regional basis and of high voltage technology. In 1962, some 500 km of transmission line with a tension of 800 kV were brought into use between Volgograd and the Donbass. By 1967 there were 9 000 km of line with 400–500 kV tension. The distribution of major power stations and the regional grids is shown in Fig. 10.11. Ahead lie the prospects of using d.c. for very long distance transmission, as a.c. cannot commercially be used for more than about 2 400 km (1 500 kV is suggested in *Pravda,* 6 April 1966, as a possibility) or of using super conductive cables buried in the ground and cooled with liquid helium and nitrogen (*New Scientist,* 29 February 1968, p.454).

10.4 CHEMICALS AND ASSOCIATED ACTIVITIES

The chemicals industry was regarded as one of prime importance in the early 1960's. It had previously lagged behind other major branches in the Soviet period, but the need for fertilisers, plastics, synthetic fibres, synthetic rubber and other such products has now given it a stimulus. The range of raw materials and the range of products is very large and the number of production centres too large to map usefully in this book. In view of the particular interest in petrochemicals, the major Soviet oil refineries are all shown in Fig. 10.12 and are listed in Table 10.29. Fig. 10.12 also shows the 10

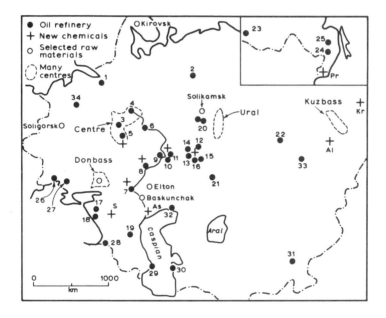

Fig. 10.12.   Oil refineries, and places in which the chemicals industry has expanded fastest during 1959-65. The ten fastest growing divisions in the R.S.F.S.R. are listed below, with 1965 increase over 1959 (1959 = 100) and map references.

Map	Division	1965	Map	Division	1965
5	*Ryazan*	*1018*	Kr	*Krasnoyarsk*	*606*
7	*Volgograd*	*887*	12	*Bashkir (A)*	*528*
8	*Saratov*	*854*	11	*Kuybyshev*	*444*
S	*Stavropol*	*689*	As	*Astrakhan'*	*391*
A1	*Altay kray*	*638*	Pr	*Primorsk kray*	*372*

Source: NkhRSFSR *1965, 92–93. See also Table 10.29 for key to numbers on map.*

Table 10.29. OIL REFINERIES OF THE U.S.S.R.

E1 NORTHWEST
   1 *Kirishi* (Leningrad)
   2 Ukhta
E2 CENTRE
   3 Lyubertsy (Moscow)
   4 *Novo-Yaroslavl'**
   5 *Ryazan'**
E3 VOLGA–VYATKA
   6 Kstovo (Gorky)
E5 VOLGA
   7 Volgograd*
   8 Saratov*
   9 Syzran'*
   10 Novokuybyshevsk*
   11 Kuybyshev*
   12 Ufa*
   13 Shkapovo*
   14 Tuymazy*
   15 Ishimbay*
   16 Salavat*
E6 NORTH CAUCASUS
   17 Krasnodar
   18 Tuapse
   19 Groznyy*

E7 URAL
   20 Perm'-Krasnokamsk
   21 Orsk
E8 WEST SIBERIA
   22 *Omsk*
E9 EAST SIBERIA
   23 *Angarsk*
E10 FAR EAST
   24 Khabarovsk
   25 Komsomol'sk
E13 SOUTH
   26 Odessa
   27 Kherson
E15 TRANSCAUCASIA
   28 Batumi
   29 Baku*
E16 CENTRAL ASIA
   30 Krasnovodsk*
   31 Fergana
E17 KAZAKHSTAN
   32 Gur'yev
   33 Pavlodar
E18 BELORUSSIA
   34 *Polotsk**

* Throughput of several million tons per year. Refineries in italics opened after about 1958.

Source: Nikitin,[4] 127 and map supplement.

divisions in the R.S.F.S.R. that have expanded their chemicals industries fastest in the 1958–65 period. Comparable data are not available for the other S.S.R.'s, but developments in chemicals are probably most rapid in Belorussia (Soligorsk, Polotsk) Transcaucasia, and parts of Kazakhstan.

Some major mineral deposits for the Soviet chemical industry are shown on Fig. 10.12: Kirovsk (apatite) Solikamsk and Soligorsk (potash) Donbass, Elton and Baskunchak (salt). There are many other raw materials, however, including wood, peat, lignite, by-products of the iron and steel industry and particularly now, oil and natural gas.

Some chemicals branches are widely dispersed, for example, wood-chemicals along the whole southern fringe of the coniferous forest zone. Fertilisers are produced in all but three Republics as well as in many R.S.F.S.R. oblasts; *per capita* production varies considerably among the Republics, figures for which are shown in Table 10.30. The high output in the Baltic Republics and Belorussia represent the attempt to improve farmlands in these less fertile areas. Uzbekistan serves the other three Central Asian Republics as well as itself. With the extension of

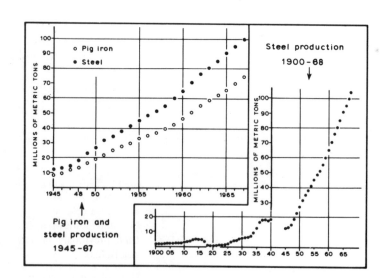

Fig. 10.13.   *Steel production from 1900-68 and pig iron since 1945 in Russia and the U.S.S.R.*

Table 10.30. FERTILISER PRODUCTION BY REPUBLICS IN 1967

	Thousands of tons	*Kilograms per inhabitant*
U.S.S.R.	40 083	176
R.S.F.S.R.	20 592	161
Ukraine	8 738	188
Lithuania	777	254
Latvia	163	71
Estonia	883	680
Georgia	508	109
Azerbaijan	666	136
Armenia	108	47
Uzbekistan	3 057	270
Turkmenistan	298	147
Kazakhstan	868	68
Belorussia	3 415	388

Source: *NkhSSSR* 1967, 252.

the oil and gas pipeline systems, the petro-chemicals industry is also becoming widespread. Older concentrations of chemicals are the four industrial regions shown in Fig. 10.12 and the Volga oilfields.

10.5 IRON AND STEEL

The growth of steel production in the U.S.S.R., shown in Fig. 10.13, has faltered since World War II, particularly in the years 1955-57. It has grown to reach an output in 1967 of over 100 million tons, one of those magic totals greeted with awe in the Soviet press. Though beyond the scope of this book it would be revealing to compare U.S. steel output with Soviet totals. Consider the following:

	U.S.A.	*U.S.S.R.*
1953	101	38
1958	77	55
1959	85	60
1960	90	65
1961	89	71
1962	89	76
1963	99	80
1964	115	85
1965	119	91
1966	122	97
1967	115	102

The 40 million population gap should not be overlooked.

Greater capacity is apparently still needed, given that the U.S.S.R. is providing some steel for most of the Comecon countries and a number of other foreign markets as well. There has been less regional shift in capacity than might have been expected from discussion a decade ago about a third and even a fourth metallurgical base in the east. Presumably the promising low cost sites east of the Ural region are too far from the main markets of the west to make them as attractive as they look in theory.

The classic considerations for the location of an iron and steel works apply in the U.S.S.R. as much as in a Western industrial country, except that strategic considerations and the course of World War II distorted the Soviet pattern of development appreciably. The main ingredients of an idealised integrated steelworks are shown in Fig. 10.14(a). The actual arrangement of the eastern Ukraine steel industry (Donets-Dnepr) is shown diagrammatically in Figs. 10.14(b) and (c). The main heavy industrial regions are shown in Fig. 10.14(d). The following points are relevant to a study of the Soviet iron and steel industry:

1. It is usually advantageous to have an integrated works making pig iron, steel and rolled steel.

2. Up to a capacity of several million tons of steel a year, economy of production costs is achieved with increase in scale, especially of blast furnace units.

3. Soviet works vary greatly both in size and age and, therefore, sophistication of their equipment.

4. Greater efficiency in the use of coal (and other sources of energy ranging from electricity and gas to charcoal) has meant a reduction of the volume of fuel to iron ore and somewhat less advantage now than previously in being located on the coalfields.

5. Ores of greatly varying iron content are used, ranging from about 60% to 25% iron.

6. Steel produced varies greatly in quality, application and price.

7. Other ingredients of the industry include manganese ore and other ferro-alloys, limestone, water and scrap steel, in all of which the U.S.S.R. is largely self-sufficient.

8. The market for steel products largely consists of a considerable number of towns of varying size, rather than a continuous surface; much steel goes to heavy engineering plant, often near the steelworks.

Considering these points, it is not surprising that production costs of steel have varied greatly, some regions having much lower costs than others, but with marked differences between works within the same region. Cost aspects of the industry will be dealt with in Chapter 12.

Table 10.31 shows the comparative performance, as regards pig iron and steel, of the R.S.F.S.R. and Ukraine over recent years and particularly the effect of the war in the 1940–50 decade. The R.S.F.S.R. total comes mainly from the Ural, West Siberia and Centre works. Pig iron production is only about 75% that of steel and this is almost exclusively transformed into steel. Dependence on scrap is increasing, as is shown in the table by the widening gap between (a) and (b) since World War II. It will be noted that the Ukraine produces a much higher ratio of pig iron to steel than the R.S.F.S.R. does and, in fact, the Ukraine is a supplier of pig iron both to the R.S.F.S.R., particularly the Centre, and to Comecon partners. In 1967, production for the main ingredients of the Soviet iron and steel industry is shown in Table 10.32.

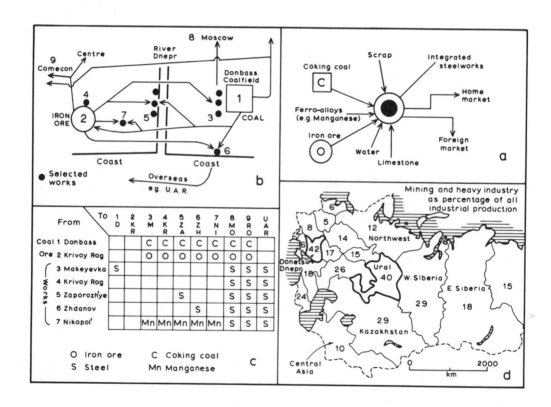

Fig. 10.14.   *The Soviet iron and steel industry. (a) Idealised iron and steel works. (b), (c) The Donets-Dnepr complex, (b) map, (c) matrix of transactions. (d) Mining and heavy industry as a percentage of all industrial production. Source: Feygin,[1] 72.*

Table 10.31. SOVIET PIG IRON (a) AND STEEL (b) PRODUCTION BY SELECTED REGIONS, 1958–67

Production in thousands of tons

(a)

	U.S.S.R.	R.S.F.S.R.	Ukraine	Transcaucasia	Kazakhstan
1940	14 902	5 260	9 642	–	–
1950	19 175	10 007	9 168	–	–
1958	39 600	18 837	20 092	671	–
1959	42 972	19 933	22 347	692	–
1960	46 757	21 589	24 174	721	274
1961	50 893	22 787	26 419	732	956
1962	55 265	25 073	28 102	787	1 303
1963	58 692	26 906	29 646	764	1 376
1964	62 377	28 784	31 264	810	1 519
1965	66 184	31 158	32 582	819	1 625
1966	70 264	32 533	35 216	814	1 701
1967	74 812	35 479	36 720	833	1 780

(b)

	U.S.S.R.	R.S.F.S.R.	Ukraine	Transcaucasia	Kazakhstan
1940	18 317	9 311	8 938	24	–
1950	27 329	18 546	8 351	121	131
1958	54 920	31 074	21 717	1 420	268
1959	59 971	33 655	24 010	1 532	288
1960	65 294	36 588	26 155	1 730	309
1961	70 751	39 897	28 083	1 887	313
1962	76 307	42 750	30 577	1 990	393
1963	80 231	44 494	32 630	2 054	426
1964	85 038	47 052	34 631	2 137	551
1965	91 021	50 058	36 980	2 175	1 123
1966	96 907	52 042	40 474	2 232	1 257
1967	102 224	54 733	42 809	2 286	1 334

Sources: *NkhSSSR* 1963, 146; *NkhSSSR* 1965, 182; *NkhSSSR* 1967, 244.

A regional breakdown of Soviet steel production beyond S.S.R. level for the 1965–67 period is bound to be approximate as data for R.S.F.S.R. economic regions are not published in the statistical yearbooks. The main basis for the estimates of the breakdown for 1967 within the R.S.F.S.R., shown in Table 10.33, are 1956 Soviet figures, also shown. Feygin[1] also provides a regional breakdown, but his figures, regional percentages of the total Soviet production, are for the whole iron and steel industry, not a single item. In 1962, according to Feygin, Donets-Dnepr had 41% of the Soviet total, Ural 31%, Centre 5·4% and West Siberia 5%.

According to Nikitin[4] the U.S.S.R. has the largest reserves of iron in the world, 90–100 × 10⁹ ton, about half in the eastern part of the country. The largest deposits are in the area of the Kursk Magnetic Anomaly (40×10^9), Krivoy Rog (Donets-Dnepr), the Kustanay basin in Kazakhstan and in East Siberia. Smaller deposits that are exploited are in the Kola peninsula (Olenegorsk), Kachkanar and Magnitogorsk (Ural). Few Soviet iron ore deposits have an iron content in excess of 50%.

Table 10.32. PRODUCTION OF INGREDIENTS OF STEEL INDUSTRY, 1967

Product	Million tons
Iron ore	170
Coking coal	150
Pig iron	75
Steel	102
Rolled steel	81

Source: *Pravda*, 25 Jan. 1968

Table 10.33. REGIONAL DISTRIBUTION OF SOVIET STEEL PRODUCTION, 1956 AND 1967

		10^3 ton 1956	Percentage	10^3 ton 1967	Percentage
	U.S.S.R.	48 698	100	102 224	100
E1	Northwest	950	2	1 500	1·5
E2–3	Centre	2 689	5·5	4 700	4·6
E5	Volga	1 655	3·5	1 000	1·0
E6	North Caucasus	966	2	1 000	1·0
E7	Ural	17 496	36	34 000	33·0
E8	West Siberia	4 151	8·5	13 000	12·6
E11	Donets-Dnepr*	18 323	37·5	42 810	41·7
E15	Transcaucasia	685	1·5	2 290	2·2
	Residue†	1 763	3·5	2 400	2·4

*Ukraine figure used
†Residue 1956: Volga-Vyatka, East Siberia, Far East, Central Asia
  Residue 1967: Uzbekistan (Central Asia) 386
               Kazakhstan 1 334
               Others (including Latvia 480, Belorussia 180) about 800

Sources: *NkhSSSR* 1959, 167; *NkhRSFSR* 1957, 80; *NkhSSSR* 1967, 244

Many ores are deep mined rather than obtained opencast. According to *New Scientist,* 20 June 1968, 615–6, the great Kursk deposits, little used up to now, are soon to be exploited. The problem of the waterlogged state of the surface rocks is being overcome and it is proposed to sink shafts near Belgorod to reach 30 000 million tons of ore with a 64% iron content. Of the Soviet manganese ore, according to Feygin,[1] Donets-Dnepr has 85% of the reserves, Transcaucasia 6%. Nevertheless, Chiatura in Transcaucasia (Georgia) now produces about 3 million tons of manganese ore (*Pravda,* 9 February 1966).

Coking coal is obtained chiefly from four fields (see Fig. 10.7): Donbass, Kuzbass, Karaganda and Pechora. The Kizel coal of the Urals is also used after suitable preparation and Georgia coal is used for the Rustavi works. One other known deposit of coking coal is the Chul'man deposit of Southern Yakutia. All major Soviet iron and steel works are shown in Table 10.34 and mapped in Fig. 10.15. Some outstanding aspects of the geography of the industry will now be noted:

1. Almost all centres producing pig iron also produce steel. Only about two-thirds of the centres listed in Table 10.33, however, produce pig iron. According to Galitskiy,[5] four mills alone account for 40% of all Soviet pig iron; they are Magnitogorsk, Novokuznetsk, Nizhniy Tagil and Zaporozh'ye. Novokuznetsk does not include here the new Zapsib works, which produced its first pig iron only in 1965.

2. The capacity and output of works varies enormously. The estimated output of steel from the places in Table 10.33 may come from more than one works in a given place. The figures are based on various sources and take into account the enlargement of several works during the 1960's, notably Novo-Lipetsk, Krivoy Rog (1·7 million ton capacity blast furnace opened in 1967), Magnitogorsk, and Nizhniy Tagil, and the establishment of others, particularly the second works at Novokuznetsk (Zapsib) and the Temirtau works near Karaganda. Very roughly, probably only a dozen places together account for about three-quarters of Soviet pig iron and two-thirds of Soviet steel. Some of the smaller producers, however, specialise in high grade steel and are more vital to the economy than their output suggests.

3. The steel works of the U.S.S.R. fall into a number of types on the basis of position in relation to iron ore, coking coal and markets. Even within regions, types can be distinguished. The following may be suggested:

(a) On coking coal: the Donbass works, Novokuznetsk, Karaganda;

(b) On or near iron ore: Krivoy Rog, Magnitogorsk, Nizhniy Tagil;

(c) At or near markets: Elektrostal', Kolpino, Volgograd. The heavy industrial areas of the Donets-Dnepr, Ural and Kuzbass are in their own right also large markets for the steel produced on the spot. Small works running largely on scrap, notably at Begovat, Komsomol'sk-na-Amure and Liyepaya, are token bases of heavy industry for economic regions away from the heavy industrial concentrations.

(d) Intermediate: Cherepovets, assembling Pechora coal and Kola iron ore at a site between Moscow and Leningrad; the Dnepr works between Krivoy Rog iron ore and Donbass coal (Fig. 10.14(b)).

(e) Coastal: Zhdanov.

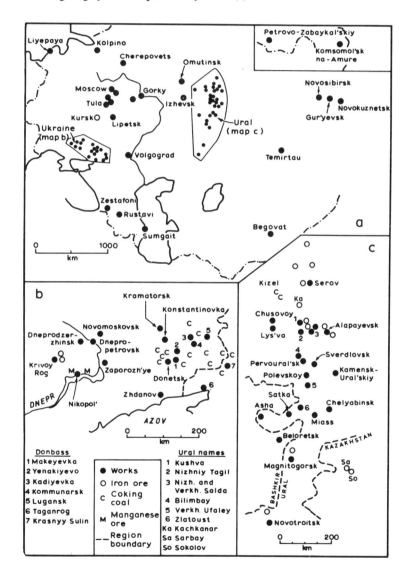

Fig. 10.15. *Iron and/or steel works of the U.S.S.R. in 1967. (a) U.S.S.R. (b) East Ukraine–North Caucasus. (c) Ural.*

Table 10.34. IRON AND STEEL WORKS OF THE U.S.S.R.

Region and works	Output	Location	Region and works	Output	Location
E1 NORTHWEST			**E8 WEST SIBERIA**		
Kolpino	u	M	Novosibirsk	1	M
Cherepovets	1	M	Novokuznetsk (2 works)	10	C
			Gur'yevsk	1	C
E2 CENTRE					
Tula	1	(C)M	**E9 EAST SIBERIA**		
Kosaya Gora	u	(C)M	Petrovo-Zabaykalskiy	u	
Elektrostal'	1	M	Krasnoyarsk	u	
E3 VOLGA-VYATKA			**E10 FAR EAST**		
Gorky	1	M	Komsomol'sk-na-Amure	u	
Kulebaki	1	(C)M			
Vyksa	u	(C)M	**E11 DONETS-DNEPR**		
Omutninsk	u	(C)M	Krivoy Rog	5	O
			Nikopol'	1	O
E4 BLACKEARTH CENTRE			Dnepropetrovsk	4	I
Lipetsk	3	M	Dneprodzershinsk	4	I
			Novomoskovsk	2	I
E5 VOLGA			Zaporozh'ye	4	I
Volgograd	1	M	Zhdanov	4	C
Beloretsk	u		Donetsk		
			Makeyevka	4	C
E6 NORTH CAUCASUS			Yenakiyevo	4	C
Krasnyy Sulin	u	C	Konstantinovka	4	C
Taganrog	1	C	Kramatorsk	4	C
			Kommunarsk	2	C
E7 URAL			Kadiyevka	2	C
Nizhniy Tagil	4	O	Lugansk	u	C
Sverdlovsk	2	O			
Chelyabinsk	4	O	**E14 BALTIC**		
Magnitogorsk	15	O	Liyepaya	u	M
Serov	1	O			
Lys'va	1	C	**E15 TRANSCAUCASIA**		
Alapayevsk	1		Zestafoni	u	C
Pervoural'sk	1		Rustavi	1	IM
Zlatoust	1		Sumgait	u	M
Novotroitsk	2	O			
Kushva	u		**E16 CENTRAL ASIA**		
Chusovoy	u		Begovat	u	M
Izhevsk	u				
Verkh: Salda	u		**E17 KAZAKHSTAN**		
Nizh: Salda	u		Temirtau	2	C
Bilimbay	u		Aktyubinsk	1	
Polevskoy	u				
Verkh: Ufaley	u				
Asha	u				
Satka	u				
Miass	u				

Output column: 1967 output of steel, estimated to nearest million tons;
  u – under half a million tons.
Location column: M – market,   C – coal,
  O – iron ore,   I – intermediate

Notwithstanding the apparent existence of an iron and steel industry in most regions, there is, in fact, almost a complete absence of steel production in the western regions of European U.S.S.R. and in Central Asia and southern Kazakhstan. Moreover, the Leningrad and Moscow industrial areas lack a metallurgical basis commensurate in capacity with their steel requirements.

10.6 ENGINEERING

The central position of engineering in the structure of a modern industrial power was well appreciated by the Communists after 1917. Before the Revolution this branch had not developed far and Tsarist Russia imported most of its machinery. Metal-working and engineering now employ over one-third of the manufacturing population and are the most widely dispersed sectors. Any self-respecting town has some form of engineering. Unfortunately very little quantitative information is available, and one is left to assume, therefore, that on the whole, the bigger the population of a town, the larger the number of people employed in engineering. It is possible to distinguish local and regional specialisms in different branches. Any Soviet atlas or economic geography textbook includes at least one map with a large number of engineering centres. Table 10.35 tabulates engineering specialisms of towns with over 350 000 inhabitants in 1965. Engineering has, however, filtered down to many medium and small towns and 'footloose' branches are, in fact, regarded as a means of bringing industry to relatively backward areas when other branches fail.

A number of features of Soviet engineering geography are listed here:

1. In pre-1917 Russia, about 90% of the engineering was in a few areas, notably the Centre (Moscow, Sornovo), the Baltic Ports (Peterburg, Tallin, Riga) and the Ukraine (Kharkov, Odessa). Branches represented then were locomotives and rolling stock (eg Kolomna), shipbuilding and the manufacture of farm equipment.

2. Although engineering has both expanded in existing works and diffused spatially to new places, the old centres reserve a special place, having tradition, skill and research facilities not

Table 10.35. BRANCHES OF ENGINEERING REPRESENTED IN TOWNS WITH OVER 350 000 INHABITANTS

Economic region	Town	Steel	General	Heavy	Machine tools	Energy	Rail	Motor vehicles	Ships	Tractors	Farm machinery
1	Leningrad	S	1		1	1			1	1	1
2	Moscow	S	1		1	1	1	1			
2	Yaroslavl'		1			1		1			
2	Ivanovo		1								
2	Tula	S	1	1							1
3	Gorky	S	1		1			1	1		
4	Voronezh		1								1
5	Kuybyshev		1		1						
5	Kazan'		1								1
5	Volgograd	S	1							1	
5	Saratov		1				1	1			1
5	Ufa		1								
6	Rostov		1					1		1	1
6	Krasnodar		1		1						
7	Sverdlovsk	S	1	1		1					
7	Chelyabinsk	S	1	1						1	
7	Perm'		1								1
7	Nizhniy Tagil	S	1					1			
7	Izhevsk	S	1		1						
8	Novosibirsk	S	1		1						
8	Omsk		1								1
8	Novokuznetsk	S	1	1							
8	Barnaul		1				1	1			
8	Kemerovo		1								
9	Krasnoyarsk	S	1								1
9	Irkutsk		1	1							
10	Khabarovsk		1								
10	Vladivostok		1								
11	Kharkov		1				1	1		1	
11	Donetsk	S	1	1							
11	Dnepropetrovsk	S	1					1			1
11	Zaporozh'ye	S	1						1		1
11	Krivoy Rog	S									
11	Makeyevka	S	1								
11	Zhdanov	S	1	1							
12	Kiev		1	1							
12	Lvov		1					1			
13	Odessa		1								1
14	Riga		1				1	1	1		
15	Baku		1	1							
15	Tbilisi		1					1			
15	Yerevan'		1					1			
16	Tashkent		1								1
16	Frunze		1								1
17	Alma-Ata		1	1							
17	Karaganda	S	1	1							
18	Minsk		1		1			1		1	

always easy to build up quickly in new areas. Feygin[1] quotes examples of regional discrepancies in skilled labour. Thus, one type of mechanic accounts for 1·8% of all persons employed in industry in the U.S.S.R. as a whole, 3·7% in the Centre, 2% in the Baltic, but only 1·4% in East Siberia and 1·2% in Kazakhstan. Central Asian figures, not given, could well be below those for Kazakhstan. Understandably then, precision engineering goods, machine tools and other such items are made in the Moscow area, turbines in Leningrad.

Moreover, various branches of engineering are interdependent, so there has been a lag between the opening up of new industrial areas and the spread of more complex and sophisticated engineering there. Some branches of engineering, such as the manufacture of locomotives and rolling stock, have diffused more than others. The lag might have been greater but for constant provision for the decentralisation of engineering in national plans and the impact of World War II, when the production of aircraft, motor vehicles and tractors as well as military supplies had to

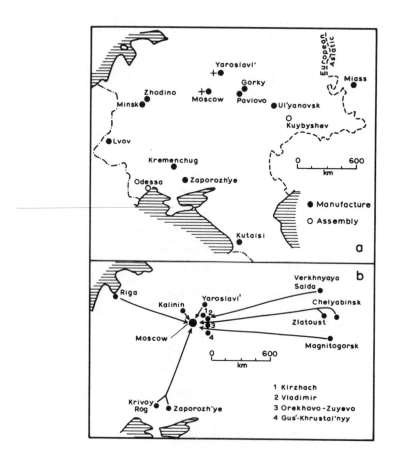

Fig. 10.16.   The manufacture and assembly of motor vehicles in the U.S.S.R. (a) Distribution of works. (b) Selected suppliers of materials and parts to the Likhachev motor vehicles works in Moscow. Main source: Lyalikov (see Bibliography), 42. The items involved are the following: Rolled steel–Krivoy Rog, Zlatoust, Chelyabinsk, Magnitogorsk; Sheet steel–Zaporozh'ye, Magnitogorsk; Instruments–Riga, Vladimir; Resins and paints–Yaroslavl'; Lamps–Kirzhach; Glass–Gus' Khrustal'nyy; Plastics–Orekhovo Zuyevo; Textiles–Kalinin.

take place east of the Volga. Then, for example, motor vehicle production began in Ul'yanovsk on the Volga and at Miass in the Ural region and tractor production at Rubtsovsk in West Siberia. Nevertheless, the newer eastern regions tend to be lacking in some branches of engineering and much machinery is carried great distances by rail.

3. Considering the great size of the U.S.S.R. and relatively inflexible rail transport system, it is desirable to produce many items in several regional centres, rather than exclusively in one place. Heavy engineering is well represented in the Donbass (eg Kramatorsk), the Ural region (eg Uralmash at Sverdlovsk) and West Siberia. Shipbuilding yards are found on the Black Sea (Nikolayev, Kherson), Baltic (Leningrad) and White Sea (Severodvinsk) as well as on each of the main river systems (eg Rybinsk, Gorky on the Volga). Bulky, clumsy machines, costly to move far by rail, must in particular be produced locally. Nikitin[4] points out, for example, that to transport a large modern crane from European U.S.S.R. to the Far East would need several wagons on a goods train and would cost more than the cost of making the crane itself.

4. As far as possible, engineering products that have only a regional or local application are made where they are needed. Thus coal-mining equipment is made in the Donbass and Kuzbass, oil equipment in Transcaucasia and the Ural region and farm and factory equipment for handling cotton in Central Asia. This principle has not always been adhered to; although much power station and transmission equipment is now required in Siberia, Leningrad is the main centre for producing some items, and Moscow, Kharkov and Riga, also in European U.S.S.R., still contribute.

5. Other trends include a growing concentration on a few branches in such places as Leningrad and Kharkov, once very cosmopolitan in an engineering sense and a tendency for some industries to farm out work to many establishments or to draw widely for components. Thus, the Moscow Likhachev motor vehicle works has some 300 connected establishments and the Kolomna diesel works 100.

6. The motor vehicles industry makes an interesting case study of diffusion. The first Russian motor vehicles were made in Moscow, Yaroslavl' and especially Gorky, where skilled labour, high grade steel and other industries were attractions. As already noted, during World War II, plants were established in safer places, including Ul'yanovsk and Miass. Decentralisation has continued, and now about a dozen places, not all large towns, make passenger cars, lorries and buses or assemble them. As a result, the motor vehicles industry is now established in about half of the 19 economic regions. Fig. 10.16(a) shows the location of the principal plants, all but one, Miass, in European U.S.S.R. Fig. 10.16(b) shows selected sources of ingredients for the Moscow Likhachev works.

10.7 OTHER SELECTED INDUSTRIES

Four very different branches of industry are studied together in this section. Data are relatively good for all of them and by contrasting the four branches it is possible to highlight some of the problems and contradictions of Soviet industrial location. The four industries are shown by regions in Table 10.36 with output *per capita* for each item spread about the national mean. Cement and leather footwear, quite dissimilar in most respects, both show a fairly balanced distribution among the regions. Timber and cotton cloth, on the other hand, show a very unbalanced distribution, with a very large part of production concentrated in a few regions and a skewed distribution of *per capita* values with most values lying below the mean. Reference to Table 10.13 in this chapter shows that the impression is confirmed numerically. Against a maximum possible correlation index of $+1.0$, which would indicate an exact shareout of production according to the population of each region, footwear scores $+0.85$ with population, and cement $+0.80$. Cotton reaches $+0.59$, but timber only $+0.02$. A breakdown of footwear, timber and cotton cloth (Tables 10.37 and 10.38 and Fig. 10.17) on the basis of 87 units (71 for the R.S.F.S.R., 3 for the Ukraine and 1 for each other Republic) shows, even in footwear, within region imbalances at oblast level not marked at economic region level. Cement data would presumably show the same since many divisions at that level do not have a cement factory.

Table 10.36. CONCENTRATION OF FOUR SELECTED BRANCHES OF INDUSTRY IN THE 19 ECONOMIC REGIONS

Cement ton/1 000 inhabitants		Leather footwear pairs/100 inhabitants		Timber m³/100 inhabitants		Cotton cloth m/10 inhabitants	
Ural	515						
Volga	428	Northwest	358				
Blackearth C.	428	Baltic	334				
Donets-Dnepr	414	Belorussia	328				
E. Siberia	391	Centre	286	Northwest	625		
Northwest	349	N. Caucasus	272	E. Siberia	613		
W. Siberia	348	Volga-Vyatka	238	Ural	336		
Kazakhstan	340	Transcaucasia	238	Far East	297		
Far East	337	Southwest	229	Volga-Vyatka	267	Centre	1 940
Baltic	314	Moldavia	218	W. Siberia	171	Baltic	314
U.S.S.R.	312	U.S.S.R.	209	U.S.S.R.	118	U.S.S.R.	306
Transcaucasia	295	Ural	197	Baltic	75	Transcaucasia	252
Centre	284	South	197	Centre	68	South	220
Central Asia	250	Donets-Dnepr	188	Belorussia	67	Northwest	204
N. Caucasus	220	Volga	176	Southwest	44	Central Asia	202
Belorussia	206	Central Asia	141	Volga	42	W. Siberia	175
Southwest	199	W. Siberia	128	N. Caucasus	21	Volga-Vyatka	151
Moldavia	174	Kazakhstan	126	Blackearth C.	12	E. Siberia	118
Volga-Vyatka	117	E. Siberia	117	Kazakhstan	10	Volga	79
South	60	Blackearth C.	92	Transcaucasia	6	N. Caucasus	30
		Far East	20	Donets-Dnepr	3	Far East	22
				Moldavia	neg.	Southwest	21
				South	neg.	Kazakhstan	20
				C. Asia	neg.	Belorussia	10
						Ural	9
						Donets-Dnepr	9
						Blackearth C.	6
						Moldavia	6

neg. – negligible.

Source: *NkhSSSR* 1965, 208, 215, 225, 237

How may the contrast between the four branches be explained?

1. Raw materials. Limestone and other rocks containing lime are widely found in nature and occur in every region of the U.S.S.R. Leather, similarly, is widespread and easily transported. Forest, in contrast, is found in one main zone (see Fig. 10.18) and cannot be cut elsewhere; cotton production is confined to three of the 19 regions and largely to one only, Central Asia. Little of it is manufactured where it is grown, but, like leather, it is reasonably easy to transport.

2. *Per capita* variation reflects differing regional requirements to some extent. The regions with heavy industry, hydroelectric constructions, road building schemes and so on, would presumably have a higher *per capita* consumption of cement. Similarly, but for a different reason, more timber is consumed for construction in the timber producing areas than outside, where other materials become more competitive. There is no reason, however, to assume that either leather footwear or cotton goods vary much in *per capita* consumption among regions.

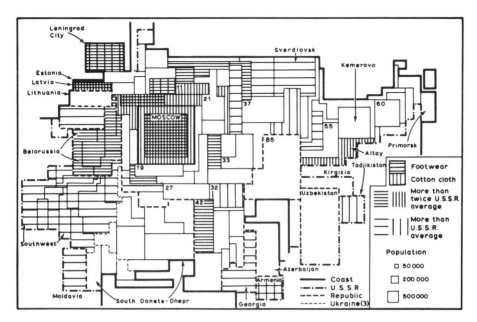

Fig. 10.17.   The distribution of manufacture of leather footwear and cotton cloth. The map highlights divisions
producing per capita quantities above the national average of one and/or the other of these items.
Key to selected places: 11 Ivanovo, 19 Tula, 21 Gorky, 27 Voronezh, 32 Volgograd, 33 Kuybyshev,
37 Chelyabinsk, 42 Rostov, 55 Novosibirsk, 60 Irkutsk, 85 Kazakhstan.

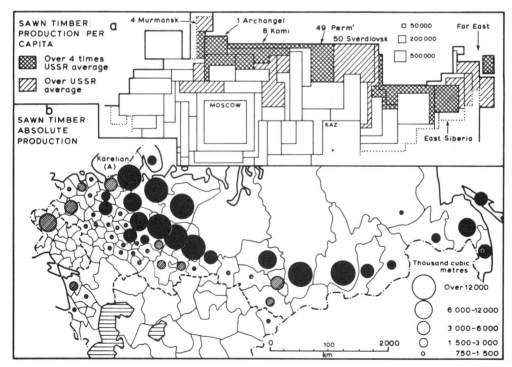

Fig. 10.18.   Sawn timber by region of the R.S.F.S.R. (a) Per capita output on a base map with divisions
proportional in area to their populations. (b) Absolute production. Circles are proportional in area to
the amount of sawn timber produced in the divisions they represent in 1965. Circles of divisions with a
per capita output above the national average are black. No circle is shown in divisions with only a
very small output.

Table 10.37. DIVISIONS WITH A TIMBER OUTPUT ABOVE NATIONAL MEAN OF 118 CUBIC METRES PER 100 INHABITANTS

Division	Output	Division	Output
RR7 Karelian (A)	2 379	RR69 Sakhalin	488
RR1 Archangel	1 535	RR58 Tyumen'	454
RR8 Komi (A)	1 519	RR65 Khabarovsk	452
RR60 Irkutsk	878	RR50 Sverdlovsk	450
RR2 Vologda	860	RR66 Amur	330
RR57 Tomsk	807	RR5 Novgorod	320
RR22 Kirov	767	RR61 Chita	266
RR14 Kostroma	756	RR23 Mariysk (A)	240
RR59 Krasnoyarsk	589	RR4 Murmansk	234
RR49 Perm'	561	RR64 Primorsk	211
RR62 Buryat (A)	553	RR12 Kalinin	177
		RR21 Gorky	148

NkhSSSR 1965, 209   RR: division of R.S.F.S.R.
NkhRSFSR 1965, 108–11 (A):   A.S.S.R.

3. Differences in regional production patterns of leather footwear and cotton goods, therefore, reflect different economic history, largely pre-Soviet, setting patterns little changed since 1917. The manufacture of cotton textiles, other textiles and factory made clothing in the Centre and Northwest perpetuates the concentration of decades ago, shown broadly in Fig. 10.1.

Several branches of industry have not been described at all. For non-ferrous metals, very little data are available. For the food industry, distribution is on the spot (sugar beet, cotton ginning) intermediate, or at markets (Leningrad, Moscow). The fishing industry is orientated towards the Far East ports, the Barents Sea and, to a lesser extent, Baltic and Black Sea and declining Caspian. Fish farming is developing fast and in 1965, according to *The Times,* 23 September 1965, about one million tons were being produced annually.

Table 10.38. DIVISIONS WITH LEATHER FOOTWEAR AND COTTON CLOTH *per capita* OUTPUT ABOVE THE NATIONAL MEAN

Leather footwear (pairs per 100 inhabitants)		Cotton cloth (metres per inhabitant)	
Division	Output	Division	Output
RR3 Leningrad City	1 047	RR11 Ivanovo	1 408
RR12 Kalinin	769	RR10 Vladimir	547
RR22 Kirov	652	RR12 Kalinin	242
RR42 Rostov	634	RR15 Moscow	153
RR34 Penza	505	Estonia	109
RR15 Moscow City	493	RR25 Chuvash (A)	101
RR20 Yaroslavl'	489	RR18 Smolensk	79
RR14 Kostroma	448	RR53 Altay	62
Estonia	444	RR20 Yaroslavl'	52
RR16 Orel	380	RR32 Volgograd	46
Latvia	358	RR3 Leningrad	44
RR52 Udmurt (A)	347	RR51 Chelyabinsk	41
Belorussia	328	Armenia	40
RR51 Sverdlovsk	309	Tadjikistan	31
RR39 Tatar (A)	301	Mean of U.S.S.R.	30·5
Lithuania	281		
RR28 Kursk	278		
RR49 Perm'	271	RR : division of R.S.F.S.R.	
Georgia	244	(A) : A.S.S.R.	
Armenia	244		
Southwest	229		
RR56 Omsk	226		
Moldavia	218		
Mean of U.S.S.R.	209		

Source: *NkhRSFSR* 1965, 12–14, 135, 148–9.

10.8 INDUSTRY IN THE 1966-70 FIVE YEAR PLAN: SUMMARY[6]

PROPOSALS FOR INDUSTRY

Various fundamental improvements in industry are required in productive efficiency, technical level, structure, quality and other aspects. The following aims are outlined:

1. Increase the volume of industrial production 47-50%. Capital (producer) goods (group A) by 49-52%, consumer goods (group B) by 43-46%.
2. On the basis of heavy industry, perfect the structure of industrial production. Improve the main branches of heavy industry and deliver to agriculture more equipment, fertilisers and insecticides. Speed up the development of light and food industries.
3. Greater productivity. Use innovations from foreign countries.
4. Develop physics, chemistry, electrophysics, electronics and other branches.
5. Increase the utilisation and productivity of equipment.
6. Increase specialisation and cooperation, especially in engineering. Standardise parts.
7. Make better use of raw materials and fuel. Cut fuel consumption in metallurgical plants, avoid the wastage of steel in rolling mills and generally use energy more efficiently.
8. Raise the productivity of labour by 33-35%.

Notes follow on certain key industries:

Electricity

Construct 64-66 million kW of new capacity. Thermal power stations with 2·4 million kW capacity and 300 MW units should be built. Large quantities of electricity should be transmitted from the eastern regions to European U.S.S.R., the grid in the European part completed and higher voltages introduced.

Oil and gas

New fields in West Siberia and western Kazakhstan should be developed and a large increase achieved in old fields. The capacity for storing gas under the ground should be raised and 25 000 km of new pipelines built. Oil refining capacity to be increased and improved. The search for oil and gas should be promoted in European U.S.S.R., especially in areas where these are most needed.

Coal

By 1970, 28% should be extracted by opencast methods. Coal output should be raised without an increase in the size of the labour force. New productive capacity for 165 million tons of coal should be provided. Oil shale production to reach 28 million tons and peat 92 million tons.

Metallurgical industries

The quality and variety of products to be improved. New facilities for the enrichment of ores. Continuous processes in factories. In non-ferrous metallurgy, the output of aluminium to be doubled.

The output of chemicals and petrochemicals should be doubled. Concentrated fertilisers, synthetic rubber, detergents should be increased and the quality of motor tyres improved. The iron and steel, oil and wood industries should provide more raw materials for the chemicals industry.

Table 10.39 shows the 1965 production and 1970 target for selected industrial items.

DEVELOPMENT BY REPUBLICS

The rate of expansion of industry planned for the 15 Republics varies greatly. Unfortunately the R.S.F.S.R. is not subdivided, so the exercise of comparison is valid largely for the other Republics. Further, since the faster growth is mainly in the less developed Republics, a large relative increase in one Republic, even when converted to *per capita* to eliminate differences in population size, may mean a small increase in absolute terms.

Table 10.39. 1966–70 FIVE YEAR PLAN TARGETS FOR SELECTED BRANCHES OF INDUSTRY

	1965	*1970*
Electricity (10^9 kWh)	507	840–850
Oil (10^6 ton)	243	345–355
Gas (10^9 m^3)	129	225–240
Coal (10^6 ton)	578	665–675
Pig iron (10^6 ton)	66	94–97
Steel (10^6 ton)	91	124–129
Rolled steel (10^6 ton)	71	95–99
Steel pipes (10^6 ton)	9	14–15
Mineral fertilisers (10^6 ton)	31·3	62–65
Plastics, etc. (10^3 ton)	821	2 100–2 300
Chemical fibre (10^3 ton)	407	780–830
Motor vehicles (10^3 units)	616	1 360–1 510
Heavy	380	600–650
Light	201	700–800
Tractors (10^3 units)	355	600–625
Agricultural machines (10^6 roubles)	1 446	2 500
Timber (10^6 m^3)	337	350–365
Cellulose (10^6 ton)	3·2	8·4–9
Paper (10^6 ton)	3·23	5–5·3
Cement (10^6 ton)	72·4	100–105
Cloth (10^9 m^2)	7·5	9·5–9·8
Leather footwear (pairs x 10^6)	486	610–630
Meat (state purchases) (10^6 ton)	4·8	5·9–6·2
Fish, etc. (10^6 ton)	5·8	8·5–9
Raw sugar (10^6 ton)	8·9	9·8–10
Radios (10^6 sets)	5·2	7·5–8
Televisions (10^6 sets)	3·7	7·5–7·7
Household refrigerators (10^6 units)	1·7	5·3–5·6

Source: *Pravda,* 20 Feb. 1966

Table 10.40. COMPARATIVE GROWTH OF INDUSTRY IN THE REPUBLICS DURING THE 1966–70 FIVE YEAR PLAN

Economic region	*Republic*	*1966– 1970*	*1965– 1966*	*1966– 1967*	*1967– 1968*
1–10	R.S.F.S.R.	150	108	110	108
11–13	Ukraine	150	108	109	108
14	Lithuania	170	112	113	111
14	Latvia	150	111	111	109
14	Estonia	150	108	109	108
15	Georgia	160	111	108	108
15	Azerbaijan	160	107	108	104
15	Armenia	180	112	114	107
16	Turkmenistan	160	110	112	105
16	Uzbekistan	160	109	109	104
16	Tadjikistan	180	109	111	105
16	Kirgizia	170	114	118	111
17	Kazakhstan	170	109	113	109
18	Belorussia	170	113	113	112
19	Moldavia	170	.107	111	113

Sources: *Pravda,* 20 Feb. 1966, 25 Jan. 1968, 26 Jan. 1969.

Development in the Soviet context means two different things. First, some regions and Republics, with a rural and/or colonial hangover, need industry and services to bring up their standard of living. Secondly, some regions are promising in terms of resources, but under-used and undersettled. They need an infrastructure of communications and settlements as well as new services and industry. The eastern regions, those lying east of the Volga and Ural regions, have cheap supplies of fuel, electricity and raw materials.

Increases of industrial production proposed for the period 1966-70 and actual increases claimed to have been achieved each year from 1966 to 1968 are shown in Table 10.40. Although this table does not reveal much, it suggests that some of the less developed Republics are being given a face-lift, whether or not they have low cost resources to exploit. Lithuania, for example, is getting more attention than the more heavily industrialised Latvia and Estonia. Much of the advantage given to the Central Asian and Transcaucasian Republics will be offset by the faster than average natural increase of population in these parts of the U.S.S.R.

EASTERN AND WESTERN U.S.S.R.

In the plan emphasis is given to the share of industrial production accounted for by the eastern regions.

The energy industry should be developed as well as branches of industry requiring large quantities of energy, particularly non-ferrous metals and chemicals. The timber industry should also be developed.

The share of the national total of Soviet production provided in 1970 by the eastern regions should be as follows (they have about 52

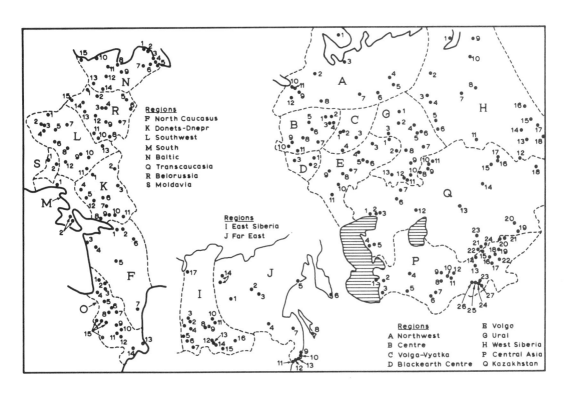

Inside the figure:

Regions
F North Caucasus
K Donets-Dnepr
L Southwest
M South
N Baltic
Q Transcaucasia
R Belorussia
S Moldavia

Regions
I East Siberia
J Far East

Regions
A Northwest   E Volga
B Centre   G Ural
C Volga-Vyatka   H West Siberia
D Blackearth Centre   P Central Asia
                      Q Kazakhstan

Fig. 10.19.   Selected places in which major industrial developments have been mentioned in the 1966-70 Five Year Plan. Source: Atlas razvitiya khozyaystva i kul'tury SSSR, 50 (Moscow, 1967).

million people or 22–23% of the total population of the U.S.S.R.):

45% of coal (77% of this opencast)
35% of natural gas
16% of oil
28% of electricity
65% of aluminium
58% of copper
28% of cellulose
31% of board (*karton*).

Living conditions in the eastern regions should be good and people should be attracted to settle there permanently. The rate of house construction should be faster than the average for U.S.S.R. as a whole and cultural standards and amenities should be improved.

When the 1966–70 Five Year Plan was announced in February 1966, a considerable number of places was mentioned specifically with reference to individual developments. The list has been 'tidied up' and the places mapped in *Atlas razvitiya khozyaystva i kultury SSSR* 1967, p. 50. Approximately 200 different places are referred to, some more than once, as having specific industrial projects. In addition, various improvements in transportation media are shown (see Chapter 11). Unfortunately, no idea of the comparative scale of projects is given. The engineering development at Novgorod could hardly be comparable with the engineering development at Leningrad; each gets one mention. Nevertheless it is useful to reproduce the list of places since many small towns have come into the news for the first time. The list has understandably been compiled to play down development in most R.S.F.S.R. regions and to magnify that in the smaller non-Russian regions. However, Siberia is well represented, although the Ukraine, considering its size, has relatively few places. Table 10.41 shows the places grouped into 19 regions, referred to for convenience from A to S. All places are pinpointed in Fig. 10.19.

1. In European U.S.S.R. and the Ural, the large productive forces and manpower reserves should be overhauled and used better. New industries consuming large quantities of energy should not be located here and existing ones should be curtailed. (This seems to contradict actual specific plans for expanding iron and steel production in the Ukraine, Ural and elsewhere.)

2. New enterprises should be encouraged in medium and small towns. Female labour should be utilised more.

3. Links between Republics and economic regions should be strengthened, in particular east-west routes. The mid-Siberian railway should be completed and new lines of communication provided between Central Asia and European U.S.S.R. Gas pipelines are needed between Central Asia and the Centre (Moscow region) and between West Siberia and European U.S.S.R.

4. Regional planning should be improved, local patriotism discouraged.

Table 10.41. THE LOCATION OF SELECTED INDUSTRIAL ESTABLISHMENTS DUE FOR CONSTRUCTION DURING 1966–70

Key to codes

BLD	Building materials	LIGHT	Light industry
CHEM	Chemicals industry	NONFE	Non-ferrous metals industry
COAL	Mining hard coal	NONFEORE	Non-ferrous ores and noble metals
DIAM	Extraction of diamonds	OIL	Extraction of oil
ENG	Engineering and metal-working	OILREF	Oil refinery
FEORE	Extraction of iron ore and ferro-alloys	SHALE	Oil shales
FOOD	Food industry	STEEL	Iron and steel industry
GAS	Extraction of natural gas	TEPS	Thermal electric power station
HEPS	Hydroelectric power station	WOOD	Manufacture of wood and paper

Table 10.41. contd

Frequency of mention of branches

1	Chemicals	47	10	Iron and steel	13
2	Engineering	40	11	Gas	11
3	Light	28	12	Oil	10
4	Thermal electric	28	13	Non-ferrous manufacturers	10
5	Building	25	14	Coal	8
6	Hydroelectric	19	15	Non-ferrous ores	8
7	Wood	17	16	Iron ore	6
8	Food	17	17	Diamonds	2
9	Oil refining	15	18	Oil shales	1

A NORTHWEST
A1	Serebryanskaya	HEPS
A2	Kondopoga	WOOD
A3	Archangel	WOOD
A4	Ukhta	OIL
A5	Voy-Vozh	GAS
A6	Syktyvkar	WOOD
A7	Kotlas	WOOD
A8	Cherepovets	STEEL
A9	Kirishi	TEPS, OILREF
A10	Leningrad	ENG
A11	Kolpino	ENG
A12	Novgorod	ENG, CHEM

B CENTRE
B1	Yaroslavl'	OILREF
B2	Kostroma	TEPS
B3	Ivanovo	ENG
B4	Vichuga	ENG
B5	Konakov	TEPS
B6	Moscow	CHEM
B7	Ryazan'	ENG, OILREF
B8	Kaluga	ENG
B9	Fokino	BLD
B10	Bryansk	ENG
B11	Orel	ENG

C VOLGA-VYATKA
C1	Gorky	ENG
C2	Bor	BLD
C3	Cheboksary	HEPS, LIGHT
C4	Saransk	ENG

D BLACKEARTH CENTRE
D1	Lipetsk	STEEL
D2	Voronezh	ENG
D3	Kursk	ENG, LIGHT, FOOD, FEORE

E VOLGA
E1	Karmanov	TEPS
E2	Ufa	OILREF
E3	Nizhne-Kamsk	HEPS
E4	Ul'yanovsk	ENG, LIGHT
E5	Tol'yatti	ENG
E6	Kuybyshev	OILREF
E7	Vol'sk	BLD
E8	Saratov	CHEM, LIGHT, HEPS
E9	Balashov	LIGHT
E10	Kamyshin	LIGHT
E11	Volgograd	ENG, OILREF

F NORTH CAUCASUS
F1	Rostov	ENG
F2	Shakhty	LIGHT
F3	Novorossiysk	BLD
F4	Krasnodar	LIGHT
F5	Stavropol'	CHEM
F6	Volgodonsk	FOOD
F7	Chirkeysk	HEPS

G URAL
G1	Berezniki	CHEM
G2	Perm'	CHEM
G3	Chaykovskiy	LIGHT
G4	Nizhniy Tagil	STEEL
G5	Sverdlovsk	STEEL, CHEM, BLD, FOOD
G6	Asbest	BLD, TEPS
G7	Chelyabinsk	STEEL
G8	Katav-Ivanovsk	BLD
G9	Magnitogorsk	STEEL
G10	Iriklin	TEPS
G11	Orsk	STEEL
G12	Gay	FEORE
G13	Orenburg	LIGHT

H WEST SIBERIA (H1–H10 are in Tyumen')
H1	Novyy Port	GAS
H2	Berezovo	GAS
H3	Verkhnyaya Konda	WOOD
H4	Shaim	OIL
H5	Tavda	WOOD
H6	Tyumen'	BLD, LIGHT
H7	Ust'-Balyk	OIL
H8	Megion	OIL
H9	Tazovskiy	GAS
H10	Tarko-Sale	GAS
H11	Omsk	CHEM, OILREF
H12	Rubtsovsk	ENG
H13	Barnaul	ENG, CHEM
H14	Iskitim	BLD
H15	Kemerovo	COAL, STEEL, CHEM, BLD, LIGHT

Table 10.41. contd

H16	Asino	WOOD		L6	Kamenets-Podol'skiy	BLD
H17	Leninsk-Kuznetskiy	LIGHT		L7	Rovno	CHEM
H18	Tashtagol	STEEL		L8	Vinnitsa	ENG, CHEM
				L9	Belaya Tserkov'	CHEM
I EAST SIBERIA				L10	Tripol'sk	TEPS
I1	Achinsk	NONFEORE, NONFE		L11	Cherkassy	CHEM, LIGHT
I2	Bogushany	WOOD		L12	Ladyzhensk	TEPS
I3	Yeniseysk	WOOD		L13	Chernigov	LIGHT
I4	Krasnoyarsk	HEPS, NONFE, CHEM, BLD				
				M SOUTH		
I5	Chernogorsk	STEEL, LIGHT		M1	Odessa	ENG
I6	Sayano-Shushensk	HEPS		M2	Crimea	CHEM(2)
I7	Kyzyl	NONFE				
I8	Maklakovo	WOOD		**N BALTIC**		
I9	Bratsk	NONFE, WOOD		N1	Tallin	ENG, WOOD
I10	Ust'-Ilimsk	HEPS		N2	Maardu	CHEM
I11	Korshunovo	FEORE		N3	Kiviyli	CHEM
I12	Usol'ye-Sibirskoye	CHEM		N4	Kokhtla-Yarve	CHEM
I13	Angarsk	CHEM, OILREF		N5	Narva	BLD, SHALE
I14	Irkutsk	NONFE		N6	Novopribaltiskaya	TEPS
I15	Selenga	WOOD		N7	Tartu	LIGHT
I16	Chita	TEPS, LIGHT		N8	Boldury	WOOD
I17	Noril'sk	NONFEORE, NONFE		N9	Plyavin'skaya	HEPS
				N10	Klaypeda	ENG
J FAR EAST				N11	Shyaulyay	ENG
J1	Vilyuysk	HEPS		N12	Kedaynyay	CHEM, FOOD
J2	Ust'Vilyuysk	GAS		N13	Alitus	ENG
J3	Yakutsk	TEPS		N14	Vil'nyus	TEPS, ENG
J4	Zeysk	WOOD, HEPS		N15	Baltiysk	FOOD
J5	Magadan	TEPS, LIGHT, FOOD				
J6	Pauzhest	TEPS		**O TRANSCAUCASIA**		
J7	Komsomol'sk-na-Amure	WOOD		O1	Tkvarcheli	COAL
J8	Yuzhno-Sakhalinsk	TEPS, FOOD		O2	Ingurskaya	HEPS
J9	Khrustal'nyy	NONFEORE		O3	Tkibuli	COAL
J10	Tetyukhe	COAL		O4	Bortsikhskaya	HEPS
J11	Primorskiy	CHEM		O5	Borzhomi	FOOD
J12	Vladivostok	BLD		O6	Tbilisi	ENG
J13	Nakhodka	FOOD		O7	Rustavi	CHEM
J14	North Siberia	DIAM(2)		O8	Madneuli	NONFEORE
				O9	Shamkhorskaya	HEPS
K DONETS-DNEPR				O10	Kirovabad	NONFE
K1	Kremenchug	ENG, OILREF, FOOD		O11	Razdan	NONFEORE
K2	Sumy	ENG		O12	Terterskaya	HEPS
K3	Kharkov	ENG		O13	Sumgait	CHEM
K4	Ingulets	FEORE		O14	Ali-Bayramlinskaya	TEPS
K5	Nikopol'	TEPS, STEEL		O15	Armenia	TEPS, BLD(2), CHEM
K6	Pavlograd	COAL				
K7	Nikitovka	NONFEORE, NONFE		**P CENTRAL ASIA**		
K8	Zhdanov	STEEL		P1	Cheleken	OIL
K9	Donetsk	ENG, COAL		P2	Nebit-Dag	OIL
K10	Uglegorsk	TEPS, COAL		P3	Okarem	GAS
K11	Lugansk	CHEM		P4	Darvaza	GAS
K12	Zaporozh'ye	TEPS		P5	Bezmein	BLD
				P6	Maryyskaya	TEPS
L SOUTHWEST				P7	Bayram-Ali	GAS
L1	Yavorov	CHEM		P8	Chardzhou	OILREF
L2	Stebnik	CHEM		P9	Gazli	GAS
L3	Kalush	CHEM		P10	Bukhara	LIGHT
L4	Ivano-Frankovsk	TEPS, ENG		P11	Yuzhnyy-Mobarek	GAS
L5	Ternopol'	LIGHT		P12	Navoi	TEPS, CHEM
				P13	Bekabadskaya	TEPS

Table 10.41. contd

P14	Tashkent	BLD, FOOD		Q16	Yermak	TEPS, COAL, STEEL
P15	Charvakskaya	HEPS		Q17	Pavlodar	ENG, CHEM, OILREF
P16	Namangan	CHEM, LIGHT		Q18	Leninogorsk	NONFE
P17	Fergana	CHEM		Q19	Alma-Ata	LIGHT, FOOD
P18	Mayli-Say	ENG, BLD		Q20	Kapchagayskaya	HEPS
P19	Toktogul'skaya	HEPS		Q21	Dzhambul	LIGHT
P20	Belovodskoye	FOOD		Q22	Chimkent	OILREF
P21	Kant	BLD		Q23	Karatau	CHEM
P22	Osh	LIGHT		Q24	Sas-Tobe	TEPS
P23	Vaksh	CHEM				
P24	Yavan	CHEM, BLD		R	BELORUSSIA	
P25	Dushanbe	LIGHT		R1	Grodno	CHEM
P26	Regar	NONFEORE		R2	Lida	BLD
P27	Nurekskaya	HEPS		R3	Dzerzhinsk	ENG
				R4	Minsk	ENG
Q	KAZAKHSTAN			R5	Polotsk	ENG, CHEM, OILREF
Q1	Gur'yev	OILREF		R6	Lukoml'	TEPS
Q2	Dossor	OIL		R7	Mogilev	CHEM
Q3	Makat	OIL		R8	Gomel'	ENG, CHEM
Q4	Zhetybay	OIL		R9	Bobruysk	CHEM
Q5	Uzen'	OIL		R10	Svetlogorsk	WOOD
Q6	Shubar-Kuduk	FOOD		R11	Mozyr'	OILREF
Q7	Aktyabinsk	BLD		R12	Soligorsk	CHEM
Q8	Dzhetygara	CHEM, BLD		R13	Pinsk	LIGHT
Q9	Lisakovskiy	FEORE		R14	Berezanskaya	TEPS
Q10	Rudnyy	FEORE		R15	Brest	ENG
Q11	Kustanay	CHEM, LIGHT				
Q12	Chelkar	FOOD		S	MOLDAVIA	
Q13	Dzhezkazgan	NONFEORE, NONFE		S1	Ungeny	FOOD
Q14	Karaganda	CHEM		S2	Rybnitsa	BLD
Q15	Ekibastuz	TEPS				

REFERENCES

1. FEYGIN, Ya. G. et al., *Zakonomernosti i faktory razvitiya ekonomicheskikh rayonov SSSR,* 166, 189 (Moscow, 1965)
2. HOOSON, D. J. M., 'Soviet industrial growth—where next?' *Survey,* No 57, Oct. 1965
3. POWELL, R. P., 'Economic Growth in the U.S.S.R.' *Scient. Am.,* **219**, No 6, 17–23, 1968
4. NIKITIN, N. P. et al., *Ekonomicheskaya geografiya SSSR,* 118 (Moscow, 1966)
5. GALITSKY, M. I. et al., *Ekonomicheskaya geografiya transporta SSSR,* 17 (Moscow, 1965)
6. Main source: *Pravda,* 20 Feb. 1966

BIBLIOGRAPHY

ADAMCHUK, V. A., 'The Problem of Creating a Kazakhstan Metallurgical Base' *Soviet Geogr.,* **5**, No 6, 1964
BELYANCHIKOV, K., 'Tret'ya metallurgicheskaya baza SSSR', *Pravda,* 11 Sept. 1958
CHERNYKH, A. V., *Neftyanaya i gazovaya promyshlennost' SSSR* (Moscow, 1964)
EBEL, R. E., *The Petroleum Industry of the Soviet Union* (Royer and Roger, American Petroleum Institute, 1961)
KHOREV, B. S. and ROGOV, N. A., 'On Ways of Developing Former Handicraft Industries' (As Illustrated by Gorky oblast) *Soviet Geogr.,* **4**, No 4, 31–46, 1963
LONSDALE, R. E. and THOMPSON, J. H., 'A Map of the U.S.S.R.'s Manufacturing' *Econ. Geogr.,* **36**, No 1, 36–52, 1960
LYALIKOV, N. I., *Ekonomicheskaya geografiya SSSR* (Moscow (Uchpedgiz), 1960)
NOVIKOV, V. P., 'The Kursk Anomaly—A Promising Iron-Ore Base for the Iron and Steel Industry of the Urals' *Soviet Geogr.,* **10**, No 2, 43–86, 1969
SHABAD, T., *Basic Industrial Resources of the U.S.S.R.* (Columbia University Press, New York and London, 1969)
SHIMKIN, D. B., *The Soviet Mineral—Fuels Industries, 1928–58: A Statistical Survey* (U.S. Department of Commerce, Washington D.C., 1962)
STANLEY, E. J., *Regional Distribution of Soviet Industrial Manpower: 1940–60* (F. A. Praeger, New York, 1968)

11

Communication channels

11.1 NON-SPATIAL ASPECTS OF COMMUNICATION

Communications in the U.S.S.R. are considered in this chapter only in terms of the channels, networks and media for carrying goods and passengers. The actual movement on the network is considered in Chapter 12.

EMPLOYMENT IN TRANSPORT

In 1966, 7 364 000 persons were employed in transport, 9·2% of total Soviet employment; Table 11.1 compares 1960 with 1966. Transport workers are naturally found in every part of the country, but in 1962 according to Feygin[1] ranged from 15% to 8%, with highest proportions in Kazakhstan, East Siberia, the Far East, the Northwest and South, and lowest in the Centre, Ural, Donets-Dnepr and Baltic. A wider range still is found at oblast level. There appear to be at

Table 11.1. EMPLOYMENT IN TRANSPORT IN 1960 AND 1966 IN THOUSANDS

	1960	1966
All transport	6 279	7 364
Rail	2 348	2 317
Water	322	347
All other*	3 609	4 700

*In 1965, road was 1 800 000
Source: *Strana sovetov za 50 let*, 219.

least two reasons for such considerable regional differences, first, variations in density of population and average route per person and secondly, the nature of the regional economy and products.

COMPARATIVE LENGTH

It will become clear in the next chapter that the movement of goods in the U.S.S.R. has for many decades been predominantly by rail. The following distances (Table 11.2), therefore, give comparative lengths of media that are actually used with vastly varying degrees of intensity.

Sea route length is roughly the sea distance from Leningrad to Leningrad around the U.S.S.R., via Suez, plus link routes to individual groups of ports. In the event of the Suez Canal being closed, the equivalant distance via South Africa is about 57 000 km. Inland waterway distance includes unmodified rivers of varying capacity, regulated rivers, including reservoirs, and navigation canals. The rail system for general use is distinguished from lines belonging to industrial and other establishments. Much of the route even on the general system is single track; in 1966, 27 000 km, about 20%, was electrified. Of the road length, 132 300 km or only about one-third, had a hard cement or bituminous surface. Of the air routes, 157 900 km were defined in 1965 as of union importance. The oil and gas pipelines have a considerable range in diameter and, therefore, capacity (Table 11.2).

Table 11.2. LENGTH OF TRANSPORT ROUTE
IN KILOMETRES

Route	Length
Sea (via Suez)	50 000*
Sea (via South Africa)	57 000
Waterway	142 700
Rail route	131 400
Feeder rail	114 000
Road	379 000
Air	435 000
Oil pipline	28 200
Gas pipeline	41 800

* Not strictly comparable.
Source: *NkhSSSR* 1965, 460, 474, 480, 490–2.

COMPARATIVE COST

The cost of transporting goods and passengers by four different media, in kopeks per 10 ton-kilometres and per 10 passenger-kilometres is shown in Table 11.3. The relationship of the various media to one another differs greatly between goods and passengers. It differs greatly, also, from the structure for the transportation of goods in West Europe and the United States. The values in Table 11.3 are only broadly helpful, for first, the length, duration and scope of the journeys on the various media differs greatly; secondly, the actual cost per ton or passenger unit of distance, *sebestoimost',* is not necessarily realistic since charges are fixed arbitrarily. According to Feygin[1] rates (*tarify*) do not correspond to cost (*sebestoimost'*). Galitsky[2] remarks that even after tariff reforms, rates are not realistic and not sensitive enough to be useful

indicators of the transport factor on the distribution of productive activities. At this stage it must be noted that both before and after 1917,

Table 11.3. TRANSPORT COSTS BY DIFFERENT
MEDIA

	Goods		Passengers	
	Kopeks	Rail =100	Kopeks	Rail =100
Rail	2·32	100	5·38	100
Sea	1·36	59	37·7	700
Inland waterway	2·42	104	13·1	244
Road	56·9	2 450	9·4	174

Source: *NkhSSSR* 1967, 514.

rail freight rates have been stepped-up at certain regional boundaries to protect some areas (eg, transport of Siberian grain to European Russia).

Feygin[1] states that within each of the transport media there are great differences in real cost due to different conditions of route, traction, environment and so on. For this reason, electric traction on busy lines and diesel traction elsewhere have almost replaced steam traction. Road surface quality is an important influence on road transport costs. In general, costs are lower on busy routes than on little used ones, particularly where maintenance and operation of the route is necessary. Length of journey also affects relative costs of different media. This is illustrated in Table 11.4, which though for 1961, gives an idea of the contrasts between road and rail. The distances are short by Soviet standards but the superiority of rail is soon established with

Table 11.4. COSTS IN ROUBLES PER TON OF TRANSPORTING SELECTED GOODS OVER DIFFERENT DISTANCES BY ROAD AND RAIL IN 1961

		10 km	20 km	50 km	100 km	200 km
Coal (hard)	Road	1·8	2·5	3·0	5·4	10·4
	Rail	0·6	0·6	0·7	0·9	1·3
Cement	Road	0·9	1·4	2·9	5·4	10·3
	Rail	1·3	1·4	1·5	1·7	2·7
Cloth	Road	1·0	1·5	3·0	5·4	10·3
	Rail	2·7	2·7	2·9	3·3	4·1
Confectionery	Road	1·0	1·5	3·1	5·5	10·4
	Rail	2·4	2·5	2·6	2·9	3·4

Source: Feygin,[1] 265

bulk items and even items that need more complicated handling.

COMPETITION AND COMPLEMENTARITY OF MEDIA

Since the whole transportation system of the U.S.S.R. is operated by the State there is theoretically no possibility of different companies competing in the provision of the same medium, or even of different media, offering competitive freight services and charges. The apparently superfluous duplication of services between any pair of places should not be allowed to occur. Nevertheless, it has often happened in the Soviet period that two or more means of taking a particular cargo between a given pair of places have been provided. Thus, for much of its length, the Volga is followed fairly closely by at least one railway. Similarly, an oil pipeline follows the Trans-Siberian railway closely from the Ural region to Lake Baykal and it is possible to ship goods between Leningrad and Vladivostok either by rail, or by sea, or even by air. In the Soviet context, however, the apparently competing services are merely alternative ones, sometimes necessary because one of the media (particularly sea routes and inland waterways) may be seasonally blocked. More recently, they have come to be regarded as supplementary; oil pipelines have relieved heavily used stretches of railway of oil traffic and electricity transmission lines save coal hauls. In 1961 (Feygin[1]) it was claimed that an electricity grid system could eventually save the railways the movement of 400 000 million ton-km a year, roughly equal to all the coal they were carrying at that time. With a few exceptions, however, there has not yet been a choice between road and rail, since the road system is provided largely either to cater for short distance movement to and from railways and within towns, or to serve thinly populated or physically difficult areas where railways have not been built.

In addition to the more conventional transport media discussed, the U.S.S.R. is using or experimenting with such forms as powerful helicopters and airships. The AN-22 aircraft (*Pravda,* 16 June 1965) offers possibilities that should not be underestimated for greatly increasing the share of traffic carried by air. Its capacity is 80 tons of cargo or 720 passengers and its range 5 000 km with that load or 11 000 km with 45 tons. It has a speed of 740 km/h, take off and landing requirements of only 1 100 and 800 m and does not need a concrete runway. It is hardly necessary to recall, also, that the U.S.S.R. was the first country to test in flight a supersonic commercial passenger aircraft.

11.2 SPATIAL ASPECTS OF COMMUNICATIONS

GENERAL

The spatial distribution and variations in each of the systems will now be considered. The text is mainly a commentary of the maps. In Chapter 3, Fig. 3.5, the inward looking nature of Comecon was shown diagrammatically. In this fairly closed trading system, land links, especially rail, are shorter and more reliable than peripheral sea links. The situation is similar to that in North America, but quite different from West Europe with its world-wide sea connections, or an Atlantic community. In the land based system, almost all transactions may be carried out by land media and sea routes tend to be more devious alternatives; in the ocean based system, land routes are only the beginning and end parts of long distance sea journeys. Within the U.S.S.R. itself the dependence on rail varies from less than 70% in some regions to over 95% at the other extreme. Table 11.5 shows the relative importance of different media in the early 1960's.

SEA

Since sea routes are largely independent of fixed channels it is meaningless to give a specific length to each of the routes used, though a rough idea could be given by summing distances between all pairs of ports linked by regular shipping services. Some idea of the great distances involved is given in Table 11.6. The Northern Sea Route, the first route in Table 11.6, is only open for two or three months a year. Ice obstructs movement for varying lengths of time in nearly all other sea areas in the Arctic Ocean, but ice breakers are

Table 11.5. RELATIVE IMPORTANCE OF DIFFERENT TRANSPORT MEDIA BY 19 ECONOMIC REGIONS

All figures percentages of total

	Economic region	Sea	River	Rail	Road	Pipeline
E1	Northwest	3	8	85	4	–
E2	Centre	–	8	85	5	2
E3	Volga-Vyatka	–	14	76	3	7
E4	Blackearth Centre	–	1	96	3	1
E5	Volga	1	12	71	3	13
E6	North Caucasus	4	5	83	6	3
E7	Ural	–	9	86	3	2
E8	West Siberia	–	4	83	3	10
E9	East Siberia	–	5	89	3	4
E10	Far East	22	6	67	5	1
E11	Donets-Dnepr	1	2	92	5	–
E12	Southwest	–	–	95	5	–
E13	South	19	3	69	9	–
E14	Baltic	4	3	83	9	–
E15	Transcaucasia	20	–	70	8	2
E16	Central Asia	11	1	77	10	2
E17	Kazakhstan	–	1	92	6	–
E18	Belorussia	–	3	90	7	–
E19	Moldavia	–	–	89	11	–
	U.S.S.R.	2	6	84	4	4

Source: Feygin,[1] 237.

becoming increasingly effective in keeping channels open. The closure of the Suez Canal in 1956-7 and again in 1967 has added great distances to Soviet routes diverted as a result; both the Cape of Good Hope and the Panama Canal routes are used as alternatives. The principal Soviet seaports are indicated in Figs. 3.5 and 11.1.

Table 11.6. SEA DISTANCES ROUND THE U.S.S.R.

Route	Distance km
Leningrad – Vladivostok via Murmansk	14 800
Leningrad – Vladivostok via Suez	22 800
Leningrad – Vladivostok via South Africa	30 000
Odessa – Vladivostok	17 400
Leningrad – Murmansk	4 300
Vladivostok – Magadan	2 600

INLAND WATERWAYS AND COASTAL NAVIGATION

The inland waterway and coastal navigation system of European U.S.S.R. forms a complex network illustrated in Fig. 11.1(a). It is possible for small vessels to navigate between any places on the system, but for the most part sea and inland navigation are distinct. The layout is highlighted by the topological nature of the map. The remaining inland waterways of the U.S.S.R. are more simple systems, several of great total length, but all reaching only one sea or ocean, in contrast to the 'five seas' of the European system. One problem, freezing, affects the system almost everywhere.

The development of the system, both past and future, is closely connected with the development of hydroelectric power dams and

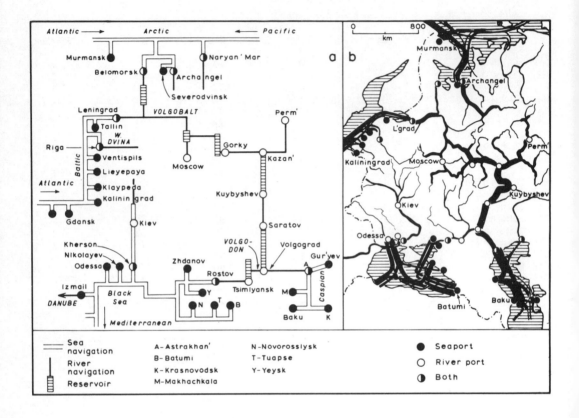

Fig. 11.1.   Coastal and inland waterways of European U.S.S.R. Selected sea and/or river ports are shown.
The same Soviet ports are shown on maps (a) and (b). The thickness of routes in (b) is roughly
proportional to the traffic carried. Source of (b): Galitskiy,[2] 73.

reservoirs, in places with irrigation and increasingly with water supply. As with other media, much of the total traffic on the system passes along only a small part of the waterways, for many river courses, counted in the total as navigable, are of very limited usefulness. The volume of traffic on different parts of the European system is shown roughly by the width of routes in Fig. 11.1(b). This system carries about two-thirds of the total ton-kilometres credited to inland waterways. Understandably, much of the investment in improving waterways in the 1960's has been put into the Volgobalt Canal between Cherepovets and Leningrad.

RAIL

The rail system is dealt with more fully than the others because of its outstanding role in Soviet transport, although it is now diminishing in relative importance.

The rail system of Russia in 1917 was fairly well developed roughly within the triangle Leningrad-Omsk-Rostov-on-Don. Beyond this, individual lines already reached far out into Transcaucasia, Central Asia and Siberia. The first two regions were then, as now, connected by ferry across the Caspian (Baku-Krasnovodsk) but the second two were not connected by a reasonably direct rail link. The loose ends of the system in 1917 are shown in Fig. 11.2(b).

Between 1917 and 1967 the length of route on the Soviet system had almost doubled (72 000 km to 133 000 km). Some new lines had been built to close up the network within the Leningrad-Omsk-Rostov triangle, but most of the construction was on the fringes of this or well beyond. A comparison of Figs. 11.2(b) and 11.3 shows the main features of construction in new areas over the period. The complete network of European U.S.S.R. is not shown as this can be found now in many atlases, both Soviet and Western. Instead some features of distance and connectivity are briefly noted and are supported by numerical data. Detailed maps of the Moscow and Donbass rail systems are given in Figs. 11.4(b) and 11.4(c).

The Soviet transportation system has the longest scheduled rail services in the world, but since the bulk of the population is in the western third of the country, most journeys are far

shorter than the extreme ones. The concept of average length of journey is worth consideration, but difficult to calculate meaningfully. The selected pairs of rail distances in Table 11.7 illustrate what might be called:
1. extremely long distances (European U.S.S.R. to Far East). These are mostly over 8 000 km.
2. Longer interregional journeys, ranging between about 3 000 and 6 000 km.
3. Journeys within European U.S.S.R., many of which are under 1 000 km.

Table 11.7. DISTANCES OF SELECTED RAIL JOURNEYS IN THE U.S.S.R. IN KM

1. European U.S.S.R.–Far East

Vladivostok–Murmansk	10 446
Vladivostok–Leningrad	9 515
Vladivostok–Brest	10 314
Vladivostok–Lvov	10 565
Vladivostok–Moscow	9 216
Vladivostok–Tbilisi	10 814

2. European U.S.S.R.–Mid-Siberia and Central Asia

Irkutsk–Moscow	5 068
Krasnoyarsk–Moscow	3 989
Novosibirsk–Moscow	3 228
Alma Ata–Moscow	4 064
Tashkent–Moscow	3 374

3. Within European U.S.S.R.

Leningrad–Moscow	680
Leningrad–Donetsk	1 708
Leningrad–Volgograd	1 742
Leningrad–Lvov	1 438
Leningrad–Pechora (Kozhva)	1 904

Few places, of course, are joined by straight line distances; some pairs of places may be linked by lines greatly in excess of the direct distance. The reason for this will usually be the presence of an insurmountable or difficult physical obstacle (the sea, a mountain range) or the lack of a direct rail connection because of absence of sufficient traffic. Table 11.8 shows journeys between selected pairs of places in three ways. The first distance is a 'straight' line (great circle for bigger distances), the second the actual recommended rail distance in the late 1950's, the third, an index

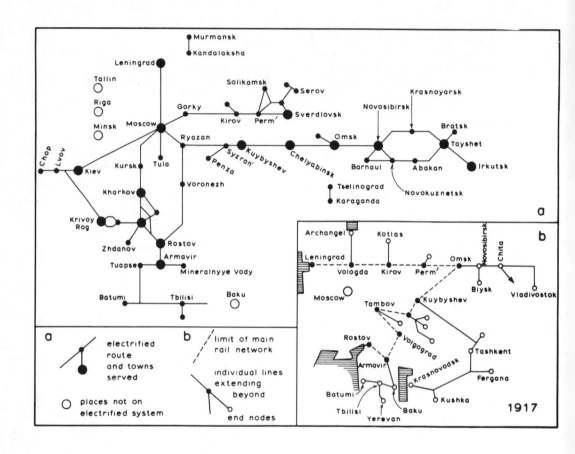

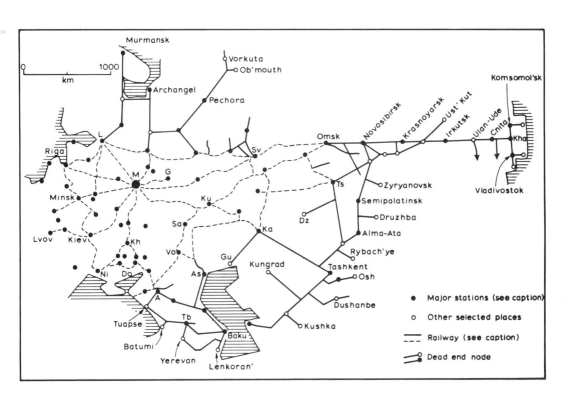

Fig. 11.3.   *Rail system of the U.S.S.R. Within the outer broken lines, scale is correct. Beyond them, the network is represented topogically with scale greatly reduced east of Novosibirsk. All major lines are shown outside the outer broken line, but only selected lines are shown within.*

The map also shows (black dots) all places classed as major stations (krupnyye stantsii) in Spisok stantsiy zheleznodorozhoy seti SSSR, 406-07. The selected routes shown by broken line join places considered in Table 11.8.

Key to places on map:

A	*Armavir*	*G*	*Gorky*	*Kha*	*Khabarovsk*	*Ni*	*Nikopol'*
As	*Astrakhan'*	*Gu*	*Gur'yev*	*Ku*	*Kuybyshev*	*Sv*	*Sverdlovsk*
Do	*Donetsk*	*Ka*	*Kandagach*	*L*	*Leningrad*	*Tb*	*Tbilisi*
Dz	*Dzhezkazgan*	*Kh*	*Kharkov*	*M*	*Moscow*	*Ts*	*Tselinograd*

Table 11.8. DETOURS ON SELECTED RAIL JOURNEYS IN THE U.S.S.R.

Route	Direct	Rail	Detour	Route	Direct	Rail ·	Detour
Leningrad–Archangel	750	1 223	163	Donetsk–Armavir	420	544	129
Leningrad–Sverdlovsk	1 780	2 077	117	Donetsk–Nikolayev	440	599	136
Leningrad–Moscow	630	680	108	Armavir–Volgograd	500	664	133
Leningrad–Minsk	690	866	126	Tbilisi–Armavir	480	858	179
Leningrad–Riga	500	604	121	Tbilisi–Baku	450	552	123
Moscow–Archangel	990	1 174	119	Baku–Armavir	880	964	110
Moscow–Gorky	400	492	123	Baku–Volgograd	1 020	1 628	160
Moscow–Sverdlovsk	1 410	1 691	120	Volgograd–Saratov	320	427	133
Moscow–Kuybyshev	870	1 104	127	Saratov–Tashkent	2 110	2 470	117
Moscow–Saratov	720	905	126	Kuybyshev–Sverdlovsk	750	1 120	150
Moscow–Kharkov	650	822	127	Kuybyshev–Tashkent	1 920	2 270	118
Moscow–Kiev	750	904	120	Kuybyshev–Saratov	350	445	127
Moscow–Minsk	680	800	118	Sverdlovsk–Omsk	810	907	112
Moscow–Riga	830	972	117	Sverdlovsk–Tselinograd	920	1 130	123
Riga–Minsk	400	525	131	Omsk–Novosibirsk	600	630	105
Kiev–Minsk	440	622	141	Omsk–Tselinograd	450	764	170
Kiev–Kharkov	410	500	122	Tselinograd–Alma Ata	980	1 318	134
Kiev–Nikolayev	400	593	148	Tashkent–Alma Ata	690	999	145
Kiev-Lvov	460	579	126	Alma Ata–Novosibirsk	1 390	1 687	121
Kharkov–Saratov	710	980	138	Novosibirsk–Tselinograd	860	1 162	135
Kharkov–Donetsk	* 250	318	127	Novosibirsk–Krasnoyarsk	610	767	126
Kharkov–Nikolayev	450	564	125	Krasnoyarsk–Irkutsk	840	1 079	140
Donetsk–Volgograd	500	616	123	Irkutsk–Khabarovsk	2 220	3 397	153

of detour or circuitousness calculated as DIRECT/RAIL × 100. A more exhaustive study of such distances between all pairs of 19 places, one representing each of the 19 economic regions, showed mostly low indices within the dense network of European U.S.S.R. (eg Moscow-Minsk 120, Moscow-Leningrad 108). At the other extreme, the highest indices, representing a rail detour more than twice the direct distance were Tbilisi-Kishinev (Moldavia) 216 and Tbilisi-Tashkent (not using Caspian ferry) 203. Still greater indices of detour are found between many places of secondary importance (eg Kungrad-Gur'yev-Astrakhan' in Fig. 11.3). These are guides to where further links may be desirable in the system. Some of the new railway lines under construction or consideration in the late 1960's are shown in Table 11.9 at the end of this chapter.

Certain centres, thanks to their size, have come to occupy advantageous positions as the rail network has evolved, through having reasonably direct rail links. Moscow is particularly privileged in this respect as it is the centre of a radial system, the pattern of which is discernible for many hundreds of kilometres

away. Many places can be reached from Moscow along trunk routes which are not only nearly direct, but also double track and electrified. Many secondary centres are linked by cross-country routes that may not have excessive detours, but nevertheless run across the trunk routes. As an example, the rail links between Minsk and Moscow, and Minsk and Kursk, are compared on the same scale in Fig. 11.4(a). The relative distances are:

	Minsk–Moscow	Minsk–Kursk
Rail	800	790
Direct	680	630
Detour index	118	125

The Minsk-Moscow line is superior to the Minsk-Kursk line(s) in at least three ways: it is more direct, it is double track all the way and it follows a recognised traffic flow. The Minsk-Kursk traffic can follow any of several alternative routes, but each uses part of the busy Moscow-Kiev and/or Moscow-East Ukraine lines, shown heavily in Fig. 11.4(a).

As will be shown in the next chapter, the

volume of traffic handled on the Soviet rail system has increased enormously not only since 1917, but even since 1945. Although the system has been extended, the increase has largely been achieved on existing lines. Great emphasis has been placed on improving the quality of track, signally and marshalling yard facilities and, as in Western industrial countries, a transformation in the means of traction has been achieved since the mid-1950's, as is shown here:

Traction	*All figures are percentages*			
	1958	*1965*	*1966*	*1967*
Electric	15	40	42	} 92
Diesel	11	45	47	
Steam	74	15	11	8

Sources: *NkhSSR* 1965, 464
Strana sovetov za 50 let

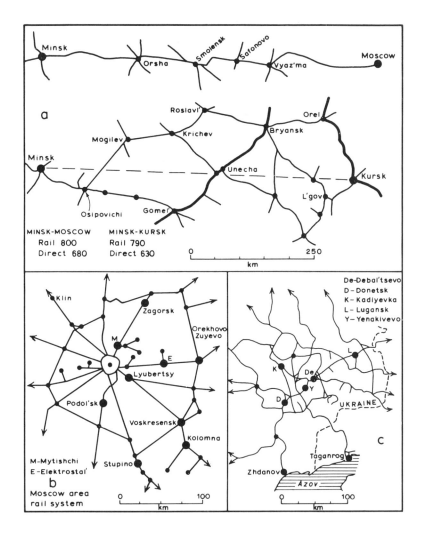

Fig. 11.4. *(a) Contrasting layout of Minsk-Moscow and Minsk-Kursk railway lines. (b), (c) Detailed maps ((b), topological) of the Moscow area and Donbass area rail systems.*

The policy has been to electrify the routes and to introduce diesel traction on less used routes. The proportion electrified by 1966 was 27 000 km or 20%, more than twice the length in 1958. The electrified system is shown topologically in Fig. 11.2(a). Different sources give somewhat different versions of the exact lines electrified. The routes in operation for general use in the U.S.S.R. are supported by a further 114 000 km of line belonging to individual enterprises, which, however, carry far less traffic.

Most developed countries have built almost no new railway lines for several decades and are indeed closing lines, but Soviet planners are still putting down new lines. Those listed in the 1966-70 Plan are given in Table 11.9 and mapped in Fig. 11.7. Many are filling gaps in the existing network to reduce detours. Some are penetrating new areas. Among these, for example, is the Tyumen'–Surgut line, 700 km in length, across marsh and peat lands, through forests and across two sizeable rivers. Tayga or mountain conditions confront the builders of new lines almost anywhere in Siberia. Yet Feygin[1] suggests that the route length in the eastern part of the U.S.S.R. should be at least doubled; this implies the further building of some 20 000 km.

ROAD

There is much evidence to show that road transport has a very different role in the U.S.S.R. from that in either the Western industrial countries such as the United States and France, or the more advanced developing countries such as Mexico and Brazil. The small number of vehicles in circulation per thousand inhabitants, the relatively high ratio of goods vehicles to passenger cars, the small share of goods traffic taken by road, the short average length of road journey, the high cost of road freight charges and the layout of the road system all point to a very characteristically Soviet view of road transport.

The road system of most of the U.S.S.R. was recognised as deplorable until very recently. The total length of 'road' over which motor vehicles may pass is enormous (1 364 000 km in 1965), but less than one-third (379 000 km) had a hard surface in that year. Of this, only 132 000 km was properly macadamised or cemented. The fact, however, that the hard surface roads have doubled in length since the early 1950's and the finished surface roads between 1959 and 1965 alone, emphasises not only the hitherto inadequate state of the system, but a new appreciation of the need for better roads.

In the U.S.S.R. the private car has been almost non-existent and commuter and service contacts between town and adjoining country by car are rare. Inter-city road links are apparently also poor. The role of road transport, then, has been mainly as follows: first, to take within-town traffic (only three towns, Moscow, Leningrad and Kiev have undergrounds) secondly, to serve as feeders to railways, thirdly, to link places separated by terrain across which rail construction would be extremely difficult, particularly in the Caucasus area and Central Asia and fourthly, to open up thinly populated areas in which too little traffic could be expected to make rail construction worthwhile. The last two functions are not entirely mutually exclusive. Roads such as the Trans-Caucasus highways and those into Yakutia have strategic as well as economic origins. The recent improvement of a number of inter-city main roads (eg Moscow–Minsk, Moscow–Kharkov), gives alternative routes to railways and suggests that a more integrated road system for the U.S.S.R. is on the way.

AIR

Since an air service can theoretically be provided between any pair of suitable airports it is unrealistic to map an air network. The map of scheduled air services, however, gives an idea of the pattern of traffic. All other things being equal, the frequency of services, or rather of carrying capacity between any pair of places, would be expected to be related to their size and the distance between them. Great reservations have, however, to be added. For example, administrative centres, particularly of S.S.R.'s, would probably generate more passenger traffic than other centres of comparable size. Alternative means of transport would also affect air traffic. In the last resort, some places depend exclusively on air transport for contacts with the rest of the country. In the Soviet context it seems important to distinguish the routine system of passenger and freight links from the special use of air transport to develop inaccessible areas, serving, for example, to open up the diamond fields in Yakutia and the new areas of oil exploration in the Ob' lowlands. Thus the M1-6 helicopter has been the only means of transport in parts of Tyumen' oblast (*Pravda,* 27 July 1966).

PIPELINES AND ELECTRICITY TRANSMISSION

The movement of oil and gas by pipeline and electricity by transmission line needs extensive special purpose networks. In contrast to the other systems, used for general purposes and, ideally, integrated to serve the whole country, there is less immediate advantage in, or possibility of, making pipelines or transmission lines into integrated systems. The gas pipeline system still tends to link specific gas deposits with a limited number of market terminals. The oil pipeline system is more integrated since much of its input comes from the one Volga-Ural area. The electricity grid started life as a large number of separate local or regional networks, but the advantages of a national system have long been appreciated. Developments in long distance transmission are making it feasible even for the U.S.S.R. to contemplate one main system, reaching from East Europe to East Siberia. This topic has been discussed in Chapter 10.3 and illustrated in Fig. 10.11.

One of the most spectacular aspects of the development of the Soviet economy has been the growth since the early 1950's of both oil and gas pipelines. The two systems are separate in function and very different in layout. The growth in length of pipeline in use between 1945 and 1966 is shown in Fig. 11.5. The length of oil pipeline increased six times between 1950 and 1966, but the gas pipeline increased 23 times over the same period. Figures for selected years in kilometres are:

Year	Oil	Gas
1950	5 400	2 300
1955	10 400	4 900
1960	17 300	21 000
1965	28 200	41 800
1966	29 500	47 400
1967	32 400	52 600

Sources: *NkhSSSR* 1965, 491 and *Strana sovetov za 50 let,* 179, *NkhSSSR* 1967, 572.

The oil and gas pipelines are both becoming so complicated that it is difficult to show them in detail on an ordinary map. The topological map in Fig. 11.6 loses accuracy of distance but retains the correct relationship of places on the systems. To the system shown diagrammatically in Fig. 11.6 should be added not only the Central Asia to Moscow pipeline, already in use in 1968, but also parts of the West Siberia to Centre (Moscow) and Northwest (Leningrad) system; *Pravda,* 17 August 1968, reported the construction in the Komi A.S.S.R. of part of the pipeline with a large (122 cm) diameter. Pipelines planned for 1966-70 are listed in Table 11.9.

The U.S.S.R. has been linked to Comecon partners for some time by electricity transmission lines and oil pipelines. In 1967 a pipeline called *Bratstvo* (Brotherhood) to carry Ukraine (Bitkov) natural gas into Czechoslovakia was under construction (*Pravda,* 19 January 1967).

11.3 NEW LINES OF COMMUNICATION IN THE 1966-70 FIVE YEAR PLAN: SUMMARY

The system of transport and communications should be improved to satisfy the needs of the national economy. A unified automated transportation network should be created, with the

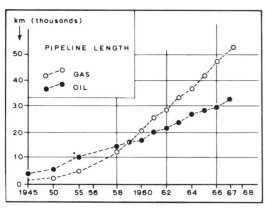

Fig. 11.5.   The length of oil and gas pipline in the U.S.S.R. since 1945.

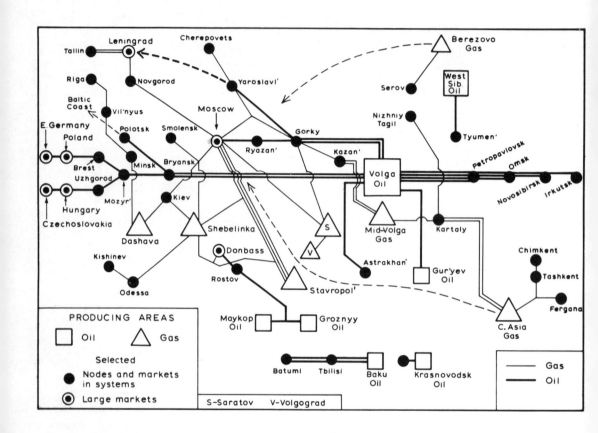

Fig. 11.6. *The oil and gas pipeline systems of the western part of the U.S.S.R. All the major pipes are shown but details of small branches are omitted. The map is topological, and scale diminishes sharply in Siberia. Pipes under construction in the late 1960's are shown by broken lines.*

economic opening up of new regions in mind. The correct means of transport should be used for a given haul. Delivery should be speeded up, and terminal facilities improved. Automation and computer techniques should be developed.

1. Railways. The volume of goods carried should go up by 23%. Steam traction should be replaced entirely. 7 000 km of new lines are to be built and 10 000 km more lines electrified. Labour productivity on the railways is to go up 23–25%.
2. Water. Sea transport will increase by 80% and port capacity by 40%. Fuller use should be made of the Siberian rivers and of the Volgobalt system.
3. Pipelines. The length of pipelines should be doubled, with the construction of 12 000 km of new lines.
4. Roads. An increase here of 70% in the volume of goods handled and the introduction of more passenger services. Roads, particularly in rural areas, should

be improved. 63 000 km of hard surface is to be put on existing roads.

Table 11.9 shows all the main improvements to communications in the 1966–70 Five Year Plan. The lines in the western part of the U.S.S.R. are located in Fig. 11.7. The overwhelming share of developments in the western half of the area of the U.S.S.R. is extraordinary. Only about 10% of the new rail construction and electrification is in the eastern half and almost none of the pipeline length. The new lands, scene of much rail construction, have now ceased to be the pioneer frontier of the country. The electrification of the South-Siberian Railway from Kartaly to Pavlodar is the main feature of development. North of the Trans-Siberian Railway, on the other hand, there are several rail spurs, as well as oil and gas pipelines in West Siberia. In terms of distance, the longest project is the gas pipeline from Central Asia to Moscow. In detail, as might have been predicted, several railways fill short but critical gaps in the rail system.

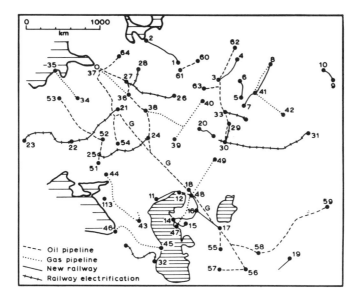

Fig. 11.7.   *Key map to new communications in western U.S.S.R., 1966-70 Five Year Plan. Source:* Atlas razvitiya khozyaystva i kul'tury SSSR, 50.

Table 11.9. NEW TRANSPORT LINES 1966–70

New railway	1 Mikun'–2 Archangel 3 Ivdel–4 Serginy 5 Tavda–6 Uray 7 Tyumen'–8 Surgut 9 Asino–10 Belyy Yar 11 Astrakhan'–12 Gur'yev 13 Krasnodar to coast 14 Shevchenko–15 Uzen' 16 Beynau–17 Makat–18 Kungrad 19 Dushanbe–boundary 20 Chishmy–Beloretsk
Rail electrification	21 Moscow–22 Kiev–23 Chop 24 Penza–25 Kharkov 26 Kirov–27 Cherepovets–28 Konosha 29 Chelyabinsk–30 Kartaly–31 Pavlodar 32 Lenkoran'–Yerevan 33 Sverdlovsk–Kurgan
Oil pipelines	34 Polotsk–35 Ventispils 36 Yaroslavl'–37 Leningrad 38 Bor–39 Kuybyshev–40 Perm' 8 Surgut–41 Tobol'sk–42 Omsk 43 Groznyy–44 Trudovaya 45 Baku–46 Batumi 47 Zhetybay–48 Kul'sary–49 Orsk
Gas pipelines	51 Shebelinka–52 Kursk–53 Viln'yus 54 Voronezh–Moscow ring 55 Darvaza–18 Kungrad 56 Bayram-Ali–57 Ashkhabad 58 Bukhara–59 Alma Ata 24 Penza–38 Gorky–36 Yaroslavl' 60 Voy-Vozh–61 Syktyvkar 62 Berezovo–63 Berezniki–29 Chelyabinsk–30 Kartaly 36 Yaroslavl'–27 Cherepovets–64 Petrozavodsk

Not shown in Fig. 11.7.

New railways	three short spurs north from Trans-Siberian in East Siberia
Rail electrification	Irkutsk–Chita
Oil pipeline	Ust'-Vilyuysk–Yakutsk Erri (Sakhalin)–Komsomol'sk-na-Amure

REFERENCES

1. FEYGIN, Ya. G. *et al., Zakonomernosti i faktory razvitiya ekonomicheskikh rayonov SSSR,* 219–20, 229, 234, 237, 247–8 (Moscow, 1965)
2. GALITSKIY, M. I. *et al., Ekonomicheskaya geografiya transporta SSSR,* 26 (Moscow, 1965)

BIBLIOGRAPHY

LEBED, A. and YAKOVLEV, B., *Soviet Waterways,* Series 1, No 36, Institute for the Study of the USSR (Munich, 1956)
ORLOV, B. P., *Razvitiye transporta SSSR 1917–1962* (Moscow, 1963)
Spisok stantsiy zheleznodorozhnoy seti SSSR (Transzheldorizdat, Moscow, 1957)
Glavnoye upravleniye geodezii i kartografii Ministerstva geologii SSSR, *Atlas avtomobil'nykh dorog SSSR* (Moscow, 1967)
YEGOREVA, V. V., 'The Economic Effectiveness of the Construction of Pioneering Railroads in Newly Developed Areas' *Soviet Geogr.,* 5, No 4, 1964

12

Regional differences in production costs, and interregional traffic flows

Great differences were observed in the regional production of many items in Chapters 9 and 10. Between two extremes, complete regional self-sufficiency and complete specialisation in one locality, lie a whole range of possibilities. At one extreme, it is essential or desirable to provide services such as primary education, health services, or bakeries, in every community. At the other extreme it may be advantageous or even necessary to concentrate production in one or two places for the whole national market: diamonds are mined mainly in one locality in the Far East and tea and citrus fruits are produced almost exclusively in Georgia. The degree of interregional exchange depends on the commodity produced and on transport conditions. Where production costs are equal among regions, the region with the best transport facilities will be the one that serves the widest area.

12.1 SPATIAL DIFFERENCES IN PRODUCTION COSTS

A basic consideration for planners in deciding which resources to develop is the cost of production of given items at different places. The real usefulness of this depends on the ability under the Soviet system to assess relative production costs. It is assumed here that the

methods used are satisfactory, but this matter is itself debatable. Different production costs for many goods and services would seem to depend on one variable in particular, the productivity of an individual. For example, a coal miner in the Kuzbass produces on average two or three times as much coal per shift as one in the Donbass. Similarly, a state farm worker in Kazakhstan may produce several times as much grain as one in Belorussia and a doctor or teacher in a densely populated urban environment may be able to serve more patients or schoolchildren than one working in an area of dispersed rural settlement.

Such differences in productivity stem also from organisational and technological variations. On the whole, state farm workers tend to be more productive than collective farm workers even in the same environmental area, growing the same things, because the organisation and capitalisation of state farms is superior. Similarly, the cost of producing a ton of steel is three to four times as high in some small, old mills in the Ural region as it is at the Magnitogorsk works, though the raw materials used do not differ substantially. It would have been equally valid to consider different production costs separately for each item under different sections in this book, but it has been decided to consider selected items together in this chapter for comparative purposes.

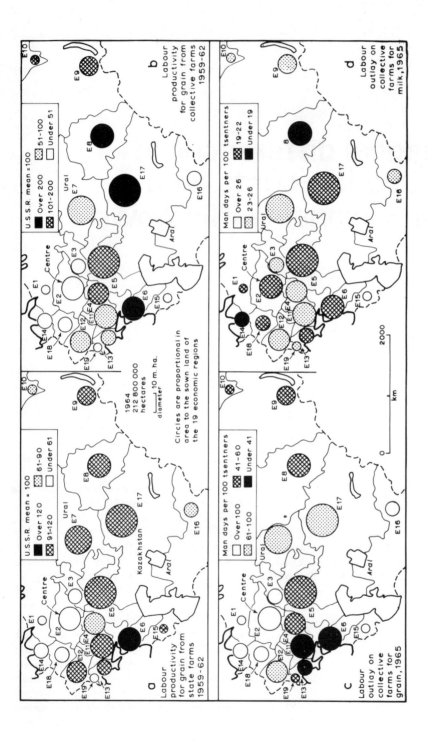

*Fig. 12.1.   See maps for topics covered. Source for (a) and (b): Feygin.[3] Note that the means of 100 for state farms (sovkhoz) and collect-
ive farms (kolkhoz) do not represent the same absolute index of labour productivity. For the key to the economic region (E)
names and numbers, see Table 12.1.*

AGRICULTURE

Productivity per worker per man-day for grain production varies greatly from one region to another on both collective and state farms. During 1959-62, if the U.S.S.R. mean for a kolkhoz was 100, then the Kazakhstan index was 265 and that of West Siberia 221 compared with 40 for Transcaucasia, 35 for the Baltic, 27 for the Northwest and 20 for the North (now part of the Northwest). The regions with the lowest index did not in fact grow much grain, but the discrepancy was still two to three times between Kazakhstan and the Blackearth Centre or Southwest, all of which are major grain regions. The range for sovkhozes was again great: from 155 for the North Caucasus to 16 for the North.

tivity in Transcaucasia or Central Asia was about seven times lower than in the North Caucasus. The range in milk production per worker was however less than twofold. The greater efficiency of sovkhozes compared with kolkhozes within the same regions should also be noted. They are roughly twice as efficient for grain, and 50% more efficient for potatoes, beef and milk. For sugar beet, however, there is little difference. Kolkhoz grain and milk variations are mapped in Figs. 12.1(c) and (d).

According to *NDSE*[1] the procurement prices paid to kolkhozes for wheat before 1965 ranged from 71 roubles per ton in Kazakhstan to 85 in the northern part of European U.S.S.R. In that year they were changed to give a bigger range, from 76 for most of the Ukraine and Moldavia

Table 12.1. LABOUR OUTLAY ON THE PRODUCTION OF SELECTED BASIC ˙ AGRICULTURAL ITEMS IN 1967 BY REGIONS. MAN DAYS PER 10 TSENTNERS PRODUCED ON KOLKHOZES (K) AND SOVKHOZES (S)

Economic region		Grain		Sugar beet		Potatoes		Beef		Milk	
		K	*S*	*K*	*S*	*K*	*S*	*K*	*S*	*K*	*S*
E1	Northwest	11	7	—	—	8	6	88	62	19	12
E2	Centre	7	4	3	3	5	4	90	70	17	13
E3	Volga-Vyatka	8	4	5	5	5	4	109	75	23	17
E4	Blackearth Centre	3	2	2	2	5	3	98	78	22	16
E5	Volga	3	2	4	3	5	5	92	67	20	16
E6	North Caucasus	2	1	2	2	9	7	78	66	17	14
E7	Ural	4	2	8	5	6	5	90	64	21	14
E8	West Siberia	3	2	3	2	5	4	68	60	16	13
E9	East Siberia	3	2	7	9	5	4	81	62	20	15
E10	Far East	3	2	4	5	6	6	84	67	20	15
E11	Donets-Dnepr	3	2	2	2	7	7	126	77	21	13
E12	Southwest	5	4	3	3	8	7	137	99	23	15
E13	South	2	1	3	3	14	12	108	69	19	14
E14	Baltic	6	5	4	3	4	4	53	41	13	10
E15	Transcaucasia	13	7	5	5	15	13	190	126	32	22
E16	Central Asia	13	8	2	2	13	9	129	96	24	20
E17	Kazakhstan	4	2	2	3	8	8	78	73	18	15
E18	Belorussia	9	7	6	6	6	6	82	65	20	16
E19	Moldavia	5	3	3	3	13	14	117	85	23	16

Source: *NkhSSSR* 1967, 489-90.

Figs. 12.1(a) and (b) show indices for sovkhoz and kolkhoz differences, on a base map with the units drawn proportional in area to their cropland.

Data for 1967 show the same features in greater detail. Table 12.1 shows the magnitude of regional differences in productivity both for kolkhoz and sovkhoz workers. Grain produc-

(Kazakhstan 80) to 130 in the northern part of U.S.S.R. The U.S.S.R. weighted means were 74 and 83 respectively. The effect of the change, then, was to recognise regional discrepancies in labour productivity and to subsidise the less fortunate kolkhozes. Similar changes were made for rye.

Examples of regional differences are given by

Feygin[2] for costs of production of timber (*drevesina*) and raw sugar (*sakhar pesok*). Costs, ranging about the U.S.S.R. mean of 100, are shown in Table 12.2. Wage differences for sugar beet workers are mapped in Fig. 12.2(c). Note that the U.S.S.R. weighted mean of 100 stands near the figure for the main producing areas of southern European U.S.S.R., but the small producing areas in the east are highly subsidised and unproductive in terms of labour output.

Table 12.2. REGIONAL DIFFERENCES IN PRODUCTION COSTS OF TIMBER AND OF SUGAR BEET IN EXTREME ECONOMIC REGIONS

Timber		Sugar beet	
East Siberia	78	Kiev	89
West Siberia	83	Kharkov	89
Leningrad	87	Podol'sk	90
Volga-Vyatka	90	Dnepr	92
Northwest	100	Lvov	101
South Ural	134	Volga-Vyatka	180
Far East	156	Far East	186
Lvov	170	East Siberia	214
Kazakhstan	195	Kuzbass	221

U.S.S.R. mean 100.

COAL

Coal production costs presumably vary from one mine to another within coalfields. There are, however, also big overall contrasts between different fields. The location of the fields will be found in Fig. 10.7. Since opencast mining is almost inevitably lower in cost than coal from beneath the surface, there is a marked initial contrast here. Table 12.3 shows that output per miner in the Kuzbass was about twice that in the Donbass by the early 1960's. Four times more coal, mainly opencast, but mainly inferior grade, is produced per worker in East Siberia than in the Donbass. Mining areas requiring very low capital outlay and having very high output per worker are Ekibastuz in Kazakhstan and Kansk-Achinsk in East Siberia. In the early 1960's output per worker here was six times as high as in deep mines in the Karaganda coalfield, itself not one of the poorest in performance. According to data in Galitskiy,[4] apparently for the mid-1950's, shown in Table 12.4, the relative cost (*sebestoimost'*) of mining a ton of coal compared

Table 12.3. PRODUCTIVITY PER MINER IN THREE COAL MINING AREAS (U.S.S.R. = 100)

	1950	1959	1962
East Siberia	158	272	280
Kuzbass	122	135	132
U.S.S.R.	100	100	100
Donbass	75	66	66

Source: Feygin,[3] 27.

with the U.S.S.R. mean of 100, after conversion of the coal into conventional fuel units, then had very great regional variations. The gap between fields appears from Table 12.3 to be widening. Commonsense suggests that if machinery for the extraction of coal is limited in availability, what there is will be sent to high productivity coalfields, not low productivity ones. In Table 12.5, 1962 data for coal basins and individual deposits emphasise the low productivity of Donbass coal workers in terms of actual tonnage extracted, regardless of the quality of the coal and show the overwhelming tendency for other fields to have improved their positions in relation to the Donbass since the interwar period. Mechanisation has not helped to level out productivity differences between fields; as in Britain, it appears to have magnified them.

The U.S.S.R. has 60% of the world's peat reserves. For decades now, peat has been cut for fuel for domestic heating and electricity generation, but it is very costly to extract, even compared with high cost coal. It has been emphasised, therefore, (eg *Pravda,* 10 September

Table 12.4. RELATIVE COST OF EXTRACTING ONE TON OF COAL IN SELECTED AREAS (U.S.S.R.= 100)

West (all deep)		East (deep)		East (opencast)	
Moscow	172	Far East	170	Ural (mixed)	113
Pechora	124	E. Siberia	95	Far East	54
Donbass	111	Karaganda	77	Kuzbass	35
		Kuzbass	71	E. Siberia	30
				Karaganda	28
				Ekibastuz	23

Source: Galitskiy.[4]

1966) that it should from now on be used as a raw material for the chemicals industry, as a substitute for various items. It can be used both to enrich the soil and as fodder for livestock.

	West and South			East	
	1937	*1962*		*1937*	*1962*
Ural	131	243	East Siberia	157	420
C. Asia	70	175	Ural	131	243
Moscow	119	168	Kuzbass	174	199
Georgia	78	112	Karaganda	130	187

Donbass 100.
Source: Feygin.[3]

OIL AND GAS

Productivity per worker is less relevant as a guide to efficiency in the oil and gas industry than in the coal industry. Production costs in oil and gas are discussed in Soviet sources both directly and in terms of capital outlay. The figures in Table 12.6 for 1950 and 1961 are revealing. The base is the cost of extraction in the Volga region. In just over a decade, costs in Transcaucasia had risen from being little more than twice as great as Volga costs to being more than five times as great. This trend has probably continued in the 1960's, though not so quickly.

Table 12.6. COMPARATIVE OIL PRODUCTION COSTS IN SELECTED REGIONS (VOLGA = 100)

Region	*1950*	*1958*	*1961*
Volga	100	100	100
Ural	123	146	153
Ukraine	795		255
North Caucasus	172		338
Central Asia and Kazakhstan	220	412	425
Transcaucasia	224	522	508
Northwest			627
Far East	498		735
U.S.S.R.	196	244	213

Sources: Feygin[3] for 1950 data, Nikitin, N. P. *Ekonomicheskaya geografiya SSSR*, 99 (Moscow, 1966) for 1958, 1961 data.

The estimates for capital outlay in the oil industry in roubles per ton narrow the gap between the regions, but the Volga remains the cheapest at 27 compared with 45 for Azerbaijan and over 80 for Siberia and the Far East, where sheer remoteness makes exploration difficult. Rouble per ton indices are shown in Fig. 12.2(a) for selected regions and smaller Republics. Comparable data for gas (roubles per 1 000 m^3) are given in Fig. 12.2(b). In this case, Uzbekistan and Turkmenistan have slightly lower indices than the Volga.

No less striking than the contrast in production costs of coal, oil and gas in different regions is the average difference between coal, oil and gas themselves. According to *Pravda*, 5 September 1965, the cost of producing oil is only one-sixth that of producing the equivalent amount of coal; the coal : gas ratio is 30 to 1. As the three fuels become more and more mutually replaceable, so the planners must be tempted more and more to reduce the Soviet coal producing capacity, whatever the social implications.

HYDROELECTRICITY

Striking variations in the capital outlay needed to produce a given amount of electricity in different hydroelectric stations are recorded by Vedishchev.[5] Even without taking into account the smaller stations in European U.S.S.R., the cost in kopeks of generating 10 kWh in 1962 was 1·2 kopeks on the Volga system stations compared with expected amounts of 0·3–0·5 on the Yenisey system in East Siberia (Bratsk, Krasnoyarsk) and Central Asia (Nureks, Vaksh) and 0·25 at Sayan on the upper Yenisey near Abakan.

One aspect of hydroelectric power stations, the cost of construction of reservoirs, shows very marked regional differences, according to Feygin.[2] The outlay for 1 million kWh in thousands of roubles for selected regions in the early 1960's is shown in Table 12.7.

IRON AND STEEL INDUSTRY

Regional differences in the production costs of iron ore, coke, pig iron and steel have received

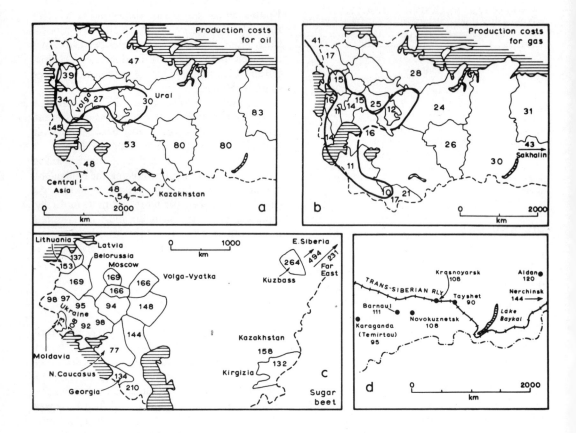

Fig. 12.2.   Comparative production costs in 1962 for (a) oil in roubles of capital outlay per ton and (b) gas in roubles per 1 000 m³. Source: Feygin,[3] 45. (c) Comparative sugar beet production costs (see Table 12.2). (d) Proposed sites for steel works according to Pravda, 11 Sept. 1958, with relative pig iron production costs, Magnitogorsk = 100.

Table 12.7. OUTLAY FOR RESERVOIR CONSTRUCTION PER MILLION KILOWATT HOURS OF ELECTRICITY IN THOUSANDS OF ROUBLES

Region	Outlay	Region	Outlay
Central Asia	1	Volga	14
North Caucasus	2	Ural	35
Northwest	3	Ukraine and Moldavia	47
Kazakhstan	5	Centre and	
East Siberia	7	Volga-Vyatka	58
West Siberia	14	U.S.S.R. mean	14

much attention from Soviet economists. The work of Livshits, now somewhat out of date, is nevertheless important enough to mention in this section. It is supplemented by more recent data from *Pravda* and other sources.

Production costs of pig iron and steel vary greatly from region to region and from plant to plant according to Livshits,[6] as Table 12.8 shows. The cost (in roubles per ton) of producing pig iron is very high not only at Lipetsk and Tula but also at Rustavi in Georgia (489 compared with 100 for Magnitogorsk, Ukraine pig iron can be brought here more cheaply) Cherepovets in the North region at 613, and in older, smaller works in the Ural: Beloretsk 530, Verkhne-Sinyachikhinsk 523, Alapayevsk 422, Nizhne-Saldinsk 414, Chusovoy 400, Asha 367, Serov 359.

In theory, even taking transport costs into account, Magnitogorsk pig iron is cheaper (238 roubles per ton) in Moscow than pig iron from Zaporozh'ye (353), Zhdanov (362), the Donbass works (data not provided) and Lipetsk (463). Kuznetsk pig iron (335 roubles per ton) is cheaper in Moscow than Lipetsk pig iron (463). Moreover, it can be argued that at the same per kilometre freight charge as from Magnitogorsk to Moscow, Magnitogorsk pig iron could be cheaper in the Donbass than Donbass pig iron itself. Such a haul is certainly rarely made and obviously there is no question of decreasing output in the eastern Ukraine. Surprisingly, however, capacity has been greatly expanded in European U.S.S.R., but presumably the new plants will in some cases

Table 12.8. COST TO NEAREST ROUBLE OF PRODUCING ONE TON OF PIG IRON AND STEEL IN SELECTED MILLS OF THE U.S.S.R. IN 1956

Mill	Cost of pig iron (R./ton)	Cost of ore (R./ton)	Cost of fuel (R./ton)	Magnitogorsk cost = 100	Cost of steel (R./ton)	Magnitogorsk = 100
Ural						
1 Magnitogorsk	169	39	119	100	229	100
2 Nizhniy Tagil	253	106	127	149	358	156
3 Chelyabinsk	284	118	134	168	422	185
West Siberia						
4 Stalinsk*	220	135	79	130	271	119
Ukraine						
5 Makeyevka	333	105	188	197	426	186
6 Yenakiyevo	354	107	193	209	n.a.	
7 Zhdanov	329	111	188	194	435	190
8 Dneprodzerzhinsk	293	89	187	173	n.a.	
9 Dnepropetrovsk	337	79	212	199	391	171
10 Krivoy Rog	311	82	189	184	n.a.	
11 Zaporozh'ye	323	101	186	191	402	176
Centre						
12 Lipetsk	447	138	251	265	–	–
13 Tula	521	151	297	308	–	–

n.a. not available.　　　– no production.　　　* now Novokuznetsk.
Mill name, if different from town name: 2 Novo-Tagil; 4 Kuznets; 5 Kirov; 7 Azovstal'; 8 Dzerzhinsk; 9 Petrovsk; 11 Zaporozhstal'; 12 Novo-Lipetsk; 13 Novo-Tulsk.
Source: Livshits,[6] 226–31.

be much more efficient than the older ones. Even so, in 1956, pig iron in the newly opened works in Cherepovets cost 613 roubles per ton compared with 333 at Makeyevka in the same year, the high cost being partly due to the great distance over which initially costly coking coal (Pechora) and iron ore (Olenegorsk) have to come.

The cost of pig iron from the new works at Lipetsk was expected to be 22% higher than that at Magnitogorsk, and pig iron from Krivoy Rog 36% higher, or in 1956 terms, 206 and 230 roubles per ton respectively. If, however, the fuel alone cost 188 roubles per ton at Makeyevka (and the move there 110 roubles) it is surprising (especially since coal has to go by rail from the Donbass to Lipetsk) that such a low figure can be envisaged for Lipetsk, even if Kursk iron ore is very cheap, without there having been either a fundamental change in relationship of regional coal and iron ore prices since 1956, or an omission in the calculation to make Lipetsk appear more favourable than it really is.[7] Possibly the cost of enriching ore in the orefields is not taken into account. It appears, then, that the policy is to expand output in European U.S.S.R. even if cheaper pig iron or steel could be obtained from the Ural region and from places farther east. The demand in East Europe may influence policy and too great a concentration of expansion in Siberia may be considered undesirable.

Table 12.9. LABOUR PRODUCTIVITY IN DONETS-DNEPR IRON AND STEEL WORKS

	Pig iron	Steel
Zaporozh'ye	100	100
Zhdanov	97	76
Makeyevka	75	60
Dneprodzerzhinsk	74	67
Alchevsk	74	87
Donetsk	64	31
Dnepropetrovsk	49	40
Yenakiyevo	42	31

Source: Feygin[3], 29

The U.S.S.R. must, however, eventually produce the cheapest steel it can if it is to achieve high living standards and compete outside the Communist bloc. Since the early 1960's economic, rather than social and strategic, considerations have been taken into account. Considerable attention has understandably been given to choosing sites at which production costs are lowest in the new third metallurgical base (see *Pravda*, 11 September 1958). Thus, taking the cost of producing one ton of pig iron at Magnitogorsk to be 100 units, then the cost at the following sites would be: Tayshet 90, Karaganda 95, Novokuznetsk (West Siberia) 108, Krasnoyarsk 108, Barnaul 111, Aldan 120, Nerchinsk 144. The great drawback of the third base is that it is not only distant from European U.S.S.R. but as far as it could be from seaports and outlets to overseas markets (contrast U.S.A.). The cost merely of moving the pig iron to ports in European U.S.S.R. from these interior sites adds 30–40% to the cost at the mills.

Table 12.10.
IRON ORE PRODUCTION COSTS

Deposit	Cost (R./ton)
1 Krivoy Rog (quartzite)	55·7
2 Rudnogorskoye	27·0
3 Mikhaylovskoye	42·2
4 Korshunovskoye	56·9
5 Nizhne-Angarskoye	58·0
6 Sokolovsko-Sarbayskoye	62·7
7 Kachkanarskoye	75·6

Source: Feygin[3], 46.

Feygin[3] quotes big discrepancies in labour productivity in iron and steelworks in the Donets-Dnepr region itself still existing in 1962. In Table 12.9, productivity is expressed in terms of the Zaporozhstal' works at Zaporozh'ye. Prepared iron ore production costs similarly vary greatly among deposits, for natural, locational and organisational reasons. Prepared ore costs around 1960 in roubles per ton are shown in Table 12.10.

12.2 RELATIVE IMPORTANCE OF DIFFERENT TRANSPORT MEDIA

The total amount of goods carried in the U.S.S.R. in a year expressed in ton-kilometres is an astronomical number; in 1966 it was

2 918 000 million. In more comprehensible terms, for each single inhabitant, one ton of goods was moved about 12 000 km. Comparable quantities are carried in the Western trade system, but much of the distance is covered by oceanic shipping hauls, whereas in the U.S.S.R., most is by land. The ton-kilometres handled on the Soviet system have increased more than fourfold between 1950 and 1966 and have roughly doubled between 1957 and 1966. That the growth of goods traffic is not entirely within the control of the planners is suggested by the fact that the planned increase of about 4–5% for 1967 over 1966 was greatly exceeded, being 9%, a case where overfulfilment of a production target is of doubtful merit. The 1967 figure was 3 179 000 million ton-km, which in turn rose by some 7% to 3 419 000 in 1968.

Table 12.11 shows the share of ton-kilometres handled by each of the main forms of goods transport. It should not be overlooked that the figures along each row are percentages of a constantly increasing absolute amount. The movement of goods by air is not shown since it has never been more than 0·1% of the total. The movements of gas by pipeline and of various fuels converted into electricity are not shown since they are not easily comparable. Each, however, would claim a few per cent of an enlarged overall total. For comparison, the relative share of

passenger-kilometres accounted for in 1967 by each of the media is as follows (Source: *NkhSSSR* 1967, 514): rail 52·3%, sea 0·4%, river 1·2%, road 34·2%, air 11·9%.

The overwhelming importance of the rail system in the postwar period is evident from Table 12.11. Since the late 1950's, however, there has been a very marked decline in the relative importance of rail, though the absolute volume of goods carried has increased enormously. Contrary, perhaps, to what would be imagined or expected, the relative importance of road transport has changed little since the late 1950's and the inland waterways continue the slow downward trend that started a century ago with the railway era. Sea transport and oil (and gas) pipelines have been the forms most impressively increasing their share.

The split expected in the use of the various media in 1980 (Feygin[3] p.265) is:

Rail	54·0%
Sea	16·5%
Inland waterway	5·3%
Road	9·3%
Pipeline (Oil)	14·5%

This estimate was however made in about 1960 and will no doubt have been revised.

Table 12.11 does not reveal the vastly different average length of haul in the different

Table 12.11. RELATIVE IMPORTANCE OF DIFFERENT TRANSPORT MEDIA IN GOODS HAULS (PERCENTAGE OF TON–KILOMETRES CARRIED)

	Rail	Sea	River	Oil pipe	Road
1945	83·9	9·1	5·0	0·7	1·3
1950	84·4	5·6	6·5	0·7	2·8
1955	83·4	5·9	5·8	1·3	3·6
1958	81·2	6·6	5·3	2·1	4·8
1959	80·8	6·5	5·3	2·4	5·0
1960	79·8	7·0	5·3	2·7	5·2
1961	78·4	8·0	5·3	3·0	5·3
1962	77·8	8·2	5·2	3·5	5·3
1963	76·1	9·8	5·0	3·9	5·2
1964	73·7	11·8	4·9	4·4	5·2
1965	70·6	14·1	4·8	5·3	5·2
1966	69·2	15·1	4·7	5·7	5·3
1967	67·8	16·7	4·5	5·3	5·7
1968	66·5	*n.a.	4·5	6·3	*n.a.

*n.a.– not available

Sources: *NkhSSSR* 1965, 457, *Strana sovetov za 50 let*, 169, *Pravda*, 25 Jan. 1968, 26 Jan. 1969.

sectors. The following figures for 1967 (Source: *NkhSSSR* 1967, 513 *et seq*) need no elaboration:

Sea	2 013 km
Rail	830 km
Inland waterway	477 km
Road	16 km

Oil and natural gas 'journeys' by pipeline each probably average several hundred kilometres.

Table 12.12 illustrates both the relative volume of selected goods carried by rail, and their average haul length. Again, there is great variation in the length of individual hauls around the mean for each item. About 80% of all the ton-kilometres carried on the Soviet rail system are accounted for by the eight classes of item listed in Table 12.12. Hauls of over 3 000 km were 4–5% of all hauls around 1960, but they accounted for 23% of the ton-kilometres and 26% of the cost of movement. In particular, 15% of the timber carried went over 3 000 km, as did 12% of the grain and 7% of the oil.

Table 12.12. GOODS CARRIED BY RAIL, 1967

Product	Percentage of ton-km	Percentage of ton	Mean length of haul in km
Coal and coke	18·6	23·3	671
Oil	15·1	10·0	1 255
Timber	11·5	5·8	1 652
Mineral building materials	11·5	23·8	402
Iron and steel	9·2	6·3	1 201
Ores	5·8	8·3	587
Grain	4·2	3·4	1 021
Fertilisers	2·5	2·0	1 046
All	100	100	830

Source: *NkhSSSR* 1967.

The composition of goods carried by sea transport is very different from that of rail goods. Oil and oil products accounted for nearly 50% in 1965, building materials, ores and coal, each about 10%. Inland waterways, in contrast, handled mainly timber (35%) floated as rafts or carried on boats, building materials (about 45%) and oil (about 10%).

Feygin[3] puts goods into three classes according to length of haul. The criteria for the three hauls are under 25%, 25%–50% and over

50%, composed of interregional hauls, combined with mean distances of less than 500 km, 500 km–1 000 km or over 1 000 km.

1. Short haul: peat, firewood, oil shales, bricks and stones, rye flour, cattle, milk, lime, sand and clay, reinforced concrete.
2. Medium haul: coal, coke, iron and manganese ore, cement, salt, furniture, maize, wheat flour, some animal fodder, scrap metal.
3. Long haul: crude oil, oil products, pig iron, rails, pipes, roundwood and sawn timber, fertilisers, sugar, vegetable oils, grain, fish, machinery, potatoes, meat, ginned cotton, non-ferrous ores and metals.

Table 12.13. DISTANCES OVER WHICH FUEL IS MOVED IN EUROPEAN U.S.S.R.

From	To Odessa	Voronezh	Gorky	Riga	Minsk	Leningrad	Moscow
Stavropol'*	1 270					700	
Dashava*		1 400	630	1 040			600
Donbass†	1 060	1 681	1 210	1 625	1 500	507	896
Kuzbass†	3 500	4 023	4 100	4 200	3 200		
Vorkuta†		2 373					

*gas   †coal
Source: Feygin,[3] 212.

Table 12.13 gives specific examples of the distance over which fuel is moved in European U.S.S.R.

The interregional movement of goods in the U.S.S.R. is so varied and complex that it defies description and summarisation in a single map, table or chapter. It is, however, one of the basic considerations of planning, since in any but the simplest of economic systems some movement of goods is essential. The ever increasing quantities of ton-kilometres handled are not of any merit *per se*. One basic set of planning decisions, therefore, concerns which natural resources to develop for which markets, given contrasting on-the-site production costs plus calculable transport costs to different markets. Planners have had to watch the movement of items and to weigh up the validity of long hauls. The question of the degree of regional self-sufficiency and regional specialisation for different items is closely related. Notwithstanding the attention of planners to the movement of goods, many undesirable and anomalous flows of goods have been allowed and subsequently often reported and criticised in retrospect in both academic and popular publications.

It must be stressed that what constitutes an interregional haul as opposed to a within region or local haul depends on the regional system used. Some examples of movements of coal (Fig. 12.3(a)) will suffice to show how arbitrary the concept of regions is, especially in view of the tendency to modify regions and to gerrymander economically. The mutilation of the southern part of the Ural region by the transference of the Bashkir A.S.S.R. to the Volga is a ludicrous operation illustrated in Fig. 12.3(b).

In Fig. 12.3(a), the rail distance within the Northwest region from the Pechora basin to Leningrad (flow 1) of about 1 900 km in length, greatly exceeds that from the Pechora basin into parts of the adjoining Ural and Volga-Vyatka regions. Furthermore, the haul from the Donbass to Leningrad (about 1 700 km), which crosses three regional boundaries, is less than that from the Pechora basin to Leningrad, crossing none. A second example of an anomaly is that Tula coal and Donbass coal are both sent into the Blackearth Centre region (flows 2). Donbass coal, however, also goes to the Centre region and, therefore, passes Tula coal coming the other way. Tula and Donbass coal both run parallel to reach Leningrad. In this instance, the grade of coal differs between the two sources; nonetheless, the situation is dubious. The third anomaly is illustrated by flows 3: Pechora coal reaches the Ural, while Kizel coal reaches the Northwest. In this case, each coal source lies close to the boundary of the other region. Some deficit regions, eg Volga-Vyatka in flows 4 appear to draw coal indiscriminately from a number of regions, disregarding to some extent relative costs.

There is so much incredibly muddled thinking and so many irrelevant conclusions are drawn about regions, what they produce and what they send to and receive from other regions that one has to resort to a simple example to show how Soviet economists are fighting a 'paper tiger' much of the time. Fig. 12.3(c) shows several fictitious economic regions and some factories producing a particular manufactured item. Production costs are assumed to be the same in every factory, and transport costs to a market uniformly spread over area increase with distance at a constant rate. In case 1, a high index of regional self-sufficiency is likely to be recorded. In case 2, which differs from case 1 only because the regional limits have been shifted, there will be a great deal of interregional exchange. The reader wishing to follow up the points made in this paragraph should refer to Feygin.[3] His chapter, 'The transport factor and the development of economic regions' is not available in English.

The purpose of the remainder of the chapter is to describe the overall pattern of goods flows and to outline the characteristics of individual flows.

12.3 FLOWS OF GOODS

A study of the pattern of the interregional movement of goods in the U.S.S.R. must take into consideration the following:

1. The great territorial extent of the U.S.S.R.

2. The differing distribution and, more important, the actual number, of places of origin of different goods.

3. The differing distribution of number of places of receipt of goods (markets).

4. From 2 and 3 it is theoretically possible to conceive the following kinds of origin-destination correspondences: one-to-one, one-to-many, many-to-one, many-to-many. 'One' many be taken rather loosely as a few or several, while, 'many' could extend to each household or even individual in the U.S.S.R.

Each item carried on the Soviet transport system naturally has its own pattern of flow, whether it is an agricultural product, a manufactured item, a newspaper, or even a service rather than a material object. Only a selected number of items will be studied: those for which adequate data are available and which are major items in terms of ton-kilometres recorded.

The distribution of places of origin of a

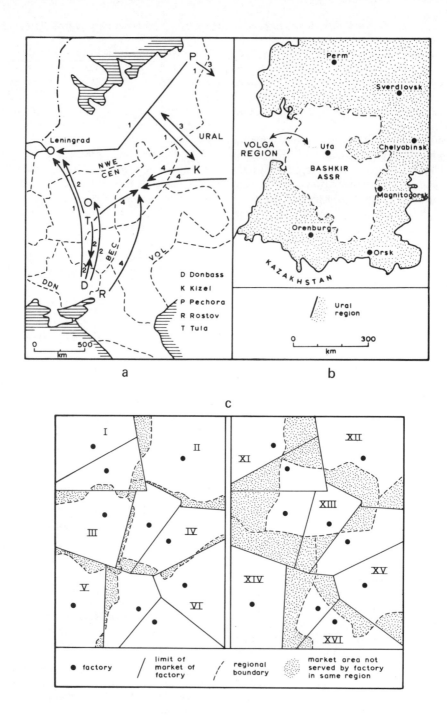

Fig. 12.3.   Regional and interregional anomalies. (a) Selected flows of goods, discussed in text. (b) The effect of detaching the Bashkir A.S.S.R. from the Ural region. (c) The relationship of factories and their market areas to economic regions. Regions are numbered I-VI in case 1 and XI-XVI in case 2.

particular item may depend on the actual occurrence of this in nature (minerals, climatic conditions for plants) or the establishment of man-made producing centres (factories, mines). Not all available sources of a particular item may however be places of origin. For example, Soviet timber is cut in a large number of localities but these in total still cover only a very small part of the total potential forest. The destination of flows of goods may be no more than a few factories or it may be the whole population of the U.S.S.R. The consumption of iron ore, for example, takes place in a few dozen iron and steel works, unevenly distributed by region. The consumption of paper, bread or glass generally corresponds to the distribution of population. Four situations are shown diagrammatically in Fig. 12.4.

summarised in Table 12.14. Both goods despatched and goods received are shown, but there is no indication whether or not regional boundaries are crossed. Since only quantities in excess of 1 million tons are shown, the absolute importance of different goods is emphasised at the expense of detail for the smaller Republics.

The actual places of origin of goods on the ground vary greatly over the area of the U.S.S.R. Even when a population base is used rather than an area base, there are great *per capita* differences, at least at oblast level, if not S.S.R. level, between administrative divisions. For this reason it seems invalid to construct a gravity model of expected flows based on distances between, say, the centres of oblasts, weighted according to their populations. Fortunately a reasonably good picture of the origin of goods

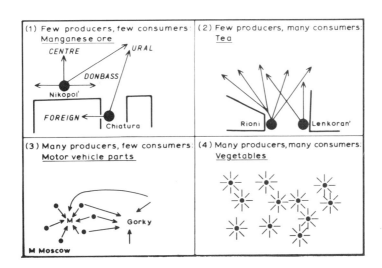

Fig. 12.4.   Examples of correspondences between producers and consumers.

What has been described above is not peculiar to the U.S.S.R., but it becomes particularly relevant in a study of the geography of the U.S.S.R. because of the size of the country. Moreover, interregional flows, theoretically at least, are not left to sort themselves out, but have to be centrally planned.

In 1967, the total number of tons of goods handled by the railways (as opposed to the ton-kilometres), was 2 605 million tons. The relative importance of the 15 Republics and of selected major commodities in this respect is

journeys is given in Fig. 12.5, based on Republic and R.S.F.S.R. oblast data. The data are for 71 divisions of the R.S.F.S.R., together with the 14 other Republics. The Ukraine and Kazakhstan are poorly shown, but the remaining Republics generate goods traffic of the same order as R.S.F.S.R. oblasts. It should be noted that the map shows goods despatched, not goods received. Many items are sent to destinations within the same unit. The difference between goods despatched and goods received is, however, substantial in many divisions and will be

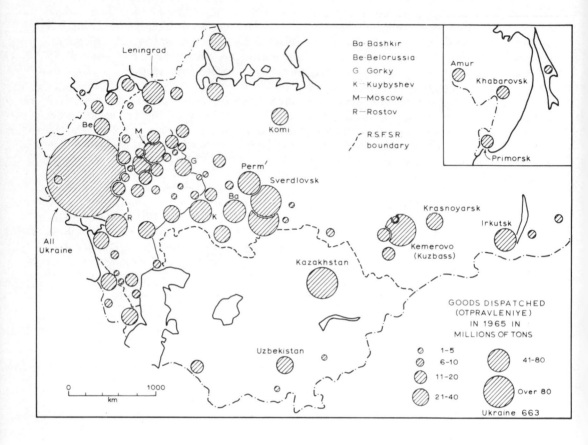

Fig. 12.5.   Tonnage of goods despatched in 1965 from Republics and from oblast level divisions of the R.S.F.S.R.
Source: NkhSSSR 1965, 46, 354-7.

outlined below. The divisions along the coasts and the Volga (indicated) would be inflated by the addition of waterborne traffic and some Volga divisions in particular by pipeline movement.

Table 12.14. GOODS SENT OUT AND RECEIVED BY REPUBLICS IN 1967 (IN MILLIONS OF TONS)

Goods sent out Republic	Coal	Oil	Tim-ber	Iron Steel	Grain	Ferti-lisers
R.S.F.S.R.	313	197	137	93	54	29
Ukraine	227	21	6	59	17	11
Belorussia	2	7	3	1	2	3
Uzbekistan	3	6	–	1	–	2
Kazakhstan	46	6	–	5	11	2
Georgia	4	1	–	2	1	–
Azerbaijan	–	13	–	1	–	–
Lithuania	–	–	–	–	–	1
Moldavia	–	–	–	–	–	–
Latvia	–	–	2	–	–	–
Kirgizia	2	–	–	–	–	–
Tadjikistan	2	–	–	–	–	–
Armenia	–	–	–	–	–	–
Turkmenistan	–	8	–	–	–	–
Estonia	–	–	–	–	–	1
Goods Received						
R.S.F.S.R.	347	143	83	99	50	23
Ukraine	187	44	35	43	18	13
Belorussia	8	9	5	5	5	4
Uzbekistan	4	9	4	2	3	3
Kazakhstan	34	12	8	5	4	1
Georgia	5	9	2	1	2	–
Azerbaijan	–	5	1	2	1	–
Lithuania	4	7	2	1	1	2
Moldavia	2	2	2	–	–	–
Latvia	3	12	2	2	1	1
Kirgizia	3	1	1	–	–	–
Tadjikistan	–	1	–	–	–	–
Armenia	–	2	–	–	–	–
Turkmenistan	–	2	–	–	–	–
Estonia	–	2	2	–	–	–

– Less than 1 million tons.
Source: *NkhSSSR* 1967, 525–30.

With regard to the actual weight despatched, in 1967, the Ukraine in total provided 27%. Though an oblast breakdown is not available it is reasonable to expect some 200 million tons of coal and steel from Donetsk oblast alone, and tens of millions of tons of iron ore from Krivoy Rog. Similarly, Karaganda oblast presumably accounts for much of the Kazakhstan total. Of the divisions within the R.S.F.S.R., in 1965, the

following accounted for goods (millions of tons) despatched in the quantities shown: Kemerovo (Kuzbass), 145; Sverdlovsk (Ural), 112; Chelyabinsk (Ural), 82. At the other°extreme, some predominantly rural divisions (eg Orel, Chuvash A.S.S.R., Kabardino-Balkarsk A.S.S.R.) generated little traffic in terms of weight, and some, off the rail system altogether (eg Magadan) produced none. Even light industrial oblasts such as Ivanovo and Kostroma produced very little. For their population, Moscow (51 million tons) and Leningrad (46 million tons) also accounted for relatively little.

Lack of space makes it impossible to map also volume of goods received within divisions, but the balance, calculated in terms of an absolute gain or deficit, is worth noting briefly, even though the nature of incoming and outgoing goods in any division differs. Moscow received 44 million tons more than it despatched, Krasnodar 27 million, and Leningrad 21 million.

The data discussed so far do not give an idea of the actual volume or composition of goods traffic between individual pairs of divisions. Some idea of the general pattern of rail flows and the relative importance of individual rail routes is shown in Fig. 12.6. Although only selected routes in European U.S.S.R. can be shown on this scale, the map emphasises the heavy traffic on many of the east–west lines between European U.S.S.R. and Lake Baykal, and the heavy volume carried over short distances around Moscow and the Donbass. Selected items are now discussed individually:

1. COAL

The movement of coal is now described in some detail both for its own interest and to illustrate the drawbacks of using within and between region movements of goods as a concept. The following points must be considered:

(a) Coal varies in quality and application, from anthracite and coking coal to lignite and brown coal. Some apparently absurd counterflows may be justified for this reason.

(b) Several regions produce no coal at all. Of the coal producing regions, some are deficient (eg Central Asia), some roughly self-sufficient (eg Far East) and some have a large surplus (eg West Siberia).

(c) Production costs of the same grade of coal vary appreciably among coalfields.

(d) The *per capita* consumption of coal varies greatly among regions.

(e) Given the size and shape of the regions and the location within them of the relatively small coal producing districts, parts of some coal producing regions are closer to coalfields in adjoining regions than to coalfields within their own regions. Hauls across regional boundaries are in these circumstances valid.

Table 12.15 shows the main interregional movements of coal in the U.S.S.R. in the early 1960's. At that time the U.S.S.R. was producing about 500 million tons of coal. The eight principal source regions of interregional coal are listed at the head of the columns. The main receiving regions are the rows.

The data in the table are supported by the maps in Fig. 12.7(a) showing the main interregional flows and Fig. 12.7(b) showing the specific rail lines over which coal is moved in the western part of the U.S.S.R. The main sources of interregional coal are the Kuzbass and Karaganda, which particularly supply the Ural,

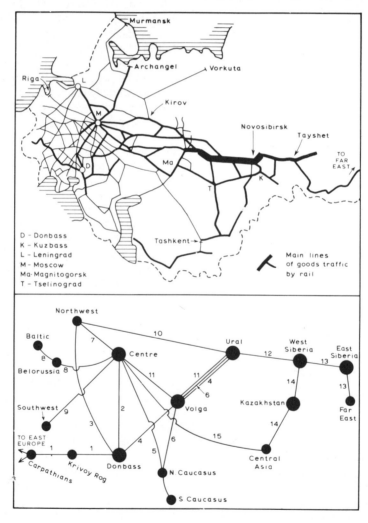

Fig. 12.6.   Rail flows. Upper map: Main flows of goods traffic by rail. The thickness of flow is roughly proportional to the volume of traffic. Source: Galitskiy,[4] 69. Lower map: Main interregional flows.

Table 12.15. INTERREGIONAL MOVEMENT OF COAL IN THE EARLY 1960's

From / To	*Northwest* E1	*Centre* E2	*N. Caucasus* E6	*Ural* E7	*W. Siberia* E8	*E. Siberia* E9	*Donets-Dnepr* E11	*Kazakhstan* E17
E1 Northwest		3·2		2·0			7·8	
E2 Centre			22·5	1·6			4·4	
E3 Blackearth Centre		9·0	17·5		·		3·6	
E4 Volga-Vyatka		1·3		9·7	2·2	2·6		
E5 Volga			17·5	1·3	3·1			4·0
E7 Ural	2·8				37·9			46·8
E8 West Siberia						13·1		
E10 Far East						2·5		
E12 Southwest							8·9	
E13 South	2·1						3·7	
E14 Baltic	3·5						3·0	
E16 Central Asia								5·5
E17 Kazakhstan					9·0	2·6		
Other (6, 9, 11, 15, 18, 19)	1·5	2·9	3·1	0·3	3·3	1·0	4·2	0·2
Total to other regions	9·9	16·4	70·3	7·4	55·9	19·2	35·6	56·5
Total within own region	90·1	83·6	29·7	92·6	44·1	80·8	64·4	43·5
Share of national total	3·7	6·0	5·5	12·0	17·6	6·3	33·6	6·9
Absolute amount (U.S.S.R. 500 million tons)	19	30	27	60	88	32	168	35

At the foot of the table, the percentages delivered outside the region and within the region are shown. The values in the table are percentages of the amount sent from each region and are therefore comparable in columns but not across rows. The relative and absolute amounts accounted for by each of the regions are shown in the two lowest rows. In absolute amount, the following are among the main interregional flows (millions of tons):

West Siberia	–	Ural	35
Kazakhstan	–	Ural	16
Donets-Dnepr	–	Southwest	15
Donets-Dnepr	–	Northwest	13
West Siberia	–	Kazakhstan	8
Donets-Dnepr	–	Centre	7
Donets-Dnepr	–	South	6
Donets-Dnepr	–	Blackearth Centre	6
North Caucasus	–	Centre	6

Source: Galitskiy,[4] 80.

and the Donbass, which supplies most of the coal deficient regions of European U.S.S.R. A more detailed consideration of coal flows reveals, however, that the zone of competition between the Donbass and the two Eastern fields is displaced far towards the former. The general effect is for a westward orientation of coal flows. The situation is illustrated diagrammatically in Fig. 12.8. Cases 1 and 2.

2. IRON AND STEEL

Interregional steel flows in Table 12.16 are for the early 1960's. The amount of iron and steel (including scrap) carried by rail was about 115 million tons, less than a quarter of the weight of coal carried. In contrast to coal, there are fewer major surplus regions of iron and steel. The main ones are the Donets-Dnepr, Ural and West

Siberia. The proportion reaching destinations outside the originating region was between 60 and 70% in all five regions shown in the table, but the absolute amount sent by the Volga and Kazakhstan is small. The wide variety of grades and types of steel presumably accounts for the apparent exchange of metals between regions. Fig. 12.9 shows the main rail movements of iron and steel. Iron ore interregional rail flows are given by Budtolayev.[8] Most of the ore carried is accounted for by within region flows.

3. OTHER ITEMS

The general direction of movement of other important goods in the Soviet economy can be obtained from Soviet sources. Fig. 12.10 shows the movement of grain in the early 1960's. The pattern of oil and gas movement may be deduced from the diagram in Fig. 11.6, though oil is moved by rail, waterway and road as well as by pipeline. The movement of timber is in the first place in a southerly direction from the

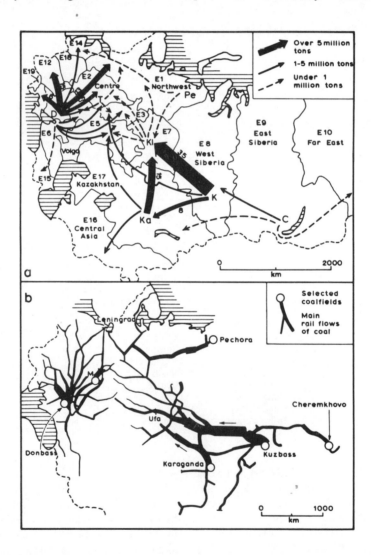

Fig. 12.7.   Coal flows in the U.S.S.R. (a) interregional tonnage carried per year, early 1960's. D = Donbass, K = Kuzbass, Ka = Karaganda, Kl = Kizel, Pe = Pechora, T = Tula. (b) actual lines of distribution of coal.

Table 12.16. INTERREGIONAL MOVEMENT OF IRON AND STEEL

	From	*Volga*	*Ural*	*West Siberia*	*Donets-Dnepr*	*Kazakhstan*
To						
E1	Northwest	4·5	5·5		4·0	
E2	Centre	10·1	9·0	3·5	6·8	
E3	Volga-Vyatka	3·9	7·3	3·9	2·4	12·2
E5	Volga		8·9	3·6	5·0	21·7
E6	North Caucasus		1·7		7·5	
E7	Ural	15·0		20·2	2·2	7·6
E8	West Siberia	7·1	7·1			
E9	East Siberia			10·8		
E10	Far East			6·6		
E12	Southwest				5·6	
E13	South				5·7	
E14	Baltic		2·5		4·5	
E17	Kazakhstan		3·2	5·3		
	Total to other regions	66·2	61·8	69·0	60·8	60·7
	Total within own region	33·8	38·2	31·0	39·2	39·3
	Share of national total	3·3	26·7	6·5	38·1	2·3

Regions not considered: 4, 11, 15, 16, 18, 19

Source: Galitskiy,[4] 118

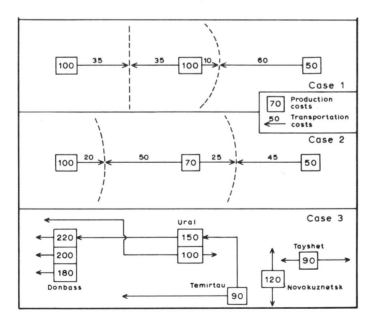

Fig. 12.8. *The combined effect of on the spot production costs plus transport costs on the pattern of interregional goods flows. Case 3 illustrates diagrammatically pig iron and steel, discussed in section 1 of this chapter.*

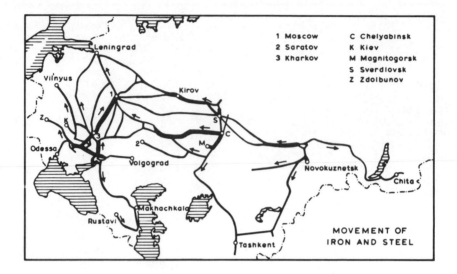

Fig. 12.9.   *Movement of iron and steel in the U.S.S.R. Only selected rail movements are shown. Widths of lines are only roughly proportional to the tonnage carried. Source: Galitskiy,*[4] *133.*

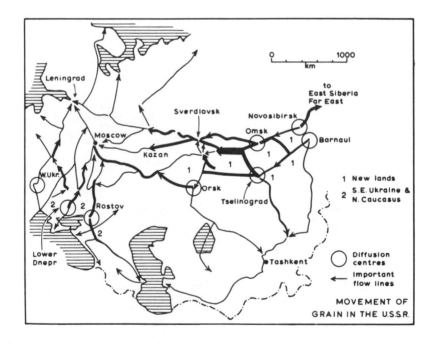

Fig. 12.10.   *Movement of grain in the U.S.S.R. in the early 1960's. Source: Galitskiy,*[4] *159.*

coniferous forest into the steppe and desert areas of the south, and secondly, from east to west, the abundant low cost timber of Siberia supplementing that derived from the Northwest to supply European U.S.S.R. Even such a bulky and perishable commodity as cement is frequently carried across regional boundaries. For example, according to Galitskiy,[4] North Caucasus cement

vegetables, industrial crops, cereals and livestock, have been weighted approximately according to their shares of total agricultural output. The sum of the 19 X 4 values in Columns 1–4 of the table is 1 000. In Column 5 each region is given a hypothetical per thousand share of the Soviet agricultural output. The (known) population share in per thousand of each region is then

Table 12.17. REGIONS OF DEFICIT AND SURPLUS IN AGRICULTURAL PRODUCTS

		1	*2*	*3*	*4*	*5*	*6*	*7*
		Vegetables and potatoes	*Industrial crops*	*Grain*	*Livestock*	*Per thousand of total agricultural output*	*Per thousand of population*	*5–6*
	Economic region							
E1	Northwest	7	2	1	10	20	51	−31
E2	Centre	33	9	8	28	78	116	−38
E3	Volga-Vyatka	13	2	5	12	32	36	− 4
E4	Blackearth Centre	11	12	12	18	53	35	+18
E5	Volga	16	12	31	42	101	76	+25
E6	North Caucasus	8	14	24	37	83	58	+25
E7	Ural	13	2	18	28	61	72	−11
E8	West Siberia	10	3	13	26	52	47	+ 5
E9	East Siberia	6	0	7	18	31	31	0
E10	Far East	3	7	1	5	16	24	− 8
E11	Donets-Dnepr	16	15	17	37	85	84	+ 1
E12	Southwest	36	14	15	41	106	88	+18
E13	South	4	6	8	15	33	25	+ 8
E14	Baltic	10	1	3	15	29	31	− 2
E15	Transcaucasia	2	3	2	18	25	49	−24
E16	Central Asia	3	19	3	31	56	74	−18
E17	Kazakhstan	5	3	26	45	79	52	+27
E18	Belorussia	22	3	3	19	47	37	+10
E19	Moldavia	2	3	3	5	13	14	− 1
	U.S.S.R.	220	130	200	450	1 000	1 000	0

goes by rail to many places in southern European U.S.S.R. and Far East cement is taken as far as West Siberia; 46% of Volga cement goes to other regions as does one-third of that produced in the Ural.

Table 12.17 is an attempt to put a quantity to the amount of surplus or deficit of agricultural products in each of the 19 regions. Since the calculations depend on weightings for different branches in the early 1960's, not available for later years, corresponding agricultural data have been used. Four branches (see Chapter 9)

subtracted from the agricultural per thousand. An 'assumed' surplus or deficit is then obtained and placed in Column 7.

STEPS

1. (a) Sum areas under potatoes and vegetables in each region.
   (b) Express these as per thousand of Soviet total.
2. Express area under industrial crops in per thousand of Soviet area.

3. (a) Sum volumes of grain output for 1962-64 inclusive and find mean annual output during this period for each region.

   (b) Express these as per thousand of Soviet total.

4. Find cattle equivalent units per region:

   (a) Sum pigs, sheep and goats in each region and divide by six (to reduce to cattle comparability). Horses are not considered since they are largely part of the farm 'machinery' rather than output.

   (b) Add the new pigs-sheep-goats units to the cattle numbers.

   (c) Express the new values as per thousand of Soviet total.

5. Reduce the four sets of per thousand values to give weights of 220, 130, 200 and 450 respectively to the four groups of items.

REFERENCES

1. *New Directions in the Soviet Economy,* 456–57 (U.S. Government Printing Office, Washington, 1966)

2. FEYGIN, Ya. G. *et al., Problemy ekonomicheskoy effektivnosti razmeshcheniya sotsialisticheskogo proizvodstva v SSSR,* 122 (Moscow, 1968)

3. FEYGIN, Ya. G. *et al., Zakonomernosti i faktory razvitiya ekonomicheskikh rayonov SSSR,* 27–8, 205, 253 (Moscow, 1965)

4. GALITSKIY, M. I. *et al., Ekonomicheskaya geografiya transporta SSSR,* 79, 139 (Moscow, 1965)

5. VEDISHCHEV, A. I., *Problemy razmeshcheniya proizvoditel'nykh sil SSSR,* 65–72, 79 (Moscow, 1963)

6. LIVSHITS, R. S., *Razmeshcheniye chernoy metallurgii SSSR,* 236–44 (Moscow, 1958)

7. LIVSHITS, R. S., *Razmeshcheniye chernoy metallurgii SSSR,* 355 (Moscow, 1958) casts some doubt on the cheapness of Lipetsk pig iron. He quotes

figures for future outlook, taking into account adjusted iron ore bases for some works and gives the following figures for cost per ton of pig iron at works and (in brackets) price in Moscow after rail haul; Magnitogorsk 255 (324), West Siberian 314 (429), Zhdanov 370 (403), Krivoy Rog 290 (323), New Lipetsk 415 (430). The calculation for Lipetsk appears to be based on the assumption that poor grade Kursk quartzites will be used. In 1953–54, however, high grade iron ore was found here (56–67%) though at a depth of 400–500 m. This would presumably lower costs considerably.

8. BUDTOLAYEV, N. M., NOVIKOV, V. P. and SAUSHKIN, Yu. G., 'On methods of building a territorial (spatial) model of the national economy of the USSR' *Soviet Geogr.,* 6, No 9, 56–66, 1965

BIBLIOGRAPHY

BRENNER, M. M., *Ekonomika neftyanoy promyshlennosti SSSR* (Moscow, 1962)

DANILOV, A. D. and MUKHIN, G. I., *Razmeshcheniye otrasley narodnogo khozyaystva SSSR* (Gosplanizdat, Moscow, 1960)

Ekonomicheskiye svyazi i transport *Vop geogr.,* No 61 (Moscow, 1963)

KAZANSKIY, N. N. and LASIS, Yu. V., 'Methods of Forecasting Freight Flows in Planning a Transportation Net' *Soviet Geogr.,* 4, No 7, 3–18, 1963

LIVSHITS, R. S., *Ocherki po razmeshcheniyu promyshlennosti SSSR* (Gospolitizdat, Moscow, 1954)

NIKITIN, N. P., *Ekonomicheskaya geografiya SSSR* (Moscow, 1966)

PROBST, A. Ye., 'Calculation of the Economic Effect of Regional Productive Specialization' *Soviet Geogr.,* 5, No 2, 32–41, 1964

TSAPKIN, N. V. and PERECELEGIN, V. I. (eds), *Planirovaniye narodnogo khozyaystva SSSR,* 158 (Uchebnoye posobiye, Moscow, 1967)

TURETSKIY, Sh. Ya., *Ocherki planovogo tsenoobraniya SSSR* (Moscow, 1959)

VARLAMOV, V. A. and KAZANSKIY, N. N., 'Forecast of Average Length of Haul on Soviet Railroads' *Soviet Geogr.,* 4, No 7, 19–26, 1963

WILLIAMS, E. W., *Freight Transportation in the Soviet Union* (Princeton University Press, 1962)

13

Achievements and
future prospects

The purpose of this chapter is to examine some of the problems and anomalies that have arisen since the late 1920's when the Five Year Plans began, or which have remained from before the Soviet period. For a considerable time it could be said that the Communist regime has in reality, as opposed to its professed aims, sacrificed not only the consumer in general, but also some regions at the expense of others, in its drive to establish heavy industry. There is considerable evidence, some of it indirect, to suggest that regional discrepancies both in productivity per worker and in availability of public services and even individual purchasing power are as great as in any capitalist or underdeveloped country. It is not the purpose of this chapter to criticise this situation, but to present some evidence and to examine, particularly in the light of demographic trends, the future prospects for evening out regional differences.

13.1 WHAT DO THE REGIONS CONTRIBUTE?

No figure for the value of total production of all goods in each region is readily available in Soviet sources. An approximation that at least allows the 19 regions to be ranked in order of estimated *per capita* production of goods can be achieved in a somewhat devious way. The *per capita* production has already been given for many items by region at various stages in the book. Table 13.1 is a summary of all goods produced. It has already been pointed out that the contribution of each region to the national total of any given product can be divided by the population of that region to give an index about a national mean of 100 for the apparent surplus or deficit of that region. Such figures have been used in Table 13.1. In this way population is held constant. A grand total for each region has been obtained by summing along each row the index for each item. Since some items are much more important than others, columns have been weighted to give roughly the relative importance of each item. Weightings used are shown at the foot of Table 13.1. The figures have been calculated so that a hypothetical region which produced exactly the same share of every item as it had of population would score 100, or a multiple of 100, in each column, and exactly 2 000 in the final consensus column. A miscellaneous column has been added to allow some subjective correcting for such products as non-ferrous and precious metals, fish and furs, or publishing items, found for example, more in such regions as the Centre or Far East than in the Southwest or Belorussia.

Table 13.2 shows the regions ranked according to *per capita* output in Column 11 of Table 13.1. Note that by holding population constant, differences in size have been eliminated and, with reference to Table 13.1, that the grand total of the consensus column does not reach 38 000, which might be expected with 19 regions and an average score of 2 000. This is because of the reduction to *per capita* terms.

Table 13.1. SUMMARY OF SOVIET PRODUCTION BY REGIONS

Economic region	Timber	Agriculture	Fuel	Electricity	Iron and steel	Engineering	Chemicals	Cement	Textiles and food	Miscellaneous	Consensus
	1	2	3	4	5	6	7	8	9	10	11
E1 Northwest	520	154	135	98	78	294	294	110	196	240	2 119
E2 Centre	57	268	72	84	69	396	302	90	432	280	2 050
E3 Volga-Vyatka	222	356	51	67	56	195	111	36	194	160	1 448
E4 Blackearth Centre	12	606	9	50	177	58	118	138	206	160	1 534
E5 Volga	36	532	1 029	133	53	198	420	150	184	200	2 935
E6 North Caucasus	19	572	480	60	69	155	206	69	242	200	2 072
E7 Ural	248	340	169	227	1 060	404	424	177	152	240	3 441
E8 West Siberia	146	444	657	133	226	173	173	100	173	300	2 435
E9 East Siberia	522	400	348	274	26	96	64	126	129	240	2 225
E10 Far East	250	268	300	75	16	84	42	104	125	280	1 544
E11 Donets-Dnepr	2	405	711	168	962	404	202	131	154	200	3 339
E12 Southwest	46	482	96	36	0	69	69	63	206	120	1 187
E13 South	0	528	0	64	0	120	80	20	200	160	1 172
E14 Baltic	65	374	78	77	0	129	64	100	193	160	1 240
E15 Transcaucasia	6	204	294	78	98	102	204	92	143	200	1 421
E16 Central Asia	0	304	117	43	10	66	198	78	132	240	1 188
E17 Kazakhstan	8	608	219	73	46	58	58	108	96	280	1 554
E18 Belorussia	49	508	39	46	0	108	81	65	136	120	1 152
E19 Moldavia	0	372	0	40	0	67	0	53	200	120	852
Consensus total											34 908

Weightings:	1	Timber	100	7	Chemicals	200
	2	Agricultural items	400	8	Cement	100
	3	Fuel	300	9	Textiles and food	200
	4	Electricity	100	10	Miscellaneous	200
	5	Iron and steel	200	11	Consensus	2 000
	6	Engineering	200			

Source: *NkhSSSR* 1965, *NkhRSFSR* 1965.

Table 13.2. THE REGIONS RANKED ACCORDING TO THEIR *per capita* CONTRIBUTION TO TOTAL SOVIET PRODUCTION

Rank	Region	Production	Rank	Region	Production
1	Ural	187	11	Blackearth Centre	84
2	Donets-Dnepr	182	12	Volga-Vyatka	79
3	Volga	160	13	Transcaucasia	77
4	West Siberia	133	14	Baltic	68
5	East Siberia	121	15	Central Asia	65
6	Northwest	115	16	Southwest	65
7	North Caucasus	113	17	South	64
8	Centre	112	18	Belorussia	63
9	Kazakhstan	85	19	Moldavia	46
10	Far East	84		U.S.S.R.	100

On paper, then, the extremes are the Ural region and Moldavia, the former turning out about four times as many goods per inhabitant as the latter. The ratio is about 3:1 for the Urals and Donets-Dnepr against such prominent regions as the Southwest and Central Asia. The following points should be considered:

1. The 10 R.S.F.S.R. regions fall in the top 12 regions. Only the Donets-Dnepr and Kazakhstan, themselves heavily settled by Russians, reach as high as the R.S.F.S.R. regions.
2. The Centre and Northwest might justifiably be raised somewhat to allow for their special service contribution on behalf of the U.S.S.R. as a whole.
3. It is the middle regions, both in length of settlement by Russians and in location, that come highest (see Fig. 13.1).

related to the natural resources of the region and to the population/resource balance. Feygin[1] lists seven of the 19 regions as possessing limited natural resources: Centre, Volga-Vyatka, Baltic, Blackearth Centre, South, Belorussia and Moldavia. The present author would add the Southwest and possibly Transcaucasia.

From the evidence presented it must be assumed that some regions are making a greater *per capita* contribution to the Soviet economy than others. Do they, in return, have a higher standard of living than those making a more modest contribution? Or is the discrepancy in production evened out to give uniform purchasing power and health, educational and other services? Do the more prolific regions subsidise the poorer ones? Why is the discrepancy there at all? Mainly, it may be assumed, on account of the availability and

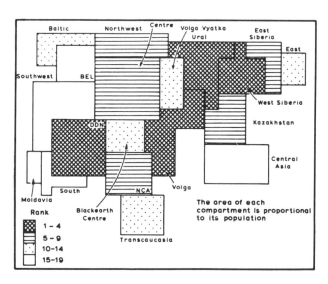

Fig. 13.1.   The estimated per capita *contribution of the 19 economic regions to total Soviet production. The regions are shaded according to their ranking in Table 13.2. Note that already in the table the differing size of the regions has been eliminated. In the topological map,* per capita *position is shaded on compartments proportional to people, not area.*

Per capita achievement falls off drastically towards East Europe, southwards in the main non-European areas of Transcaucasia and Central Asia, and towards the extreme east.

Fig. 13.1 shows the distribution of regions on the basis of their consensus rank in Table 13.2. To some extent the level of achievement reached by each region according to the evidence given is

accessibility of natural resources and of their production costs. Is there a case for planners to move people from the poorer into the more prosperous regions?

Exact data are difficult to obtain. Feygin[1] gives *per capita* national income figures for Republics, set against an R.S.F.S.R. index of 100. Estonia (115) and Latvia (113) are higher, the Ukraine (89) not far below, but Belorussia (63) Central Asia (average 56) and Transcaucasia (average 66) are notably lower. Given that the R.S.F.S.R. average covers such depressed areas as the Blackearth Centre, some high oblasts might be expected to score 130–140; a discrepancy of 3:1 between extremes may be inferred, one roughly comparable with extremes found between states in the U.S.A.

13.2 MULTIVARIATE ANALYSIS FOR 87 AREAS

This section is an attempt to show the relationship between several demographic, economic and prosperity variables. From the data used, a regionalisation on demographic and

data in Soviet sources. The factors actually obtained are at least as valid as single variables used elsewhere and are at least new.

The 13 variables used are fully described in Table 13.3(a). Their values are given in the data matrix in Table 13.3(b) after appropriate modification to *per capita* terms to eliminate size differences between areas. Divisions with extreme values on selected variables are shown in Table 13.4. All 13 are included in full in Table 13.3 since they are not readily available to Western geographers not in direct touch with Soviet sources. As an example, variable 12, doctors per population, is mapped in Fig. 13.2; this single distribution, like each of the others, is of interest in its own right. For example, in contrast to Moscow, a semicircle of oblasts to the west (Smolensk) south (eg Orel) and east (eg

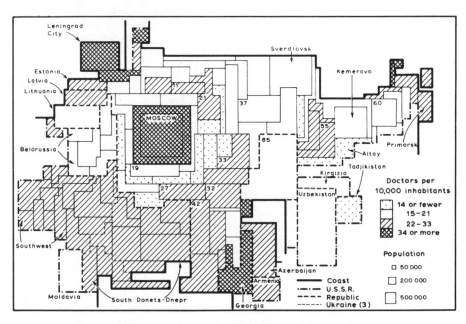

Fig. 13.2.   Doctors per 10 000 inhabitants. The area of each division on the map is proportional to the population of the division. Note, the dots and heavy shading are the extremes. Key to numbers on the map: 11 Ivanovo, 19 Tula, 21 Gorky, 27 Voronezh, 32 Volgograd, 33 Kuybyshev, 37 Chelyabinsk, 42 Rostov, 55 Novosibirsk, 60 Irkutsk, 85 Kazakhstan.

economic criteria can be derived for 87 regions. Unfortunately, not many revealing variables are available, and those that have been chosen, therefore, do an inadequate job in characterising the U.S.S.R. on a basis of development, or material well-being. This, however, is the fault not of the author but of the lack of published

Chuvash A.S.S.R.) is among the most poorly provided with medical services in the U.S.S.R. There is also a contrast between Transcaucasia (high proportion of doctors) and Central Asia (low proportion).

The meaning of most of the variables chosen is obvious, but the following points should be

Table 13.3.

(a) *Description of the variables used, to characterise development and well-being in 87 divisions of the U.S.S.R.*

1 Density of population, persons per square kilometre, January, 1966 (S1, 12–14, S2, 12–13).

2 Urban population as a percentage of total population, January 1966 (S1, 12–14, S2, 11).

3 Natural growth of population (*yestyestvennyy prirost naseleniya*) 1965 per 10 000 inhabitants (S1, 20–4, S2, 46–7).

4 Population change 1959–64, 1959 = 100 (S5, 12–14, S6, 12).

5 Growth of industrial base (*tempy rosta valovoy produktsii vsey promyshlennosti*) 1958–65, 1958 = 100 (S1, 50–1, S2, 128).

6 Growth of productivity of industrial labour (*tempy rosta proizvoditel'nosti truda v promyshlennosti*) 1958–65, 1958 = 100 (S1, 71–2, S2, 146–7).

7 Mean income of kolkhoz family (*denezhnyye dokhody kolkhozov (sel'khozarteley) v raschete na*

odin kolkhoznyy dvor) in tens of roubles in 1963 (S5, 316–18, S6, 347).

8 Retail turnover of state and cooperative trade (*roznichnyy tovarooborot . . .*) in tens of roubles per inhabitant, 1965.

9 Portable radio sets (*translyatsionnykh radiotochek . . .*) per 100 inhabitants, 1966 (1965 for areas outside R.S.F.S.R.) (S1, 365–6, S2, 518).

10 Students in higher education (*vysshiye uchebniye zavedeniya: chislennost' studentov*) per 10 000 total population in 1965/66 (S1, 469–70, S2, 694).

11 Specialists (*spetsialisti s vysshim obrazovaniyem, zanyatykh v narodnom khozyaystve*) per 1 000 total population, 1966 (S1, 405–6, S2, 578–9).

12 Doctors (*vrachi*) per 10 000 total population in 1964 (S3, 485, S4, 734).

13 Hospital places (*chislo bol'nichnykh mest*) per 10 000 inhabitants 1965/66 (S1, 508, S2, 748).

(b) *Data matrix for 13 variables in 87 regions*

Population (millions)	Division	1	2	3	4	5	6	7	8	9	10	11	12	13
1 404	1 Archangel	2	66	108	108	166	142	91	55	20	8	15	19	10
1 308	2 Vologda	9	44	69	100	195	167	93	45	20	6	13	15	11
5 028	3 Leningrad	59	87	40	108	165	146	138	75	30	51	52	60	12
714	4 Murmansk	5	96	127	118	167	131	104	72	21	5	23	36	12
724	5 Novgorod	13	49	29	97	201	167	89	46	22	5	14	16	10
875	6 Pskov	16	37	6	93	229	162	68	41	24	9	14	16	11
700	7 Karelian (A)	4	71	126	105	154	136	101	57	13	13	18	22	12
966	8 Komi (A)	2	65	143	116	149	135	94	64	17	3	16	21	12
1 564	9 Bryansk	45	42	85	101	201	139	55	34	18	7	14	13	8
1 492	10 Vladimir	52	64	64	105	159	136	75	46	15	5	16	17	10
1 355	11 Ivanovo	57	73	49	102	127	122	89	49	21	16	17	26	10
1 736	12 Kalinin	21	52	14	97	161	139	101	46	22	7	16	18	10
964	13 Kaluga	32	46	57	102	200	157	70	39	19	5	18	16	10
870	14 Kostroma	15	49	45	97	136	138	94	44	19	11	15	16	10
11 799	15 Moscow	251	85	35	105	145	136	162	83	21	54	55	47	12
942	16 Orel	38	33	54	103	269	162	66	36	21	5	15	12	8
1 444	17 Ryazan'	37	40	39	101	229	167	52	39	19	11	15	19	9
1 098	18 Smolensk	22	42	38	97	198	139	105	43	20	10	17	21	10
1 964	19 Tula	76	67	51	102	171	149	77	46	14	10	19	17	10
1 395	20 Yaroslavl'	38	67	39	100	157	137	83	48	18	9	18	25	11
3 668	21 Gorky	49	61	60	102	170	144	58	45	17	14	19	22	11
1 775	22 Kirov	15	50	48	94	156	146	92	41	17	7	13	15	11
652	23 Mariysk (A)	28	36	106	102	191	162	48	32	17	15	17	16	10
1 009	24 Mordov (A)	39	29	107	101	285	158	54	29	15	12	14	12	7
1 177	25 Chuvash (A)	64	31	141	106	223	150	42	29	18	8	14	12	7
1 249	26 Belgorod	46	28	53	102	245	157	84	32	22	2	14	13	7
2 477	27 Voronezh	47	42	53	105	190	141	101	39	21	20	20	22	7
1 496	28 Kursk	50	27	58	102	215	155	75	31	22	7	13	15	8
1 214	29 Lipetsk	50	38	72	105	202	141	59	35	16	5	15	14	8
1 529	30 Tambov	45	32	56	100	188	145	82	33	19	8	15	13	8
801	31 Astrakhan'	18	58	86	111	162	146	237	45	15	11	20	39	10
2 163	32 Volgograd	19	62	91	113	248	167	175	48	15	12	21	27	10
2 559	33 Kuybyshev	48	69	79	111	207	147	141	47	10	18	25	28	9
1 543	34 Penza	36	39	71	102	186	141	97	36	18	11	15	13	7
2 386	35 Saratov	24	60	76	107	214	149	195	45	17	21	22	29	9

Table 13.3 contd

Population	Division	1	2	3	4	5	6	7	8	9	10	11	12	13
1 175	36 Ulyanovsk	32	44	77	104	198	143	100	29	18	11	15	14	8
3 719	37 Bashkir (A)	26	45	145	110	221	161	88	35	11	8	14	15	8
241	38 Kalmyk (A)	3	32	191	124	246	165	323	40	16	1	14	15	10
3 082	39 Tatar (A)	45	48	117	107	180	139	79	37	12	18	18	20	8
4 218	40 Krasnodar	51	46	63	108	193	145	180	45	19	8	18	24	8
2 144	41 Stavropol'	27	38	91	110	196	132	231	45	12	10	18	27	9
3 730	42 Rostov	37	63	68	110	177	142	169	45	14	22	22	23	8
1 325	43 Dagestan (A)	26	35	277	119	194	137	51	24	11	9	13	17	7
518	44 Kabardino-B. (A)	41	44	186	118	232	130	107	37	16	9	20	22	8
510	45 Severo-Os. (A)	64	63	113	111	187	127	93	41	16	30	27	37	10
1 008	46 Checheno-Ing. (A)	52	39	193	135	205	149	87	27	10	12	15	17	7
1 081	47 Kurgan	15	38	80	108	217	169	134	40	18	10	13	12	8
2 045	48 Orenburg	17	50	116	110	184	135	155	38	14	7	15	16	9
3 106	49 Perm'	19	67	91	103	181	160	83	46	12	11	15	19	10
4 349	50 Sverdlovsk	22	80	77	107	175	146	139	52	10	18	19	21	9
3 263	51 Chelyabinsk	37	78	87	108	172	144	149	49	8	13	18	21	11
1 375	52 Udmurt (A)	33	53	106	103	209	174	84	39	14	12	18	20	10
2 766	53 Altay	11	40	86	104	186	147	103	39	18	9	12	13	9
3 033	54 Kemerovo	32	81	84	108	161	138	113	49	7	8	15	19	12
2 468	55 Novosibirsk	14	62	86	107	187	142	111	44	15	25	23	24	10
1 807	56 Omsk	13	50	118	108	197	158	108	44	15	19	17	27	9
782	57 Tomsk	3	57	83	103	172	146	124	47	20	54	20	25	11
1 292	58 Tyumen'	1	45	115	109	176	136	101	47	15	7	14	15	10
2 919	59 Krasnoyarsk	1	58	101	109	209	153	146	51	15	13	17	18	10
2 254	60 Irkutsk	3	69	119	111	199	158	140	50	10	20	18	21	10
1 095	61 Chita	3	57	126	104	159	146	232	43	12	6	13	19	10
771	62 Buryat (A)	2	43	136	112	181	145	146	46	11	16	16	16	10
213	63 Tuvinsk	1	37	227	117	255	155	142	40	14	6	16	20	11
1 607	64 Primorsk	10	72	109	109	203	132	195	58	14	22	20	24	10
1 300	65 Khabarovsk	2	79	111	109	189	147	245	59	19	22	21	27	12
781	66 Amur	2	62	98	105	188	152	363	48	18	12	14	20	11
261	67 Kamchatka	1	76	142	115	189	190	210	83	21	5	26	40	13
318	68 Magadan	0	87	113	125	190	141	210	114	23	5	33	44	14
640	69 Sakhalin	7	81	108	97	151	156	175	81	14	5	21	29	14
631	70 Yakutsk (A)	0	56	155	122	248	179	140	71	15	7	22	22	13
694	71 Kaliningrad	46	69	118	109	216	140	175	52	11	16	22	30	13
19 507	72 Donets-Dnepr	87	71	70	108	177	142	110	41	18	14	21	24	10
20 166	73 Southwest	75	34	81	105	194	142	66	41	18	14	21	24	10
5 843	74 South	51	53	84	111	199	142	144	41	18	14	21	24	10
2 986	75 Lithuania	45	45	102	108	224	123	78	42	6	15	18	21	9
2 262	76 Latvia	35	62	38	106	200	127	108	62	9	14	25	31	12
1 285	77 Estonia	28	63	42	105	199	128	138	64	7	16	26	29	11
4 548	78 Georgia	64	47	141	109	161	128	50	34	8	17	30	34	9
4 660	79 Azerbaijan	52	50	301	119	163	124	63	29	8	13	20	24	9
2 194	80 Armenia	72	55	233	118	196	129	73	35	6	16	26	27	8
10 581	81 Uzbekistan	23	35	289	118	180	128	189	32	11	15	16	17	9
2 652	82 Kirgizia	13	38	246	121	203	135	170	33	10	11	17	18	9
2 579	83 Tadjikistan	17	35	300	121	185	117	136	28	8	11	14	14	9
1 914	84 Turkmenistan	4	49	302	119	151	125	211	33	10	10	16	21	9
12 129	85 Kazakhstan	4	48	204	124	212	138	184	41	10	11	16	18	10
8 633	86 Belorussia	41	39	111	105	207	144	60	36	18	11	18	21	9
3 368	87 Moldavia	98	28	142	113	211	125	93	31	14	10	15	18	9

Sources: S1 *NkhRSFSR* 1965   S2 *NkhSSSR* 1965
          S3 *NkhRSFSR* 1964   S4 *NkhSSSR* 1964
          S5 *NkhRSFSR* 1963   S6 *NkhSSSR* 1963

Table 13.4. EXTREME VALUES FOR VARIABLES 1, 2, 7, 8–FIRST COLUMN ACTUAL VALUES, SECOND COLUMN, U.S.S.R. MEAN = 100

1 *Density of population (persons/km)*				2 *Urban (percentage)*			
15	Moscow	251	785	4	Murmansk	96	180
87	Moldavia	98	307	3	Leningrad	87	163
72	Donets-Dnepr	87	272	68	Magadan	87	163
54	Kemerovo	32	100	80	Armenia	55	103
13	Kaluga	32	100	74	South	53	100
67	Kamchatka	1	3	87	Moldavia	28	53
70	Yakutsk (A)	0	0	26	Belgorod	28	53
68	Magadan	0	0	28	Kursk	27	51

7 *Kolkhoz income (roubles per family)*				8 *Retail turnover (per capita)*			
66	Amur	3 630	297	68	Magadan	114	254
38	Kalmyk (A)	3 230	264	67	Kamchatka	83	185
31	Astrakhan'	2 370	194	15	Moscow	83	185
57	Tomsk	1 240	101	62	Buryat (A)	46	101
24	Mordov (A)	540	44	2	Vologda	45	100
43	Dagestan (A)	510	42	36	Ul'yanovsk	29	65
78	Georgia	500	41	25	Chuvash (A)	29	65
23	Mariysk (A)	480	39	43	Dagestan (A)	24	53
25	Chuvash (A)	420	34				

(A) = A.S.S.R.

borne in mind; first, kolkhozes now account for about half of Soviet farm land under cultivation, but they vary greatly from regions to region in relation to sovkhozes; secondly portable radio sets are a relatively new article and there is no reason to expect that the innovation has had a chance to spread over all regions with equal intensity. Radios do not therefore serve as a good guide to purchasing power.

Table 13.5 is a correlation matrix showing the Pearson product moment *r* values for each pair of variables. Table 13.6(a) shows factors derived from the correlation matrix. Table 13.6(b) shows the loadings on the first three factors. The first factor contains 33% of all the variation and picks out the strong relationships between urbanisation, health services, education and sales. It confirms the marked contrast between town and country in the U.S.S.R. and suggests that from the urbanisation variable some other well-being variables can be predicted fairly closely. Although literacy is now almost universal in the U.S.S.R., the quality of educational opportunities offered in towns is superior, since specialised teaching, with its costly and complex

facilities, often has to be concentrated in urban places. Potentially satisfactory children from rural areas may never be reached and brought into the higher education system. Town children, then, tend to have the best job opportunities.

The extreme individual weightings for the 87 regions on Factors I and II are given in Table 13.7 and mapped in Figs. 13.3 and 13.4. Factor I highlights the extremes of urban and rural. At the urbanised end, it groups indiscriminately the big urban agglomerations of Moscow and Leningrad, the thinly populated special, sophisticated Far East, and the resort orientated Severo-Osetinsk A.S.S.R. in the North Caucasus. In contrast, extreme rurality is found in the Blackearth Centre between Moscow and the Donbass, in the Volga-Vyatka between Moscow and the Ural region and in the Caucasus and Central Asia. Some oblasts of the Southwest would certainly also fall here if this region were divided into oblasts for the purposes of this exercise. It must be emphasised that what happens at the macro-level of regions and oblasts, does also on a smaller scale. One example will have to suffice to illustrate this point. In Armenia, according to *Pravda*, 25 March 1966,

Table 13.5. CORRELATION MATRIX OF PEARSON PRODUCT MOMENT VALUES. THE 13 VARIABLES CORRELATED ARE DISPLAYED AND DESCRIBED FULLY IN TABLE 13.3, $n = 87$

Variable	1	2	3	4	5	6	7	8	9	10	11	12	13
1 Pop. density	1·00												
2 Urban	0·03	1·00											
3 Nat. growth	−0·19	−0·20	1·00										
4 Pop. change	−0·11	0·04	0·77	1·00									
5 Industrial growth	−0·10	−0·51	0·07	0·15	1·00								
6 Productivity growth	−0·25	−0·08	−0·26	−0·19	0·45	1·00							
7 Kolkhoz income	−0·28	0·29	0·18	0·34	−0·04	0·06	1·00						
8 Retail turnover	−0·05	0·77	−0·25	0·07	−0·27	0·11	0·36	1·00					
9 Radio sets	0·07	0·01	−0·54	−0·41	0·01	0·35	−0·07	0·25	1·00				
10 Students	0·42	0·34	−0·13	−0·04	−0·23	−0·19	0·07	0·20	0·09	1·00			
11 Specialists	0·53	0·56	−0·13	0·13	−0·22	−0·14	0·14	0·60	0·17	0·69	1·00		
12 Doctors	0·27	0·67	−0·09	−0·19	−0·30	−0·14	0·30	0·68	0·15	0·56	0·88	1·00	
13 Hospital beds	−0·16	0·69	−0·14	−0·01	−0·32	0·11	0·34	0·80	0·12	0·12	0·40	0·53	1·00

Table 13.6. FACTORS AND FACTOR LOADINGS

(a) *Factors*

	Factor I	*Factor II*	*Factor III*
Value of factor	4·34	2·42	2·03
Percentage	33%	18·5%	15·5%
Cumulative	33%	51·5%	67%

(b) *Factor loadings*

	Variables	*Factor I*	*Factor II*	*Factor III*
1	Populations density	−0·26	0·21	−0·77
2	Urban percentage	−0·85	−0·08	0·17
3	Natural growth	0·25	−0·87	−0·04
4	Pop. change 1959–64	−0·03	−0·86	0·04
5	Industrial growth	0·47	0·06	0·20
6	Industrial productivity growth	0·11	0·42	0·59
7	Kolkhoz income	−0·33	−0·42	0·47
8	Retail turnover	−0·84	0·02	0·40
9	Radios	−0·22	0·70	0·16
10	Students	−0·58	0·04	−0·51
11	Specialists	−0·85	−0·02	−0·34
12	Doctors	−0·89	−0·13	−0·11
13	Hospital places	−0·73	−0·03	0·48

(c) *Variables loading most strongly on Factors I and II*

	Ranked Factor I				*Ranked Factor II*	
12	Doctors	−0·89		3	Natural growth	−0·87
2	Urban	−0·85		4	Pop. change	−0·86
11	Specialists	−0·85		9	Radios	−0·70
8	Retail turnover	−0·84				
13	Hospital places	−0·73				
10	Students	−0·58				

Table 13.7. INDIVIDUAL WEIGHTINGS OF EXTREME AND MEAN DIVISIONS ON FACTORS I AND II

Rank	Factor I		Rank	Factor II	
1	Moscow	−18·1	1	Turkmenistan	−6·1
2	Leningrad	−16·9	2	Tadjikistan	−6·0
3	Magadan	−12·1	3	Azerbaijan	−5·1
4	Kamchatka	−7·3	4	Uzbekistan	−5·1
5	Murmansk	−6·8	5	Kirgizia	−4·7
6	Sakhalin	−6·6	6	Kazakhstan	−4·6
7	Khabarovsk	−5·2	7	Checheno-Ingush (A)	−4·3
8	Severo-Os. (A)	−4·5	8	Armenia	−4·2
9	Tomsk	−4·3	9	Dagestan (A)	−3·7
10	Latvia	−4·2	10	Kalmyk (A)	−3·5
11	Estonia	−4·0	11	Tuvinsk (A)	−2·6
12	Kaliningrad	−4·0	12	Magadan	−2·3
13	Ivanovo	−3·5	13	Kabardino-Balkarsk (A)	−2·3
14	Astrakhan'	−3·3			
15	Primorsk	−2·9			
16	Karelian (A)	−2·7			
17	Donets-Dnepr	−2·3			
18	Yaroslavl'	−2·3			
19	Kuybyshev	−2·2			
20	Chelyabinsk	−2·2			
	Vladimir	0·0		Krasnoyarsk	−0·1
	Kalinin	0·1		South	0·2
	Southwest	0·3		Novosibirsk	0·2
				Omsk	0·2
67	Ryazan'	3·0			
68	Uzbekistan	3·0			
69	Tuvinsk (A)	3·3	69	Yaroslavl'	2·0
70	Kirgizia	3·3	70	Bryansk	2·1
71	Altay	3·4	71	Mariysk (A)	2·1
72	Moldavia	3·5	72	Mordov (A)	2·2
73	Ul'yanovsk	3·7	73	Moscow	2·4
74	Penza	3·8	74	Leningrad	2·4
75	Tambov	4·0	75	Kostroma	2·5
76	Bryansk	4·1	76	Kaluga	2·7
77	Lipetsk	4·2	77	Kirov	2·7
78	Kurgan	4·3	78	Tambov	2·7
79	Tadjikistan	4·6	79	Smolensk	2·8
80	Bashkir (A)	4·6	80	Vologda	3·0
81	Checheno-Ingush (A)	4·9	81	Kalinin	3·4
82	Kursk	4·9	82	Kursk	3·4
83	Orel	5·6	83	Orel	3·5
84	Chuvash (A)	6·1	84	Belgorod	3·5
85	Belgorod	6·1	85	Ryazan'	3·6
86	Dagestan (A)	6·1	86	Novgorod	4·2
87	Mordov (A)	7·1	87	Pskov	5·3

(A) = A.S.S.R.

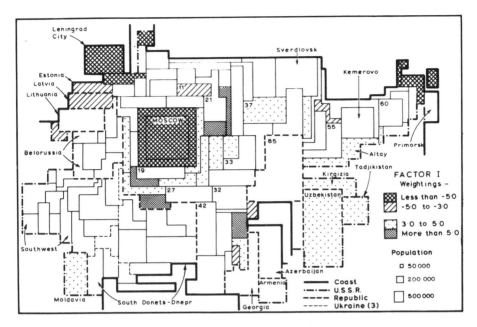

Fig. 13.3.   *Individual weightings of 87 divisions on Factor I. Note the heavy crossed lines and dots are at the extremes. Divisions with scores between – 3·0 and +3·0 are in white.*
Key to numbers on map: 11 Ivanovo, 19 Tula, 21 Gorky, 27 Voronezh, 32 Volgograd, 33 Kuybyshev, 37 Chelyabinsk, 42 Rostov, 55 Novosibirsk, 60 Irkutsk, 85 Kazakhstan.

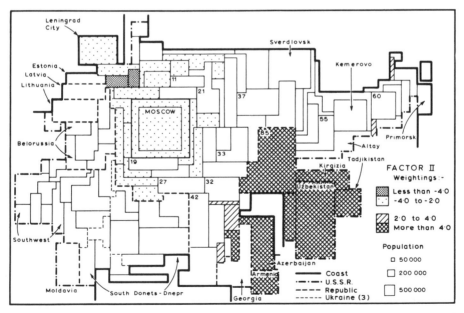

Fig. 13.4.   *Individual weightings of 87 divisions on Factor II. Note the heavy crossed lines and dots are at the extremes. Divisions with scores between –2·0 and +2·0 are in white.*
Key to numbers on the map: 11 Ivanovo, 19 Tula, 21 Gorky, 27 Voronezh, 32 Volgograd, 33 Kuybyshev, 37 Chelyabinsk, 42 Rostov, 55 Novosibirsk, 60 Irkutsk, 85 Kazakhstan.

three towns, Yerevan, Leninakan and Kirovakan, with only 40% of Armenia's population, had 75–80% of the Republic's gross industrial production and industrial workers. Since the motor vehicle has not yet spread the influence of the town into the country and since distances between towns are considerable, a stark contrast between town and country is again suggested.

Factor II picks out the areas of population growth. Note that the urban variable is almost unconnected with this factor (loading −0·08). In other words, although urban areas are still attracting population from rural areas, their effect on the immigrants once established in the towns is to dampen down growth. Thus at one extreme the 'heartland' of old Russia, the northern two thirds of European U.S.S.R. with its Great Russian population, in Pskov, Novgorod, Ryazan', Belgorod, even Moscow, contrasts with the Asian S.S.R.'s and various A.S.S.R.'s at the other extreme. The Russians are lagging in the population race, as Asiatic U.S.S.R. experiences a population explosion.

It would be misleading to suggest that the 13 variables and the 87 divisions used do justice to the complexity of U.S.S.R. The author would have been glad to use far more data had it been available and in the correct form. An example of an interesting variable, available only for larger towns of the R.S.F.S.R. (*NkhRSFSR* 1963, pp. 551–2) is the amount of housing space available per population in 1964. The median space is some 85 square metres per 10 people, but the extremes range from Moscow (112) and Leningrad (98) to Izhevsk (Ural, only 70) and Murmansk (Northwest, 69).

13.3 POPULATION PROJECTIONS

Attempts to project present population trends into the future have often proved hopelessly inaccurate in retrospect. Nevertheless some indication of the way the population of the U.S.S.R. might fare over the next few decades is thought provoking This section presents two alternative courses, neither of which is likely to happen exactly, but either of which seems a possibility, given demographic trends since World War II.

The first projection takes the population of each of the 19 economic regions in 1966 and adds to it annually (analogous to compound interest) the amount expected from its 1965

Table 13.8. POPULATION PROJECTION WITH NO MIGRATION

	Economic region	Population in millions						Percentage of total	
		1966	1976	1986	1996	2006	2016	1966	2016
E1	Northwest	11·8	12·6	13·5	14·4	15·5	16·6	5·1	3·9
E2	Centre	26·6	27·7	28·8	30·0	31·2	32·5	11·6	7·6
E3	Volga-Vyatka	8·3	9·0	9·7	10·5	11·4	12·3	3·6	2·9
E4	Blackearth Centre	8·0	8·5	9·0	9·5	10·1	10·7	3·4	2·5
E5	Volga	17·7	19·5	21·6	23·8	26·3	29·1	7·6	6·8
E6	North Caucasus	13·5	15·0	16·7	18·7	20·8	23·2	5·8	5·4
E7	Ural	15·2	16·6	18·2	19·9	21·8	23·8	6·6	5·6
E8	West Siberia	12·1	13·3	14·5	15·9	17·4	19·0	5·2	4·4
E9	East Siberia	7·3	8·2	9·2	10·4	11·7	13·2	3·1	3·1
E10	Far East	5·5	6·2	6·9	7·7	8·6	9·6	2·4	2·2
E11	Donets-Dnepr	19·5	20·9	22·4	24·0	25·8	27·6	8·4	6·4
E12	Southwest	20·2	21·8	23·7	25·6	27·7	30·0	8·7	7·0
E13	South	5·8	6·3	6·9	7·4	8·0	8·7	2·5	2·0
E14	Baltic	7·2	7·7	8·3	8·9	9·6	10·2	3·1	2·4
E15	Transcaucasia	11·4	14·2	17·6	21·9	27·2	33·8	4·9	7·9
E16	Central Asia	17·7	23·6	31·3	41·8	55·6	74·0	7·6	17·2
E17	Kazakhstan	12·1	14·8	18·0	22·0	26·8	32·6	5·2	7·6
E18	Belorussia	8·6	9·6	10·7	12·0	13·4	14·9	3·7	3·5
E19	Moldavia	3·4	3·9	4·4	5·1	5·9	6·7	1·5	1·6
	U.S.S.R.						428·5	100	100

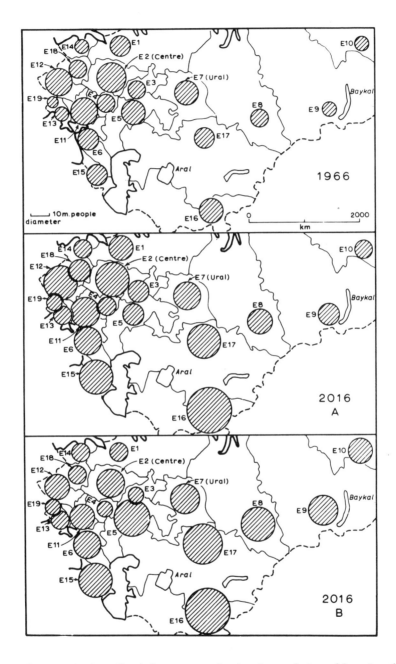

Fig. 13.5. Population projections. The circles are proportional to the populations of the regions they represent: 1966 population; 2016 projection A (natural increase with no migration); 2016 projection B (natural increase with selected migration).

Table 13.9. PROPORTION OF POPULATION MOVING BETWEEN REGIONS

	From	To	5 Volga	7 Ural	8 W. Siberia	9 E. Siberia	10 Far East	17 Kazakhstan
1	Northwest		0·002	0·001	0·002	0·002	0·001	0·002
2	Centre		0·002	0·001	0·002	0·002	0·001	0·002
3	Volga-Vyatka		0·002	0·001	0·002	0·002	0·001	0·002
4	Blackearth Centre		0·002	0·001	0·002	0·002	0·001	0·002
11	Donets-Dnepr		0·002	0·001	0·002	0·002	0·001	0·002
12	Southwest		0·002	0·001	0·002	0·002	0·001	0·002
13	Belorussia		0·002	0·001	0·002	0·002	0·001	0·002

Table 13.10. POPULATION PROJECTION WITH SELECTED MIGRATION

	Economic region	Population in millions			Percentage of total	
		1966	1991	2016	1966	2016
E1	Northwest	11·8	10·9	10·0	5·1	2·3
E2	Centre	26·6	22·9	19·7	11·6	4·5
E3	Volga-Vyatka	8·3	7·9	7·5	3·6	1·7
E4	Blackearth Centre	8·0	7·2	6·5	3·4	1·5
E5	Volga	17·7	28·3	41·5	7·6	9·4
E6	North Caucasus	13·5	17·7	23·2	5·8	5·3
E7	Ural	15·2	21·8	29·9	6·6	6·7
E8	West Siberia	12·1	20·8	31·1	5·2	7·0
E9	East Siberia	7·3	15·6	26·4	3·1	5·9
E10	Far East	5·5	10·1	16·0	2·4	3·7
E11	Donets-Dnepr	19·5	18·1	16·7	8·4	3·8
E12	Southwest	20·2	19·1	18·2	8·7	4·2
E13	South	5·8	7·1	8·7	2·5	2·0
E14	Baltic	7·2	8·6	10·2	3·1	2·3
E15	Transcaucasia	11·4	19·6	33·8	4·9	7·6
E16	Central Asia	17·7	36·2	74·0	7·6	16·7
E17	Kazakhstan	12·1	26·4	49·3	5·2	11·8
E18	Belorussia	8·6	8·8	9·0	3·7	2·1
E19	Moldavia	3·4	4·8	6·7	1·5	1·5
	U.S.S.R.		331·9	438·4	100	100

natural increase rate. At one extreme the Centre only had an increase rate of 4·4 per thousand, compared with 28·6 per thousand for Central Asia at the other. Results at the end of 10 year periods are shown in Table 13.8. The effect of this projection is to reduce the relative share of most of European U.S.S.R., to leave the share of Siberia somewhat lower than it is now, but to increase the share of Transcaucasia, Central Asia and Kazakhstan. Their combined 1966 share of 17·7% would rise in 2016 to 32·7% or nearly one-third of the total Soviet population. Central Asia would increase four times from its current 18 million to some 74 million in 2016.

The second projection assumes the same natural increase rate for each region as before, but also allows for the movement each year of some population from selected regions into other selected regions. The yearly transactions are shown in Table 13.9. Regions not shown in this table change as under the first projection. Results of the second projection are shown in Table 13.10. This time the eastern regions increase their relative share and the seven regions made to 'export' population either diminish or change little. Fig. 13.5 shows the population as in 1966, then in 2016 according to the first and second projections.

13.4 LONG TERM TRENDS IN THE U.S.S.R.

It is becoming increasingly fashionable and respectable to predict trends over several decades ahead. In the West, particularly the U.S.A., the business of predicting has become highly professional. Kahn[2] has discussed methods, projections, and scenarios for the next 30-50 years. Several Soviet papers on the question of prediction in geography are in *Soviet Geography: Review and Translation;*[3] in one Pokshishevskiy writes about economic geography in the year 2000 as follows:

> 'Urban population will tend to live in middle-size cities rather than gigantic urban complexes or excessively small settlements. Farm yields will be increased through more intensive use of the land. Conventional fuels and hydroelectricity will not be challenged by atomic power except in remote areas lacking other energy sources. Heavy industry will continue a gradual eastward shift beyond the Urals but will not be matched by an equal flow of population, which will remain concentrated in the European part of the country.'

Pokshishevskiy suggests a population of 330 million ±25 million of which 75% would be urban. His estimate of 13% for Transcaucasia and Central Asia does not agree with about 20% suggested in the previous section (Table 13.8). Pokshishevskiy expects that the proportion of urban dwellers living in large cities (over 500 000) will actually diminish as a result of policy. There will be a more rational approach to the use of both renewable and non-renewable resources and the U.S.S.R. could become a major exporter of food. Reafforestation should be carried out correctly.

Pokshishevskiy foresees seven iron and steel regions: Ukraine, Ural, Kuzbass, Central European U.S.S.R. (Cherepovets, Lipetsk), Kazakhstan, Baykal (Tayshet) and the Soviet Far East. Waterways in the dry areas of the U.S.S.R. would be under engineering control and northern rivers diverted as required into the interior basins of the Caspian and Aral Seas. On the other hand, diversion of the bigger Siberian rivers, starting from the Ob', would be undesirable, since large areas with mineral and other resources would be flooded. Much of the hydroelectric potential of Siberia will be harnessed and electricity will be transmitted westwards over long distances.

The long anticipated uplift for the Soviet consumer is not overlooked. Pokshishevskiy sees the growth of light industry and of services over the next decades as a way of justifying the perpetuation of the preponderance of Soviet population in western U.S.S.R. He might have added that the 'footloose' tertiary or non-goods sector of the economy has been absorbing more and more employees in the advanced Western countries for some time.

Zvonkova and Saushkin[4] discuss prediction in more general terms. In their view 'Prediction, in the sense of the study of the virtually unknown but inevitable future, is one of the timeliest and most complex problems of modern science'.

REFERENCES

1. FEYGIN, Ya. G. *et al., Zakonomernosti i faktory razvitiya ekonomicheskikh rayonov SSSR*, 39, 146 (Moscow, 1965)
2. KAHN, H. and WIENER, A. J., *The Year 2000* (Macmillan, New York, 1967)
3. POKSHISHEVSKIY, V. V., 'The economic geography of the U.S.S.R. by the year 2000' *Soviet Geogr.*, 9, No 9, 770–6, 1968 and other papers in the same number
4. ZVONKOVA, T. V. and SAUSHKIN, Yu. G., 'Problems of long-term geographic prediction' *Soviet Geogr.*, 9, No 9, 755–65, 1968

BIBLIOGRAPHY

BUDTOLAYEV, N. M. *et al.*, 'Problems of Economic Development of the West and East of the Soviet Union' *Soviet Geogr.*, 5, No 1, 3–15, 1964
SLASTENKO, Ye. N., 'The Distribution of Productive Forces and the Effacing of Differences between Town and Countryside' *Soviet Geogr.*, 5, No 2, 24–32, 1964

14

The economic regions

14.1 OVERVIEW OF THE 19 ECONOMIC REGIONS

This section contains numerical data to characterise the 19 economic regions of the U.S.S.R. and to support the verbal account of their main features, problems and prospects. The following tables are included:

Table 14.1 defines the 18 variables selected to characterise the 19 regions. Some of the variables have been used elsewhere in the book, especially in Chapter 2.

Table 14.2 presents the data for the variables in a 19 region × 18 variable data matrix.

Table 14.3(a) is the 18 × 18 matrix of Pearson product moment correlation indices (r), rounded to two decimal places. Table 14.3(b) shows the five most highly correlated pairs in the matrix.

Table 14.4(a) shows the strength of the first three factors derived from the correlation matrix. Together they account for 70% of all variation among the 18 variables. The loadings of the 18 variables on each of the first three factors are shown in Table 14.4(b).

Table 14.5 shows the weightings of the 19 regions on Factors I and II.

The weightings on Factors I and II are shown in graph form in Fig. 14.1; the horizontal axis is scaled according to the score of each region on Factor I, the vertical axis to the score on Factor II. Since the two factors combined account for 67% of all the variation of 18 variables, they give a reasonably good multivariate view of the similarity of regions to each other. The closer the regions to one another on the graph, the more similar they are to one another. A different set of variables would, of course, give a different picture, but the larger the number of variables taken into account, the nearer the consensus would be to the reality of the situation, providing the variables chosen were representative. The individual weightings (scores) of the regions on Factors I and II are mapped in Fig. 14.2, first on an area base, secondly on a population base.

Factor I is very close indeed to the variable 'residual urban population'(-0.95), discussed in Chapter 8. It groups industrial variables, services (hospital beds) and livestock orientated farming, to form a development variable. The highly urbanised regions lie at one end, the highly rural, at the other, on the weightings. The ranking of the regions on this factor can be seen in Table 14.5. Six of the seven most highly developed regions are in the R.S.F.S.R., but five of the six least developed are not in the R.S.F.S.R. Note that the presence of a minus sign before the more highly developed regions has nothing to do in itself with their development.

Factor II brings out a different arrangement of the regions, emphasising the aspects of length of settlement, structure of population and organisation of agriculture. This time certain regions of European U.S.S.R. are at one extreme and Asiatic U.S.S.R. comes at the other. The Far

Table 14.1. DESCRIPTION AND SOURCES OF VARIABLES USED TO CHARACTERISE REGIONS

Reference number given to variable	Source	Date	Description of data
1	S1(a), 12	1964	Area in hectares per 10 inhabitants
2	S1(a), 12	1940–59	Population change 1940–59 (1940 = 100)
3	S1(a), 12	1959–64	Population change 1959–64 (1959 = 100)
4	S1(a), 39	1964	Natural increase of population per thousand inhabitants
5	A1, A2	various	Favourability of physical conditions for agriculture (consensus based on altitude, temperature, precipitation and soil. Maximum 20)
6	S1(a), 278	1964	Sown area (*posevnyye ploshchadi*) in hectares per 100 inhabitants
7	S2, 74	1958–62	Value of livestock farming production as a percentage of value of total farming production
8	S1(a), 401	1964	Money income of kolkhozes in roubles per kolkhoz household (*dvor*)
9	S1(a), 274–5, 276–7	1964	Sown area under kolkhoz farms as a percentage of total sown area under farms
10	S2, 75	1962	Industries other than agriculture and the food industry as a percentage of combined production of agriculture and industry
11	S1(a), 13–17	1965	Residual* urban population as a percentage of total population
12	S1(c), 133	1962	Production workers in manufacturing per thousand inhabitants (total population)
13	S1(a), 508	1959–64	Exploitation of basic funds of state and cooperative enterprises (except kolkhozes) in tens of roubles per inhabitant during 1959–64
14	S1(c), 133	1961	Electricity output in tens of kW per inhabitant
15	S2, 72	1962	Production of basic branches of industry (electricity, engineering, chemicals) as a percentage of total industrial production of region
16	S1(a), 129	1958–64	Rate of industrial growth 1958–64, 1958 = 100
17	S1(b), 580	1963/64	Persons in higher educational establishments per 10 000 total population
18	S1(a), 739	1964	Hospital beds available per 10 000 total population

* Residual here means that part of the urban population that remains in each region after a number of urban dwellers equal to 30% of the rural population has been subtracted from the total urban population (Chapter 8).

Sources;
S1(a) *NkhSSSR* 1964   S2 *Zakonomernosti i faktory razvitiya ekonomicheskikh rayonov SSSR*
S1(b) *NkhSSSR* 1963   A1 *Atlas SSSR*
S1(c) *NkhSSSR* 1961   A2 *Atlas sels'kogo khozyaystva*

Table 14.2. DATA MATRIX FOR THE 19 REGIONS

Variables (see Table 14.1 for description)

Economic region	1	2	3	4	5	6	7	8	9	10	11	12	13	14	15	16	17	18
E1 Northwest	158	97	106	8	11	25	58	917	65	76	63	164	113	161	34	156	234	111
E2 Centre	18	95	103	6	15	53	48	847	61	78	57	174	96	124	35	146	261	102
E3 Volga-Vyatka	32	94	100	10	14	83	45	588	82	73	32	128	60	109	49	164	97	88
E4 Blackearth Centre	21	86	103	7	16	140	44	1 186	72	38	14	71	54	66	39	179	92	74
E5 Volga	39	103	109	12	13	162	47	1 409	57	59	37	115	93	251	41	189	124	86
E6 N.Caucasus	27	110	114	12	13	124	49	1 673	58	44	31	82	70	83	26	170	119	80
E7 Ural	129	133	107	11	12	114	49	1 239	47	73	55	134	97	317	37	165	114	98
E8 W. Siberia	92	124	106	11	10	163	47	1 708	35	62	46	113	107	244	39	165	154	97
E9 E. Siberia	573	133	111	14	5	108	56	1 698	38	63	45	106	133	253	31	184	121	97
E10 Far East	1 150	150	112	13	6	46	51	1 973	26	53	64	123	146	119	24	179	124	117
E11 Donets-Dnepr	11	109	108	9	15	74	48	1 365	78	66	59	146	90	264	32	162	132	99
E12 Southwest	13	95	106	10	16	65	43	764	90	37	14	63	42	48	24	172	115	85
E13 South	19	102	112	10	16	118	43	1 483	67	38	39	81	84	94	29	179	158	94
E14 Baltic	27	112	107	9	15	73	58	1 148	70	53	40	111	80	59	23	188	132	103
E15 Transcaucasia	17	116	117	24	8	21	37	660	72	43	35	65	58	135	23	155	136	81
E16 Central Asia	75	125	123	29	7	26	32	1 765	66	29	18	44	52	64	18	166	120	89
E17 Kazakhstan	228	151	129	22	9	358	46	2 053	14	33	31	56	114	106	21	191	96	97
E18 Belorussia	24	90	105	13	15	71	44	635	66	50	20	72	52	49	30	188	101	88
E19 Moldavia	10	116	114	16	16	58	30	1 079	87	21	4	43	38	24	10	181	87	88

Table 14.3.

(a) 18 × 18 correlation matrix with Pearson product moment r values rounded to two decimal places

Variable

	1	2	3	4	5	6	7	8	9	10	11	12	13	14	15	16	17	18
1	1·00																	
2	0·65	1·00																
3	0·17	0·67	1·00															
4	−0·08	0·52	0·85	1·00														
5	−0·67	−0·75	−0·52	−0·59	1·00													
6	−0·09	0·36	0·39	0·08	−0·05	1·00												
7	0·34	0·07	−0·37	−0·60	−0·13	0·11	1·00											
8	0·52	0·75	0·60	0·31	−0·54	0·52	0·12	1·00										
9	−0·63	−0·77	−0·42	−0·19	0·67	−0·60	−0·39	−0·74	1·00									
10	0·10	−0·14	−0·62	−0·58	−0·05	−0·17	0·69	−0·24	−0·14	1·00								
11	0·44	0·28	−0·20	−0·36	−0·32	−0·10	0·71	0·20	−0·45	0·78	1·00							
12	0·16	−0·13	−0·58	−0·65	0·03	−0·20	0·71	−0·14	−0·13	0·94	0·86	1·00						
13	0·72	0·59	−0·17	−0·17	−0·58	0·28	0·70	0·58	−0·81	0·51	0·81	0·57	1·00					
14	0·16	0·30	−0·19	−0·32	0·16	0·16	0·41	0·23	−0·39	0·65	0·66	0·58	0·59	1·00				
15	−0·13	−0·42	−0·70	−0·60	0·17	0·09	0·43	−0·25	−0·02	0·74	0·36	0·62	0·20	0·49	1·00			
16	0·21	0·22	0·26	0·10	0·03	0·49	0·04	0·36	−0·26	−0·47	−0·39	−0·48	0·04	−0·21	−0·25	1·00		
17	−0·05	−0·23	−0·26	−0·35	0·01	−0·31	0·40	−0·17	−0·03	0·55	0·62	0·67	0·35	0·18	0·22	−0·64	1·00	
18	0·60	0·44	−0·03	−0·20	−0·33	−0·11	0·59	0·28	−0·46	0·48	0·78	0·62	0·77	0·29	−0·03	−0·11	0·50	1·00

(b) Highest correlations in (a)

				Correlation
10	Industries other than agriculture and food as percentage of all industry	12	Industry as percentage of all population	+0·94
12	Manufacturing	11	Residual urban	+0·86
3	Population change 1959–64	4	Natural increase	+0·85
11	Residual urban	13	Basic funds per capita	+0·81
13	Basic funds	9	Kolkhoz as percentage of all farms (sovkhoz would be +)	−0·81

Table 14.4.

(a) *Relative strength of first three factors*

	Factor I	Factor II	Factor III
	6·58 or 36·5%	5·52 or 30·5%	1·95 or 11%

(b) *Loadings of variables on first three factors*

Variables	Factor I	Factor II	Factor III
1	−0·48	0·59	0·11
2	−0·25	0·91†	0·11
3	0·32	0·83†	0·21
4	0·47	0·66†	0·42
5	0·33	−0·73†	−0·33
6	−0·00	0·48	−0·71
7	−0·81*	−0·07	−0·28
8	−0·21	0·83†	−0·18
9	0·52	−0·75†	0·22
10	−0·85*	−0·43	−0·02
11	−0·95*	0·02	0·18
12	−0·89*	−0·41	0·05
13	−0·87*	0·46	−0·08
14	−0·68*	0·07	−0·15
15	−0·50	−0·52	−0·43
16	0·29	0·45	−0·64
17	−0·58	−0·35	0·44
18	−0·76*	0·23	0·27

*Chief variables loading on Factor I
†Chief variables loading on Factor II

Table 14.5. INDIVIDUAL WEIGHTINGS OF REGIONS ON FACTORS I AND II

	Region	Factor I	Region	Factor II
1	Northwest	−10·1	Centre	−7·8
2	Far East	−9·5	Volga-Vyatka	−7·7
3	Centre	−7·9	Northwest	−5·0
4	East Siberia	−6·8	Southwest	−4·6
5	Ural	−6·5	Blackearth Centre	−4·4
6	West Siberia	−5·7	Belorussia	−3·7
7	Donets-Dnepr	−4·6	Donets-Dnepr	−3·4
8	Volga	−1·5	Baltic	−1·7
9	Baltic	−0·8	South	−0·7
10	Volga-Vyatka	−0·2	Volga	−0·6
11	Kazakhstan	1·8	Ural	0·0
12	South	2·1	Transcaucasia	0·5
13	North Caucasus	3·1	Moldavia	0·8
14	Transcaucasia	5·5	North Caucasus	0·8
15	Belorussia	5·7	West Siberia	1·5
16	Blackearth Centre	6·4	East Siberia	6·2
17	Southwest	7·7	Central Asia	6·3
18	Central Asia	8·8	Far East	9·6
19	Moldavia	12·7	Kazakhstan	13·8

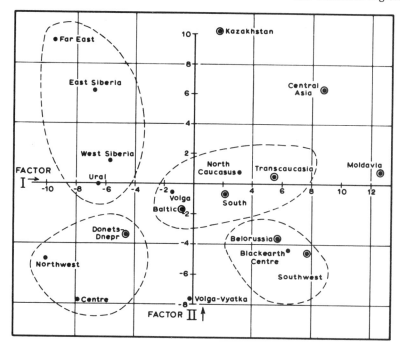

Fig. 14.1.   *Individual weightings of the 19 economic regions on Factors I (horizontal) and II (vertical).*
Regions not in the R.S.F.S.R. are shown with a large dot.

East, Kazakhstan and Central Asia, very different in development, are very similar in the aspects covered by Factor II.

Since the first two factors together account for 67% of all the variation in 18 variables they are sufficient to give a rough classification of the 19 regions. It is possible to see which regions are similar to which others by their positions on the graph. Thus, Blackearth Centre, Southwest and Belorussia are very similar, as might be expected. So too, however, are the Volga and Baltic, a fact that might easily be overlooked. The Centre and Central Asia are extremely different, as are the Far East and the Southwest.

Unfortunately, the regions themselves are so large and have so many contrasts within them, that they provide too coarse a network to form the basis for a regionalisation of the U.S.S.R. Nevertheless, they are used widely in the U.S.S.R. and do therefore affect Soviet planning. They will be described in the following order:

1. Developed, old
   Northwest
   Centre
   Donets-Dnepr

2. Developed, new
   Ural
   West Siberia
   East Siberia
   Far East

3. Middle
   Volga
   Volga-Vyatka
   Baltic
   South
   North Caucasus

4. Underdeveloped
   Belorussia
   Blackearth Centre
   Southwest
   Moldavia
   Transcaucasia
   Central Asia
   Kazakhstan

Much of the information contained in this chapter has been put in tabular form in various other chapters already. There are at least two reasons, however, why it is desirable to include at

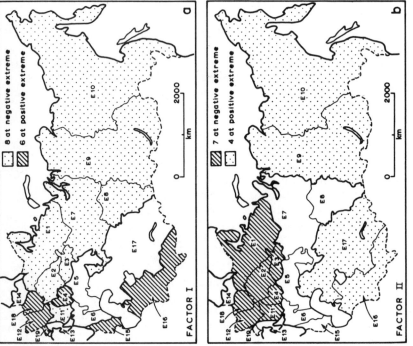

Fig. 14.2. *Individual weightings of the 19 economic regions on (a) Factor I and (b) Factor II. (c) and (d) are based on the same data as (a) and (b), but have a population, not area, base. Note: the shading between (b) and (d) is reversed.*

FACTOR I

▨ 8 at negative extreme
▧ 6 at positive extreme

E18 E12 E14 E11 E4 E3 E13 E1 E2 E5 E6 E7 E9 E10 E8 E17 E16 E15

FACTOR II

▨ 7 at negative extreme
☐ 4 at positive extreme

E18 E12 E14 E11 E4 E3 E13 E1 E2 E5 E6 E7 E9 E10 E8 E17 E16 E15

FACTOR I

2 500 000 inhabitants in 1964-5

▨ 7 at negative extreme
▧ 6 at positive extreme

Baltic Northwest Centre Volga Vyatka Ural East Siberia Far East West Siberia
Southwest BEL DDN Volga Kazakhstan
Moldavia South Blackearth Centre NCA Central Asia
16 Transcaucasia

FACTOR II

▨ 7 at negative extreme
▧ 5 at positive extreme

Baltic Northwest Centre Volga Vyatka Ural Siberia Far East West Siberia
Southwest BEL DDN Volga Kazakhstan
Moldavia South Blackearth Centre NCA Central Asia
Correct contiguity is preserved Transcaucasia

least a brief verbal description of each of the 19 regions. First, this is the form familiar to most geographers. Secondly, it allows the regions to be considered in an integrated fashion, as planning entities. Each of the 19 regions is treated in turn. The order in which they are dealt with is based to some extent on the desirability of having similar ones next to each other in the sequence and on the length of time each region has formed part of the Russian Empire. In reality the regions do not exist in a linear sequence but in a two dimensional relationship, if thought of areally, or in a multidimensional one if conceived on a multivariate basis. Many of them merge imperceptibly into each other and their boundaries are entirely arbitrary.

Each region is dealt with in roughly the same order of topics, but more space is devoted to the

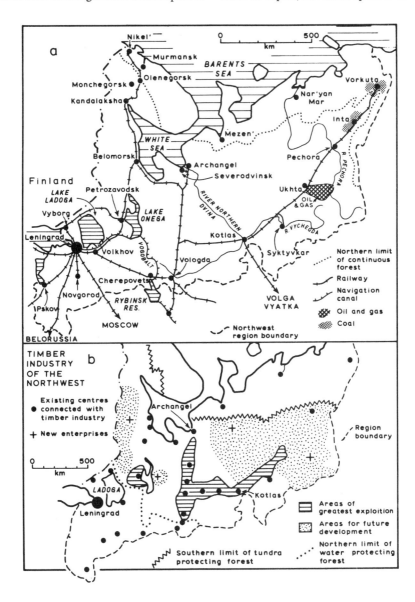

Fig. 14.3. *The Northwest (a) Key map of places referred to in the text (b) The timber industry of the Northwest. Source:* Al'tman.[1]

larger regions. The following features are considered, where appropriate: size and limits, latitude and physical features, material resources, economic activities, population, transportation network and flows of goods, regional surpluses and deficiencies, special problems, and future prospects.

14.2 THE NORTHWEST

The Northwest occupies roughly the northern third of European U.S.S.R. It is fifth in area among the regions but eleventh in population (11 855 000 in 1968). About 30% of the population is in Greater Leningrad (3 750 000) 40% in Leningrad oblast including the town. The places mentioned in this section are shown in Fig. 14.3(a).

The region is relatively closed to the west by the Soviet-Finnish boundary, and to the east by the high though narrow northern Urals. There is rail access to each of the neighbouring regions to the south but none directly into the Ural region. To the north the region is open to the oceans and the northwest extremity (Murmansk) is ice free all the year. The southern limit of the Northwest region coincides roughly with the watershed between Arctic and other drainage systems. The Northwest lies roughly between 55°N. and 70°N. By European standards, it has long cold winters, with a long snow cover, though little permafrost. Precipitation is adequate for crop farming, but the growing season is short. Soils are in general poor. Sown area occupies only a small proportion of total area, even in the most favourable southwest part (Pskov oblast about 20%, Novgorod and Leningrad oblasts about 10%). Further north it thins out to become negligible. Rye, wheat and flax are the principal crops in the southwest, but further north oats and barley are grown. There is a strong emphasis on dairy farming and fodder crops are grown in addition to the cereals mentioned. Potatoes and other vegetables are cultivated particularly around Leningrad.

Although much of the forest in the Northwest has already been cut, coniferous forest still covers extensive tracts and there is now concern about reafforestation. Indeed the forests remain the principal natural resource of the region. Fig. 14.3(b) shows aspects of the timber industry in the Northwest. Forests alongside the railways have been most heavily exploited. The forest in the southwest is now conserved to protect water supply, while that in the extreme north is protected to hold back the gradual incursion of the tundra. In the north, the forest thins out and disappears to make way for the tundra coastlands of the Arctic, with reindeer herding the main land use.

The Northwest has abundant water resources, though few sites for large hydroelectric power stations. It has been planned to divert headwaters of the Pechora and the North Dvina south into the Volga system. Energy minerals consist mainly of the high grade but costly Pechora basin coal seams, currently mined at Inta and Vorkuta, and of apparently small oil and gas deposits southeast of Ukhta. These are supplemented by wood, peat and oil shales (Slantsy near Leningrad). Other minerals are found mainly in the Kola Peninsula at Nikel' (nickel ore) Olenegorsk (iron ore) and Kirovsk (apatite).

Basically the Northwest is one of the most urbanised and sophisticated regions, with its economy depending primarily on timber and on such products as paper and cellulose. In addition, Leningrad has a wide range of industries, including engineering (particularly electrical, shipbuilding) textiles and clothing and chemicals. Leningrad is also an educational and cultural centre second in importance only to Moscow. Non-ferrous metal smelting uses regional minerals (Monchegorsk (nickel), Volkhov (aluminium)). The Cherepovets integrated iron and steel works uses regional coking coal and ore and is an attempt to fill the empty area north of Moscow. Though it has been enlarged several times it still only produces about 1% of all Soviet steel. A new gas and chemicals plant will help to boost the status of Novgorod.

The three largest towns of the region, Leningrad, Archangel (population 313 000) and Murmansk (296 000) are all ports. The railway system of the region has developed largely in response to the need to link these with areas further south. The Moscow–Archangel line was completed in 1898 but the Murmansk line not until 1916. The railway to the Pechora coalfield was only completed in 1942. The rail system is supplemented by waterways, both improved natural ones (eg the North Dvina) and completely artificial ones (Volgobalt).

The Northwest has a surplus of timber and wood products, of certain minerals and of engineering goods. According to Al'tman,[1] it sends out '94% of its apatite concentrate output, 30% of its timber and 50% of its paper and paperboard'. It is, however, deficient in almost all kinds of food and agricultural raw materials, in energy (particularly oil) and many manufactured goods. For example, 24% of its grain, 36% of its meat and 50% of its milk come from other regions. Nevertheless, it appears to make a contribution to the national economy roughly proportional to its share of total population. Relatively, however, the Northwest has declined in the last few decades in its absolute importance. Natural population growth is slow, there is little in-migration and the war was a setback particularly to Leningrad. More important, perhaps, Siberia has nearly all the material resources which were for a long time a monopoly of the Northwest, and in Siberia they are found in much larger quantities and are often cheaper to exploit. The Northwest still scores on its relative proximity to the rest of European U.S.S.R., to Comecon partners and to the outside world via its sea-ports. In the 1950's and 1960's it has had relatively high *per capita* investment, which indicates that Soviet planners by no means feel it to be in serious decline.

14.3 THE CENTRE

The Centre is the largest of the 19 regions in population (26 763 000) but only ninth in order of size. As in the Northwest, much of the population is in one centre, Greater Moscow (6 590 000), which has about 25% and Moscow oblast with Moscow itself (11 989 000) about 45%. The Centre shares boundaries with seven other regions and nowhere do its limits follow a physical obstacle of any kind, or even a marked change in land use. The region does however derive some unity from the presence of Moscow roughly in the centre and from the distinct radial pattern of the rail system; it could be described as a nodal region.

The Centre lies roughly between 52° and 60° N., the latitude of the British Isles, or of Quebec province. It consists of hill country in the west, rarely over 300 metres in height, but often with considerable variations locally in relative relief, and of broad gently undulating valleys in the east. Vegetation ranges from coniferous forest in the north, through mixed coniferous and broadleaf forest and forest-steppe. Conditions of soil quality, drainage and length of growing season improve generally from northwest to southeast across the region. This is reflected in great contrasts in sown area varying at oblast level from about 10% under crops in Kostroma to 70% in Orel. While the chernozem or chernozem-like soils of the southern part give almost continuous cultivation in places, both the quantity and reliability of precipitation diminish from north to south.

Agriculture in the Centre is characterised by the relatively highly developed livestock sector based both on dairying and meat production from cattle, pig and poultry raising, on a basis of cereals, grasses and other fodder crops. Within the region, however, there are many local specialisms. Around Moscow, vegetable growing and dairying are particularly developed (Fig. 14.4(a) area 1). To the north and west of Moscow (area 2), much of the land is still forested, rural settlements tend to be small and scattered and the only outstanding special crop is flax. To the south (area 3) cereals, including wheat and rye, and potatoes are predominant. In the extreme south hemp is also cultivated. It has been suggested (*Pravda,* 4 March 1966) that the Meskchera lowland, fertile, but currently ill-drained in places, could be improved for dairying purposes.

There is little irrigation in the Centre, but in some districts improved drainage of land is needed. Several reservoirs have been built on the Volga, but the hydroelectric power stations supplied by these are small. The water supply for urban and industrial needs, adequate now, is expected to need supplementing in the future. The Centre has few mineral resources. The limited supply of local wood, peat and hydroelectric power is supplemented by high cost lignite from the Moscow field around Tula. There are no other minerals either metallic or non-metallic, of any consequence.

The industries of the Centre are dependent on other regions in almost every way. In the early 1960's the region was only providing about one-third of its energy needs locally. This share is tending to diminish, not surprisingly, since

Moscow coalfield coal costs in Moscow roughly twice Donbass or Kuzbass coal and several times Volga oil or Stavropol' gas. Industry depends for its success on adding value to 'imported' materials. The region survives industrially thanks to its early start, tradition of skilled manufacturing, large force of skilled labour and its plant. Its central position, difficult to assess in quantitative terms, must also be an advantage, for a large part of the Soviet national market is still within 1 000 km of Moscow. The fact that it has the national capital and the centre of national planning should also be taken into account.

There is some heavy industry in the Centre. Pig iron is produced at Tula and steel from local or imported pig iron, or from scrap, is made here and in the Moscow area (particularly Elektrostal'). The chemicals industry has also grown in this area, particularly since the late 1950's thanks to oil and gas supplies from outside. Moscow itself, the coalfield area, and Yaroslavl' are the main centres. The engineering industry is widely represented and within the region local specialisms may be distinguished: for example, precision engineering in Moscow, railway equipment at Kolomna, textile machinery at Ivanovo. Light industry is well developed and it is in textiles, including cotton, wool, linen and silk, that the Centre produces its biggest surplus. Factory based textile manufacturing has been established for over a century in places such as Ivanovo to the northeast of

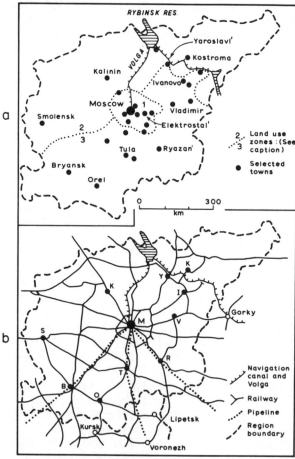

Fig. 14.4.   (a) Key map to places mentioned in text. The three land use zones are:
1 Suburban vegetables and dairying
2 Flax, dairying and meat
3 Cereals, potatoes, dairying and milk
(b) The rail system of the Centre. All railway lines are shown but only selected pipelines.

Moscow, and much of Soviet textile capacity is still in a zone between Moscow and Ivanovo. The manufacture of clothing and the processing of agricultural products is much more widespread in the Centre. Moscow itself is also a printing and publishing centre.

The cultural, educational, research and administrative role of Moscow should not be forgotten. Greater Moscow dominates the urban scene in the Centre and is many times larger than the next towns in size Yaroslavl' (population 507 000), Ivanovo (415 000) and Tula (384 000). It is the most developed and sophisticated place in the U.S.S.R. in many respects and probably among the most affluent. The Centre, however, also contains some of the most backward parts, notably Smolensk, Bryansk and Orel oblasts and about one-third of the population of the region is still rural.

The transportation network of the Centre is better illustrated by Fig. 14.4(b) than described verbally. Most of the main lines, some already electrified, radiate from Moscow. Movement between other pairs of places is often indirect and relatively slow. Moscow itself may be avoided by use of an outer ring railway (see Fig. 11.4(b)). The rail system is supplemented by relatively good roads, running in various directions from Moscow and by several oil and gas pipelines and electricity transmission lines bringing in fuel and power from the south and east (see Fig. 11.6).

It is hard to conceive a region less like the well-balanced, self-sufficient model that Soviet planners have aspired to. Scarcely any item except perhaps potatoes and vegetables, flax and milk, is adequate to meet the needs of the region. The inventory of goods flowing into the Centre is not unlike that received by Britain or West Germany, but large quantities of coal must be added. In return, the Centre pays by providing a surplus for other regions of textile, engineering and other manufactured goods, as well as services such as administration, higher education and research.

Like the Northwest, the Centre is less important now that it was before 1917 or even in the 1930's, for its population is growing only slowly, and movement of population into Moscow is controlled. Whereas the Northwest has considerable natural resources, however, the Centre has few. Moreover it is ironical that the

very industries the Centre possesses are those that could equally easily be located in many other regions.

The prospects for the Centre are certainly not obvious. Some factories are obsolete, particularly in the textile areas; others are small in scale, particularly on the metallurgical side. The development of petrochemicals and the existence of growth sectors in engineering around Moscow point to a gradual transformation of the nature of industry in the Centre, although even now it is unlikely that Soviet strategic thinking would allow an excessive concentration of sophisticated engineering in one place. Meanwhile, plans to bring in more energy continue to be implemented. By the late 1960's, gas was being piped direct from Central Asia and there are plans for a pipeline from West Siberia to the capital.

14.4 BALTIC–BELORUSSIA–BLACKEARTH CENTRE–VOLGA-VYATKA

These four regions are for convenience treated together to avoid repetition of the many features they have in common. Distinctions between them will be noted. Their ranks in order of area and population in the 19 economic regions are:

| | Rank | | |
	Area	Population	Population in thousands
Volga-Vyatka	12	13	8 288
Belorussia	14	12	8 820
Baltic	15	15	7 359
Blackearth Centre	17	14	7 948

They are close both in area and in population. In Fig. 14.5 the four regions are shown as a rim zone around the Leningrad–Moscow core, or as four small regions between bigger, mostly more developed ones (see inset map in Fig. 14.5). The Northwest and Centre merge imperceptibly into the four regions. The Baltic region and Belorussia terminate abruptly in the west against the Baltic Sea and Poland, but on the south and east, Belorussia, Blackearth Centre and Volga-Vyatka again merge into other Soviet regions. Only the Poles'ye in the south of Belorussia forms a thinly peopled zone separating the Belorussians from the western Ukrainians.

Like the Centre, the four regions lie between

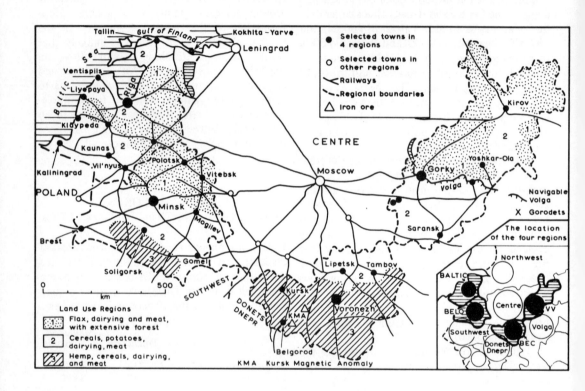

Fig. 14.5.　Key to map of the four economic regions: Baltic, Belorussia, Blackearth Centre and Volga-Vyatka.

50° and 60°N. There are, however, considerable temperature differences between north and south in summer, and between west and east in winter, and an increase in continental characteristics east from the Baltic. Precipitation in general is adequate if not abundant for agriculture, but is more limited and unreliable in the Blackearth Centre. Mixed coniferous and broadleaf forest formerly occupied the Baltic and the northern parts of Belorussia and the Volga-Vyatka. This gives way southwards to broadleaf forest, then mixed forest-steppe. Even in the Blackearth Centre, however, the continuous steppe occurs only locally. Soils are mostly poor or only moderately good in the Baltic, Belorussia and Volga-Vyatka, but they are fertile in the Blackearth Centre. There are many areas still to be improved by drainage, particularly in Belorussia. In northern areas, only about 20% of the land is cultivated (Estonia 17%, Kirov 21%) and even in Belorussia, only about 30%. In contrast, the Blackearth Centre is about two-thirds cultivated (Kursk and Lipetsk each 70%). Forest of varying composition and economic usefulness covers much of the remaining land, but only the Volga-Vyatka has a surplus of forest products.

In terms of crop and livestock emphasis, the Blackearth Centre contrasts with the other three regions in being more orientated towards crops. The Baltic and Belorussia specialise in dairying in particular and livestock in general. In Fig. 14.5 the dotted area is to a considerable extent forested. Farming has an emphasis on dairying and flax cultivation (Area 1). The second zone (2) in Fig. 14.5 is concerned mainly with cereal and potato cultivation and with livestock farming, both dairying and meat, based on cattle and pig raising. Wheat and rye are the principal cereals. Additional crops in this zone are sugar beet and hemp, particularly in Lithuania (in the south of the Baltic region) Belorussia and the Chuvash A.S.S.R. (in the south of the Volga-Vyatka). The Blackearth Centre has a somewhat longer growing season and hotter summers and in addition to all the items mentioned for the other three regions it specialises in sugar beet (especially in Kursk and Belgorod) maize and sunflowers.

The four regions have no immediate water supply problems. Eventually the Blackearth Centre might benefit from some form of irrigation. In the other three regions, however, a superabundance of moisture is in places the problem. Only the Volga on its way through the Volga-Vyatka region is important for navigation. It has been dammed above Gorky (at Gorodets) to provide a moderate sized hydroelectric station. According to *Pravda,* 28 September 1968, work has started on another at Cheboksary (Chuvash A.S.S.R.) below Gorky, to have a capacity of 1 400 MW. The regions are very poorly endowed with fuel deposits. Only Estonia, with oil shales (Kokhtla-Yarve) and Belorussia, with the prospect of natural gas, have any local base at all. Nor are other minerals of importance at the moment, though Belorussia has large potash deposits at Soligorsk and near Kursk and Belgorod in the Blackearth Centre is the famous Kursk Magnetic Anomaly. Both are being developed in the 1966–70 Five Year Plan.

The four regions share the basic problem of the Centre, a lack of raw materials. In contrast to the Centre, however, they contain no major industrial concentration and only a few individual industrial centres of size. The chemicals industry is almost non-existent, and the metallurgical industry is largely confined to Lipetsk, which has an integrated iron and steel works. Light engineering is mostly restricted to Gorky, which has now, however, lost its former near monopoly of motor vehicle manufacture, and to Minsk, Voronezh, and the Baltic ports, particularly Riga. The manufacture of textiles is fairly widespread in the Baltic region, and of paper and wood in the Volga-Vyatka, Belorussia and the Baltic. There seems little prospect that any new major industrial concentrations will emerge in these regions. Nevertheless, by Soviet standards they are densely populated and are indeed overpopulated rurally. They contain some of the most depressed areas in the U.S.S.R., particularly the three A.S.S.R.'s of the Volga-Vyatka (Mariysk, Mordov and Chuvash) Belgorod and Kursk, and parts of Belorussia. The policy in the late 1960's seemed to be to remedy the situation as far as possible by linking many towns to the gas pipeline system to bring in gas from Dashava, Shebelinka, Stavropol' and the Volga. The oil pipeline west from the Volga also crosses the regions in places.

The larger towns are clearly still growing industrially, with prospects for light engineering and consumer goods. There are several small growth centres worth noting, including Kokhtla-Yarve (oil shales) Klaypeda (oil port) Polotsk (oil refinery) Soligorsk (fertilisers) and Lipetsk (iron and steel).

Although the regions are adequately served with railways, Fig. 14.5 suggests that the radial lines from Moscow and to a lesser extent Leningrad tend to dominate the rail system particularly of the Blackearth Centre and Volga-Vyatka. In a sense, each region seems to be an intermediate zone between Moscow and other places, and much rail traffic in the regions must be between points of origin and destination outside. Several lines terminate at Baltic ports, of which the most southerly are ice free and form one of the main outlets for Soviet seaborne trade. Belorussia lies between Moscow and Poland, the Blackearth Centre between Moscow and the Donets-Dnepr, and the Volga-Vyatka between Moscow and the Urals.

In conclusion, the lack of mineral resources in the four regions must be re-emphasised. If the regions are to pay their way towards achieving a high standard of living they, like the Centre, will have to transform materials from other regions and attract high value added branches. Other regions, however, including much of the Ukraine, Transcaucasia and Central Asia, also aspire to such industries. A second possibility is to embark on a long term improvement of land resources, including both the forests and the cropland and to bring these as yet neglected sectors to prominence. By the standards of Scandinavia or Central Europe, the 32 million people of the four regions are sitting on big reserves of such assets as timber and land suitable for dairying. It is being suggested that at 450 roubles per hectare the Poles'ye is well worth reclaiming; 35 000 km^2 might be gained, timber reserves and fisheries would benefit, navigation would be improved and the Dnepr system better controlled. There are hints also that underlying the Pripyat depression are oil deposits (*Pravda*, 15 August 1965).

14.5 THE URAL

The Ural region, now seventh in area and sixth in population (15 262 000) has undergone various changes in the 1960's. First, it has lost the oil producing Bashkir A.S.S.R. to the Volga region.

Secondly, it has gained the predominantly agricultural Kurgan oblast from West Siberia. Thirdly, for a time it had the territorially vast Tyumen' oblast; this has now reverted to West Siberia (see Fig. 14.6). This example of Soviet manipulation of economic regions was discussed in Chapter 12 and shown in Fig. 12.3(b). The *raison d'etre* of the Ural region is the mineral bearing north-south Ural Mountain range, which in fact divides the region into two halves, linked by several railways across the relatively low Middle Ural, and by a line passing to the south.

Without Tyumen' oblast, the region extends between about 50° and 62°N. It is characterised by long cold winter conditions, accentuated by the high ground of the range. Except in the south, precipitation is considerable. To the west of the range, the coniferous forest belt extends south of Perm', and merges into mixed forest. In the extreme south, the vegetation is steppe, but the coniferous forest extends far south along the range itself. To the east of the mountains, the birch is the only broadleaf tree species found widely and there is a sharper transition from coniferous forest to steppe. Except in the steppes of the south (Orenburg and Kurgan oblasts) soils are generally moderate or poor and sloping ground further hinders cultivation. As a result, there is a striking contrast in cultivated area expressed as a percentage of total area; Perm' 12%, Sverdlovsk 8%, but Orenburg 51% and Kurgan 42%. There is some compensation in the north, however, for the Ural region has extensive reserves of timber.

The urban concentrations of the Ural are large enough to attract around them specialised vegetable growing and dairying. The more hardy rye and oats, accompanied by dairying and some flax cultivation, give way in the agricultural southern part of the region to spring wheat and cattle raising with both dairying and meat production.

Except in the south the Ural region has abundant supplies of water, being drained by large tributaries of the Volga (Kama, Chusovaya) and the Irtysh (Tavda, Tura). The region has a considerable number of small and medium sized hydroelectric stations and two large ones on the Kama (Krasnokamsk, Votkinsk). Nevertheless, almost all the large energy requirements of the region are satisfied from other sources. The region itself has several deposits of brown coal

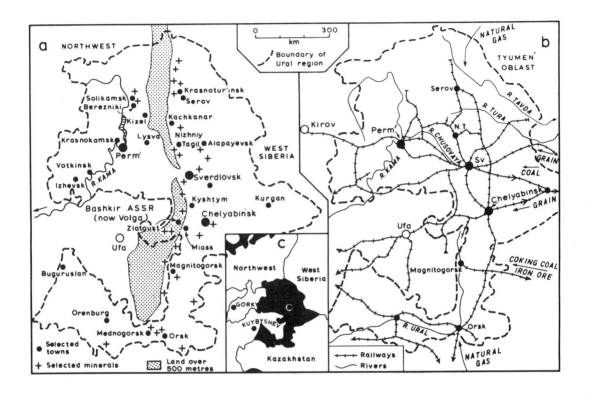

Fig. 14.6.   *Ural region: (a) Key map to places mentioned in text. (b) The rail system. (c) Location of the Ural region.*

and some hard coal, but only that of Kizel is suitable for coking. A little oil is produced in the extreme southwest at Buguruslan, but the former large reserves in the Bashkir A.S.S.R. have of course, been transferred to the Volga region.

The Ural range also has a large number of other minerals, some 20 of which are of economic importance. With the discovery of minerals further east in recent decades, however, it has declined relatively and is no longer the outstanding mineral region of the U.S.S.R. Its inventory does include iron ore in several places, manganese ore (but secondary to that of the Donets-Dnepr and Transcaucasia), copper ore, nickel ore, bauxite, gold, salt, potash salt and asbestos.

The Ural region is one of the oldest industrial regions. From early in the 18th century until late in the 19th, there developed and flourished one of the greatest iron smelting regions in the world. Numerous easily accessible deposits of ore, abundant charcoal for smelting, and water in mountain streams, provided the ingredients. Peter the Great and subsequent Russian leaders supplied the necessary initiative and the rivers were the means of access to markets in European Russia. The major problem was labour supply. Technicians were brought from Central Europe. Metal working developed and armaments and agricultural implements were widely manufactured. The region then stagnated technologically from the latter part of the 19th century until the first Five Year Plan. With heavy investment here in the 1930's, a link with Kuzbass and later Karaganda coking coal supplies and the threat of occupation of the Donbass area, the Ural region became the key to Soviet victory in World War II. By the late 1960's it shared with the Donets-Dnepr the leading place in iron and steel production and heavy engineering. In addition, the processing of non-ferrous metals and of non-metallic minerals, together with the manufacture of chemicals and of paper and wood products, make it reasonably diversified.

Like the Northwest and Centre, the Ural region is highly urbanised, but it is not dominated by a single very large centre. Both Sverdlovsk and Chelyabinsk, with neighbouring towns, have about 1 million inhabitants. Nizhniy Tagil and Magnitogorsk are particularly associated with the iron and steel industry, Perm' with

chemicals. Many smaller centres specialise, for example, in steel production in Lys'va, Zlatoust and Serov, chemicals in Berezniki, non-ferrous metals in Krasnotur'insk, Kyshtym and Mednogorsk, mining in Kizel and Kachkanar and motor vehicles in Miass.

The rail system of the Ural region is dominated by several east-west lines, two of which converge on Sverdlovsk and one of which passes through Chelyabinsk. On the eastern side there is also a north-south line running almost the whole extent of the region. Traffic is heavy on most lines and several routes are already electrified (Fig. 14.6(b)).

By Soviet standards the Ural region can now no longer be thought of as possessing superabundant natural resources. The region does not have a sound food base, though new lands in the south have been opened up since 1953. The modern iron and steel industry depends almost entirely on coal from outside the region. Moreover, the higher grade iron ore deposits (eg at Magnitogorsk) are being depleted: fortunately nearby deposits in Kazakhstan (Rudnyy near Kustanay) are near at hand. Oil and gas now come into the region from West Siberia and Central Asia. Many of the traditional mineral deposits are limited or suspect. Light industry is poorly represented. Altogether, then, the region currently draws on many other regions for a wide range of materials and manufactured goods, for which it pays with its surplus of metals and machines. Its long term usefulness and prosperity depend on a shift to branches of industry that require relatively less in terms of materials and more in terms of skilled manpower.

14.6 WEST SIBERIA

With Tyumen' oblast, West Siberia (Fig. 14.7) is fourth in area among the 19 regions but ninth in population (12 201 000). It coincides fairly closely with the drainage basin of the Ob'-Irtysh. It is closed in the northwest by the high Northern Ural Range. In the north there is little traffic out into the Arctic Ocean and in the east, little movement across into East Siberia. The region is, however, open to the south.

West Siberia lies mainly between $50°$ and $70°N$. Apart from the high, rugged Altay mountain district of the extreme south, it

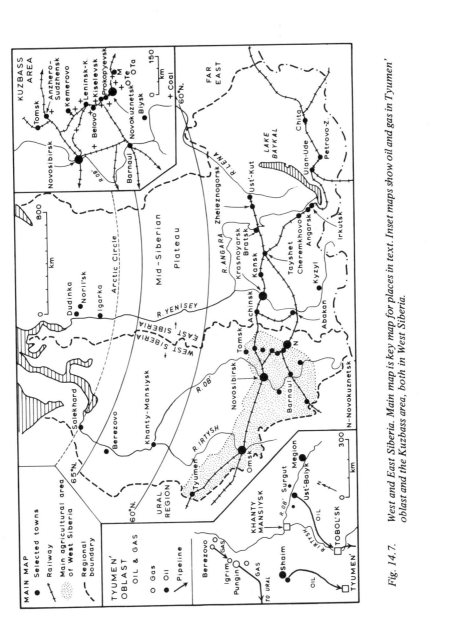

Fig. 14.7. West and East Siberia. Main map is key map for places in text. Inset maps show oil and gas in Tyumen' oblast and the Kuzbass area, both in West Siberia.

consists of some hill country and low mountain ranges (eg Kuznetskiy Alatau) flanking this, and the great West Siberian Lowland, the flatness of which is interrupted by occasional low hills and ridges, with a local relative relief rarely in excess of a few tens of metres. Much of this vast lowland area is marshy. North of a line roughly through Tyumen', Omsk and Tomsk, there is almost no cultivation at all and the less swampy areas remain covered with coniferous forest. In the extreme north, this thins out to give way to tundra. In the extreme south, however, there is a considerable area of steppe country (Barabinsk and Kuludinsk steppes) with reasonable to good chernozem and associated soils. About 30% of Omsk oblast and of the Altay kray are under cultivation. Mixed farming, with an emphasis on dairying, was developed by Russian settlers in the 19th century. There was much slack to be taken up, however, when the new lands project was initiated in 1953, and this area specialised in spring wheat cultivation. In the 1960's there has been a reversion to livestock farming to some extent. The southern fringe of the coniferous forest is now being exploited intensively. With its cereals, dairy products, meat, wool and timber, West Siberia is still a region of surplus for products of the land.

Like the Northwest, West Siberia has abundant supplies of water, vast quantities of which drain to the Arctic. There have been plans to divert water south into Kazakhstan and even into Central Asia. So far this has only been done for industrial and domestic supply to Karaganda. The first mineral to be exploited on a large scale in West Siberia was the coal of the Kuzbass field (Fig. 14.7). The Kuzbass has both surface and deep mines and includes excellent deposits of coking coal. The coal is generally cheap to mine, but regional needs are still limited, and much is exported to the Ural region, eastern Kazakhstan, Central Asia and even European U.S.S.R. Some non-ferrous metals and iron ore are now produced in West Siberia. The second great mineral discovery in West Siberia has been oil and natural gas; official Soviet estimates describe oil reserves as very large. These exist in many localities, but particularly along the Ob', east from its confluence with the Irtysh at Khanty-Mansiysk. Gas deposits occur mainly to the northwest, along the west side of the lower Ob'. There is already a gas pipeline from Berezovo into the Ural region. If West Siberian oil and gas are developed on a large scale, outlets in European U.S.S.R. and beyond the U.S.S.R. will no doubt be sought. Eventually pipeline links with the existing system must be provided.

Industrially, West Siberia is relatively young. Omsk, Novosibirsk, Barnaul and Tomsk are centres of mixed manufacturing, but the Kuzbass centres, Novokuznetsk, Prokop'yevsk and Kemerovo, are predominantly associated with coal mining, iron and steel and heavy engineering. Between the early 1930's and 1960's, one large works, the Kuznetsk integrated works, dominated the iron and steel industry. At first this works used Ural ore but more recently it has been able to use local ores (Temirtau, Tashtagol). A second large works, the Zapsib, is now working in the same vicinity. The exact size of the West Siberian contribution to Soviet iron and steel production is not revealed in Soviet Yearbooks, but it is about 10%; it might well have been more by now but for the distance from markets.

In general, West Siberia is well off in terms of its population/resource balance, and its resources are not only large, but low cost. Thus the region produces or will be producing low cost grain, meat, coal, steel, timber, gas and oil. It lacks light industry and is, therefore, dependent on other regions for such items as textiles, light machinery and motor vehicles. Without doubt, however, its future prospects are bright and it already shows signs of providing some contribution to Soviet cultural and technological development in its Akademgorod at Novosibirsk.

14.7 EAST SIBERIA

Although East Siberia has lost the vast Yakut A.S.S.R. to the Far East it is larger in area than West Siberia, but has fewer people. It coincides roughly now with the drainage area of the Yenisey river. Though like West Siberia in a general way, it differs in many secondary respects, some of which will be mentioned.

East Siberia lies mainly between 50° and 70°N. The southern part is extremely rugged, consisting of a number of high ranges, separated by deep basins. Most of the remainder consists of the Mid-Siberian plateau, which is 400–1 500 m above sea level, dissected by many deep valleys.

The platform ends abruptly in the west, where it overlooks the Yenisey river and West Siberian lowland. Mean temperatures are very low on account of the long, cold winter, which is to be expected at these latitudes but is accentuated by the additional altitude of the plateau and the remoteness of the region from the Atlantic or Pacific. Most of the area is in the zone of continuous or partial permafrost.

Agriculturally, East Siberia is less favoured than West Siberia. It has a number of areas suitable in places for cultivation, mainly in valleys and plains linked now by the Trans-Siberian Railway. Cereal cultivation, with spring wheat and rye, predominates to the west of Lake Baykal, but livestock farming, with cattle and sheep, is practised to the east. Altogether, however, only about 2–3% of each of the oblast level divisions of East Siberia is cultivated, and there seems barely sufficient food for the seven million inhabitants of the region. Timber reserves, so far hardly exploited, are vast since much of the region as far north as the Arctic circle is forested; Krasnoyarsk kray alone has 20% of all Soviet timber reserves. One of the principal assets of East Siberia is its deep narrow valleys, carrying large perennial rivers such as the Yenisey and Angara. There are several sites suitable for very large scale hydroelectric stations. One of these, Bratsk, is the world's largest hydroelectric power station. Another is under construction at Divnogorsk near Krasnoyarsk, with a proposed

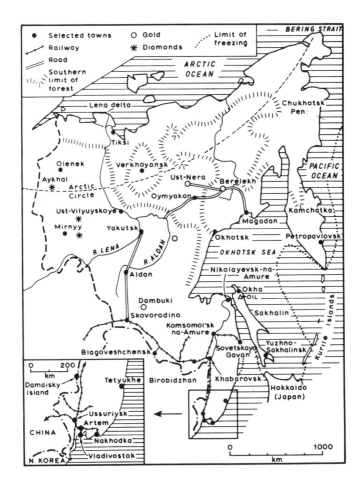

Fig. 14.8.   The Soviet Far East: Key Map. Inset map shows Vladivostok area in greater detail.

capacity of 6 million kW; two 500 MW generators were installed there in 1967 (*Pravda,* 25 January 1968). According to *Pravda,* 17 January 1967, other sites on which work has started or is planned are Ust'-Ilimsk (4 million kW) and Sayansk (6 million kW); Nazarov (1.8 million kW) and Tom-Usinsk (1.2 million kW) are thermal stations.

East Siberia also has very large coal deposits, including proved reserves of easily extracted but generally low grade coal both at Cheremkhovo and Kansk-Achinsk. Since the energy needs of the region are small at the moment, the usefulness of starting large-scale exploitation of the hydroelectricity and the thermal electricity from regional coal may be questioned. A possibility is to put metallurgical industries in the region to supply steel, aluminium and other metals, for movement west, and possibly, if and when trading conditions improve with East Asia, to Japan and China. East Siberia is also a secondary supplier of iron ore, gold, tin and non-ferrous metals and it has been worthwhile establishing smelting facilities at Noril'sk almost 70°N., to exploit local nickel. Krasnoyarsk and Irkutsk are the largest centres of East Siberia and each has a number of associated smaller centres. Movement in the region is still very much east–west, but the older Trans-Siberian Railway has been supplemented by a new line, Kuzbass–Abakan–Tayshet, while the Tayshet–Bratsk–Ust'Kut spur offers penetration towards the heart of Siberia.

East Siberia, then, may be thought of as less developed than West Siberia, but abundant in energy sources, metals and timber. At present its light industrial base is weak and its potential for food production appears limited.

14.8 THE FAR EAST

The Far East region now includes Yakut A.S.S.R., which for some decades was thought of as part of East Siberia (see Fig. 14.8). It is now by far the largest economic region of the U.S.S.R., covering over a quarter of the area, but it is only eighteenth in population. Its five and a half million people contrast with many times this figure for the equivalent Western part of Anglo-America. Though it is similar in some respects to the two Siberias, it is much further

from European U.S.S.R., is very much a world apart, involved in Far Eastern affairs, and is much more difficult to integrate into national life even than the Baykal area. Moreover, it does not possess such favourable resources as West Siberia, and to exploit its gold, fisheries and other resources the region appears to have been heavily subsidised.

From the latitude of Northern Japan at Vladivostok, the Far East extends far into the Arctic. It borders China in the south, but has few rail or road links in that direction. The Trans-Siberian Railway is the only important land link with the rest of the U.S.S.R. The north coast is ice bound nearly all the year. Access to the long Pacific coast is difficult because high ranges lie behind the coast and the closed Okhotsk Sea is itself frozen much of the year. Rugged conditions, short growing season, marsh, permafrost and poor soils combine to make farming difficult except in a few small favoured localities. The total cultivated area of the Far East is about 1/300 of the total area, and reaches no more than 4% even in Amur oblast and Primorsk kray. Wheat, rice and soybeans are the main crops. Fodder crops form the basis of dairying, and large areas support relatively small reindeer herds. Fishing is gaining importance; it includes both crab fishing near to the coasts of Kamchatka and the Kurile Islands, and fishing further afield in the Pacific itself. As yet little has been done to exploit the hydroelectric resources of the Far East, but the Amur offers a large potential; however it is followed by the Soviet–Chinese boundary for much of its course. The Lena and its tributaries also have a large potential.

The Far East has coal and oil deposits, but production costs seem in general high and these energy resources are exploited exclusively for regional needs. Other minerals include non-ferrous metals (Tetyukhe) gold at several places (eg Dambuki, Ust'-Nera, Berelekh) diamonds (Mirnyy, Aykhal) and the discovery of oil at Ust-Vilyuyskoye by the Lena in Yakutia.

The Trans-Siberian Railway serves the southern part of the Far East and reaches the coast at the ports of Vladivostok, Nakhodka and Sovetskaya Gavan'. The rest of the region depends on road, river and sea links and the remotest parts may be initially developed by air transport. Although the Far East is one of the most highly urbanised regions, this is because of lack of a rural farming population, rather than the growth of industry. Most industry still takes the form of processing, preparing and servicing, for example saw-milling, canning and some engineering. The small steel works at Komsomol'sk-na-Amure depends on pig iron from elsewhere and on scrap.

The Far East is at present a political and strategic asset to the U.S.S.R. rather than an economic one. Its surplus of fish products, furs, gold and timber seems unlikely to pay for the investment that has gone into the region. Perhaps the future of the Soviet Far East lies in the strengthening of trade with Japan and other countries of East Asia. Recognition of its need to act to some extent independently of central planners in Moscow, has been the delegation of some decision making on trade to regional planners. In the late 1960's there was talk of allowing the Japanese to invest capital in some enterprises, a move that would hardly be welcomed by the Chinese.

14.9 THE VOLGA

This region, long a frontier of the Russians against the open steppes and semi-desert, was under-used even in the inter-war period. It has gained in relative importance since the development of oil, gas and hydroelectricity started, and since World War II, when it occupied a valuable strategic position. Its central position in relation to population in a country becoming more and more integrated has also helped the Volga region to become more important; almost all traffic flows between European and Asiatic U.S.S.R. pass through it somewhere. During its life as a recognised economic region the region has changed in size and shape several times. At present it is an ungainly shape, justified only by the presence of the Volga, the main inland waterway of European U.S.S.R., which passes through it from north to south (Fig. 14.9).

The Volga region is very diverse physically, culturally and economically. From north to south it contains forest of various mixes, forest steppe, steppe, semi-desert and desert. It includes some of the best farmland in the U.S.S.R., especially in the more humid northwest, but extensive areas with saline soil provide in

contrast almost useless natural pasture land. Culturally, the region is characterised by the presence in three A.S.S.R.'s of Tatars, Bashkirs and Kalmyks among an otherwise predominantly Russian population. Economically, the region contains pockets of very rural population, especially in the Tatar A.S.S.R. and around Ul'yanovsk. It also contains such sophisticated urban centres as Kazan', Kuybyshev and Volgograd and booming oil centres.

Agriculturally the Volga region is an asset, for its farmland is less densely populated than elsewhere in European U.S.S.R. In most years climatic conditions are satisfactory and a surplus of grain, meat and other livestock products is, therefore, achieved; on the other hand, industrial crops are not grown to any great extent and vegetables and potatoes are essentially for local use. There are possibilities for irrigation and improvement of water supply to livestock in the south. Timber is cut in the north, but most of the region is deficient in forest and the Volga carries large quantities of timber southwards, especially from the Volga-Vyatka region.

More than any other river in the U.S.S.R., the Volga with its tributary the Kama, have been subjected to Soviet 'hydromania'. Several of the largest dams and artificial reservoirs in the world now affect most of the course of the Volga. The two stations near Kuybyshev and Volgograd each generate the electrical equivalent of several million tons of coal. The installed capacity in MW and the dates (start to installation of first turbine) are as follows: Kuybyshev 2 300 (1950–55) Volgograd 2 563 (1950–58) Saratov 1 290 (1956–67); compare Gorky (Volga-Vyatka region) 520 (1947–55). Some electricity is transmitted outside the region. Navigation on the Volga has been improved by the reservoirs and in 1952 access was achieved by the Volga-Don canal to the Black Sea area. So far, little appears to have been done to use Volga water for irrigation, although the reservoirs have affected local climate favourably in places. Through extra evaporation and greater loss of water seeping away, the Volga system is taking less water than previously into the Caspian Sea, and the shallow northern part of this may find itself above sea level in a matter of decades. Supplementary water could however be brought in from the Arctic rivers.

Far more important in terms of energy than

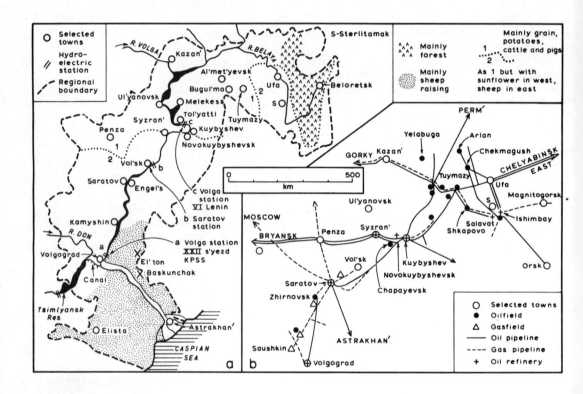

Fig. 14.9.   Volga region: (a) Key map and land use zones. (b) Details of oil and gas fields, and pipelines.

the hydroelectric stations has been the discovery in many localities of both oil and natural gas. The oil and gas industries have already been discussed in Chapter 10 and the pipeline systems and flows described in Chapters 11 and 12. Fig. 14.9(b) shows places directly concerned with oil, gas and petrochemicals. In addition, the Volga region now specialises in several branches of engineering, Volgograd deals with agricultural machinery and Saratov and Kuybyshev are the principal centres. Some light industry has been introduced into the region (eg textiles at Kamyshin) and food processing is carried out in many places.

Although discovery of oil in West Siberia has deflated the Volga's near monopoly of Soviet oil, the region is undoubtedly one in which future investment will be placed in large quantities, since it has large resources. Kurnikov[2] is enthusiastic about the possibilities of the region; Paleyev[3] discusses its transport problems. Hooson[4] has described it as an emerging focal region in the Soviet Union.

14.10 THE CAUCASUS

The Greater Caucasus Range has given its name to two economic regions, North Caucasus and Transcaucasia. Fig. 14.10(b) shows the position of the Greater Caucasus Range in relation to them.

NORTH CAUCASUS

This region is predominantly Russian, but in the east contains four A.S.S.R.'s with partly non-Russian populations. Physically there is a striking contrast between the high range of the Caucasus in the south and the hill country and lowlands of the rest of the region. The Caucasus range is still crossed only by roads and access to Transcaucasia by rail is confined to the extremities. Precipitation diminishes eastwards in the region, both along the Caucasus and across the lowland. In the west, the 50 cm of rain around Krasnodar and Stavropol' is adequate for farming and the 100 cm falling on the mountains themselves allows a forest cover in the west. In the extreme east of the region, however, semi-desert conditions prevail.

Agriculturally the western part of the North Caucasus is one of the most favoured parts of the U.S.S.R. With consistent rainfall, good soils and warm summers it is suitable for maize and rice as well as winter wheat. The sunflower and sugar beet are also widely grown. In the foothills, lower valleys and flanks of the Caucasus Range, deciduous fruits and the vine are cultivated. Pastoral activities replace crop farming both in the drier lowland and in the higher parts of the Caucasus and seasonal transhumance between these two areas is still practised; sheep are the main form of livestock here, in contrast to cattle in the predominantly arable areas.

The North Caucasus has limited hydro-electric and forest resources. Its mineral wealth, however, is considerable. High grade coal is mined north of Rostov in the eastern extremity of the Donbass coalfield and is sent over considerable distances. Oil has been exploited for some decades at several localities, including areas along the Caspian coast, as well as Groznyy and Maykop. To this asset have recently been added the apparently very large gas reserves of Stavropol' and Krasnodar. In addition, non-ferrous metals are mined within the central Caucasus range.

Processing and manufacturing are fairly well represented in the region. Iron and steel making and heavy engineering are found in the Rostov area, oil refining and petrochemicals at several places associated with the oilfields and branches of the food industry in many towns. An additional asset of the region is its tourist attractions connected with the mountain scenery, the thermal resorts around Pyatigorsk, and the coastal resorts on the Black Sea. Altogether the North Caucasus gives the impression of being both well balanced and also near average in many respects for the U.S.S.R.

TRANSCAUCASIA

Territorially this region is considerably smaller than the North Caucasus, though in population there is little difference. Physical contrasts within the region are sharper and environmental conditions more varied. Culturally, also, Transcaucasia is characterised by diversity, having three main non-Russian peoples, the Georgians, Azerbaijanians and Armenians, several smaller

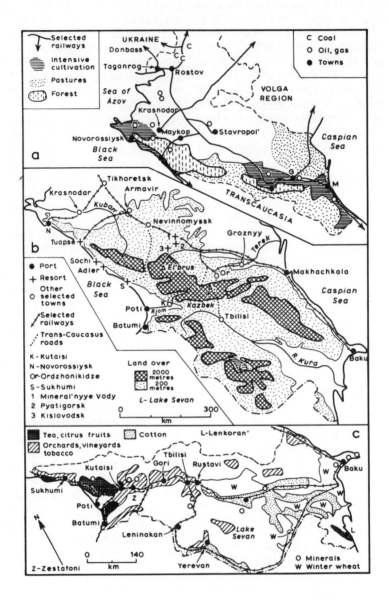

Fig. 14.10. The Caucasus regions: (a) Key map for North Caucasus. (b) North Caucasus and Transcaucasia. (c) Land use and other aspects of Transcaucasia.

ethnic groups, plus about a million Russians and Ukrainians.

The Greater Caucasus is more abrupt on its southern side than its northern; there are few wide valleys and there is little scope for grazing or forestry. The Greater Caucasus overlooks a long depression which separates it from the lower, more plateau-like Lesser Caucasus. The depression, drained in the east by the Kura and its tributaries, and in the west by the smaller Rioni system (the Kolkhida lowland) widens towards the Caspian and Black Seas. The most striking contrast between the two lowlands is in precipitation, which ranges from well over 100 cm by the Black Sea to no more than 20 cm around Baku on the Caspian.

The two main areas of intensive cultivation in Transcaucasia are the so-called humid subtropical lowlands and hillsides of the Kolkhida, and the more dispersed irrigated lands in the semi-desert and desert lowlands of the Kura. The Kolkhida conditions are repeated in the much smaller Lenkoran' lowlands at the extreme southeast of Transcaucasia. In the hot, humid areas mentioned, exceptional in the U.S.S.R., it is possible to grow tea, citrus fruits, and other bush and tree crops. In the irrigated Kura lowlands, cotton and fodder crops are cultivated. In many suitable less humid but unirrigated localities, especially on the foothills of the Greater Caucasus, the vine and orchards of warm temperate fruit are found. Elsewhere wheat, maize and barley are widely grown in Transcaucasia but conditions of cultivation are made difficult by steep slopes, poor soil and meagre rainfall. Altogether only about one-sixth of the region is under crops. Much of the rest is poor quality forest, or natural pastures in the lowlands or higher ranges. Both cattle and sheep are raised and there is a meat–wool orientation.

Although there is a considerable variety of minerals in Transcaucasia, there are now no deposits of more than regional significance, apart from the Chiatura manganese ores. Even the famous Apsheron Peninsula and associated offshore oil wells account for less than 10% of Soviet oil. Gas, coking coal, iron ore, and non-ferrous metals are all extracted, but in limited amounts. The hydroelectric potential of the region is considerable. Even so, the energy base of Transcaucasia is clearly suspect, since a life saving gas pipeline has lately been completed across the Greater Caucasus Range between Stavropol' and Tbilisi (via Groznyy) to take natural gas into the region.

Industrially Transcaucasia gives the impression of being well diversified, a desirable attribute for such a relatively remote part of European U.S.S.R. The integrated iron and steel works at Rustavi, though using regional ingredients, produces high cost steel and even then does not satisfy regional needs. The petrochemical industries of Baku also work on high cost oil. Light industry and engineering are fairly widespread.

The somewhat limited specialisms of Transcaucasia, which include its famous resorts, as well as items such as tea, fruits, manganese and wool, are hardly adequate to compensate for its requirements of food and manufactures from other regions. It appears to have high educational standards and medical facilities, yet deplorably low kolkhoz incomes and an all round low *per capita* productivity by Soviet standards. The devious access to regions to the north and the general remoteness of a dead end region make Transcaucasia, like the Soviet Far East, strategically vulnerable yet necessary to subsidise in some way.

14.11 UKRAINE-MOLDAVIA

Once considered together as the South, the Donets-Dnepr, Southwest, South and Moldavia now form smaller and more manageable entities, although still arbitrary ones. The Ukraine with Moldavia is roughly similar to France in both area and population. Here the comparison ends, for there is neither the presence of a single dominant centre, nor the sophisticated industrial and service structure of France. Fig. 14.11(a) is a key map of places mentioned in this section, while Fig. 14.11(b) shows economic activities of the four regions.

DONETS-DNEPR

The eastern part of the Ukraine is among the top regions of the U.S.S.R. in degree of urbanisation and industrialisation. It is the most developed of the non-Russian regions of the U.S.S.R.; in fact a large share of the population is Russian. The strength and importance of the region lie not only in its coal, iron ore and natural gas deposits and modern industrial establishments, but also in a sound agriculture.

The Donets-Dnepr consists of lowland and low hill country interrupted only by the Donets ridge in the extreme east. The Dnepr passes through the west of the region; the Severnaya Donets drains the eastern part. Most of the region falls within either the wooded steppe or steppe belts. Soils are mainly fertile chernozem. Mean annual precipitation ranges from about 55 cm in the north to about 40 cm along the Sea of Azov coast. It is susceptible to considerable year to year fluctuations, but in most years brings enough moisture to support good yields by Soviet standards. Of the field crops grown, sugar beet is the main industrial crop in the northwest, the sunflower in the southeast; winter wheat and grain maize both occupy a larger area than sugar

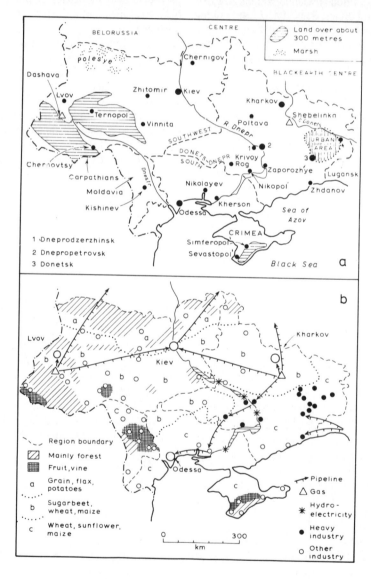

Fig. 14.11.   *The Ukraine and Moldavia: (a) Key map to places. (b) Economic activities.*

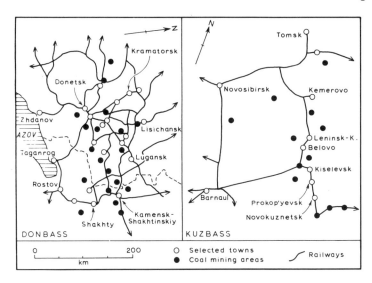

Fig. 14.12. Comparison of the Donbass and Kuzbass (West Siberia) areas.

beet. Fodder crops are also widely grown and both dairying and beef production are strongly represented. Other products of the region include hemp, tobacco, flax and potatoes, as well as fruits. Specialisation in vegetables, milk and fruit is found in the vicinity of urban areas of the Donbass and Lower Dnepr. The Donets-Dnepr probably now roughly supports its own population in agricultural products, but in favourable years may provide some surplus of grain.

The main *raison d'être* of the heavy industrial complex in the Donets-Dnepr region has been the presence of one of Europe's largest coalfields. The exposed Donbass coalfield extends some 250 km from Kramatorsk in the northwest to Shakhty in the adjoining North Caucasus region. In Fig. 14.12 the Donbass is compared with the Kuzbass. There is a much larger concealed coalfield as well. Coal mining centres are located in the many narrow, often steep-sided valleys flanking the Donets Ridge. Many of the shallower more accessible seams have now been worked, but the need for high grade coal including coking varieties gives the Donbass a key role in European U.S.S.R. Other minerals in the coalfield area include salt and mercury. The second mineral asset of the region has been the Krivoy Rog iron ore. This has now been worked for nearly a century and the higher grade reserves have already been depleted,

though there are abundant deposits of lower grade ore. A welcome third mineral has been the manganese ore at Nikopol'. Since World War II, both oil (west of Poltava) and natural gas (Shebelinka) have been discovered. Shebelinka is now one of the most productive gas fields in the U.S.S.R.

With the help of foreign capital and the construction of railways it became possible to build up tsarist Russia's main modern heavy industrial base in the Ukraine. Immediately before World War I, after some four decades of growth, this produced about 75% of Russia's iron and steel, 3 million tons a year. Works were built in the coalfield itself (eg Donetsk) on the Dnepr (eg Dnepropetrovsk) and on the iron ore at Krivoy Rog. During the 1920's the existing heavy industrial establishments were modernised and enlarged, and new works were added (eg Zaporozh'ye, Zhdanov).

After the severe damage suffered during World War II, the Donets-Dnepr industrial complex was restored and again expanded. The associated engineering industry, however, does not have the sophistication of that of the Centre or Ural regions. Steel products for construction and heavy machinery do not have the value added that the electrical, precision and transport branches do in the regions mentioned. Nor does the Donets-Dnepr account for much of the high grade steel of the country. The weakness, then, of the Donets-Dnepr heavy industrial base, lies first in the lack of diversity and sophistication of associated industries, and secondly in the high cost of extracting the coal, of enriching the ore and of actually producing steel (Chapter 12). The problem arising from the almost complete absence of light industry and of employment possibilities for women in industry at all is particularly acute.

Altogether, however, the evidence suggests that the Donets-Dnepr is one of the best regions in terms of *per capita* output of goods. Particularly striking is the contrast with its other major partner in the Ukraine trio, the Southwest. The Donets-Dnepr appears still to be used as a source of food (sugar beet, grain) for other regions (Centre) and countries of East Europe, of fuel (coal and natural gas), and semi-manufactured goods such as pig iron, for more industrialised regions.

THE SOUTHWEST

The western part of this region has changed hands on several occasions in the 20th century and much of it was not firmly in Soviet control until 1945. The Southwest, therefore, is less integrated in Soviet life than the Donets-Dnepr. Its proximity to the western boundary of the U.S.S.R. has made it vulnerable strategically and less attractive for investment in strategic industries.

Physically there are greater contrasts in the Southwest than in the Donets-Dnepr. The Eastern Carpathians pass through the south-western part of the region; they exceed 1 000 m for much of their length. Much of the central part is broken by the hill country of the Volyno-Poldol'sk Upland. In the north, in contrast, the relatively low lying and ill-drained Poles'ye, shared with Belorussia, still forms an obstacle to cultivation, settlement and movement. Most of the Southwest was originally broadleaf forest, with patches of steppe along the southern fringe. Coniferous species appear, however, in the higher Carpathians. Both the Poles'ye and the Carpathians are still heavily forested, but much of the rest of the Southwest has been cleared for farming and the grey forest soils, or in the south the chernozems, are on the whole satisfactory for cultivation. In the central

oblasts, as much as 60–70% of the land is farmed. Throughout the region, precipitation is adequate, varying from about 45 cm in the east to over 100 cm in the Carpathians.

About 65% of the population is still rural; most of it is found in collective, rather than state, farms. Much of the urban population lives in relatively small towns. In the northern part of the region, winter wheat and rye are the main cereals. These are supplemented by flax and potatoes. Through the centre of the region runs the sugar beet belt. In some districts, sugar beet occupies as much as 10% of the cultivated land. Wheat and maize are grown, and, as in the Donets-Dnepr, dairying and beef production are supported by fodder crops. In places, particularly in the small area of lowland beyond the Carpathians, orchards, vines and tobacco are cultivated. The total farm output of the Southwest is roughly equal to that of the Donets-Dnepr. In spite of the agricultural emphasis of the economy of the region, it has little surplus to send to other regions, although its few specialisms, particularly sugar, are in excess of regional needs.

The mineral resources of the Southwest, though by no means insignificant, are small compared with those of territorially larger regions even in European U.S.S.R., such as the Northwest and Volga. Oil and natural gas both occur to the south of Lvov. The oil is extracted in small quantities for local needs and the gas is sent further afield, not only within the region to Kiev, but also to Belorussia. Small amounts of coal, peat, salt and phosphates are also extracted.

Industrially the Southwest is one of the least developed regions; some towns have light engineering, textiles and wood manufacture, but many have only food industries. The so-called growth sectors of industry are hardly represented. There is no evidence of a heavy industrial base, desirable for a region with 20 million people, at least according to the thinking of Soviet planners. Only Kiev and the Lvov area have the appearance of growth 'poles'.

The future of the Southwest apparently lies in the establishment of more light industry, the improvement of agriculture and the exploitation of a position on routes between the major industrial regions of the U.S.S.R. and the southern members of Comecon in East Europe. Already one branch of the oil pipeline from the Volga into East Europe crosses the region.

THE SOUTH

This region covers the coastal lowlands of the Black Sea and includes the Crimea, and is more modest in size, population and resources than the other two regions of the Ukraine. It falls mainly in the steppe belt and is particularly dry in the North Crimea. Wheat, the sunflower and maize are the chief crops, but the flanks of the mountains of the Crimea are used for fruit and vine cultivation. Odessa, Nikolayev and Kherson, three seaports, are the principal outlets of the Ukraine on the Black Sea and the only centres of industrial importance. Together they manufacture a considerable range of items, specialising in shipbuilding, which is concentrated mainly in Nikolayev. The southern coast of the Crimea is one of the three main resort areas of the U.S.S.R. and differs both in appearance and in function from the rest of the South.

MOLDAVIA

Though physically a continuation of the Southwest and South, Moldavia differs culturally from the Ukraine, and has the status of a Soviet Socialist Republic. It is one of the most agricultural of all parts of the U.S.S.R. Its industries are almost exclusively connected with agricultural processing. Most of the area is suitable for cultivation and particularly favourable for viticulture. The future of Moldavia, in its remote corner of European U.S.S.R., lies in greater specialisation in viticulture and other branches of agriculture to which it is suited.

14.12 CENTRAL ASIA[5]

Selected features of Central Asia are shown in Fig. 14.13 on maps shared with Kazakhstan. The inclusion of the two regions on the same map was made to emphasise the similarity between Southern Kazakhstan and Central Asia. Central Asia consists of four republics, Uzbekistan, Kirgizia, Tadjikistan and Turkmenistan. Together these have nearly 20 million inhabitants. The population is basically non-Russian. It consists of peoples with Asian languages or Asian branches of the Indo-European family, quite unlike Slavonic langu-

ages. The region was Moslem until the influence of the Russian Orthodox Church in the 19th century and of Communism in the 20th. Formerly a Russian colony, Central Asia was put on an equal footing with the rest of the U.S.S.R. in the 1920's and local people were given positions of responsibility in the Communist Party and in planning. Nevertheless, there are probably about a million Russians and Ukrainians in the area, especially in the towns. The influence of the Russian language is growing, especially for higher education and technology. Today, Central Asia is still backward by Soviet standards, though advanced compared with most of the world's underdeveloped countries, including those such as Iran, Afghanistan and Pakistan, lying immediately to the south. It has one feature that must be causing concern for Russian planners, the highest birthrate of any large area in the U.S.S.R.

Physically, Central Asia consists of two clearly distinct parts, a western lowland desert area and an eastern rugged mountainous area interrupted by deep valleys. Only on some of the higher ranges is precipitation considerable. From these, rivers drain into the desert to the west and to the north into Kazakhstan. Irrigation is possible in localities fed by these rivers and having suitable soils. There is a series of oases stretching from Central Turkmenistan in the west to the Chinese border in the east. Their general distribution is shown in Fig. 14.13(b) Some (eg the Fergana valley) are in deep mountain valleys, some (eg Tashkent) along the foot of the mountains and some far out in the desert (eg Tashauz on the River Amu-Dar'ya). All are characterised by long summers with very high temperatures. Much of the economic wealth of Central Asia depends on the production of these oases. Cotton is the main specialism of the more southerly oases; it is proposed to raise cotton production to 10–11 million tons in the 1970's. The vine and various other deciduous fruits as well as rice, maize, sugar beet and alfalfa are also grown. Many of the oases have existed for centuries. Some have been extended during the Soviet period and others created. Much water of potential agricultural use is still wasted because it still flows into the Aral Sea. The Karakum Canal has been built to carry water west from the Amu-Dar'ya into Turkmenistan. Away from the oases there is little possibility for

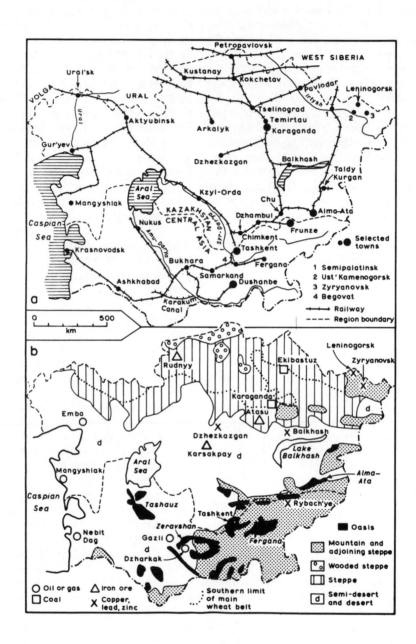

Fig. 14.13. Central Asia and Kazakhstan: (a) Key map and railways. (b) Land use and minerals.

cultivation and farming is limited to stock rearing, either on the poor natural pastures of the desert and semi-desert lands or on the difficult slopes of the mountain area. The emphasis is on sheep raising, particularly for lambskins (*karakul* skins). Previously transhumance was widely practised in Central Asia and Kazakhstan, but Soviet policy has been to settle nomadic pastoralists. The` improvement of the pastoral industry depends on the provision of more water supply facilities and on a closer link with fodder supplies from the area of intensive cultivation on the oases, which, even after the most elaborate and costly irrigation projects, could themselves never occupy more than a few per cent of the total area.

Central Asia is apparently well endowed with various minerals. Oil and coal are available in relatively limited amounts, but natural gas reserves have proved to be very large indeed. These are in the vicinity of Bukhara, at Gazli and Dzharkak. Gas is already piped not only to places such as Tashkent and Fergana, but also into southern Kazakhstan and to the industrial centres of the southern Ural. In the late 1960's, pipes were also being laid to take Central Asian gas to Moscow. The completion of the first stage in 1967 was announced in *Pravda,* 25 January 1968. Other minerals in Central Asia include salt, sulphur and non-ferrous metals. There are already several large hydroelectric stations and the rivers Naryn and Vakhsh provide potential sites for very large stations with low construction costs. The Nurensk station on the Vakhsh is to have a capacity of 2 700 MW.

Central Asia is still predominantly rural, but since the late 1920's considerable efforts have been made to develop industry. Some attempt has been made to decentralise cotton, woollen and silk textiles from the Moscow area, but Central Asia, with only a few per cent of the Soviet total output, has failed to break the near monopoly of the Centre. Light engineering is fairly widespread and there are the beginnings of a chemicals industry, particularly the manufacture of fertilisers. On the other hand, the small Begovat steelworks, using local scrap together with pig iron from other regions, is barely a token presence of heavy industry. The processing of agricultural products is still one of the principal branches of industry.

Urban growth has been greatest and fastest in the Republic capitals and Tashkent now has about one million inhabitants. Though located in Uzbekistan, it appears to be fairly cosmopolitan and a growing cultural focus for this part of the U.S.S.R., as well as a showpiece for visitors to the country.

14.13 KAZAKHSTAN

The only reason for keeping Kazakhstan in its present form as one of the economic regions appears to be that as a Soviet Socialist Republic it cannot be broken up and apportioned to adjoining regions, the Volga, Ural, West Siberia and Central Asia. The reason for its unsuitability as a single planning region is that the central part is almost uninhabited. To the north of about 50°N. conditions are very similar to those in West Siberia and to the south of about 45°N. the desert, mountain fringes, and oases are very similar to Central Asia.

The northern part of Kazakhstan consists mainly of steppe country with some intrusions of forest from the north. The steppe merges into semi-desert southwards. Long a grazing area, the Kazakhstan steppe was brought into cultivation in the years after 1953, at first almost exclusively as a wheat monoculture area with large state farms, mechanised methods and much temporary labour. Harvests varied from very good, given the physical conditions, in some years, to almost nothing in others, when precipitation fell too far below the meagre average. There have been signs of soil erosion, however, and warnings of a new dust bowl from various quarters. Soviet data for Kazakhstan show a gradual shift to a diversity of cereal crops, to the introduction of fodder crops and to a strengthening of livestock. In most years since 1953, however, Kazakhstan has provided some surplus of grain, a surplus sent not only to adjoining regions but even into such grain deficient regions as the Centre, Northwest and Far East (see Fig. 12.10 for grain flows). Cultivated land is abundant but low yielding in northern Kazakhstan and scarce but very productive in southern Kazakhstan, which receives some of the rivers from the mountains of Central Asia, including the Syr-Dar'ya and the smaller Chu. As in Central Asia, cotton, tobacco, fruits and maize are cultivated; cotton yields are not so high as in oases further south in Central

Asia. The vast intervening arid lands of Kazakhstan are nearly all natural pastures, though in places, as around the Aral Sea, they support only a very low density of stock, mainly sheep.

Kazakhstan already occupies a prominant position in the Soviet economy for its mineral products. The small, but relatively low cost, coking coal reserves of Karaganda supply steelworks in the Ural region as well as local and regional needs. Ekibastuz, to the northeast of Karaganda, has much larger reserves of coal, as yet little used. Oil has been extracted in the Emba fields for some decades, but never in large quantities. Apparently much larger reserves have recently been found at Mangyshlak and a railway now reaches this part of southwest Kazakhstan from Gur'yev. Kazakh iron ore deposits at Rudnyy are particularly useful for the steelworks of the Ural region, especially Magnitogorsk, where local iron ore is quickly being used up. Other reserves of iron ore in Central Kazakhstan at Karsakpay and Atasu now apparently supply the Temirtau steelworks at Karaganda. Buyanovskiy[6] proposes that a new iron and steel works should be placed by Lake Balkhash, itself transformed into a fresh water lake.

Kazakhstan is particularly important in the Soviet economy for its non-ferrous metals. Data are not readily available for these, but it may be assumed that a considerable proportion of Soviet copper, lead, zinc and silver comes from the region. The copper is extracted and smelted at Dzhezkazgan and Balkhash. The other non-ferrous metals come mainly from the mountainous extreme east of Kazakhstan. An aluminium smelting plant was completed at Pavlodar in the 1959–65 Plan.

Kazakhstan is more highly urbanised than Central Asia, but gives the impression of still being a region of rapid transition and change. A major industrial complex, Karaganda, with its new integrated steelworks (Temirtau) and a distinguished cultural centre, the national capital, Alma-Ata, contrast with new agricultural centres, remote mining encampments and remnants of Kazakh nomad farmers. Towns in Kazakhstan are mostly growing fast and railways are still being constructed to give the rail system some semblance of completeness. Compared with any region in European U.S.S.R. or any country of West Europe, Kazakhstan has a very favourable population/resource balance. At present it is largely a source of food and raw materials for other regions, but it is the one region into which there appears to have been no slowing down of immigration in the post war period, and its birthrate is one of the highest in the U.S.S.R.

14.14 SUMMARY

Although the 19 economic regions have been referred to throughout the book, they have been used because data are available for them, not because they reflect the geographical reality of the U.S.S.R., which remains as elusive as ever. *Faute de mieux*, Fig. 14.14 is an attempt to portray the state of the U.S.S.R. in the late 1960's. Table 14.6 shows in very broad terms the material resource position and degree of development in terms of population and industry in 16 areas of greatly differing size, function and appearance.

About 95% of the population of the U.S.S.R. is in less than half of the territory, in areas 1 to 13. Roughly during 1910 to 1970 the population increased from 160 million people to 240 million people. Of the absolute increase about five-eighths was in areas to the west of the Ural (area 4). Feygin[7] proposes moving six million people eastwards. It is not difficult to calculate, however, that unless about three-quarters of a million people are moved east each year, the absolute gap between west and east will widen, since the west gains each year by about two and a quarter million, the east by about three-quarters of a million.

There is good reason to shift some population eastwards because many material resources are situated east of the Urals; for example (Nekrasov[8]) 90% of the coal reserves, 60% of the hydroelectric potential and 70% of the timber, as well as most of the non-ferrous metals, gold and diamonds and much oil and gas. From a strategic and political point of view, also, it is increasingly desirable to give the appearance of filling up an empty area, as Chinese strength grows and world opinion swings against the countries with vast material resources and relatively few people. Since the first Five Year Plan (1928–32) the main incentive to move east has been low production costs, arising largely either from the

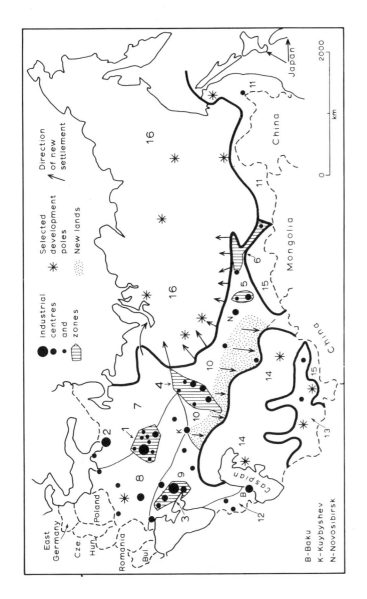

Fig. 14.14. Development regions of the U.S.S.R.

Table 14.6. SUMMARY TABLE OF STATE OF THE U.S.S.R., LATE 1960's

Area	Material Resources					Period of development	Human Achievements			
	Water	Energy	Metals	Food	Forest		Population density	Urban	Industry	Services
1 Moscow area	1	0	0	0	1	OLD/C19–20	HH	HH	HH	G
2 Leningrad	1	0	0	0	0	OLD/C18–20	HH	HH	HH	G
3 Donbass-Dnepr	1	1	1	0	0	C19–20	H	HH	HH	M
4 Ural	1	1	1	0	1	C18/1930's	H	HH	HH	M
5 Kuzbass area	1	2	1	0	1	1930's	H	H	H	M
6 Krasnoyarsk-Baykal	2	2	1	0	1	1950's	L	HH	H	M
7 Northwest	2	1	0	1	2	OLD	H	LL	L	M
8 Mid-European U.S.S.R.	2	0	0	2	1	OLD	L	L	L	P
9 Caucasus-Volga	1	2	0	2	0	C19–20	L	H	L	M
10 New lands	1	2	2	2	1	C19/1950's	L	HH	L	P
11 East of Baykal	2	1	1	0	2	C20	HH	H	LL	M
12 Transcaucasia	1	2	1	0	0	OLD/C20	H	LL	L	M
13 Central Asia	0	2	1	0	0	OLD/C20	LL	H	L	P
14 Arid U.S.S.R.	0	1	1	0	0	C20	LL	LL	LL	P
15 Mountains of south	2	1	1	0	1	–	H	H	LL	P
16 Empty U.S.S.R.	2	2	2	0	2	–	LL	H	L	P

Material resources
2 – Abundant
1 – Satisfactory
0 – Deficient

Period of development
C18 – 18th century
C19 – 19th century
C20 – 20th century

Population/industry
HH – Very high
H – Considerable
L – Slight
LL – Very low

Services
G – Good
M – Medium
P – Poor

abundance of land or the ease of extraction of minerals and high labour productivity. It seems out of place, then, to propose after all that has been quoted and argued in this book that the low cost resources of the east are losing their attractiveness. The following instances may, nevertheless, be given:

1. The vast estimated coal reserves of Siberia are difficult to move west, either by rail, or in the form of electricity. Coal needs can mainly be satisfied in the west and by area 10 in Fig. 14.14.
2. Oil and natural gas in West Siberia are being exploited and moved south and west, but further finds of oil in the Volga-Ural and North Caspian area and of gas in places in European U.S.S.R. may well keep the Siberian finds in a reserve role.
3. The hydroelectric potential of the big Siberian rivers is impressive, but slow and costly to harness, and the electricity difficult to transmit west; resulting interference with the natural landscape is also causing concern.
4. There is a growing disenchantment with the new lands area (roughly area 10 dotted). Unpredictable, usually low, yields, the danger of soil erosion and the eventual high cost of providing permanent farming facilities and services for farm population, appear to have turned attention back towards the older farm lands of European U.S.S.R. and the prospects of irrigation in Central Asia and southern Kazakhstan.
5. Timber is abundant in Siberia, but a good reafforestation programme in the northern half of European U.S.S.R. and in the Urals could provide abundant timber at a time when, presumably, diminishing amounts are being used as fuel and in construction.

The scene for the 1970's and 1980's, then seems to be set for a big face lift in European U.S.S.R. and Central Asia and a consolidation of the general surplus area stretching from the southern Ukraine through the Volga and Ural to the Kuzbass and Lake Baykal. There will be a gradual extension of the continuously settled area into the West Siberian lowland, as suggested by the arrows in Fig. 14.14. Eleswhere, there will be local developments, as suggested by the symbols in Fig. 14.14, in, for example, the Poles'ye, the northern Caspian or central Yakutia.

The major direction of flows of goods until the 1930's was north–south in European U.S.S.R. This has been replaced by an east–west flow, consolidated by new railways and pipelines, as well as the electrification of the Trans-Siberian Railway.

Between about 1930 and 1960, area 10, containing areas 4, 5 and 6, was particularly favoured in terms of capital investment. Almost without exception, its towns grew faster than the Soviet average growth of urban population. It provided a surplus of food, minerals and heavy industrial goods. Now, however, the disadvantages of the relative remoteness of this interior belt, in a U.S.S.R. more outward looking than before, although not easily expressed in quantitative terms, must not be overlooked.

REFERENCES

1. AL'TMAN, L. P. and DOLKART, M. L., 'Problems of economic development in the Northwest economic region during the Five Year Plan 1966–70' *Soviet Geogr.*, 9, No 1, 11–23, 1968
2. KURNIKOV, F. D., 'The basic tendencies of development of the industrial complex of the Volga region' *Soviet Geogr.*, 8, No 2, 107–17, 1967
3. PALEYEV, Yu. N., 'Transport problems of the Volga region in connection with development of its productive forces' *Soviet Geogr.*, 8, No 2, 117–25, 1967
4. HOOSON, D. J. M., 'The Middle Volga–an Emerging Focal Region in the Soviet Union' *Geogrl J.*, 126, Part 2, 180–90, 1960
5. Almost all the papers in *Soviet Geogr.*, 9, No 6, 1968 are on aspects of Central Asia.
6. BUYANOVSKIY, M. S., 'Balkhash-Ili, a potential major industrial complex' *Soviet Geogr.*, 6, No 8, 3–15, 1965
7. FEYGIN, Ya. G. *et al.*, *Zakonomernosti i faktory razvitiya ekonomicheskikh rayonov SSSR*, 174 (Moscow, 1965)
8. NEKRASOV, N., 'Razmeshcheniye proizvoditel'nykh syl' *Pravda*, 19 Apr. 1966, 2

BIBLIOGRAPHY

ADAMCHUK, V. A., 'The Problem of Creating a Kazakhstan Metallurgical Base' *Soviet Geogr.*, 5, No 6, 20–35, 1964

GELLER, S. Yu. *et al.*, 'The Transformation of Nature and Development of the Natural Resources of Arid Areas' *Soviet Geogr.*, 5, No 7, 1964

HOOSON, D. J. M., *A New Soviet Heartland?* (Van Nostrand, Princeton, 1964)

KARSTEN, A. A., 'The Virgin Lands Kray and its Prospects of Development' *Soviet Geogr.*, 4, No 5, 37–47, 1963

KOMAR, I. V., *Ural* (Moscow, 1959)

KROTOV, V. A. *et al.*, 'The role of Eastern Siberia in solving some of the economic problems of the Pacific basin' *Soviet Geogr.*, 9, No 2, 142–4, 1968

KUTAF'YEV, S. A. *et al.*, *Rossiyskaya sovetskaya federativnaya sotsialisticheskaya respublika* (Moscow, 1959)

NAZAREVSKIY, O. R., *Kazakhskaya SSR* (Geografgiz, Moscow, 1957)

NESTERENKO, A. A. *et al.*, *Ukrainskaya SSR* (Geografgiz, Moscow, 1957)

NIKITIN, N. P., *Ekonomicheskaya geografiya SSSR* (Moscow, 1966)

PAVLENKO, V. F., 'The Transport-Geography Situation and Inter-Regional Links of Central Asia' *Soviet Geogr.*, 4, No 9, 27–34, 1963

PETROV, M. P., *Pustyni SSSR i ikh osvoyeniye* (Moscow, 1964)

PROBST, A. Ye., 'Further Productive Specialisation of the Central Asian Region' *Soviet Geogr.*, 5, No 6, 11–20, 1964

SOCHAVA, V. B., 'Geographical Problems of Development of the Tayga (Northern Forest)' *Soviet Geogr.*, 5, No 7, 1964

SOCHAVA, V. B., 'Modern Geography and Its Tasks in Siberia and the Soviet Far East' *Soviet Geogr.*, 9, No 2, 80–105, 1968

Soviet Geogr., 5, No 5, 1964 contains various papers on Siberia (transportation, water-management, dust storms)

TAAFFE, R., *Rail Transportation and the economic development of Soviet Central Asia* (University of Chicago, Department of Geography Research, Paper No 64, 1960)

15

Soviet foreign relations

15.1 SOVIET FOREIGN TRADE

INTRODUCTION

In absolute terms, tsarist Russia was one of the major trading countries of the world before World War I. It had strong connections with Germany and other countries of central Europe as well as with several of its neighbours in Asia. Its imports were predominantly manufactured goods, its exports raw materials and food, including oil, timber, grain and livestock products. Considering the large total population of Russia, however, *per capita* trade even then was relatively small.

In the interwar period Soviet planners were aiming as far as possible to achieve self-sufficiency in raw materials, food and manufactured goods. With the inward looking policy of the Communist Party in an unfriendly, non-communist world, foreign trade was regarded as an evil, necessary at times, but to be avoided as far as possible. Vital equipment and raw materials were imported as required. They were paid for by whatever could with least inconvenience be spared at a time when many Russian traditional surplus items were scarce and when central planning did not cater for export goods. For a time in World War II this pattern changed as war materials were received from the U.S.A. through devious routes via Murmansk, through Iran, or in other ways, while trade otherwise came to a standstill.

Out of the chaos of World War II, the U.S.S.R. emerged with several so-called satellites. With the Communist coup in Czechoslovakia in 1948 and the withdrawal of Yugoslavia from close dependence on the U.S.S.R., the postwar arrangement of Soviet partners was established. Throughout the 1950's, the U.S.S.R. traded heavily with its East European partners and (after 1949) with Mao's China. From about 1960 trade with China fell off sharply, while that with East Europe continued to rise in the 1960's (see Table 3.3).

Over the first 50 years since 1917, the value and the volume of Soviet foreign trade have both increased. Total Soviet gross national product has also increased several times in this period. It is difficult to calculate an import coefficient (value of imports as percentage of total value of gross national product) to assess the changing importance of Soviet trade to the total economy. It has probably never been far from about 2%, compared with some 5% for the U.S.A., 15–20% for France, West Germany and the United Kingdom and about 45% for the Netherlands and Norway, according to figures quoted by Hill.[1] The basic composition of Soviet foreign trade since 1913 and in selected postwar years is revealed in Table 15.1. The main conclusion is that processed and manufactured items have occupied a growing share both of exports and of imports.

Soviet policy towards foreign trade in particular and international relations in general has certainly not remained static. Nevertheless there has been a widespread theoretical dislike of

Table 15.1. PERCENTAGE OF THE VALUE OF SOVIET FOREIGN TRADE MADE UP OF RAW MATERIALS OR OTHER GOODS

Exports	*1913*	*1950*	*1958*	*1963*
Raw materials	64	39	40	35
Manufactured and semi-manufactured goods	36	61	60	65
Imports				
Raw materials	44	40	36	26
Manufactured and semi-manufactured goods	56	60	64	74

Source: *NkhSSSR* 1963, 551–2.

foreign trade, counterbalanced by a pragmatic indulgence in it, both out of economic necessity and political intrigue. The arguments against foreign trade have been the size and wide range of resources of the U.S.S.R., the danger of dependence on foreign (or since World War II, non-socialist) powers and the difficulty of incorporating unpredictable and uncontrollable forces into centralised national plans. Fear of attack, and the strategic desirability of self-sufficiency, contributed more to discourage foreign trade in the interwar period than in the postwar period. Moreover, a distinction, sharp at first, now less marked, between socialist and non-socialist partners, has been made either explicitly or implicitly.

The arguments against foreign trade have been counterbalanced by the fact that there has rarely been a time when the Soviet economy has not needed to import some kind of capital goods such as machinery, equipment, or vehicles. In the early 1960's, for example, it was looking for equipment for its lagging chemicals industry and for computers, in Western countries. The U.S.S.R. has also been short of raw materials such as rubber, industrial diamonds and tin, none of which could easily be replaced. Owing to fluctuations in Soviet agriculture, food products, including grain from Canada and even the U.S.A. have been purchased in certain years, particularly since 1963. Finally, the U.S.S.R. itself does not grow fully tropical crops such as coffee, cocoa beans or bananas. The Soviet consumer has done without these except when gratuitously provided with Cuban cigars or West African cocoa.

The U.S.S.R. has generally preferred to trade on a bilateral basis, if possible with a barter arrangement, with non-Communist countries and trade figures have often shown a very close correspondence between the value of Soviet imports from and exports to any given country, although there have been exceptions, such as Malaya and Canada. This situation is changing, and may have existed simply for organisational reasons. Nevertheless, the Soviet economy has not been geared in any sense to build up exports, which have come in a haphazard if fortunate manner rather than by any definite plan. Unplanned surpluses could usefully be disposed of as exports. At times, as in the early 1930's, foodstuffs for export were virtually commandeered from collective farms. It is becoming obvious, however, that a more positive attitude towards exports is ensuring not only that such high quality items as furs, caviare and crabmeat are marketed abroad, but also that timber, oil, manganese ore and many other goods are now being produced specifically for export to socialist partners and the non-communist world. Further, the U.S.S.R. is not averse to playing an *entrepôt* role; in the 1950's Chinese metallic ores were refined and then re-exported. Egyptian cotton and Cuban sugar may also be re-exported.

TRADING PARTNERS OF THE U.S.S.R.

Table 15.2 shows the 25 countries with the greatest absolute value of trade with the U.S.S.R. in 1966, exports and imports combined. The total value in that year was 15 079 million roubles (exports 7 957, imports 7 122). The 25 countries listed accounted for almost 90% of the

Table 15.2. SOVIET FOREIGN TRADE IN 1966

(See also Table 3.3)

Rank	Country	Percentage share	Rank	Country	Per capita value in roubles
1	East Germany	15·8	1	Mongolian People's Republic	180
2	Czechoslovakia	10·8	2	Bulgaria	149
3	Poland	9·2	3	East Germany	140
4	Bulgaria	8·1	4	Czechoslovakia	116
5	Hungary	6·1	5	Finland	93
6	Romania	4·7	6	Hungary	91
7	Cuba	4·5	7	Cuba	91
8	Great Britain	3·0	8	Iceland	88
9	Finland	2·8	9	Poland	44
10	Japan	2·8	10	Romania	38
11	Yugoslavia	2·4	11	Yugoslavia	19
12	India	2·3	12	Canada	16
13	Canada	2·2	13	Austria	15
14	United Arab Republic	2·1	14	Sweden	14
15	China	1·9	15	North Korea	13
16	West Germany	1·9	16	Malaysia	12
17	France	1·7	17	Cyprus	12
18	Italy	1·5	18	United Arab Republic	12
19	Mongolia	1·3	19	Denmark	11
20	North Korea	1·1	20	Belgium	10
21	Austria	0·7	21	Norway	10
22	Argentina	0·7	22	Netherlands	9
23	Netherlands	0·7	23	Great Britain	8
24	Sweden	0·7	24	Syria	7
25	U.S.A.	0·7	25	Greece	7

Source: *Vneshnyaya torgovlya SSSR za 1966 god–statisticheskiy sbornik,* 11–16 (Moscow, 1967)

total. The Comecon countries (six in East Europe plus Mongolia) took 56·0% of the total, the remaining socialist countries (China, Cuba, North Korea, North Vietnam, Yugoslavia) another 10·5%. The remaining one-third was, by Soviet definition, 21% with 'industrially developed' countries and 12·5% with 'developing' countries.

A very different picture (Table 15.2, Column 2) emerges if trade value is expressed in terms of roubles per inhabitant of the population of the partner (1966 figures). Mongolia heads the list. Finland and Iceland come high. Interestingly, of the 10 largest countries in the world in population (excluding the U.S.S.R. itself) only three score above 1 rouble per inhabitant, Great Britain 8, West Germany 5 and Japan 4. Why does the U.S.S.R. have the particular set of trading partners given in the list? Opinion in the West is not uniform. In the 1950's it was often assumed that it used its limited trading capacity and requirements to influence various non-socialist countries politically. In other words, the desire to establish trading links and toeholds such as embassies, missions and teams of experts in particular countries determined the items received by the U.S.S.R. Nove[2] put a strong case against this, stressing the economic rather than the political or strategic motives behind Soviet trade. He pointed out, however, that where there were alternative sources of a required item, the U.S.S.R. would choose a partner more likely to be politically valuable in some way; for example, it would obtain fish from Iceland rather than Norway and cocoa beans from Ghana, once it became independent in the 1950's, rather than from areas still controlled by France or Britain in West Africa. To some extent, Soviet trade was and still is affected by the embargoes on the sale of certain strategic items, especially by the

U.S.A., and by the unwillingness of regimes in some countries (eg Spain, South Africa) to become involved with the U.S.S.R.

The direction of Soviet foreign trade and the choice of partners is an increasingly complex field of study, undertaken preferably in conjunction with study of Soviet diplomatic connections, aid programmes, airline and shipping services. Without any statistical backing, it is tempting to suggest that there seems to be a tendency to trade with small countries that are islands (eg Iceland, Cyprus, Cuba) or with countries that are immediate neighbours (Finland, Afghanistan, all but two of the Comecon partners—see Fig. 3.3). When it comes to the point, political ends can be satisfied through the centralised nature of Soviet decision making and pressure put even on powerful countries. For example, when France withdrew from N.A.T.O. in 1966, Soviet trade organisations began to 'buy French' and in a year French exports to the U.S.S.R. roughly doubled (*The Times*, 17 July 1968).

ITEMS OF SOVIET FOREIGN TRADE

Table 15.3 shows the relative importance of selected main categories of trading items covering some 90% of total trade. At first sight

the facts are contradictory since the U.S.S.R. appears to import and export the same kinds of thing. This may, however, be explained in several ways. First, the categories are mostly large and contain very different items; under machinery and equipment, petrochemicals equipment may be imported while bulldozers are exported. Secondly there is in fact some manipulation in certain items; for example, sugar is both imported and exported (not presumably back to its source country). Thirdly, the U.S.S.R. is territorially so large that an item needed at one end of it might be in surplus at the other end; for example, it might be convenient (or cheaper) to carry Canadian wheat from Vancouver to Vladivostok to supply the Soviet Far East region, while selling surplus Ukraine wheat in East Europe. Indeed, in the late 1960's, the U.S.S.R. and Japan were negotiating on lines that suggest the southern part of the Soviet Far East may become commercially more closely linked with nearby Japan than with European U.S.S.R. Lumber in exchange for machinery was the first step, made in a 163 million dollar deal in July 1968 (*The Times*, 30 July 1968).

The U.S.S.R. emerges from the figures shown as heavily dependent on the outside world for goods that are either entirely manufactured or considerably processed. Its exports still come primarily from its land and mines, evidence of

Table 15.3. MAIN CATEGORIES OF SOVIET FOREIGN TRADE IN 1966

	Item	Percentage of Imports	Percentage of Exports
1	Food	19·6	9·2
2	Furs		0·8
3	Textile raw materials	4·8	5·2
4	Wood and products	1·9	7·0
5	Non-metallic minerals		1·1
6	Ores and concentrates	8·7	20·1
7	Fuel and electricity	2·4	16·4
8	Chemical products	6·4	3·8
9	Machinery and equipment	32·4	20·8
10	Consumer goods	16·4	2·4
	Items 1– 4 Land	26·3	22·2
	Items 5– 7 Mines	11·1	27·6
	Items 8–10 Manufactured goods	55·2	27·0

Note: the values do not add up to 100 since only selected groups are shown.

Source: *Vneshnyaya torgovlya SSSR za 1966 god-statisticheskiy sbornik,* 19 (Moscow, 1967)

the great scale of Soviet resources, and the consequent favourable population/resource balance compared with that of most countries in the world. A consideration of items exchanged with individual trading partners shows a dichotomy, with Soviet farm and mineral products going mainly to the more industrialised partners, whether socialist or capitalist, and manufactured goods going to the developing countries, again regardless of political regime.

Table 15.4 shows the destination of selected items of export, either large in value, or heavy in weight. Soviet machinery and equipment goes both to developing countries, where it is exchanged for food and raw materials and to the industrialised Comecon partners, which themselves sell other types of machinery to the U.S.S.R. Coal goes mainly to Comecon partners but also to countries such as Denmark, Italy and Japan that produce little or none themselves.

Crude oil and oil products exports, which in 1966 accounted for nearly a third of the national output, went to many countries (see Table 15.4). Iron ore, pig iron and manganese are sent mainly to Comecon countries, but even Britain imports some. Japan, China and Britain are among the main purchasers of timber and its products. Wheat, which is both imported and exported, came in 1965–66 (in millions of metric tons) from Canada (7·8), Argentina (2·2), Australia (1·4) and even France (0·4) but went to certain Comecon partners almost exclusively.

Soviet imports of machinery and equipment come mainly from Comecon partners, particularly East Germany and Czechoslovakia, but also from West Germany, Japan and Britain. Of the raw materials received, Malaysia is the main supplier of rubber, Mongolia and Australia of wool. Of foodstuffs, Brazil now supplies most of the coffee, Ghana the cocoa and Cuba the raw sugar (two millions tons).

Table 15.4. SELECTED EXPORT ITEMS BY COUNTRY IN 1966

Machinery and equipment: total 1 654 in millions of roubles

1	Bulgaria	288	6	Hungary	109
2	Czechoslovakia	137	7	East Germany	108
3	Poland	130	8	India	90
4	United Arab Republic	120	9	China	76
5	Cuba	110	10	Mongolia	74

Coal: total 22·4 million tons   *Iron ore: total 26·0 million tons*

1	East Germany	5·9	1	Poland	7·9
2	Bulgaria	3·0	2	Czechoslovakia	7·7
3	Czechoslovakia	2·1	3	East Germany	2·6
4	Japan	1·6	4	Hungary	2·6
5	Italy	1·4	5	Romania	2·4

Crude oil: Total 50·3 million tons   *Oil products and diesel fuel: total 34·0 million tons*

1	Italy	8·0	1	Sweden	6·9
2	Czechoslovakia	6·4	2	Finland	4·5
3	East Germany	6·1	3	Poland	2·1
4	Cuba	3·8	4	Japan	2·0
5	Poland	3·3	5	Cuba	2·0
6	West Germany	3·3			
7	Japan	2·8			
8	Bulgaria	2·6			
9	Finland	2·6			
10	Hungary	2·5			
11	Brazil	2·2			

TRADE WITH THE COMECON PARTNERS

In Chapter 3 the Communist countries of East Europe were compared with the 19 economic regions of the U.S.S.R. Their heavy dependence on trade with the U.S.S.R. was noted and their own interdependence implied. In view of the lack of appropriate information, it is a matter of speculation and guesswork as to the precise content and value of flows of goods between East European countries and individual economic regions of the U.S.S.R. The following notes, then, merely give an idea of the kind of items traded between individual East European countries and the U.S.S.R. in total; some more detailed origins and destinations are suggested.

1. *East Germany* is now one of the most highly industrialised countries in the world and the largest trading partner of the U.S.S.R. Machinery and equipment make up about 60% of its exports to the U.S.S.R.; items that figure prominently are ships, railway rolling stock, construction equipment and machinery for food processing and light manufacturing. Clothing, furniture and other consumer goods also go to the U.S.S.R. Although East Germany takes some machinery from the U.S.S.R. (under 10% of its imports) it receives mainly metal ores, rolled steel (about 20%) timber, cotton, wool and various food items. It is not difficult to deduce, then, that East Germany has strong links with many of the economic regions of the U.S.S.R.

2. *Czechoslovakia* is very similar to East Germany in its trade relations with the U.S.S.R. Equipment and machinery make up over 50% of its exports; motor vehicles of various kinds, electric locomotives and factory equipment are major items. Ores and metals (not specified in detail) also go to the U.S.S.R. Clothing and footwear are exported in large quantities. Although Czechoslovakia receives farm machinery and other engineering items from the U.S.S.R. (about 15% of its imports) like East Germany, it acquires mainly coal (though less than East Germany) oil, iron ore, rolled steel and non-ferrous metals. From Soviet farms it obtains cotton, wheat and barley in particular.

3. *Poland* sends to the U.S.S.R. far less machinery and equipment than the two preceding countries (about 35% of its exports) some light manufactured goods and certain food products. It imports little coal, but takes oil and oil products, ores and processed metals and some grain. Poland is not as highly industrialised as several Soviet economic regions; it is larger than East Germany or Czechoslovakia and within Comecon, more balanced and self-sufficient.

4. *Hungary* About 50% of Hungary's exports to the U.S.S.R. are machinery and equipment, including particularly transportation items; most of the remainder is made up of consumer manufactured goods and specialised food products. Hungary receives some machinery and equipment from the U.S.S.R., but mainly oil, metals and chemicals products, as well as some grain and cotton.

5. *Romania* The pattern of Romanian trade with the U.S.S.R. differs considerably from that of the four preceding countries. Less than 20% of its exports are machinery and equipment. On the other hand, Romania exports refined oil products to the U.S.S.R. as well as rolled steel and pipes, and such items as timber, wines, clothing and furniture. Romania no doubt supplies the little industrialised Western Ukraine and Moldavia with various manufactured goods. At the same time it receives from the U.S.S.R. not only items such as cotton and minerals that it does not have at home, but also various steel products. Whereas East Germany, Czechoslovakia and to some extent Hungary complement the raw material producing regions of the U.S.S.R., Romania has less specific items to offer and trade seems to be less obvious and perhaps less vital.

6. *Bulgaria* depends very heavily on the U.S.S.R. for its foreign trade, but the role is partly reversed in that it receives much more machinery and equipment from the U.S.S.R. than it sends there. It sends tobacco, wines, fruits and other 'southern' agricultural produce, as well as cigarettes, clothing and furniture and receives agricultural and transport machinery, coal, oil and metals. To some extent, its relationship to the industrialised economic regions of the U.S.S.R. is like that of Transcaucasia and Central Asia.

CONCLUSION

Soviet foreign trade is characterised by two other features worth noting (Tables 15.5 and 15.6).

Table 15.5. ITEMS OF SOVIET FOREIGN TRADE
LARGE IN WEIGHT

Exports	*1963*	*1964*	*1965*	*1966*
Crude oil	30	37	43	50
Oil products	21	20	21	23
Hard coal	21	24	22	22
Iron ore	21	23	24	26
Pig iron and rolled steel	6	7	8	9
Grain	6	4	4	4
Imports				
Grain	3	7	6	8

Sources:
NkhSSSR 1965, 671-2
*Vneshnyaya torgovlya SSSR za 1966
god-statisticheskiy sbornik* (Moscow 1967).

First, much of it goes by land (rail, pipeline or road) into contiguous countries and secondly, the weight and/or volume of exports greatly exceeds that of imports, which means that at times Soviet ships are moving empty and can compete for traffic along certain sea lanes. It would be advantageous for the U.S.S.R. to extend its oil pipeline system beyond the Comecon partners into markets such as Austria and West Germany. Natural gas could also reach West Europe by pipeline or in liquid form by sea.

One aspect of Soviet foreign trade that would be worth investigating if data were available is the contribution made by various economic regions to the goods exported and the direction of these

to the outlets (seaports, rail heads). Most of the oil clearly comes from the Volga region, the coal, iron ore, pig iron and steel, presumably from the Donets-Dnepr and timber from the Northwest. The Far East has its own trading links with Japan, exporting regional coal, oil and timber. Just as some regions make a much bigger *per capita* contribution to the Soviet economy than others, so they do to Soviet exports.

Finally, it is appropriate to put Soviet foreign trade in world perspective. In 1938, Soviet foreign trade was a mere 1% of total world trade. Since the mid 1950's, it has been around 4-5% of total world trade (see Table 15.7). In *per capita* terms it is now only about a quarter that of the U.S.A. and less than one-tenth that of Canada.

Table 15.6. SOVIET FOREIGN TRADE CARRIED
BY DIFFERENT MEANS OF TRANSPORT
IN 1966

	Exports $\times 10^3$ *ton*	*Imports* $\times 10^3$ *ton*
Rail	55 619	9 264
Sea	90 307	12 442
River	7 118	822
Road	166	29
Pipeline	15 999	429
Air	2	1
Total	169 211	22 987

Source: *Vneshnyaya torgovlya SSSR za 1966
god-statisticheskiy sbornik,* 18 (Moscow, 1967).

Table 15.7. WORLD TRADE IN MILLIONS OF U.S. DOLLARS IN 1966 AND 1967

	Imports	*Exports*	*Imports*	*Exports*
World	215 800	203 800	227 100	214 400
U.S.S.R.	7 913	8 841	8 536	9 649
1 U.S.A.	25 445	30 013	26 813	31 243
2 West Germany	18 023	20 134	17 352	21 737
3 United Kingdom	16 107	14 132	17 186	13 869
4 France	11 843	10 889	12 381	11 380
5 Japan	9 524	9 777	11 664	10 442
6 Canada	9 316	9 551	10 057	10 553
Common Market	53 630	52 630	54 940	56 140
EFTA	33 380	27 990	35 230	28 650
East Europe	21 300	20 910	22 900	22 800

Source: *United Nations Statistical Yearbook* 1967, Table 148 and 1968, Table 151

In total value, Comecon lags behind EFTA, which has only about a quarter as many inhabitants and it lies far behind the Common Market. Since so much of the U.S.S.R.'s trade is within Comecon, its impact on total world trade is very small indeed.

15.2 SOVIET FOREIGN RELATIONS OTHER THAN TRADE

SOVIET FOREIGN AID

Table 15.8 shows the general direction of Soviet aid and technical assistance without giving more than a rough quantitative guide to relative importance. This is because there is no information about the size of projects. Presumably the 257 projects in Mongolia, with only one million people, are much smaller on average than the 256 in China, with some 700 million people. The list of other countries, actually described as the developing countries (*razvivayushchiye strany*) is not complete, since altogether 599 projects are referred to, in 31 countries, compared with 1 413 in socialist countries. The combined total, 2 012, includes all postwar projects completed, under way, or scheduled by 1967. The data in Table 15.8 are mapped topologically in Fig. 15.1.

SOVIET EMBASSIES

This subsection compares briefly the presence of Soviet embassies, legations or diplomatic relations without embassies in 1957 and 1968.

In 1957, the U.S.S.R. had relations with 58 countries (embassies in 46, legations in 3 and diplomatic relations without embassy in 9). In 1968, the same 57 countries were on the list, one, Syria, had dropped out, but there were 14 more. A few of the 1957 legations were raised to embassy status by 1968. The following are the 13 new countries, listed in descending order of population: Morocco, Tanzania, Chile, Cuba, Cameroon, Tunisia, Dominican Republic, Chad, Rwanda, Somalia, Dahomey, Central African Republic, Congo (Brazzaville), Cyprus. Ten of these are new African countries. Diplomatic connections with the rest of Europe, both East and West, are almost universal. Only Spain, Portugal, Ireland and West Berlin are missing. Of 23 countries in Latin America, Brazil, Colombia, Peru and Venezuela were among the 12 with which there were no direct relations in 1967. There were also some 20 countries in Africa with which the U.S.S.R. did not have diplomatic relations in the late 1960's, as well as several in Asia, including Japan, the Philippines, South Korea, South Vietnam and Taiwan. The information given above was

Table 15.8. DIRECTION OF SOVIET FOREIGN AID AND TECHNICAL ASSISTANCE, 1945–67

Socialist countries	Projects	Other countries	Projects	Other countries	Projects
Mongolia	257	United Arab Republic	102	Yemen	13
China	256	Algeria	74	Mali	13
Bulgaria	166	Afghanistan	59	Ceylon	11
North Vietnam	143	Iraq	49	Tunisia	6
Poland	108	India	45	Ethiopia	6
Cuba	104	Guinea	31	Nepal	6
Romania	101	Pakistan	21	Burma	5
Hungary	76	Iran	21	Cambodia	4
North Korea	58	Indonesia	20		
Yugoslavia	46	Ghana	20		
Albania	45	Syria	19		
Czechoslovakia	27	Somalia	17		
Germany	26	Sudan	14		

Source: *Strana sovetov za 50 let,* 48 (Moscow, 1967).

obtained from *The Statesman's Yearbook*, 1957 (p. 1467) and 1968–69 (p. 1534). It may be assumed that, unlike many small countries, the U.S.S.R. could afford to maintain an embassy in every country in the world. There may be various reasons why it does not. In some cases (eg Spain, South Africa, Brazil) the regimes in power have no doubt felt that to get involved with the U.S.S.R. might be politically embarrassing. In

also a study of changes during the intervening period.

In October 1957 (see Table 15.9) 12 socialist countries were mentioned, China first of all and by itself, the remaining 11, in alphabetical order (Russian alphabet). Only 15 other countries were mentioned by name. By April 1967, *Pravda* editors were more lavish in mentioning countries individually. The U.S.A. and West Germany were

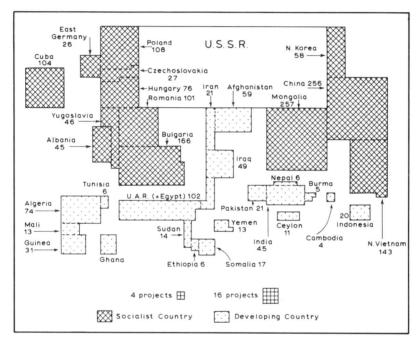

Fig. 15.1.   Distribution of Soviet foreign aid and technical assistance.

other cases, the U.S.S.R. may use the facilities of one of its Comecon partners (eg Poland or Czechoslovakia). It is quite feasible, of course, to trade with a country without having an embassy in it.

GREETINGS TO COUNTRIES OF THE WORLD IN *PRAVDA*

Until 1968 it was customary for *Pravda* to display a list of countries, with greetings to them, both in mid-April and in mid-October. A comparison of the lists of 13 October 1957 and 18 April 1967 is revealing in various ways, as is

selected for special criticism. They were followed by 12 socialist countries, listed in alphabetical order; since 1957, China had moved down into the alphabetical list and Cuba up into it. Albania had dropped out. In addition to 13 socialist countries, some 40 non-socialist countries were mentioned by name. These included many Afro-Asian countries, some new since 1957, others still with colonial status. West Europe was covered in detail, but Latin America was undivided. Like the list of Soviet diplomatic connections, the *Pravda* list gives only a rough guide to Soviet attitudes in foreign affairs. Unfortunately the mention of specific countries seems to have been dropped since April 1967.

Table 15.9. *PRAVDA* GREETINGS TO COUNTRIES OF THE WORLD IN 1957 AND 1967

(a) *October 1957*

  China

Alphabetical (Russian) order
  Albania, Bulgaria, Hungary, North Vietnam, East Germany, (West Germany), North Korea, Mongolian People's Republic, Poland, Romania, Czechoslovakia, Yugoslavia.

By area
  India, Burma, Ceylon, Cambodia

By area (contd)
England, U.S.A., France
Italy
Finland
Sweden, Norway, Denmark, Iceland
Austria
Japan
Arab East
Colonial and dependent countries.

(b) *April 1967*

Admonitions
  U.S.A., Vietnam war, West Germany

Alphabetical
  Bulgaria, Hungary, North Vietnam, East Germany, China, North Korea, Cuba, Mongolian People's Republic, Poland, Romania, Czechoslovakia, Yugoslavia.

By area (by paragraphs as in *Pravda*)
  Albania
  United Arab Republic
  Algeria
  Syria
  Burma
  Guinea, Mali, Congo (Brazzaville)
  Laos, Cambodia
  India
  Pakistan
  Indonesia
  South Vietnam
  Afghanistan
  South Korea

By area (contd)
Arab countries
South Arabia, Oman
Angola
Mozambique
Portuguese Guinea
Rhodesia
South Africa
Latin America
France
Britain
U.S.A.
Italy
Iran, Turkey
West Germany
Spain
Portugal
Austria, Sweden, Switzerland
Finland
Belgium, Holland, Greece, Denmark, Spain, Norway
Canada
Japan

COMMUNIST PARTIES AT THE CELEBRATIONS OF THE 50TH ANNIVERSARY OF THE 1917 REVOLUTION

In November 1967 communist parties from various countries in the world gathered in Moscow (also at Leningrad, Kiev and Minsk) and their representatives delivered speeches, reported in *Pravda* during 4–7 November 1967. Table 15.10 shows the countries (plus a few other institutions) represented. The U.S.S.R. was represented 15 times by its 15 Soviet Socialist Republics (italic), all quite high in the order. Some other countries were also represented twice, in most cases once in Moscow and once in another town. The top part of the list shows a subtle intermingling of S.S.R.'s, other Socialist countries (eg Poland) and non-Socialist countries (eg France, Italy). It is interesting to note, however, that China, Albania and Cuba are absent from the list. Speeches 45–49 were made at Leningrad, 50–56 at Kiev and 57–63 at Minsk. Seldom in diplomatic history can there have been a more delicate and complicated list.

SOVIET AIRLINES

Soviet International airline flights are distributed rougly as one might expect. Twenty-seven flights advertised by Aeroflot in 1968 are listed in Table 15.11 and mapped in Fig. 15.2. The Moscow–New York flight has been added. With this, Aeroflot has services to 42 countries, among which

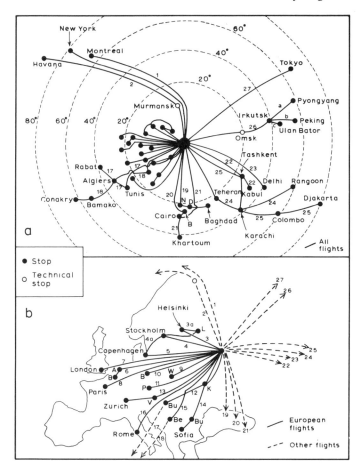

Fig. 15.2. *Aeroflot flights in January 1968. Refer to Table 15.11 for key to flights. Note: the numbering of flights is not official; it is solely for the convenience of this section of the book. (a) All flights. The map uses an oblique zenithal projection centred on Moscow. Scale is halved beyond 20° from Moscow. 20° is roughly 2200 km. The National Geographic Globe was used for the construction of the map. (b) Flights to places in Europe.*

are represented 11 of the 13 socialist countries (Albania and North Vietnam are not served). Aeroflot could not be more economical in its landings, for it serves exactly one town, either the capital, or in three cases the largest city, in each country. At home, only Leningrad, Kiev, Tashkent and Irkutsk have the privilege of being served by international services. Murmansk and Omsk are used for technical stops. In fact the International Airlines of such small countries as the Netherlands (KLM) and Switzerland (Swissair) reach more countries than Aeroflot and serve two or more airports in many of the

countries. Since the establishment of an airline between a pair of countries often requires negotiation with intervening countries, reciprocal flights and other concessions, the U.S.S.R., in its reluctance to allow other companies to fly over its vast territory, is to some extent victim of its own policy.

COVERAGE OF WORLD NEWS

To obtain a rough idea of the coverage of world

Table 15.10. ORDER OF SPEAKERS AT 50TH ANNIVERSARY OF 1917 REVOLUTION, MOSCOW 1967

1	R.S.F.S.R.	27	Tadjikistan S.S.R.	53	Venezuela
2	Poland	28	Finland	54	Guatemala
3	Ukraine S.S.R.	29	Armenia S.S.R.	55	Canada
4	East Germany	30	U.S.A.	56	Tunisia
5	Belorussia S.S.R.	31	Turkmenistan S.S.R.	57	U.S.A.(2nd)
6	North Vietnam	32	United Arab Republic	58	Switzerland
7	France	33	Estonia S.S.R.	59	Costa Rica
8	Czechoslovakia	34	Guinea	60	Martinique
9	Uzbekistan S.S.R.	35	Mali	61	Panama
10	Hungary	36	Syria	62	Iraq
11	Kazakhstan S.S.R.	37	Great Britain	63	World Trade Union
12	Bulgaria	38	Congo (Brazzaville)	64	Greece
13	Georgia S.S.R.	39	Uruguay	65	Austria (2nd)
14	Italy	40	Algeria	66	Syria
15	Azerbaijan S.S.R.	41	West Germany	67	Portugal
16	Yugoslavia	42	India	68	Australia
17	Lithuania S.S.R.	43	Tanzania	69	Belgium
18	Romania	44	Chile	70	Angola
19	South Vietnam	45	France (2nd)	71	Colombia
20	Moldavia S.S.R.	46	South Vietnam (2nd)	72	South Africa
21	Spain	47	Spain (2nd)	73	Argentina
22	Red Army Tank Corps	48	Mexico	74	Ecuador
23	Latvia S.S.R.	49	Morocco	75	Ceylon
24	Mongolia	50	Italy (2nd)	76	Guinea (2nd)
25	Kirgizia S.S.R.	51	Lebanon	77	Cyprus
26	North Korea	52	Austria	78	Denmark

Table 15.11. FLIGHTS OF SOVIET AIRLINE AEROFLOT, JANUARY 1968

1	Moscow–Montreal	16	Moscow–Rome
2	Moscow–(Murmansk)–Havana	17	Moscow–Budapest–Tunis–Algiers–Rabat
3	Moscow–Helsinki	18	Moscow–Belgrade–Algiers–Bamako[1]–Conakry[2]
3a	Leningrad–Helsinki	19	Moscow–Nicosia–Damascus–Baghdad
4	Moscow–Stockholm	20	Moscow–Beirut–Cairo
4a–5a	Leningrad–Stockholm–Copenhagen	21	Moscow–Cairo–Khartoum
5	Moscow–Copenhagen	22	Moscow–Tashkent–Kabul
6	Moscow–Amsterdam–Brussels	23	Moscow–Delhi
7	Moscow–London	24	Moscow–Teheran–Karachi–Rangoon
8	Moscow–Paris	25	Moscow–Tashkent–Karachi–Colombo–Djakarta
9	Moscow–Warsaw	26	Moscow–(Omsk)–Irkutsk
10	Moscow–Berlin	26a	Pyongyang[3]
11	Moscow–Prague	26b	Ulan Bator[4]
12	Moscow–Kiev–Budapest	26c	Peking
13	Moscow–Vienna–Zurich	27	Moscow–Tokyo
14	Moscow–Kiev–Bucharest–Sofia	28	Moscow–New York (after January 1968)
15	Moscow–Belgrade		

[1]Mali   [2]Guinea   [3]N. Korea   [4]Mongolia
Source: *ABC World Airways Guide*, Part 1, 30, Jan. 1968.

news in the Soviet press, *Pravda* was sampled. The front page of 35 numbers of *Pravda*, taken regularly at 10-day intervals in 1968 (starting 14 January 1968 and ending 19 December 1968), was studied for place mentions. These were counted and subdivided first into home and foreign mentions, then into subregions. Any place mentioned was counted once only on a given day. The maximum possible score (achieved only by the U.S.S.R.) was 35. On this basis, 1 047 home place mentions and 669 foreign place mentions were recorded. The foreign places are divided into sub-areas in Table 15.12. The most frequently mentioned foreign places are shown in Table 15.13. Frequently mentioned home places are shown in Appendix 2. It is suggested that for anyone studying the geography of the U.S.S.R. they are worthwhile learning as they are likely to appear often in the news.

Table 15.12. MENTIONS OF PLACES OUTSIDE THE U.S.S.R. IN *PRAVDA*

Big places (Institutions, continents)	46

Sub-areas

A	Socialist East Europe (including Yugoslavia)	118
B	Non-socialist Europe	129
C	U.S.A. and Canada	57
D	Latin America	23
E	Africa (excluding U.A.R.)	42
F	Southwest Asia (and U.A.R.)	75
G	South Asia	11
H	Southeast and East Asia (excluding Vietnam)	42
I	Vietnam	123
J	Australia and New Zealand	3
K	China	0
	Total	669

CATCHING UP THE U.S.A.

In the late 1950's the ebullient Nikita Khrushchev talked a great deal of the race with the U.S.A. and the possibility of overtaking it in the 1970's first in total production and then *per capita* production. This subject formed the whole theme, for example, of a book by Tikhonov.[3]

In the late 1960's less publicity was given to peaceful competition with capitalist industrial countries, which is hardly surprising since in absolute terms the gap between the two countries has widened since 1958, in spite of a faster rate of growth of national income in the U.S.S.R. In absolute terms, and even in *per capita* terms (remember the larger size of the Soviet population) the U.S.S.R. has overtaken the U.S.A. in the production of some major items, coal, iron ore, cement, locomotives and engineers. In other respects, however, it lags far behind, in road transport, most branches of chemicals and housing, not to mention consumer goods and services.

Soviet statistical publications continue to compare the achievements of the U.S.S.R. in

Table 15.13. MENTIONS OF INDIVIDUAL PLACES OUTSIDE THE U.S.S.R.

Rank	Place outside U.S.S.R. *Countries underlined*	Mentions	Rank	Place outside U.S.S.R. *Countries underlined*	Mentions
1	U.S.A.	26	20	Jordan	8
2	North Vietnam	26	21	Hungary	7
3	South Vietnam	18	22	Budapest	7
4	Hanoi	16	23	Washington	7
5	East Germany	14	24	Africa	6
6	Bulgaria	14	25	Berlin	6
7	Poland	13	26	France	6
8	Saigon	12	27	Italy	6
9	Czechoslovakia	11	28	Rome	6
10	England	11	29	United Arab Republic	6
11	New York	11	30	Japan	6
12	Israel	10	31	United Nations	5
13	West Germany	10	32	Asia	5
14	Paris	9	33	Prague	5
15	Europe	8	34	Bratislava	5
16	Near East	8	35	Helsinki	5
17	Warsaw	8	36	Syria	5
18	Finland	8	37	Amman	5
19	London	8			

Four mentions outside U.S.S.R.   Romania, Yugoslavia, Sofia, Belgium, Bonn, Uruguay, Mexico, Nigeria, Iraq, Cairo, India, Malaysia, Cambodia, Tokyo.

particular and the socialist countries in general with those of the capitalist countries. Very broad indices of success may be shown. Thus, in *Strana sovetov za 50 let* the Soviet share of 3% of all world industrial production in 1917 is contrasted with its share in 1966 of 20% and the 38% accounted for by all Socialist countries. Again whereas Russian industrial production was only 12·5% that of the U.S.A. in 1917, it was 65% of it in 1965. (If 1800 is taken as the base year instead of 1917, however, then Russian production was much bigger than American.)

The growth of productivity of industrial workers is compared in *NkhSSSR* 1967, p. 144. In comparison to a base (not specified in absolute terms) of 100 in 1950, the Soviet figure had risen to 287 in 1967, the French to 212, the German to 207, the U.S. to 171 and the British only to 150.

Many separate criteria can be taken to compare the U.S.S.R. and the U.S.A. They could be combined in some way to give an overall quantitative value for comparison. This is in fact roughly provided by national income figures. In *NkhSSSR* 1967, the capitalist definition of national income is, as would be expected, rejected. Western figures are deflated. As a result the absolute values in thousands of millions of U.S. dollars shown in Table 15.14, are claimed for 1965 and 1967 respectively.

Even the Soviet calculation leaves the U.S.A. with a *per capita* income twice as high as its own. A more generous estimate of the U.S. national income in 1967, in fact the official figure, given in the *United Nations Statistical Yearbook* is 658

thousand million, which gives a *per capita* income of 3 400 dollars, about three times the Soviet amount. West European indices are also higher.

Soviet figures used for comparative purposes with other countries are in a sense genuine, but they are selected, modified, and put in a form that makes them give the impression that overtaking the leading industrial countries, whether in *per capita* terms, or in absolute terms (for the U.S.A.), is just a matter of time, if not as imminent as Khrushchev was hoping a decade ago. Kvasha[4] gave figures showing the gap closing fast between the early 1950's and 1960. He expresses the value of Soviet capital investment as a percentage of U.S. capital investment; 1951–55 average 26%, 1959 50%, 1960 54%. Americans, understandably, have watched the Soviet performance closely. *New Directions in the Soviet Economy* (1966, pp. 107–8), considering gross national product (not national income) figures, calculates that in 1964 the Soviet gross national product was approximately 47% as large as that of the U.S.A. (Table 15.14).

'As a proportion of the United States equivalent, Soviet gross national product increased from one-third in 1950 to a plateau of around 46 or 47% since 1958. In terms of the absolute margin of the U.S. economy over the Soviet, the minimum difference was reached in 1958. Since that date the dollar gap between the United States and Soviet GNP has been progressively widening' (Table 15.15).

Table 15.14. COMPARATIVE NATIONAL INCOME AND GROSS NATIONAL PRODUCT FIGURES (THOUSAND MILLION U.S. DOLLARS)

	National income (Soviet figures)		Gross national product (U.S. figures)	National income (U.N. figures)
	1965	1967	1964	1967
U.S.A.	401	468	629	658
U.S.S.R.	248	293	293	202
West Germany	81	85	126	90
United Kingdom	64	69	104	71
France	63	77	96	87
Japan	50	66	101	92
Italy	39	43	61	53

Sources: *NkhSSSR* 1965, 87, *NkhSSSR* 1967, 142
  NDSE Part 2-A, 108
  United Nations Statistical Yearbook 1968, Table 184

Table 15.15. THE U.S.–SOVIET DOLLAR GAP 1950–64

| | *Thousand million dollars* | | | | | | |
	1950	*1955*	*1958*	*1960*	*1962*	*1963*	*1964*
U.S.A.	387	477	487	531	577	599	629
U.S.S.R.	124	174	215	237	265	272	293
Difference	263	303	272	294	312	327	336
U.S.S.R. as ratio of U.S.A.	32	37	44	45	46	45	47

Source: *NDSE* Part 2-A, 109

THE U.S.S.R. IN A WORLD CONTEXT

During the 20th century, internal troubles and external setbacks affected Russia adversely until 1945. Since then, Soviet expansion has taken new forms. For a decade, the countries of East Europe were not inappropriately regarded in the West as Soviet satellites. Even now they mostly look to the U.S.S.R. as their main trading partner, source of credit and protector. As well as establishing Comecon, the Soviet Union has spread its influence round the whole world. Its shipping and airline services, financial aid, equipment and technicians reach many parts of Asia, Africa, Latin America and even Antarctica. Its fishing, scientific and naval vessels pay frequent visits to far-flung parts of the world, hardly heard of in the U.S.S.R. before World War II. Direct involvement in Cuba since about 1960 marks the first successful Russian attempt to establish a foothold in the tropics. Interest in the treasure of the oceans, particularly the Pacific, was expressed, for example, by Batalin[5] and the need for countries to cooperate in the research of the oceans and the control of exploitation of the resources was stressed by Filippov[6] in one of the relatively few articles in *Pravda* that is not critical of non-socialist countries. In 1966 a squadron of Soviet nuclear submarines travelled 40 000 km round the world without once surfacing (*The Times*, 4 April 1966). Soviet foreign trade continues to expand, though only roughly at the rate of total world trade. The merchant shipping fleet has grown about three times in a decade, from about 3 500 000 tons in 1960 to 10 000 000 tons in 1970. The U.S.S.R. itself is becoming a leading shipbuilding power. The construction of vessels of 45 000 gross tons, under way at Leningrad in 1968, would have been inconceivable in the 1950's.

As well as exploring or influencing the tropics, the Arctic and Antarctic areas and the ocean beds around the earth's crust, the U.S.S.R. has the distinction of sharing with the U.S.A. the exploration of 'outer' space and of being alone in piercing the earth's mantle in the Kola Peninsula (*New Scientist*, 17 August 1967) in its own 'Mohole' project (eg *Pravda,* 26 April 1966).

Altogether it is remarkable that little more than 100 million Russians have managed to extend their control over nearly as many non-Russians within the U.S.S.R. and the same number of people in Comecon countries. At a very rough estimate the U.S.S.R. itself has financial resources equal to those of E.E.C., and less than half those of the U.S.A. It is ringed by hostile forces not only in the non-communist world, but even in China and Czechoslovakia. It has commitments in Cuba and West Africa, Egypt and Vietnam. It would be an understatement to say that Stalin's successors have stretched Stalin's Russia far beyond the limits sober forecasters would have suggested in 1945.

Will a compromise be worked out whereby the U.S.S.R. becomes more and more financially and technologically involved with the advanced capitalist countries of the West? Links with West European firms have already been noted. Similar involvement with Japan started in 1969, according to *The Observer*, 23 March 1969, with some 200 million U.S. dollars in a timber agreement between Japanese interests and Soviet Far East authorities. Soon 2 500 million dollars may be involved, with Japan developing various Soviet minerals as well as timber. The boundary dispute in March 1969 between the U.S.S.R. and China may be a manifestation of resentment from the Chinese because the resources of Siberia are not going their way. There have even been tentative suggestions of joint space research with the U.S.A. and the wild plan to build a dam across the Bering Strait might also involve the two countries some day. The cost of the latter was estimated in 1959 to be some 16 000 million dollars; the effect on climate would be devastating. What the effect on the world political climate would be, the mind cannot imagine.

REFERENCES

1. HILL, T. P., 'Too Much Consumption' *Nat. Westminster Bank Quart. Rev.*, 19, Feb. 1969

2. NOVE, A., 'Soviet Trade and Soviet Aid' *Lloyds Bank Rev.*, No 51, 1–19, Jan. 1959

3. TIKHONOV, I. A., *Osnovnaya ekonomicheskaya zadacha SSSR (voprosy metodologii)* (Lenizdat, 1959)

4. KVASHA, Ya. B., *Kapital'nyye vlozheniya i osnovnyye fondy SSSR i SShA*, 97 (Moscow, 1963)

5. BATALIN, A., 'Sokrovishcha okeana. Kak ikh vzyat'?' *Pravda*, 16 July 1966

6. FILIPPOV, B. *et al.*, 'Okean Zovet' *Pravda*, 30 Aug. 1968

BIBLIOGRAPHY

JACKSON, W. A. D., 'Mackinder and the Communist orbit' *Can. Geogr.*, 6 (1), 12–21, 1962

ZOLOTAREV, V. I., *Vneshnyaya torgovlya sotsialisticheskikh stran* (Vneshtorgizdat, Moscow, 1964)

Appendix 1

Factor analysis

One of the main differences between the first edition of this book and the present edition has been the use of factor analysis. Factor analysis is one of several kinds of multivariate analysis. Though first used in the 1930's, it requires very long arithmetical calculations and the number of cases and/or variables that could be handled remained small until the advent of fast electronic computers in the 1950's. Since about 1960, factor analysis (also principal components analysis) has been used very widely in various subjects, including geography. Some publications in which it has been used are listed at the end of this Appendix.

Factor analysis has both advantages and drawbacks. On the positive side, it can produce reasonably precise and comparable numerical indices about relationships and similarities out of a vast initial amount of numerical data, the complexity of which may prevent the human mind from picking out vital information. On the negative side, it is exacting about the kind of data (in a statistical sense) that it uses and the results, once presented, are there to be interpreted in a subjective way by whoever uses them. Some publications on the method are listed at the end of the Appendix.

For the purpose of showing what factor analysis does, a limited amount of data has been selected from Table 13.3(b) and processed. It has been concocted to give a set of data in Table AP1.1 (normalised in Table AP1.2) that would in fact not normally be subjected to factor analysis, but which illustrates what is actually going on. Ten divisions of the U.S.S.R. have been used. Seven variables are taken. The variables may be thought of as data that a geographer could map separately on seven different maps. The maps could then in some way be compared visually.

Table AP 1.1. DATA MATRIX
(PLACES × VARIABLES)

	1	2	3	4	5	6	7
Archangel	34	66	66	55	19	108	47
Leningrad	13	87	87	75	60	40	42
Moscow	15	85	85	83	47	35	74
Voronezh	58	42	42	39	22	53	54
Kursk	73	27	27	31	15	58	83
Volgograd	38	62	62	48	27	91	58
Saratov	40	60	60	45	29	76	60
Armenia	45	55	55	35	27	233	29
Kirgizia	62	38	38	33	18	246	38
Tadjikistan	65	35	35	28	14	300	36

1	Rural population as a percentage of total population
2, 3	Urban population as a percentage of total population
4	Retail turnover in terms of roubles per inhabitant
5	Doctors per 10 000 inhabitants
6	Natural increase of population per 10 000 inhabitants
7	Randomly ordered values

Some distributions might be similar to others; any similar pair would be highly correlated. In factor analysis the correlation matrix (Table AP1.3) shows all pairs of variables, whether positively or negatively correlated. The correlation index, referred to as r (the Pearson

Table AP 1.2. NORMALISED DATA MATRIX (MEAN = 1) (PLACES × VARIABLES)

	1	2	3	4	5	6	7
Archangel	0·77	1·18	1·18	1·17	0·68	0·87	0·90
Leningrad	0·29	1·56	1·56	1·59	2·16	0·32	0·81
Moscow	0·34	1·53	1·53	1·76	1·69	0·28	1·42
Voronezh	1·31	0·75	0·75	0·83	0·79	0·43	1·04
Kursk	1·65	0·48	0·48	0·66	0·54	0·47	1·59
Volgograd	0·86	1·11	1·11	1·01	0·97	0·73	1·11
Saratov	0·90	1·08	1·08	0·95	1·04	0·61	1·15
Armenia	1·02	0·99	0·99	0·74	0·97	1·88	0·56
Kirgizia	1·40	0·68	0·68	0·70	0·65	1·98	0·73
Tadjikistan	1·47	0·63	0·63	0·59	0·50	2·42	0·69
Mean	1·00	1·00	1·00	1·00	1·00	1·00	1·00

Table AP 1.3. CORRELATION MATRIX (V VALUES) (VARIABLES × VARIABLES)

		1	2	3	4	5	6	7
Rural	1	1·00						
Urban	2	−1·00	1·00					
Urban	3	−1·00	1·00	1·00				
Retail	4	−0·94	0·94	0·94	1·00			
Doctors	5	−0·88	0·88	0·88	0·87	1·00		
Population	6	0·49	−0·49	−0·49	−0·63	−0·52	1·00	
Random	7	−0·01	0·01	0·01	0·25	0·05	−0·72	1·00

product moment coefficient) is derived from a data matrix with (in this case) seven variables and ten areas. In the present example, rural population is (by definition) the complement of urban. Columns 1 and 2 in the data matrix therefore correlate negatively, at −1·00, a complete negative correlation. Column 2 correlates with itself, repeated in Column 3, entirely positively, at +1·00. A fairly close correspondence between the values in Columns 3 (or 2) and 4 is suggested by the fact that where the value is high (for the column) in one column, it is high in the other and low values also tend to correspond. To a lesser extent, Column 5 shows the same kind of trend and might be expected to correlate fairly highly. Columns 6 and 7 appear not to correlate with the others but, by chance, correlate between themselves negatively quite highly.

After producing the correlation matrix, factor analysis goes on to group 'families' of intercorrelated variables (Table AP1.4). When several are closely correlated, as in this example, they form what is called a factor (Table AP1.5). There are as many factors as variables, but, according to the extent of mutual inter-correlation, much of the variation may be concentrated on one or two strong factors. This is the case in the present example.

Finally, individual weightings (Table AP1.6) show numerically how close each area is to the others on the verdict of each factor (family of variables) in turn. At this stage of the process it is not easy to see what is happening, or how the areas reappear, as it were from nowhere. In the present concocted situation, variables 1–5 have been chosen to correlate highly and form a strong first factor. On the verdict of this factor, Moscow and Leningrad are similar. A consideration of the original data table will show why this is so. Look along the rows for Leningrad and Moscow. In all five columns they have very similar values. So

Table AP 1.4. FACTORS (FIRST FOUR ONLY)

I	II	III	IV
5·095	1·523	0·192	0·148

Table AP 1.5. FACTOR LOADINGS (VARIABLES × FACTORS)

		I	II	III	IV
Rural	1	0·97	0·19	0·10	0·05
Urban	2	−0·97	−0·19	−0·10	−0·05
Urban	3	−0·97	−0·19	−0·10	−0·05
Retail	4	−0·97	0·05	−0·10	0·10
Doctors	5	−0·92	−0·12	0·32	0·20
Population	6	0·65	−0·70	−0·18	0·25
Random	7	−0·19	0·95	−0·14	0·17

also do Kirgizia and Tadjikistan. Kirgizia, however, has a very different set of indices from Moscow. Quite possibly, on other variables, Moscow and Leningrad would have different values and would stand apart on another factor.

The steps in factor analysis as used in this book are shown in Fig. AP1.1 and the places in the book in which it has been used are shown in Table AP1.7.

The various conclusions may be summarised
1. The results of factor analysis are only as good/valid/meaningful as the data that go in.

2. It is possible, by selecting variables, to emphasise certain aspects of a situation. It is possible, as was done in this example, to 'cook up' a strong factor by putting in identical or very similar ingredients.

3. For the geographer factor analysis may be considered as an extension or modification of comparing distribution maps. What it does mathematically can be appreciated either geometrically (each variable occupies a dimension) or algebraically.

Table AP 1.6. INDIVIDUAL WEIGHTINGS FOR FACTORS I AND II

	I	II
Archangel	−1·46	−0·39
Leningrad	−8·82	−1·11
Moscow	−8·51	0·99
Voronezh	2·37	1·09
Kursk	5·22	3·24
Volgograd	−1·24	0·41
Saratov	−1·04	0·68
Armenia	1·87	−2·17
Kirgizia	5·11	−1·16
Tadjikistan	6·50	−1·57

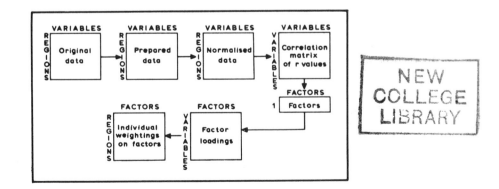

Fig. AP 1.1.   Steps in factor analysis.

Table AP 1.7.

Chapter	Tables	Place	Theme	Number of areas	Number of variables
3	3.5–3.10	U.S.S.R., Comecon	Social, economic	26 regions/countries	15
9	9.3, 9.21–9.22	R.S.F.S.R., S.S.R.'s	Physical, agricultural	87 oblasts/Republics	21
10	10.12–10.15	U.S.S.R. regions	Industrial	19 economic regions	13
13	13.3–13.7	R.S.F.S.R., S.S.R.'s	Development, well-being	87 oblasts/Republics	13
14	14.1–14.5	U.S.S.R. regions	Various human	19 economic regions	18

For the most part the data used in the above applications of factor analysis are for 1965 because at the time of writing the latest available breakdown of R.S.F.S.R. data into regions and oblasts was *NkhRSFSR* 1965.

BIBLIOGRAPHY

AHMAD, Q., *Indian Cities: Characteristics and Correlates* (The University of Chicago, Department of Geography, Research Paper No 102, 1965)

BAGGALEY, A. R., *Intermediate Correlational Methods* (Wiley, New York, 1964)

COLE, J. P. and KING, C. A. M., *Quantitative Geography* (Wiley, London, 1968) especially Chapters 6 and 7

FISHER, J. C., *Yugoslavia–A Multinational State* (Chandler, San Francisco, 1966)

GINSBURG, N. and BERRY, B. J. L., *Atlas of Economic Development*, Part 8 (University of Chicago Press, Chicago, 1961)

MOSER, C. A. and SCOTT, W., *British Towns. A Statistical Study of their Social and Economic Differences* (Oliver and Boyd, Edinburgh and London, 1961)

Appendix 2

Places in the U.S.S.R. mentioned in *Pravda*

The following is an analysis of the front page of *Pravda* sampled at 10-day intervals throughout 1968 (see Chapter 15, pp. 300–301).

Table AP 2.1. COMPOSITION OF 1 047 MENTIONS OF U.S.S.R. PLACES

U.S.S.R. itself	35
Moscow and Moscow oblast	31
'Big' places with regional connotations	61
Fifteen Soviet Socialist Republics	135
Fourteen S.S.R. capitals (not Moscow)	62
Oblasts and capitals of R.S.F.S.R. (not Moscow)	222
Oblasts and capitals of all other S.S.R.'s	100
All other towns	158
All 'small' places	170
Physical features	73
	1 047

'Big' places—eg Ural, Siberia, Zavolzh'ye
'Small' places—eg specific villages, farms, streets, buildings

Table AP 2.2. FREQUENCY OF MENTION OF SOVIET SOCIALIST REPUBLICS AND THEIR CAPITALS

Republic	Mentions	Capital	Mentions
U.S.S.R.	35	Moscow	29
R.S.F.S.R. (Russia)	13(4)		
Ukraine	21	Kiev	13
Kazakhstan	17	Alma-Ata	4
Belorussia	11	Minsk	10
Azerbaijan	9	Baku	2
Turkmenistan	9	Ashkhabad	0
Latvia	8	Riga	4
Kirgizia	8	Frunze	3
Moldavia	7	Kishinev	7
Uzbekistan	7	Tashkent	6
Estonia	6	Tallin	4
Lithuania	6	Vil'nyus	4
Tadjikistan	5	Dushanbe	4
Georgia	4	Tbilisi	2
Armenia	4	Yerevan	1

All places mentioned at least four times are shown below. Those mentioned five or more times are in the columns for comparison. The 72 Soviet places mentioned four or more times might be employed as a basic list for place-name learning since in view of their relative frequency of mention there is an advantage in knowing where (and what) they are, whereas places mentioned only occasionally can be looked up. Where oblast and oblast capital are both mentioned they have been combined.

Table AP 2.3. PLACES MENTIONED FOUR OR MORE TIMES

Rank	U.S.S.R. place	Mentions	Rank	U.S.S.R. place	Mentions
1	U.S.S.R.	35	24	Moldavia (S.S.R.)	7
2	Moscow	31	25	Uzbekistan (S.S.R.)	7
3	Ukraine (S.S.R.)	21	26	Kharkov	7
4	Leningrad	18	27	Kishinev	7
5	Kazakhstan (S.S.R.)	17	28	Estonia (S.S.R.)	6
6	R.S.F.S.R. (Russia)	13+(4)	29	Lithuania (S.S.R.)	6
7	Kiev	13	30	Bashkir A.S.S.R.	6
8	Kremlin	12	31	Tatar A.S.S.R.	6
9	Belorussia (S.S.R.)	11	32	Kuybyshev	6
10	Minsk	10	33	Krasnodar	6
11	Siberia	10	34	Rostov	6
12	Tyumen'	10	35	Chelyabinsk	6
13	Krasnoyarsk	10	36	Dnepropetrovsk	6
14	Azerbaijan (S.S.R.)	9	37	Zaporozh'ye	6
15	Turkmenistan (S.S.R.)	9	38	Tashkent	6
16	Ural (region)	9	39	Tadjikistan (S.S.R.)	5
17	Odessa	9	40	Centre (region)	5
18	Sverdlovsk	9	41	Central Asia	5
19	Volgograd (Stalingrad)	9	42	West Siberia (region)	5
20	Kirgizia (S.S.R.)	8	43	Bryansk	5
21	Latvia (S.S.R.)	8	44	Orenburg	5
22	Kemerovo	8	45	Perm'	5
23	Omsk	8	46	Kustanay	5

Four mentions U.S.S.R.: Georgia S.S.R., Armenia S.S.R., Riga, Vil'nyus, Dushanbe, Tallin, Alma-Ata, Volga (Povolzh'ye), Nizhniy Tagil, Cherepovets, Magnitogorsk, Lipetsk, Saratov, Ul'yanovsk, Dagestan A.S.S.R., Severo-Osetinsk A.S.S.R., Novosibirsk, Irkutsk, Donetsk, Poltava, R. Kuban.

Appendix 3

Transliteration and pronunciation of Russian names

With the exception of certain well-known places, all Soviet place names and certain technical terms for which no satisfactory English equivalent exists have been transliterated into English by a standard system using one English symbol for one Russian one where convenient or an unambiguous combination of two or more English symbols for one Russian one. The English equivalent of each Russian letter is given below together with a rough guide to the pronunciation of those sounds that differ appreciably from their apparent English equivalent in transliteration. Place names for which the standard transliteration has not been used are listed on p. 11.

Russian letter	*English version*	*Notes on pronunciation and transliteration*
А а	A	As *ar* in *car*.
Б б	B	
В в	V	
Г г	G	
Д д	D	
Е е	YE, E	When initial letter in word, or following another vowel, hard sign or soft sign, as *Ya* in *Yale;* elsewhere as *ay* in *say*.
Ё ё	YO	As *Yor* in *York*.
Ж ж	ZH	Almost as *s* in *pleasure*.
З з	Z	
И и	I	As *ee* in *fleet*.
Й й	Y	As *i* in *bit*.
К к	K	
Л л	L	
М м	M	
Н н	N	
О о	O	Almost as *ore* in *more*.
П п	P	
Р р	R	Always rolled in Russian.
С с	S	
Т т	T	
У у	U	As *oo* in *boot*.
Ф ф	F	
Х х	KH	As *ch* in Scottish *loch*.
Ц ц	TS	As *ts* in *bits*.
Ч ч	CH	As *ch* in *church*.

Ш ш	SH	As *sh* in *ash*.
Щ щ	SHCH	As *shch* in *Ashchurch*.
Ъ ъ	"	(hard sign) Not pronounced.
Ы ы	Y	No English sound resembles this. The sound may be approached by attempting to pronounce *ee* in *feet* and *oo* in *boot* simultaneously.
Ь ь	'	(soft sign) Not pronounced.
Э э	E	As *e* in *egg*.
Ю ю	YU	As *you* in *youth*.
Я я	YA	As *ya* in *yard*.

The following vowel combinations are pronounced as one syllable: IY, OY, YY. -A, -I, -Y, are often nominative plural endings of nouns, -IYE, -YYE, nominative plural endings of adjectives. -SKIY, -SKAYA, -SKOYE, -SKIYE are frequently attached to a noun to convert it to an adjective, with the appropriate gender and number (eg Donetskiy from Donets). In this book the practice has been to omit the ending where this may be done without ambiguity (eg Tyumen' oblast instead of Tyumenskaya oblast).

Compass points (Sever = North, Yug = South, Vostok = East, Zapad = West) used in place names as separate words (eg Severnyy Donets, North Donets) are usually translated. Where a compass point is incorporated in a word (eg Vladivostok) it is not translated.

Stressed syllable in the names of selected large towns are as follows:

Alma-Atá	Múrmansk
Arkhángel'sk	Nikoláyev
Ástrakhan'	Novokuznétsk
Barnaúl	Novosibírsk
Chelyábinsk	Petrozavódsk
Dnepropetróvsk	Rostóv-na-Donú
Donétsk	Samarkánd
Irkútsk	Sarátov
Ivánovo	Semipalátinsk
Karagandá	Sevastópol'
Kazán'	Sverdlóvsk
Khabárovsk	Tashként
Khár'kov	Ufá
Kishinév	Ul'yánovsk
Krasnodár	Vladivostók
Krivóy Rog	Volgográd
Krasnoyársk	Vorónezh
Leningrád	Yaroslávl'
Makéyevka	Yereván
Magnitogórsk	Zaporózh'ye

The learning of Soviet place names is made somewhat more interesting and less arduous when certain features of toponymy are appreciated. T. Shabad in his *Geography of the USSR, a Regional Survey* (New York, 1954) has some useful material on the subject (p.41–53). Some places, either renamed or created during the Soviet period, refer to persons, events or achievements connected with the Communist Party. Towns, for example, may be called after distinguished party members (eg Leningrad, Voroshilovsk). Many places may refer to some feature of the landscape (eg Magnitogorsk = Magnetic Mountain, Sernyy Zavod = Sulphur Mill, Solikamsk = Salt deposits on the River Kama, Belaya Tserkov' = White Church). The ending of a word may be a geographical term (-gorsk means mountain, -gorod, -grad, town). Some confusion may be caused by the fact that a large factory or mine may have a completely different name from the settlement serving it (eg in Kazakhstan copper ore from Kounradskiy goes to the nearby smelter at Balkhash).

SELECTED PLACE-NAMES WHICH HAVE BEEN CHANGED SINCE WORLD WAR II

From	To	Location
Akmolinsk	Tselinograd	Kazakhstan
Chkalov	Orenburg	Ural
Chistyakovo	Torez	Ukraine
Koenigsburg	Kaliningrad	R.S.F.S.R.
Memel	Klaypeda	Lithuania
Molotov	Perm'	Ural
Molotovsk	Severodvinsk	Northwest
Osipenko	Berdyansk	Ukraine
Proskurov	Khmel'nitskiy	Ukraine
Shcherbakov	Rybinsk	Centre
Stalinabad	Dushanbe	Tadjikistan
Stalingrad	Volgograd	Volga
Stalino	Donetsk	Ukraine
Stalinogorsk	Novomoskovsk	Centre
Stalinsk	Novokuznetsk	West Siberia
Stanislav	Ivano-Frankovsk	Ukraine
Stavropol'	Tol'yatti	Volga
Voroshilov	Ussuriysk	Far East
Voroshilovgrad	Lugansk	Ukraine

Appendix 4

Selected Data for 1969

The source of all data in this appendix was *Pravda,* 25 January 1970.

Table AP 4.1. INDUSTRIAL GROWTH BY REPUBLICS, 1968– 69, 1968 = 100

R.S.F.S.R.	107	Uzbekistan	100
Ukraine	108	Kirgizia	108
Lithuania	112	Tadjikistan	104
Latvia	107	Turkmenistan	101
Estonia	108	Kazakhstan	106
Georgia	108	Belorussia	111
Azerbaijan	105	Moldavia	109
Armenia	111		

Table AP 4.2. PRODUCTION OF SELECTED BRANCHES OF INDUSTRY, 1969 AND 1968–69 GROWTH, 1968 = 100

Electricity, kWh $\times 10^9$	689	108	Television sets, $\times 10^6$	6·6	115
Oil, ton $\times 10^6$	328	106	Refrigerators, $\times 10^6$	3·7	117
Gas, $m^3 \times 10^9$	183	107	Timber, $m^3 \times 10^6$	273	99
All coal, ton $\times 10^6$	608	102	Paper, ton $\times 10^6$	4	102
Coking coal, ton $\times 10^6$	161	105	Cement, ton $\times 10^6$	89·8	103
Pig iron, ton $\times 10^6$	81·6	104	Cloth, $m^2 \times 10^6$		
Steel, ton $\times 10^6$	110	104	Cotton	6 210	102
Rolled steel, ton $\times 10^6$	76·2	103	Woollen	617	106
Iron ore, ton $\times 10^6$	186	105	Linen	674	99·7
Fertilisers, ton $\times 10^6$	46	105	Silk	1 026	108
Motor vehicles, $\times 10^3$			Clothing, roubles $\times 10^9$	14·4	111
Lorries	505	106	Knitwear, items $\times 10^6$	363	120
Cars	294	105	Leather footwear, pairs $\times 10^6$	635	106
Buses	46	109	Meat, ton $\times 10^6$	11·6	100
Tractors, $\times 10^3$	442	104	Sugar, ton $\times 10^6$	10·3	96

Table AP 4.3. AGRICULTURE

(a) *Crop and livestock products*

Product	1966	1967	1968	1969
Total production, roubles (1965) x 10^9	77	78·1	81·6	79
Cereals, ton x 10^6	171·2	147·9	169·5	160·5
Cotton, ton x 10^6	5·98	5·97	5·95	5·71
Sugar beet, ton x 10^6	74·0	87·1	94·3	71·0
Sunflower, ton x 10^6	6·1	6·6	6·7	6·3
Potatoes, ton x 10^6	87·9	95·5	102·2	91·7
Vegetables, ton x 10^6	17·9	20·5	19·0	18·2
Meat, ton x 10^6	10·7	11·5	11·6	11·6
Milk, ton x 10^6	76·0	79·9	82·3	81·6
Eggs, x 10^9	31·7	33·9	35·7	37·0
Wool, ton x 10^3	371	395	415	390

(b) *Livestock totals,* x 10^6

	1966	1967	1968	1969	1970
Cattle	93·4	97·1	97·2	95·7	95·0
Cows	40·1	41·2	41·6	41·2	40·6
Pigs	59·6	58·0	50·9	49·0	56·1
Sheep and goats	135·3	141·0	144·0	146·1	136·6

Table AP 4.4. TRANSPORT

Goods handled in ton-kilometres, x 10^9, *and growth, 1968–69, 1968 = 100*

Rail	2 362	104
River	160	103
Road	60	104
Oil pipeline	245	113

MISCELLANEOUS NOTES

1. Krasnoyarsk hydroelectric power station capacity reached $4·5 \times 10^6$ kW.
2. Oil refineries opened or enlarged at: Angarsk, Perm', Kremenchug, Gur'yev, Kirishi.
3. Blast furnaces or other capacity opened or enlarged at: Cherepovets, Nizhniy Tagil, Chelyabinsk, Zapsib, Krivoy Rog, Yerakiyevo, Novo-Lipetsk, Karaganda, Zaporozh'ye.
4. Workers and office workers rose by 3% (2 800 000) to 87 900 000.

General bibliography

1. SOVIET STATISTICAL SOURCES

GENERAL: USSR

Narodnoye khozyaystvo SSSR v 1965 godu, Statisti-cheskiy yezhegodnik (Statistika, Moscow, 1966). Other years referred to are the yearbooks for each year from 1958–64, and the 1967 book.

GENERAL: RSFSR

Narodnoye khozyaystvo RSFSR v 1965 godu, Statisti-cheskiy yezhegodnik (Moscow, 1966). Other years referred to are the yearbooks for 1958, and 1961–64

AGRICULTURE

Sel'skoye khozyaystvo SSSR, Statisticheskiy sbornik (Gosstatizdat, Moscow, 1960)

INDUSTRY

Promyshlennost' SSSR, Statisticheskiy sbornik (Moscow, 1964)

TRANSPORT

Transport i svyaz' SSSR, Statisticheskiy sbornik (Statistika, Moscow, 1967)

TRADE

Vneshnyya torgovlya SSSR za 1966 god, Staticheskiy obzor (Moscow, 1967). Trade handbooks for 1956, 1958 and 1960–65 were also referred to.

MISCELLANEOUS

RSFSR v tsifrakh v 1966 godu, Kratkiy statisticheskiy sbornik (Moscow, 1967)
RSFSR za 50 let, Statisticheskiy sbornik (Statistika, Moscow, 1967)
Strana sovetov za 50 let, sbornik statisticheskikh materialov (Moscow, 1967)

2. SOVIET ATLASES

Bol'shoy sovetskiy atlas mira (1, Part 2, Moscow, 1937)
Atlas istorii SSSR dlya sredney shkoly, in three parts, various editions, published in Moscow
Atlas sel'skogo khozyaystva SSSR (Moscow, 1960)
Atlas SSSR (Moscow, 1962)
Atlas razvitiya khozyaystva i kultury SSSR (Moscow, 1967)

3. GENERAL TEXTS IN RUSSIAN

CHERDANTSEV, G. N. *et al., Ekonomicheskaya geografiya SSSR* (Moscow, 1958)
Ekonomicheskaya geografiya, Vop. geogr., No 41, 1957
Ekonomicheskaya geografiya SSSR v perspektive, Vop. geogr., No 57, 1962
GALITSKIY, M. I., DANILOV, S. K. and KORNEYEV, A. I. (eds), *Ekonomicheskaya geografiya transporta SSSR* (Izdatel'stvo 'Transport', Moscow, 1965)
LAVRISHCHEV, A. N., *Ekonomicheskaya geografiya SSSR, obshchaya chast'* (Moscow, 1965)
LYALIKOV, N. I., *Ekonomicheskaya geografiya SSSR* (Uchpedgiz, Moscow, 1960)
NIKITIN, N. P. *et al.* (eds), *Ekonomicheskaya geografiya SSSR* (Moscow, 1966)
SAUSHKIN, Yu. G. *et al., Ekonomisheskaya geografiya Sovetskogo Soyuza, Chast 1* (Moscow, 1967)
SHUVALOV, E. L., *Ekonomicheskaya geografiya SSSR, obshchiy obzor* (Moscow, 1965)
VEDISHCHEV, A. I., *Problemy razmeshcheniya proizvoditel'nykh sil SSSR* (Moscow, 1963)

4. BOOKS AND PERIODICALS IN ENGLISH

DEWDNEY, J. C., *A Geography of the Soviet Union* (Pergamon, Oxford Geographies, 1965) (reviewed by R. E. H. Mellor in *Geography,* 53, Part 4, No 241, 440, 1968)
EAST, W. G., *The Soviet Union* (Van Nostrand, Princeton, 1963)
GREGORY, J. S., *Russian Land, Soviet People— A Geographical Approach to the USSR* (Harrap, London, 1968)

HODGKINS, J. A., *Soviet Power—Energy resources, production and potentials* (Prentice Hall International, London, 1961)

HOLZMAN, F. D. (ed), *Readings on the Soviet Economy* (Chicago, 1962)

HOOSON, D. J. M., *A New Soviet Heartland?* (Van Nostrand Searchlight Book No 21, New York, 1964)

HOOSON, D. J. M., *The Soviet Union* (University of London Press, 1966)

JORRÉ, G., *The Soviet Union* (Longmans, London, 1967 (revised by C. A. Halstead))

KASER, M., *Comecon, Integration Problems of the Planned Economies* (Oxford Univ. Press, 1965)

LYDOLPH, P., *Geography of the U.S.S.R.* (Wiley, London, 1964)

New Directions in the Soviet Economy, Studies Prepared for the Subcommittee on Foreign Economic Policy of the Joint Economic Committee, Congress of the United States.

Part 1   Economic Policy
Part 2—A   Economic Performance
        1 Aggregate National Product
        2 Industry
Part 2—B   Economic Performance
        3 Agriculture
        4 Consumption
        5 Transportation
Part 3   The Human Resources
Part 4   The World Outside
(U.S. Government Printing Office, Washington, 1966)

Oxford University Atlas, the U.S.S.R. and Eastern Europe (Oxford Univ. Press, 1956 and later editions)

Problems of Communism, bimonthly, U.S. Information Agency

Soviet Geography: Review and Translation, English translation of Soviet geographical papers and books, appearing 10 months a year, produced by the American Geographical Society since 1960 (Broadway at 156th Street, New York, N.Y.)

5. BOOKS ON GENERAL SYSTEMS AND THE MATHEMATICAL APPROACH TO GEOGRAPHY

BERRY, B. J. L. and MARBLE, D. F. (eds), *Spatial Analysis: A Reader in Statistical Geography* (Prentice Hall, New Jersey, 1967)

CHORLEY, R. J. and HAGGETT, P. (eds), *Models in Geography* (Methuen, London, 1967)

COLE, J. P. and KING, C. A. M., *Quantitative Geography* (Wiley, London, 1968)

HAGGETT, P., *Locational Analysis in Human Geography* (Arnold, London, 1965)

The Yearbook of the Society for General Systems Research

Index